Mastering Qt 5
Second Edition

Create stunning cross-platform applications using C++ with Qt Widgets and QML with Qt Quick

Guillaume Lazar
Robin Penea

BIRMINGHAM - MUMBAI

Mastering Qt 5
Second Edition

Commissioning Editor: Kunal Chaudhari
Acquisition Editor: Larissa Pinto
Content Development Editor: Flavian Vaz
Technical Editor: Akhil Nair
Copy Editor: Safis Editing
Project Coordinator: Devanshi Doshi
Proofreader: Safis Editing
Indexer: Rekha Nair
Graphics: Jason Monteiro
Production Coordinator: Shraddha Falebhai

First published: December 2016
Second edition: August 2018

Production reference: 1230818

Published by Packt Publishing Ltd.
Livery Place
35 Livery Street
Birmingham
B3 2PB, UK.

ISBN 978-1-78899-539-9

`www.packtpub.com`

To my sisters, Christine and Patricia. To my parents, Béatrice and Claude. To my fiancé, Sophie.

– Guillaume Lazar

mapt.io

Mapt is an online digital library that gives you full access to over 5,000 books and videos, as well as industry leading tools to help you plan your personal development and advance your career. For more information, please visit our website.

Why subscribe?

- Spend less time learning and more time coding with practical eBooks and Videos from over 4,000 industry professionals
- Improve your learning with Skill Plans built especially for you
- Get a free eBook or video every month
- Mapt is fully searchable
- Copy and paste, print, and bookmark content

PacktPub.com

Did you know that Packt offers eBook versions of every book published, with PDF and ePub files available? You can upgrade to the eBook version at www.PacktPub.com and as a print book customer, you are entitled to a discount on the eBook copy. Get in touch with us at service@packtpub.com for more details.

At www.PacktPub.com, you can also read a collection of free technical articles, sign up for a range of free newsletters, and receive exclusive discounts and offers on Packt books and eBooks.

Contributors

About the authors

Guillaume Lazar is a software engineer living in France, near Paris. He has worked in different companies, from start-ups to multinationals, for the last 10 years. He took the opportunity to observe and learn many team organizations and technologies.

In 2014, he founded his own software development company at the age of 27. The current hierarchical organization that applies to most companies seems obsolete to him. With his own company, he wants to try a different approach.

Although he defines himself as a Qt framework lover, he likes to mix different technologies and platforms. He also spends time on game development, machine learning, and electronics, because "things" become "alive".

> *Working on this second edition of Mastering Qt 5 was a great pleasure. The Qt framework is constantly evolving and you can now enjoy this book using Qt 5.11. A lot of people help me to bring this new edition to life. The publisher team: Akhil Nair and Flavian Vaz. The reviewer team: Kévin Lemaire, Robin Penea, and Pavel Strakhov. By the way, Robin was also the co-author of the first edition in 2016 and this book owes him a lot.*

Robin Penea has been working in the software industry for a more than a decade. He worked in start-ups and large companies with many technologies that ranged from embedded software to web development. Armed with this experience, he wrote the Mastering Qt 5 book to spread what he loves the most about the programming craft: proper design and quality code. The teaching bug has bitten him, and he continues to share what he learned online using videos. When he is not tinkering with some new technology, he is either on a wall, rock-climbing, or playing music on his piano. You can reach him via Twitter @synapticrob.

> *This book would not have existed without Guillaume Lazar, my friend and co-author of the book. He was truly dedicated to the work. I thank our reviewers, Rohit Kumar Singh, Ray Rischpater, Quentin Canu, Christophe Dongieux, and Hugo Loi. Also my father, Calin, for always believing in me. Finally, for Flore, my girlfriend, who kept me sane during this endeavor.*

About the reviewers

Pavel Strakhov is a software architect and developer from Russia. He started working with Qt in 2011 in Moscow Institute of Physics and Technology, where it was used to build scientific image processing software. He was highly active in the Qt section of StackOverflow, helping people learn Qt and solve issues. He also worked on Qt bindings for Rust. He is the main author of the book called Game Programming Using Qt 5 / Beginner's Guide / Second Edition published in 2018 by Packt.

Kévin Lemaire is a software engineer since 2011. He lives in the north of Paris since he was born. He first studied accountancy but has quickly been interested in how softwares were makes it easier and switched to IT studies. Now he gets to work in a full Microsoft environment: C++, C#, and WPF. He also is a MCP for SQL Server 2012.

Kévin works for Arc Informatique, a French SCADA provider. He is in charge of data consistency, which starts with the acquisition of industrial equipments, to its storage in files or databases, and data enhancement with reporting.

Kévin has always been fond of Japan. Firstly through anime, then to its music, which he spends time translating as a hobby. He is a dog person and adopted a lovely Shiba Inu.

> *I want to thank Stéphanie, my lovely wife, who supported me to spend some nights working on this book. I also want to thank Guillaume for trusting me with this review. This project was a way to try to transform a hobby into something more professional, which was still a lot of fun.*

Packt is searching for authors like you

If you're interested in becoming an author for Packt, please visit `authors.packtpub.com` and apply today. We have worked with thousands of developers and tech professionals, just like you, to help them share their insight with the global tech community. You can make a general application, apply for a specific hot topic that we are recruiting an author for, or submit your own idea.

Table of Contents

Preface 1

Chapter 1: Get Your Qt Feet Wet 7
- **Qt project basic structure** 8
- **MainWindow structure** 11
- **Qt Designer interface** 14
- **Signals and slots** 16
- **Custom QWidget** 18
- **Adding a task** 22
- **Using a QDialog** 25
- **Distributing code responsibility** 27
- **Emitting a custom signal using lambdas** 28
- **Simplifying with the auto type and a range-based for loop** 32
- **Summary** 36

Chapter 2: Discovering qmake Secrets 37
- **Designing a cross-platform project** 37
  - Adding the Windows implementation 40
  - Adding the Linux implementation 46
  - Adding the macOS implementation 51
- **Transforming SysInfo into a singleton** 54
- **Exploring Qt Charts** 56
- **CpuWidget using QCharts** 59
- **Memory using Qcharts** 63
- **The .pro file in depth** 69
- **Under the hood of qmake** 73
- **Beneath Q_OBJECT and signals/slots** 76
- **Summary** 79

Chapter 3: Dividing Your Project and Ruling Your Code 81
- **Designing a maintainable project** 82
- **Defining data classes** 86
- **Storing your data in a database** 89
- **Protecting your code with a smart pointer** 97
- **Implementing the model** 104
- **Summary** 116

Chapter 4: Conquering the Desktop UI 117
- **Creating a GUI linked to a core shared library** 117

Listing your albums with AlbumListWidget 122
Creating ThumbnailProxyModel 127
Displaying the selected album with AlbumWidget 131
Enhancing thumbnails with PictureDelegate 140
Displaying a picture with PictureWidget 144
Composing your Gallery app 146
Summary 150
Chapter 5: Dominating the Mobile UI 151
Starting with Qt Quick and QML 152
Checking your development environment 159
Creating a Qt Quick project 160
Preparing your Qt Quick gallery entry point 162
Displaying albums with ListView 166
Theming the application with a QML singleton 168
Loading a database on mobile devices 172
Creating a new album from a custom InputDialog 174
Loading images with an ImageProvider 179
Displaying thumbnails in GridView 184
Swiping through full resolution images 187
Summary 190
Chapter 6: Even Qt Deserves a Slice of Raspberry Pi 191
Discovering Qt3D 191
Configuring Qt for your Raspberry Pi 196
Creating an entry point for your Qt3D code 203
Setting up the scene 206
Assembling your Qt3D entities 210
Preparing the board game 216
Crafting entities from the factory 218
Building a snake engine in JavaScript 221
Varying the HUD with QML states 229
Profiling your QML application 233
Summary 238
Chapter 7: Third-Party Libraries without a Headache 239
Creating your Qt Designer plugin 240
Configuring the project for Windows 242
Configuring the project for Linux 244
Configuring the project for Mac 245
Implementing your OpenCV filters 246
Designing the UI with FilterWidget 250
Exposing your plugin to Qt Designer 255
Using your Qt Designer plugin 258

Building the image-filter application 261
Summary 269

Chapter 8: Animations - Its Alive, Alive! 271
Creating an SDK using the Qt Plugin system 271
Creating your plugins 275
Loading your plugins dynamically 281
Using the plugins inside the application 285
Discovering the Animation Framework 289
Making your thumbnails jump 293
Fading in the picture 296
Flashing the thumbnail in a sequence 299
Summary 303

Chapter 9: Keeping Your Sanity with Multithreading 305
Discovering QThread 305
Flying over Qt multithreading technologies 311
Architecting the Mandelbrot project 315
Defining a Job class with QRunnable 318
Using QThreadPool in MandelbrotCalculator 324
Displaying the fractal with MandelbrotWidget 329
Summary 339

Chapter 10: Need IPC? Get Your Minions to Work 341
Inter-process communication techniques 341
Architecturing an IPC project 349
Laying down the foundations with an SDK 353
Working with QDataStream and QTcpSocket 357
Interacting with sockets in the worker 364
Interacting with sockets from the application 374
Building your own QTcpServer 380
Summary 389

Chapter 11: Having Fun with Multimedia and Serialization 391
Architecting the drum machine project 391
Creating a drum track 394
Making your objects serializable with QVariant 401
Serializing objects in JSON format 407
Serializing objects in XML format 412
Serializing objects in binary format 419
Playing low-latency sounds with QSoundEffect 420
Triggering a QButton with your keyboard 421
Bringing PlaybackWorker to life 424
Accepting mouse drag-and-drop events 427

Summary 429
Chapter 12: You Shall (Not) Pass with QTest 431
Discovering Qt Test 432
Executing your tests 438
Writing factorized tests with datasets 443
Benchmarking your code 447
Testing your GUI 450
Spying on your application with QSignalSpy 453
Summary 454
Chapter 13: All Packed and Ready to Deploy 455
Packaging your application 456
Packaging for Windows 457
Packaging for Linux with a distribution package 460
Packaging for Linux with AppImage 466
Packaging for OS X 468
Packaging for Android 471
Packaging for iOS 478
Summary 479
Chapter 14: Qt Hat Tips and Tricks 481
Managing your workspace with sessions 482
Searching with the Locator 482
Increasing the compilation speed 484
Examining memory with Qt Creator 484
Generating random numbers 488
Silencing unused variable warnings 489
Logging custom objects to QDebug 490
Improving log messages 491
Saving your logs to a file 493
Generating a command-line interface 494
Sending and receiving HTTP data 496
Playing with Qt Gamepad 501
Styling QML with Qt Quick Controls 2 504
Summary 511
Other Books You May Enjoy 513
Index 517

Preface

C++ is a powerful language. Coupled with Qt, you have in your hands a cross-platform framework that allies performance and ease of use. Qt is a vast framework that provides tools in many areas (GUI, threads, networking, and so on). 25 years after its inception, Qt continues to evolve and grow with each release.

This book aims to teach you how to squeeze the best out of Qt 5.11 with the new C++14 additions (lambdas, smart pointers, enum classes, and so on). These two technologies together bring you a safe and powerful development toolbox. Throughout the book, we try to emphasize a clean architecture that lets you create and maintain your application in a complex environment.

Each chapter is based on an example project that is the basis of all the discussion. Here are some tasters about what we will see in this book:

- Uncover qmake secrets
- Take a deep dive in the model/view architecture and study how you can build a complex application with this pattern
- Study QML and Qt Quick applications in mobile
- Develop Qt 3D components using QML and JavaScript
- Show how to develop plugins and SDKs using Qt
- Cover the multi-threading technologies provided by Qt
- Build an IPC mechanism using sockets
- Serialize data using XML, JSON, and binary format
- Interact with a gamepad using Qt Gamepad

We'll cover all this and much, much more.

Note that you can take a look at `Chapter 14`, *Qt Hat Tips and Tricks*, whenever you want if you want to get some development candies and see some code snippets that might make your development more pleasurable.

And most importantly, have fun writing Qt applications!

Who this book is for

This book will appeal to developers and programmers who would like to build GUI-based applications. You should be fluent in C++ and the object-oriented paradigm. Qt knowledge is recommended but is not necessary.

What this book covers

`Chapter 1`, *Get Your Qt Feet Wet*, lays the fundamentals of Qt and refreshes your memory with a todo application. This chapter covers the Qt project structure, how to use the designer, basic principles of the signals and slots mechanism, and introduces new features of C++14.

`Chapter 2`, *Discovering QMake Secrets*, takes a deep dive in the heart of the Qt compilation system: qmake. This chapter will help you understand how it works, how to use it, and how you can structure a Qt application with platform-specific code by designing a system monitoring application.

`Chapter 3`, *Dividing Your Project and Ruling Your Code*, analyzes the Qt model/view architecture and how a project can be organized by developing a custom library with the core logic of the application. The project example is a persistent gallery application.

`Chapter 4`, *Conquering the Desktop UI*, studies the UI perspective of the model/view architecture with a Qt Widget application relying on the library completed in the previous chapter.

`Chapter 5`, *Dominating the Mobile UI*, adds the missing part of the gallery application with the mobile version (Android and iOS); the chapter covers it with the use of QML, Qt Quick controls, and QML / C++ interactions.

`Chapter 6`, *Even Qt Deserves a Slice of Raspberry Pi*, continues to the road on Qt Quick application with the Qt 3D perspective. This chapter covers how to build a 3D snake game targeted at the Raspberry Pi.

`Chapter 7`, *Third-Party Libraries Without a Headache*, covers how a third-party library can be integrated in a Qt project. OpenCV will be integrated with an image filter application that also provides a custom QDesigner plugin.

`Chapter 8`, *Animations, It's Alive, Alive!*, extends the image filter application by adding animations and the ability to distribute a custom SDK to let other developers add their own filters.

`Chapter 9`, *Keeping Your Sanity with Multithreading*, investigates the multithreading facilities provided by Qt by building a multithreaded Mandelbrot fractal drawing application.

`Chapter 10`, *Need IPC? Get Your Minions to Work*, broadens the Mandelbrot fractal application by moving the calculation to other processes and managing the communication using sockets.

`Chapter 11`, *Having Fun with Serialization*, covers multiple serialization formats (JSON, XML, and binary) inside a drum machine application in which you can record and load sound loops.

`Chapter 12`, *You Shall (Not) Pass with QTest*, adds tests to the drum machine application and studies how the Qt Test frameworks can be used to make unit tests, benchmarking, and GUI events simulation.

`Chapter 13`, *All Packed and Ready to Deploy*, gives insights into how to package an application on all desktop OSes (Windows, Linux, and Mac) and mobile platforms (Android and iOS).

`Chapter 14`, *Qt Hat Tips and Tricks*, gathers some tips and tricks to develop with Qt with pleasure. It shows how to manage sessions in Qt Creator, useful Qt Creator keyboard shortcuts, how you can customize the logging, save it to disk, and much more.

To get the most out of this book

All the code in this book can be compiled and run from Qt Creator using Qt 5.11. You can do it from your preferred OS: Windows, Linux, or Mac.

About the mobile-specific chapters, either an Android or an iOS device works, but it is not mandatory (the simulator/emulator can be enough).

`Chapter 6`, *Even Qt Deserves a Slice of Raspberry Pi*, offers to build an application running on a Raspberry Pi. Although it is more fun if we can do it with a real Raspberry Pi, it is not necessary to have one to complete the chapter.

Download the example code files

You can download the example code files for this book from your account at `www.packtpub.com`. If you purchased this book elsewhere, you can visit `www.packtpub.com/support` and register to have the files emailed directly to you.

You can download the code files by following these steps:

1. Log in or register at `www.packtpub.com`.
2. Select the **SUPPORT** tab.
3. Click on **Code Downloads & Errata**.
4. Enter the name of the book in the **Search** box and follow the onscreen instructions.

Once the file is downloaded, please make sure that you unzip or extract the folder using the latest version of:

- WinRAR/7-Zip for Windows
- Zipeg/iZip/UnRarX for Mac
- 7-Zip/PeaZip for Linux

The code bundle for the book is also hosted on GitHub at `https://github.com/PacktPublishing/Mastering-Qt-5-Second-Editon`. In case there's an update to the code, it will be updated on the existing GitHub repository.

We also have other code bundles from our rich catalog of books and videos available at `https://github.com/PacktPublishing/`. Check them out!

Conventions used

In this book, you will find a number of text styles that distinguish between different kinds of information. Here are some examples of these styles and an explanation of their meaning.

Code words in text, database table names, folder names, filenames, file extensions, pathnames, dummy URLs, user input, and Twitter handles are shown as follows: "The `qmake` command is executed with the project `.pro` file."
A block of code is set as follows:

```
void MemoryWidget::updateSeries()
{
    double memoryUsed = SysInfo::instance().memoryUsed();
    mSeries->append(mPointPositionX++, memoryUsed);
```

```
if (mSeries->count() > CHART_X_RANGE_COUNT) {
QChart* chart = chartView().chart();
chart->scroll(chart->plotArea().width()
/ CHART_X_RANGE_MAX, 0);
mSeries->remove(0);
}
}
```

When we wish to draw your attention to a particular part of a code block, the relevant lines or items are set in **bold**:

```
windows {
    SOURCES += SysInfoWindowsImpl.cpp
    HEADERS += SysInfoWindowsImpl.h

    debug {
        SOURCES += DebugClass.cpp
        HEADERS += DebugClass.h
    }
}
```

Any command-line input or output is written as follows:

```
/path/to/qt/installation/5.11/gcc_64/bin/qmake -makefile -o Makefile
project.pro
```

Bold: Indicates a new term, an important word, or words that you see onscreen. For example, words in menus or dialog boxes appear in the text like this. Here is an example: "In Qt Creator, when you click on the **Build** button, qmake is invoked."

Warnings or important notes appear like this.

Tips and tricks appear like this.

Get in touch

Feedback from our readers is always welcome.

General feedback: Email `feedback@packtpub.com` and mention the book title in the subject of your message. If you have questions about any aspect of this book, please email us at `questions@packtpub.com`.

Errata: Although we have taken every care to ensure the accuracy of our content, mistakes do happen. If you have found a mistake in this book, we would be grateful if you would report this to us. Please visit `www.packtpub.com/submit-errata`, selecting your book, clicking on the Errata Submission Form link, and entering the details.

Piracy: If you come across any illegal copies of our works in any form on the Internet, we would be grateful if you would provide us with the location address or website name. Please contact us at `copyright@packtpub.com` with a link to the material.

If you are interested in becoming an author: If there is a topic that you have expertise in and you are interested in either writing or contributing to a book, please visit `authors.packtpub.com`.

Reviews

Please leave a review. Once you have read and used this book, why not leave a review on the site that you purchased it from? Potential readers can then see and use your unbiased opinion to make purchase decisions, we at Packt can understand what you think about our products, and our authors can see your feedback on their book. Thank you!

For more information about Packt, please visit `packtpub.com`.

1
Get Your Qt Feet Wet

If you know C++ but have never touched Qt, or if you have already made some intermediate Qt applications, this chapter will ensure that your Qt foundations are solid before studying advanced concepts in the following chapters.

We will teach you how to create a simple todo application using Qt Creator. This application will display a list of tasks that you can create/update/delete. We will cover the Qt Creator and Qt Designer interfaces, an introduction to the signal/slot mechanism, the creation of a custom widget with custom signals/slots, and its integration into your application.

You will implement a todo app using new C++14 semantics: lambdas, auto variables, and for loops. Each of these concepts will be explained in depth and will be used throughout this book.

By the end of this chapter, you will be able to create a desktop application with a flexible UI using Qt widgets and new C++ semantics.

In this chapter, we will cover the following topics:

- Qt project basic structure
- MainWindow structure
- Qt Designer interface
- Signals and slots
- Custom `QWidget`
- C++14 lambda, auto, and for each

Qt project basic structure

First, start Qt Creator.

By default, Qt Creator is configured to use and generate lowercase filenames (such as `mainwindow.cpp`). As this book is using the Pascal case (that is, `MainWindow.cpp`), you should disable it. Uncheck the **Tools** | **Options...** | **C++** | **File Naming** | **Lower case file names** option.

You can now create a new Qt project via **File** | **New File or Project** | **Application** | **Qt Widgets Application** | **Choose**.

The wizard will then guide you through four steps:

1. **Location**: Choose a project name and location
2. **Kits**: Target platforms that your project aims at (Desktop, Android, and so on)
3. **Details**: Input base class information and a name for the generated class
4. **Summary**: Allows you to configure your new project as a subproject and automatically add it to a version-control system

Even if all the default values can be kept, please at least set a useful project name, such as "todo" or "TodoApp." We won't blame you if you want to call it "Untitled" or "Hello world."

Once done, Qt Creator will generate several files, which you can see in the **Projects** hierarchy view:

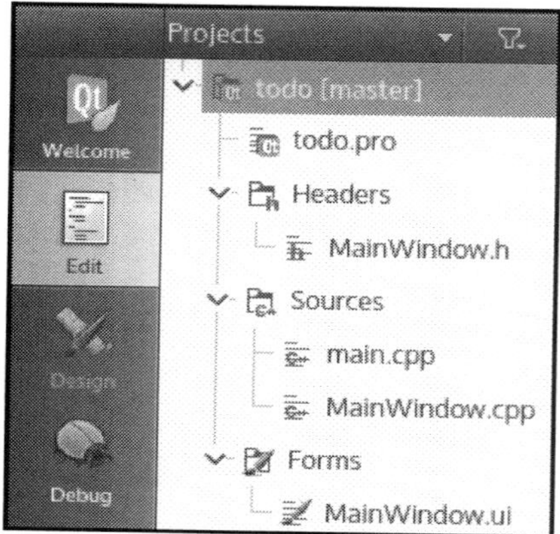

The `.pro` file is Qt's configuration project file. As Qt adds specific file formats and C++ keywords, an intermediate build step is performed, parsing all the files to generate the final files. This process is done by `qmake`, an executable from the Qt SDK. It will also generate the final Makefiles for your project.

A basic `.pro` file generally contains:

- Qt modules used (such as `core`, `gui`)
- A target name (such as `todo`, `todo.exe`)
- A project template (such as `app`, `lib`)
- Sources, headers, and forms

There are some great features that come with Qt and C++14. This book will showcase them in all its projects. For the `GCC` and `CLANG` compilers, you must add `CONFIG += c++14` to the `.pro` file to enable C++14 on a Qt project, as shown in the following code:

```
QT       += core gui
CONFIG   += c++14

greaterThan(QT_MAJOR_VERSION, 4): QT += widgets

TARGET = todo
TEMPLATE = app

SOURCES += main.cpp \
           MainWindow.cpp

HEADERS  += MainWindow.h \

FORMS    += MainWindow.ui \
```

The `MainWindow.h` and `MainWindow.cpp` files are the header/source for the `MainWindow` class. These files contain the default GUI generated by the wizard.

The `MainWindow.ui` file is your UI design file written in XML format. It can be edited more easily with Qt Designer. This tool is a **What You See Is What You Get (WYSIWYG)** editor that helps you to add and adjust your graphical components, known as widgets.

Here is the `main.cpp` file, with its well-known function:

```
#include "MainWindow.h"
#include <QApplication>

int main(int argc, char *argv[])
{
```

```
    QApplication a(argc, argv);
    MainWindow w;
    w.show();

    return a.exec();
}
```

Usually, the `main.cpp` file contains the program entry point. It will, by default, perform three actions:

- Instantiate `QApplication`
- Instantiate and show your main window
- Execute the blocking main event loop

This is the bottom-left toolbar for Qt Creator:

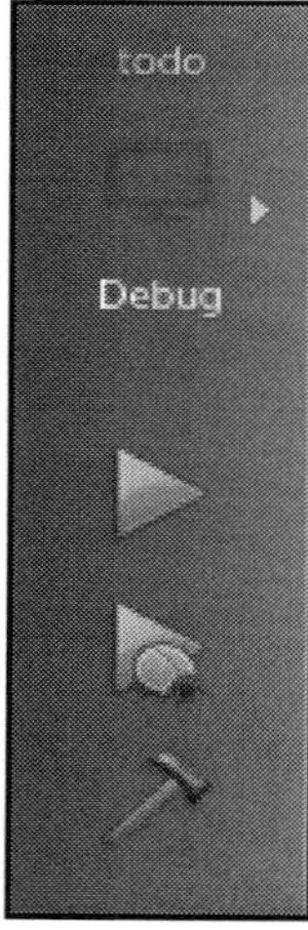

Use it to build and start your `todo` application in debug mode:

1. Check that the project is in **Debug** build mode
2. Use the hammer button to build your project
3. Start debugging using the green Play button with the little blue bug

You will discover a wonderful and beautifully empty window. We will rectify this after explaining how `MainWindow` is constructed:

- Press *Ctrl* + *B* (for Windows/Linux) or *Command* + *B* (for Mac) to build your project
- Press *F5* (for Windows/Linux) or *Command* + *R* (for Mac) to run your application in debug mode

MainWindow structure

This generated class is a perfect yet simple example of Qt framework usage; we will dissect it together. As mentioned previously, the `MainWindow.ui` file describes your UI design and the `MainWindow.h`/`MainWindow.cpp` files define the C++ object where you can manipulate the UI with code.

It's important to take a look at the `MainWindow.h` header file. Our `MainWindow` object inherits from Qt's `QMainWindow` class:

```
#include <QMainWindow>

namespace Ui {
class MainWindow;
}
```

```
class MainWindow : public QMainWindow
{
    Q_OBJECT

public:
    explicit MainWindow(QWidget *parent = 0);
    ~MainWindow();
private:
    Ui::MainWindow *ui;
};
```

As our class inherits from the `QMainWindow` class, we will have to add the corresponding `#include` at the top of the header file. The second part is the forward declaration of `Ui::MainWindow`, as we only declare a pointer.

`Q_OBJECT` can look a little strange to a non-Qt developer. This macro allows the class to define its own signals/slots through Qt's meta-object system. These features will be covered later in this chapter in the section *Signals and slots*.

This class defines a public constructor and destructor. The latter is pretty common but the constructor takes a `parent` parameter. This parameter is a `QWidget` pointer that is `null` by default.

`QWidget` is a UI component. It can be a label, a textbox, a button, and so on. If you define a parent-child relationship between your window, layout, and other UI widgets, the memory management of your application will be easier. Indeed, in this case, deleting the parent is enough because its destructor will take care of also deleting its child recursively.

Our `MainWindow` class extends `QMainWindow` from the Qt framework. We have a `ui` member variable in the private fields. Its type is a pointer of `Ui::MainWindow`, which is defined in the `ui_MainWindow.h` file generated by Qt. It's the C++ transcription of the `MainWindow.ui` UI design file. The `ui` member variable will allow you to interact with your C++ UI components (`QLabel`, `QPushButton`, and so on), as shown in the following figure:

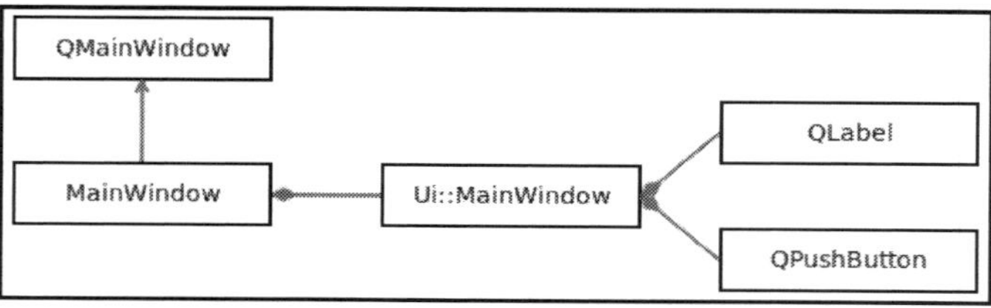

If your class only uses pointers or references for a class type, you can avoid including the header by using forward declaration. That will drastically reduce compilation time and avoid circular dependencies.

Now that the header part is done, we can talk about the `MainWindow.cpp` source file.

In the following code snippet, the first include is our class header. The second one is required by the generated `Ui::MainWindow` class. This include is required as we only use a forward declaration in the header:

```
#include "MainWindow.h"
#include "ui_MainWindow.h"

MainWindow::MainWindow(QWidget *parent) :
    QMainWindow(parent),
    ui(new Ui::MainWindow)
{
    ui->setupUi(this);
```

In many cases, Qt generates good code using the initializer list. The `parent` argument is used to call the `QMainWindow` superclass constructor. Our `ui` private member variable is also initialized.

Now that `ui` is initialized, we must call the `setupUi` function to initialize all the widgets used by the `MainWindow.ui` design file:

As the pointer is initialized in the constructor, it must be cleaned in the destructor:

```
MainWindow::~MainWindow()
{
    delete ui;
}
```

Qt Designer interface

Qt Designer is a major tool for developing Qt applications. This WYSIWYG editor will help you to easily design your GUI. If you switch between **Edit** mode and **Design** mode for the `MainWindow.ui` file, you will see the real XML content and the designer:

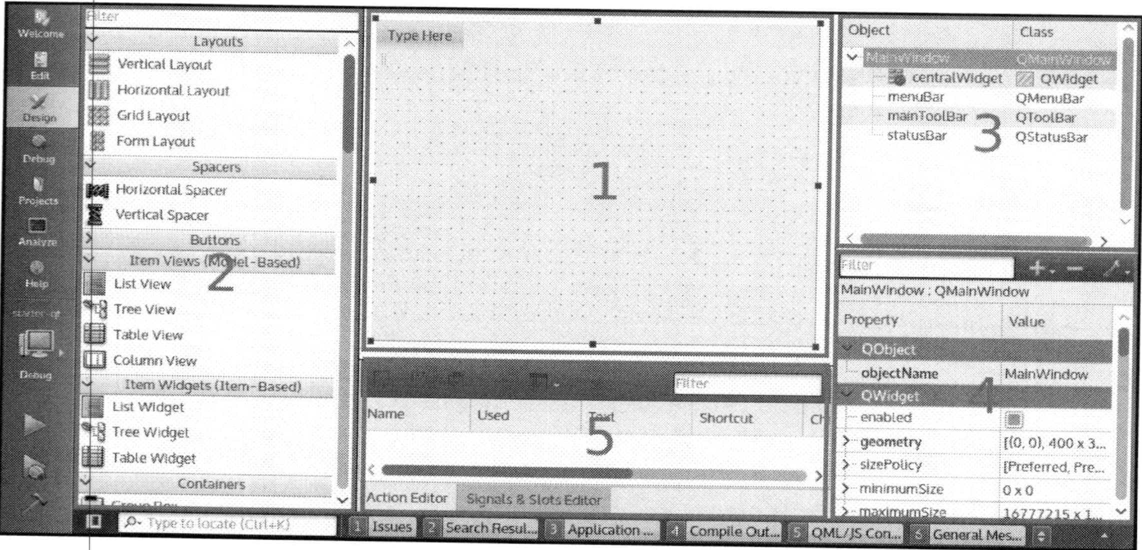

The designer displays several parts:

- Form Editor (**1**): A visual representation of the form (empty for now)
- Widget Box (**2**): Contains all the major widgets that can be used with your form
- Object Inspector (**3**): Displays your form as a hierarchical tree
- Property Editor (**4**): Enumerates the properties of the selected widget
- Action Editor/Signal & Slots Editor (**5**): Handles toolbar actions and connections between your objects

It's time to embellish this empty window! Let's drag and drop a **Label** widget from the **Display Widgets** section on the form. You can change the name and the text properties directly from the Properties editor.

As we are making a `todo` application, we suggest these properties:

- `objectName`: `statusLabel`
- `text`: `Status: 0 todo / 0 done`

This label will later display the count of `todo` tasks and the count of tasks already done. Save, build, and start your application. You should now see your new label in the window.

You can now add a push button with those properties:

- `objectName`: `addTaskButton`
- `text`: `Add task`

You should get a result close to the following:

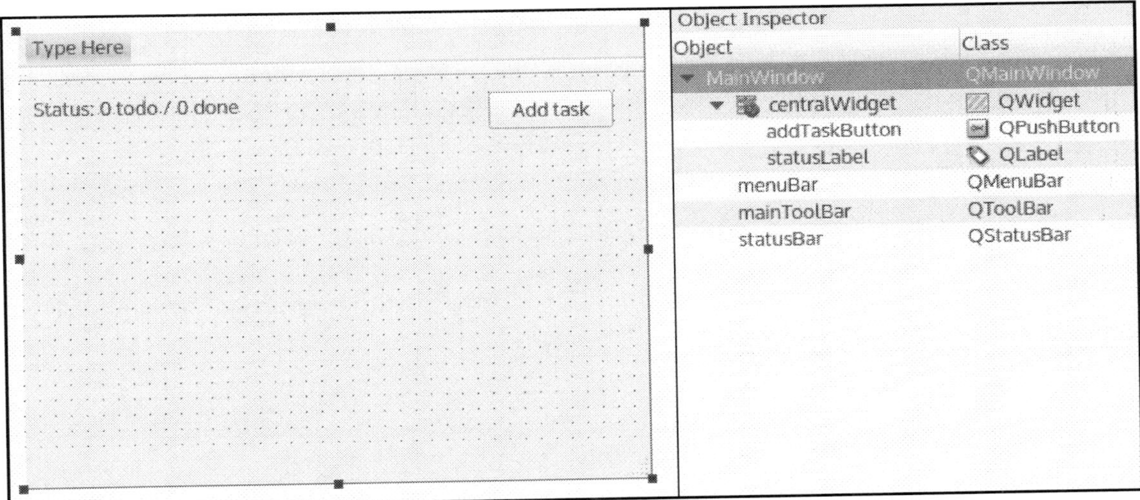

You can edit the text property of a widget directly on your form by double-clicking on it!

The design of the `MainWindow.ui` file is ready, we can now study the signals and slots.

Signals and slots

The Qt framework offers a flexible message-exchange mechanism that is composed of three concepts:

- `signal` is a message sent by an object
- `slot` is a function that will be called when this signal is triggered
- The `connect` function specifies which `signal` is linked to which `slot`

Qt already provides signals and slots for its classes, which you can use in your application. For example, `QPushButton` has `signal clicked()`, which will be triggered when the user clicks on the button. Another example: the `QApplication` class has a `slot quit()` function, which can be called when you want to terminate your application.

Here is why you will love Qt signals and slots:

- A slot remains an ordinary function, so you can call it yourself
- A single signal can be linked to different slots
- A single slot can be called by different linked signals
- A connection can be made between a signal and a slot from different objects, and even between objects living inside different threads

Keep in mind that to be able to connect a `signal` to a `slot`, their methods' signatures must match. The count, order, and type of arguments must be identical. Note that signals and slots never return values.

This is the syntax of a Qt connection:

```
connect(sender, &Sender::signalName,
    receiver, &Receiver::slotName);
```

The first test that we can do to use this wonderful mechanism is to `connect` an existing `signal` with an existing `slot`. We will add this connect call to the `MainWindow` constructor:

```
MainWindow::MainWindow(QWidget *parent) :
    QMainWindow(parent),
    ui(new Ui::MainWindow)
{
    ui->setupUi(this);
    connect(ui->addTaskButton, &QPushButton::clicked,
    QApplication::instance(), &QApplication::quit);
}
```

Let's analyze how a connection is done:

- `sender`: Object that will send the signal. In our example, the `QPushButton` named `addTaskButton` is added from the UI designer.
- `&Sender::signalName`: Pointer to the member signal function. Here, we want do something when the clicked signal is triggered.
- `receiver`: Object that will receive and handle the signal. In our case, it is the `QApplication` object created in `main.cpp`.
- `&Receiver::slotName`: Pointer to one of the receiver's `member` slot functions. In this example, we use the built-in `quit()` slot from `QApplication`, which will exit the application.

You can now compile and run this short example. You will terminate the application if you click on `addTaskButton` of your `MainWindow`.

You can connect a signal to another signal. The second signal will be emitted when the first one is triggered.

Now that you know how to connect a signal to an existing slot, let's see how to declare and implement a custom `addTask()` slot in our `MainWindow` class. This slot will be called when the user clicks on `ui->addTaskButton`.

The following is the updated `MainWindow.h`:

```
class MainWindow : public QMainWindow
{
    Q_OBJECT

public:
    explicit MainWindow(QWidget *parent = 0);
    ~MainWindow();

public slots:
    void addTask();

private:
    Ui::MainWindow *ui;
};
```

Qt uses a specific `slots` keyword to identify slots. Since a slot is a function, you can always adjust the visibility (`public`, `protected`, or `private`) depending on your needs.

We will now add this slot implementation in the `MainWindow.cpp` file:

```
void MainWindow::addTask()
{
    qDebug() << "User clicked on the button!";
}
```

Qt provides an efficient way of displaying the debug information with the `QDebug` class. An easy way to obtain a `QDebug` object is to call the `qDebug()` function. Then you can use the << stream operator to send your debug information.

Update the top of the file like the following:

```
#include <QDebug>

MainWindow::MainWindow(QWidget *parent) :
    QMainWindow(parent),
    ui(new Ui::MainWindow)
{
    ui->setupUi(this);
    connect(ui->addTaskButton, &QPushButton::clicked,
    this, &MainWindow::addTask);
}
```

Since we now use `qDebug()` in our slot, we must include `<QDebug>`. The updated `connect` now calls our custom slot instead of quitting the application.

Build and run the application. If you click on the button, you will see your debug message inside the **Application Output** Qt Creator tab.

Custom QWidget

We now have to create the `Task` class that will hold our data (task name and completed status). This class will have its form file separated from `MainWindow`. Qt Creator provides an automatic tool to generate a base class and the associated form.

Click on **File** | **New File or Project** | **Qt** | **Qt Designer Form Class**. There are several form templates; you will recognize **Main Window**, which Qt Creator created for us when we started the `todo` app project. Select **Widget** and name the class `Task`, then click on **Next**. Here is a summary of what Qt Creator will do:

1. Create a `Task.h` file and a `Task.cpp` file
2. Create the associated `Task.ui` and do the plumbing to connect to `Task.h`
3. Add these three freshly-created files to `todo.pro` so they can be compiled

Finish and voilà, the `Task` class is ready to be filled. We will jump into `Task.ui` first. Start by dragging and dropping **checkbox** (`objectName` = **checkbox**) and **Push Button** (`objectName` = **removeButton**):

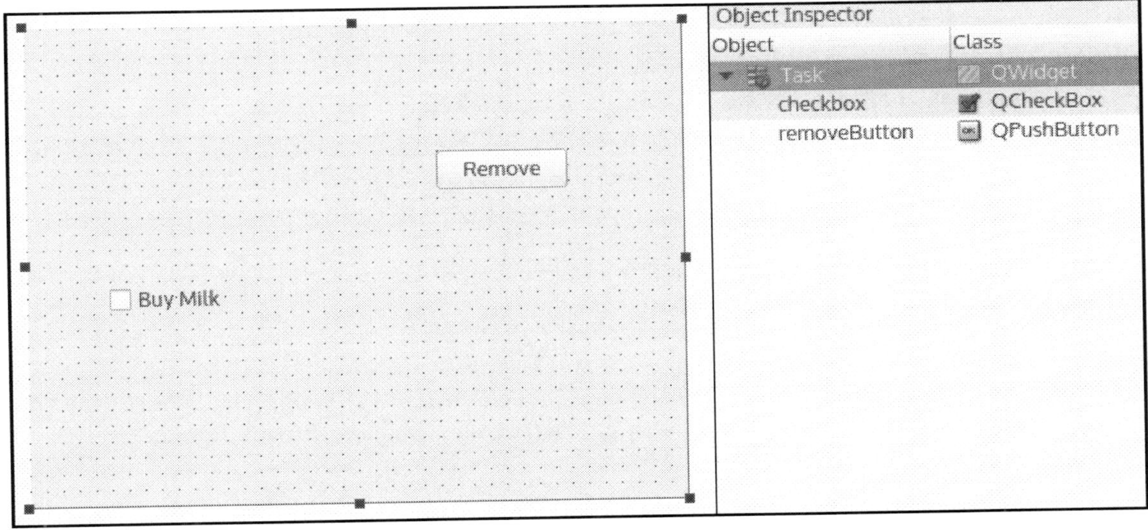

This layout looks great, let's ship it to the customers! Unless you have a pixel-perfect eye, your items are not very well aligned. You need to indicate how your widgets should be laid out and how they should react when the window geometry changes (for example, when the user resizes the window). For this, Qt has several default layout classes:

- `Vertical Layout`: Widgets are vertically stacked
- `Horizontal Layout`: Widgets are horizontally stacked
- `Grid Layout`: Widgets are arranged in a grid that can be subdivided into smaller cells
- `Form Layout`: Widgets are arranged like a web form, a label, and an input

A basic layout will try to constrain all its widgets to occupy equal surfaces. It will either change the widgets' shape or add extra margins, depending on each widget's constraints. Check Box will not be stretched but Push Button will.

In our `Task` object, we want this to be horizontally-stacked. In the **Form Editor** tab, right-click on the window and select **Lay out | Lay out Horizontally**. Each time you add a new widget in this layout, it will be arranged horizontally.

Now add a `Push Button` (`objectName` = **editButton**) just after the `checkbox` object.

The **Form Editor** window offers a realistic preview of how your UI will render. If you stretch the window now, you can observe how each widget will react to this event. When resizing horizontally, you can note that the push buttons are stretched. It looks bad. We need something to "hint" to the layout that these buttons should not be stretched. Enter the **Spacer** widget. Take **Horizontal Spacer** in the widget box and drop it after the `checkbox` object:

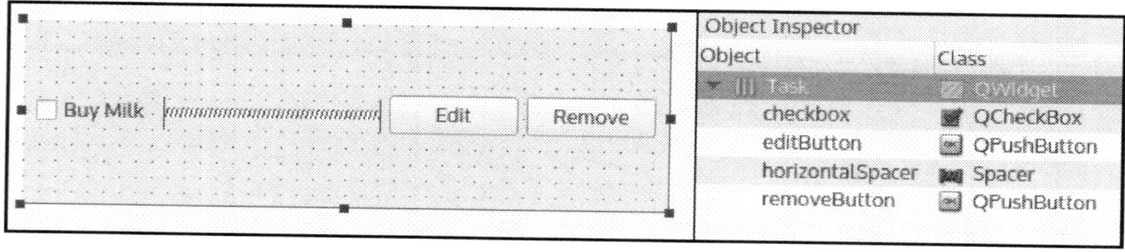

A spacer is a special widget that tries to push (horizontally or vertically) adjacent widgets to force them to take up as little space as possible. The **editButton** and **removeButton** objects will take up only the space of their text and will be pushed to the edge of the window when resized.

You can add sub layouts of any type in a form (vertical, horizontal, grid, form) and create a complex-looking application with a combination of widgets, spacers, and layouts. These tools are targeted at designing a good-looking desktop application that can react properly to different window geometries.

The Designer part is finished, so we can switch to the `Task` source code. Since we created a Qt Designer Form class, `Task` is closely linked to its UI. We will use this as a leverage to store our model in a single place. When we create a `Task` object, it has to have a name:

```
#ifndef TASK_H
#define TASK_H

#include <QWidget>
#include <QString>
```

```
namespace Ui {
class Task;
}

class Task : public QWidget
{
    Q_OBJECT

public:
    explicit Task(const QString& name, QWidget *parent = 0);
    ~Task();

    void setName(const QString& name);
    QString name() const;
    bool isCompleted() const;
private:
    Ui::Task *ui;
};

#endif // TASK_H
```

The constructor specifies a name and, as you can see, there are no private fields storing any state of the object. All of this will be done in the form part. We also added some getters and setters that will interact with the form. It's better to have a model completely separated from the UI, but our example is simple enough to merge them. Moreover, the `Task` implementation details are hidden from the outside world and can still be refactored later on. Here is the content of the `Task.cpp` file:

```
#include "Task.h"
#include "ui_Task.h"

Task::Task(const QString& name, QWidget *parent) :
        QWidget(parent),
        ui(new Ui::Task)
{
    ui->setupUi(this);
    setName(name);
}

Task::~Task()
{
    delete ui;
}

void Task::setName(const QString& name)
{
    ui->checkbox->setText(name);
```

```
}

QString Task::name() const
{
    return ui->checkbox->text();
}

bool Task::isCompleted() const
{
   return ui->checkbox->isChecked();
}
```

The implementation is straightforward; we store the information in `ui->checkbox` and both the `name()` and the `isCompleted()` getters take their data from `ui->checkbox`.

Adding a task

We will now rearrange the layout of `MainWindow` to be able to display our todo tasks. At this moment, there is no widget where we can display our tasks. Open the `MainWindow.ui` file. We will use Qt designer to create the UI:

1. Drag and drop **Horizontal layout** inside the central widget and rename it `toolbarLayout`
2. Right-click on the central widget and select **Lay out vertically**
3. Drag and drop the label, spacer, and button **inside** `toolbarLayout`
4. Drag and drop **Vertical layout** under `toolbarLayout` (a blue helper line will be displayed) and rename it `tasksLayout`
5. Add a vertical spacer under `tasksLayout` (again, check the blue helper line):

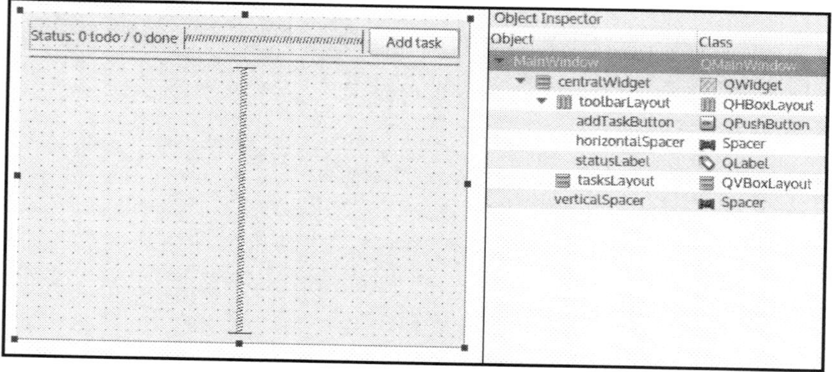

Voilà! Your `MainWindow` form is finished. Later in the chapter you will learn how to dynamically create and add some `Task` widgets to the empty `tasksLayout`.

To sum up, we have:

- A vertical layout for `centralWidget` that contains the `toolbarLayout` item and the `tasksLayout` item.
- A vertical spacer pushing these layouts to the top, forcing them to take up the smallest possible space.
- Gotten rid of `menuBar`, `mainToolBar`, and `statusBar`. Qt Creator created them automatically, we simply don't need them for our purposes. You can guess their uses from their names.

Don't forget to rename the `MainWindow` title to `Todo` by selecting **MainWindow** in the **Object Inspector** window and editing the **Qwidget** | **windowTitle** property. Your app deserves to be named properly.

Press *Shift* + *F4* in Designer mode to switch between the form editor and the source.

Now that the `MainWindow` UI is ready to welcome tasks, let's switch to the code part. The application has to keep track of new tasks. Add the following in the `MainWindow.h` file:

```
#include <QVector>

#include "Task.h"

class MainWindow : public QMainWindow
{
    // MAINWINDOW_H

public slots:
    void addTask();

private:
    Ui::MainWindow *ui;
    QVector<Task*> mTasks;
};
```

The `QVector` is the Qt container class providing a dynamic array, which is an equivalent of `std::vector`. Generally speaking, the rule says that STL containers are more customizable, but they may miss some features compared to Qt containers. If you use C++11 smart pointers, you should favor `std` containers, but we will get into that later.

In the Qt documentation of `QVector`, you may stumble upon the following statement: *For most purposes,* `QList` *is the right class to use.* There is a debate about this in the Qt community:

- Do you often need to insert objects larger than a pointer at the beginning or in the middle of your array? Use a `QList` class.
- Need contiguous memory allocation? Less CPU and memory overhead? Use a `QVector` class.

The already-added `addTask()` slot will now be called each time we want to add a new `Task` object to the `mTasks` function.

Let's fill our `QVector` tasks each time `addTaskButton` is clicked. First, we connect the `clicked()` signal in the `MainWindow.cpp` file:

```
MainWindow::MainWindow(QWidget *parent) :
    QMainWindow(parent),
    ui(new Ui::MainWindow),
    mTasks()
{
    ui->setupUi(this);
    connect(ui->addTaskButton, &QPushButton::clicked,
    this, &MainWindow::addTask);
};
```

As a best practice, try to always initialize member variables in the initializer list and respect the order of variable declarations. Your code will run faster and you will avoid unnecessary variable copies. For more information, take a look at the standard C++ documentation at `https://isocpp.org/wiki/faq/ctors#init-lists`.

The body of the `addTask()` function should look like this:

```
void MainWindow::addTask()
{
        qDebug() << "Adding new task";
        Task* task = new Task("Untitled task");
        mTasks.append(task);
        ui->tasksLayout->addWidget(task);
}
```

We created a new task and added it to our `mTask` vector. Because the `Task` object is a `QWidget`, we also added it directly to `tasksLayout`. An important thing to note here is that we never managed our new task's memory. Where is the `delete task` instruction? This is a key feature of the Qt Framework we started to mention earlier in the chapter; the `QObject` class parenting automatically handles object destruction.

In the preceding code snippet, the `ui->tasksLayout->addWidget(task)` call has an interesting side-effect: the ownership of the `task` is transferred to the layout's widget. The `QObject*` parent defined in the `Task` constructor is now `centralWidget` of the `MainWindow`. The `Task` destructor will be called when `MainWindow` releases its own memory by recursively iterating through its children and calling their destructor.

This feature has interesting consequences. First, if you use the `QObject` parenting model in your application, you will have much less memory to manage. Second, it can collide with some new C++11 semantics, specifically the smart pointers. We will get into the details about this in later chapters.

Using a QDialog

We deserve something better than an untitled task. The user needs to define its name when created. The easiest path would be to display a dialog where the user can input the task name. Fortunately, Qt offers us a very configurable dialog that fits perfectly in `addTask()`:

```
#include <QInputDialog>
...
void MainWindow::addTask()
{
    bool ok;
    QString name = QInputDialog::getText(this,
        tr("Add task"),
        tr("Task name"),
        QLineEdit::Normal,
        tr("Untitled task"),                &ok);
    if (ok && !name.isEmpty()) {
        qDebug() << "Adding new task";
        Task* task = new Task(name);
        mTasks.append(task);
        ui->tasksLayout->addWidget(task);
    }
}
```

The `QinputDialog::getText` function is a static blocking function that displays the dialog. When the user validates/cancels the dialog, the code continues. If we run the application and try to add a new task, we will see this:

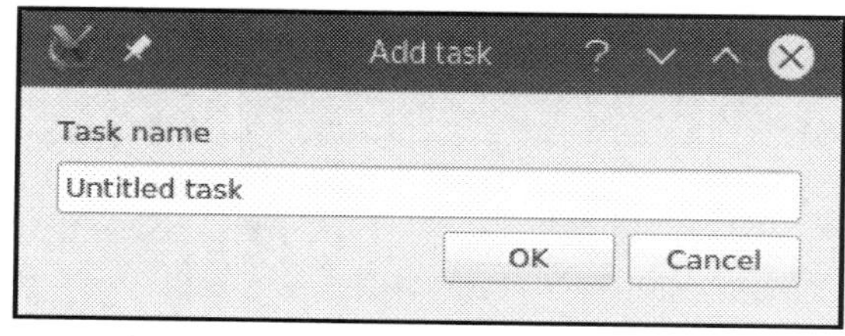

The `QInputDialog::getText` signature looks like this:

```
QString QinputDialog::getText(
  QWidget* parent,
      const QString& title,
      const QString& label,
      QLineEdit::EchoMode mode = QLineEdit::Normal,
      const QString& text = QString(),
      bool* ok = 0, ...)
```

Let's break it down:

- `parent`: This is the parent widget (`MainWindow`) to which `QinputDialog` is attached. This is another instance of the `QObject` class's parenting model.
- `title`: This is the title displayed in the window title. In our example, we use `tr("Add task")`, which is how Qt handles i18n in your code. Later, we will see how to provide multiple translations for a given string.
- `label`: This is the label displayed right above the input text field.
- `mode`: This is how the input field is rendered (password mode will hide the text).
- `ok`: This is a pointer to a variable that is set to `true` if the user presses **OK** and `false` if the user presses **Cancel**.
- `QString`: The returned `QString` is what the user has typed.

There are a few more optional parameters we can safely ignore for our example.

Distributing code responsibility

Great, the user can now specify a task name when created. What if they make an error when typing the name? The next logical step is to be able to rename the task after we create it. We'll take a slightly different approach. We want our `Task` to be as autonomous as possible. If we attach it to another component (rather than `MainWindow`), this renaming feature has to keep working. Thus, this responsibility has to be given to the `Task` class:

```
// In Task.h
public slots:
    void rename();

// In Task.cpp
#include <QInputDialog>

Task::Task(const QString& name, QWidget *parent) :
       QWidget(parent),
       ui(new Ui::Task)
{
   ui->setupUi(this);
   setName(name);
   connect(ui->editButton, &QPushButton::clicked, this, &Task::rename);
}
...
void Task::rename()
{
    bool ok;
    QString value = QInputDialog::getText(this, tr("Edit task"),
                                          tr("Task name"),
                                          QLineEdit::Normal,
                                          this->name(), &ok);

    if (ok && !value.isEmpty()) {
        setName(value);
    }
}
```

We add a public `rename()` slot to connect it to a signal. The body of `rename()` reuses what we had previously covered with `QInputDialog`. The only difference is the `QInputDialog` default value, which is the current task name. When `setName(value)` is called, the UI is instantly refreshed with the new value; there's nothing to synchronize or update, the Qt main loop will do its job.

The nice thing is that `Task::rename()` is completely autonomous. Nothing has been modified in `MainWindow`, so we have effectively zero coupling between our `Task` and the parent `QWidget`.

Emitting a custom signal using lambdas

The remove task is straightforward to implement, but we'll study some new concepts along the way. The Task has to notify its owner and parent (the MainWindow) that the removeTaskButton QPushButton has been clicked. We'll implement this by defining a custom removed signal in the Task.h files:

```
class Task : public QWidget
{
    ...
public slots:
    void rename();
signals:
    void removed(Task* task);
   ...
};
```

Like we did for the slots, we have to add the Qt keyword signals in our header. Since signal is used only to notify another class, the public keyword is not needed (it even raises a compilation error). signal is simply a notification sent to the receiver (the connected slot); it implies that there is no function body for the removed(Task* task) function.

We added the task parameter to allow the receiver to know which task asked to be removed. The next step is to emit the removed signal upon the removeButton click. This is done in the Task.cpp file:

```
Task::Task(const QString& name, QWidget *parent) :
        QWidget(parent),
        ui(new Ui::Task)
{
    ui->setupUi(this);
    ...
    connect(ui->removeButton, &QPushButton::clicked, [this] {
        emit removed(this);
    });
}
```

This code excerpt shows a very interesting feature of C++11: lambdas. In our example, lambda is the following part:

```
[this] {
        emit removed(this);
    });
```

Here, we connected the clicked signal to an anonymous inline function, a `lambda`. Qt allows signal-relaying by connecting a signal to another signal if their signatures match. It's not the case here: the `clicked` signal has no parameter and the `removed` signal needs a `Task*`. A `lambda` avoids the declaration of a verbose `slot` in `Task`. Qt 5 accepts a `lambda` instead of a slot in a `connect`, and both syntaxes can be used.

Our `lambda` executes a single line of code: `emit removed(this)`. `Emit` is a Qt macro that will trigger the connected `slot` with what we passed as the parameter. As we said earlier, `removed(Task* this)` has no function body, its purpose is to notify the registered slot of an event.

Lambdas are a great addition to C++. They offer a very practical way of defining short functions in your code. Technically, a `lambda` is the construction of a closure capable of capturing variables in its scope. The full syntax goes like this:

```
[ capture-list ] ( params ) -> ret { body }
```

Let's study each part of this statement:

- `capture-list`: Defines what variables will be visible inside the `lambda` scope.
- `params`: This is the function parameter's type list that can be passed to the `lambda` scope. There are no parameters in our case. We might have written `[this] () { ... }`, but C++11 lets us skip the parentheses altogether.
- `ret`: This is the return type of the `lambda` function. Just like `params`, this parameter can be omitted if the return type is `void`.
- `body`: This is obviously your code body where you have access to your `capture-list` and `params`, and which must return a variable with a `ret` type.

In our example, we captured the `this` pointer to be able to:

- Have a reference on the `removed()` function, which is part of the `Task` class. If we did not capture `this`, the compiler would have shouted `error: 'this' was not captured for this lambda function emit removed(this);`.
- Pass `this` to the `removed` signal: the caller needs to know which task triggered `removed`.

`capture-list` relies on standard C++ semantics: capture variables by copy or by reference. Let's say that we wanted to print a log of the `name` constructor parameter and we capture it by reference in our `lambda`:

```
connect(ui->removeButton, &QPushButton::clicked, [this, &name] {
        qDebug() << "Trying to remove" << name;
        this->emit removed(this);
    });
```

This code will compile fine. Unfortunately, the runtime will crash with a dazzling segmentation fault when we try to remove a `Task`. What happened? As we said, our `lambda` is an anonymous function that will be executed when the `clicked()` signal has been emitted. We captured the `name` reference, but this reference may be invalid once we get out of the `Task` constructor (more precisely, from the caller scope). The `qDebug()` function will then try to display an unreachable code and crash.

You really need to be careful with what you capture and the context in which your lambda will be executed. In this example, the segmentation fault can be amended by capturing `name` by copy:

```
connect(ui->removeButton, &QPushButton::clicked, [this, name] {
        qDebug() << "Trying to remove" << name;
        this->emit removed(this);
    });
```

- You can capture by copy or reference all variables that are reachable in the function where you define your lambda with the `=` and `&` syntax.
- The `this` variable is a special case of the capture list. You cannot capture it by the `[&this]` reference and the compiler will warn you if you are in this situation: `[=, this]`. Don't do this. Kittens will die.

Our `lambda` is passed directly as a parameter to the `connect` function. In other words, the `lambda` is a variable. This has many consequences: we can call it, assign it, and return it. To illustrate a "fully formed" `lambda`, we can define one that returns a formatted version of the task name. The sole purpose of this snippet is to investigate the `lambda` function's machinery. Don't include the following code in your `todo` app, your colleagues might call you a "functional zealot":

```
connect(ui->removeButton, &QPushButton::clicked, [this, name] {
    qDebug() << "Trying to remove" <<
```

```
        [] (const QString& taskName) -> QString {
            return "-------- " + taskName.toUpper();
    }(name);
    emit removed(this);
});
```

Here we did a tricky thing. We called `qDebug()`. Inside this call, we defined a `lambda` that is immediately executed. Let's analyze it:

- `[]`: We performed no capture. `lambda` does not depend on the enclosing function.
- `(const Qstring& taskName)`: When this lambda is called, it will expect a `QString` to work on.
- `-> QString`: The returned value of the lambda will be a `QString`.
- `return "------- " + taskName.toUpper()`: The body of our `lambda`. We return a concatenation of a string and the uppercase version of the `taskName` parameter. As you can see, string-manipulation becomes a lot easier with Qt.
- `(name)`: Here comes the catch. Now that the `lambda` function is defined, we can call it by passing the `name` parameter. In a single expression, we define it then call it. The `qDebug()` function will simply print the result.

The real benefit of this `lambda` will emerge if we are able to assign it to a variable and call it multiple times. C++ is statically typed, so we must provide the type of our `lambda` variable. In the language specification, a `lambda` type cannot be explicitly defined. We will soon see how we can do it with C++11. For now, let's finish our remove feature.

The task now emits the `removed()` signal. This signal has to be consumed by `MainWindow`:

```
// in MainWindow.h
public slots:
    void addTask();
    void removeTask(Task* task);

// In MainWindow.cpp
void MainWindow::addTask()
{
    ...
    if (ok && !name.isEmpty()) {
        qDebug() << "Adding new task";
        Task* task = new Task(name);
        connect(task, &Task::removed,
       this, &MainWindow::removeTask);
    ...
```

```
    }
}

void MainWindow::removeTask(Task* task)
{
    mTasks.removeOne(task);
    ui->tasksLayout->removeWidget(task);
    delete task;
}
```

`MainWindow::removeTask()` must match the `signal` signature. The connection is made when the task is created. The interesting part comes in the implementation of `MainWindow::removeTask()`.

The task is first removed from the `mTasks` vector. It is then removed from `tasksLayout`. The last step is to delete `Task`. The destructor will unregister itself from `centralWidget` of `MainWindow`. In this case, we don't rely on the Qt hierarchical parent-children system for the `QObject` life cycle because we want to delete `Task` before the destruction of `MainWindow`.

Simplifying with the auto type and a range-based for loop

The final step to a complete CRUD of our tasks is to implement the **completed** task feature. We'll implement the following:

- Click on the checkbox to mark the task as completed
- Strike the task name
- Update the status label in `MainWindow`

The checkbox click-handling follows the same pattern as `removed`:

```
// In Task.h
signals:
    void removed(Task* task);
    void statusChanged(Task* task);
private slots:
    void checked(bool checked);

// in Task.cpp
Task::Task(const QString& name, QWidget *parent) :
        QWidget(parent),
```

```
        ui(new Ui::Task)
{
    ...

    connect(ui->checkbox, &QCheckBox::toggled,
    this, &Task::checked);
}

...

void Task::checked(bool checked)
{
    QFont font(ui->checkbox->font());
    font.setStrikeOut(checked);
    ui->checkbox->setFont(font);
    emit statusChanged(this);
}
```

We define a `checked(bool checked)` slot that will be connected to the `QCheckBox::toggled` signal. In `slot checked()`, we strike out the `checkbox` text according to the `bool checked` value. This is done by using the `QFont` class. We create a copied font from `checkbox->font()`, modify it, and assign it back to `ui->checkbox`. Event if the original `font` was in bold or with a special size, its appearance would still be guaranteed to stay the same.

Play around with the font object in Qt Designer. Select `checkbox` in the `Task.ui` file and go to **Properties Editor | QWidget | font**.

The last instruction notifies `MainWindow` that the `Task` status has changed. The signal name is `statusChanged`, rather than `checkboxChecked`, in order to hide the implementation details of the task. Now add the following code in the `MainWindow.h` file:

```
// In MainWindow.h
public:
    void updateStatus();
public slots:
    void addTask();
    void removeTask(Task* task);
    void taskStatusChanged(Task* task);

// In MainWindow.cpp
MainWindow::MainWindow(QWidget *parent) :
    QMainWindow(parent),
    ui(new Ui::MainWindow),
```

```
    mTasks()
{
    ...
    updateStatus();
    }
}

void MainWindow::addTask()
{
    ...
    if (ok && !name.isEmpty()) {
        ...
        connect(task, &Task::removed, this,
                &MainWindow::removeTask);
        connect(task, &Task::statusChanged, this,
                &MainWindow::taskStatusChanged);
        mTasks.append(task);
        ui->tasksLayout->addWidget(task);
        updateStatus();
    }
}

void MainWindow::removeTask(Task* task)
{
    ...
    delete task;
    updateStatus();
}

void MainWindow::taskStatusChanged(Task* /*task*/)
{
    updateStatus();
}

void MainWindow::updateStatus()
{
    int completedCount = 0;
    for(auto t : mTasks)  {
        if (t->isCompleted()) {
            completedCount++;
        }
    }
    int todoCount = mTasks.size() - completedCount;

    ui->statusLabel->setText(
```

```
        QString("Status: %1 todo / %2 completed")
                             .arg(todoCount)
                             .arg(completedCount));
}
```

We defined a slot called `taskStatusChanged`, which is connected once a task is created. The single instruction of this `slot` is to call `updateStatus()`. This function iterates through the tasks and updates `statusLabel`. The `updateStatus()` function is called upon task creation and deletion.

In `updateStatus()`, we meet more new C++11 semantics:

```
for(auto t : mTasks)  {
    ...
}
```

The `for` keyword lets us loop over a range-based container. Because `QVector` is an iterable container, we can use it here. The range declaration (`auto t`) is the type and variable name that will be assigned at each iteration. The range expression (`mTasks`) is simply the container on which the process will be done. Qt provides a custom implementation of the `for` (namely, `foreach`) loop targeted at prior versions of C++; you don't need it anymore.

The `auto` keyword is another great new semantic. The compiler deduces the variable type automatically based on the initializer. It relieves a lot of pain for cryptic iterators such as this:

```
// without the 'auto' keyword
std::vector<Task*>::const_iterator iterator = mTasks.toStdVector().begin();

// with the 'auto' keyword, how many neurones did you save?
auto autoIter = mTasks.toStdVector().begin();
```

Since C++14, `auto` can even be used for function return types. It's a fabulous tool, but use it sparingly. If you put `auto`, the type should be obvious from the signature name/variable name.

The `auto` keyword can be combined with `const` and references. You can write a `for` loop such as this: `for (const auto & t : mTasks) { ... }`.

Remember our half-bread `lambda`? With all the covered features, we can write:

```
auto prettyName = [] (const QString& taskName) -> QString {
    return "-------- " + taskName.toUpper();
};
connect(ui->removeButton, &QPushButton::clicked,
    [this, name, prettyName] {
        qDebug() << "Trying to remove" << prettyName(name);
        this->emit removed(this);
});
```

Now that's something beautiful. Combining `auto` with `lambda` makes very readable code and opens up a world of possibilities.

The last item to study is the `QString` API. We used it in `updateStatus()`:

```
ui->statusLabel->setText(
        QString("Status: %1 todo / %2 completed")
                             .arg(todoCount)
                             .arg(completedCount));
```

The people behind Qt put a lot of work into making string-manipulation bearable in C++. This is a perfect example, where we replace the classic C `sprintf` with a more modern and robust API. Arguments are position-based only, no need to specify the type (less error-prone), and the `arg(...)` function accepts all kinds of types.

Take some time to skim through the `QString` documentation at `http://doc.qt.io/qt-5/qstring.html`. It shows how much you can do with this class and you'll see yourself using fewer and fewer examples of `std string` or even `cstring`.

Summary

In this chapter, we created a desktop Qt application from scratch. Qt is well known for its signal/slot mechanism and you must be confident using this paradigm. We also introduced some important C++14 features that will be used throughout this book.

It's now time to discover some `qmake` secrets and what really happens when you build your Qt project. In the next chapter, we will talk about how to create and organize an application with some platform-dependent code that must run on Windows, macOS, and Linux.

2
Discovering qmake Secrets

This chapter addresses the issue of creating a cross-platform application that relies on platform-specific code. We will see the impact of qmake on the compilation of your project.

You will learn how to create a system-monitoring application that retrieves the average CPU load and the memory used from Windows, Linux, and macOS. For this kind of OS-dependent application, architecture is the key to keeping your application reliable and maintainable.

By the end of this chapter, you will be able to create and organize a cross-platform application that uses platform-specific code and displays Qt Charts widgets. Moreover, qmake will not be a mystery anymore.

This chapter covers the following topics:

- Designing a cross-platform project
- Exploring Qt Charts
- The .pro file in depth
- Under the hood of qmake

Designing a cross-platform project

We want to display some visual gauges and chart widgets, so create a new **Qt widgets Application** called `ch02-sysinfo`. As already discussed in `Chapter 1`, *Get Your Qt Feet Wet*, Qt Creator, will generate some files for us: `main.cpp`, `MainWindow.h`, `MainWindow.cpp`, and `MainWindow.ui`.

Before diving into the C++ code, we must think about the software's architecture. This project will handle multiple desktop platforms. Thanks to the combination of C++ and Qt, most of the source code will be common to all targets. However, to retrieve both the CPU and memory usage from the OS (operating system), we will use some platform-specific code.

To successfully achieve this task, we will use two design patterns:

- **Strategy pattern**: This is an interface that describes functionalities (for example, retrieve CPU usage) and specific behaviors (retrieve CPU usage on Windows/macOS/Linux) will be performed into subclasses that implement this interface.
- **Singleton pattern**: This pattern guarantees a single instance for a given class. This instance will be easily accessible with a unique access point.

As you can see in the following diagram, the `SysInfo` class is our interface with the strategy pattern and is also a singleton. The specific behavior from the strategy pattern is performed in the `SysInfoWindowsImpl`, `SysInfoMacImpl`, and `SysInfoLinuxImpl` classes, subclassing `SysInfo`:

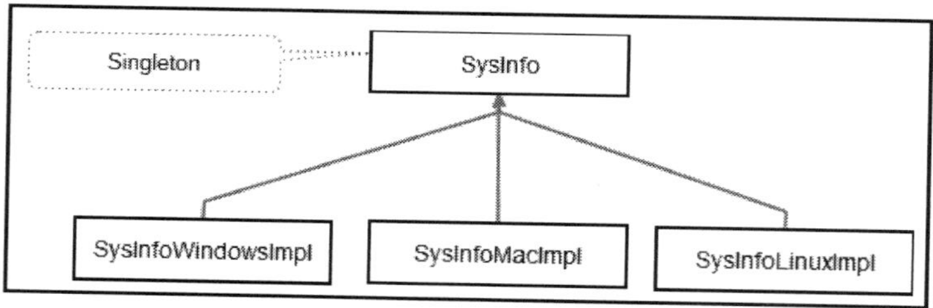

The UI part will only know and use the `SysInfo` class. The platform-specific implementation class is instantiated by the `SysInfo` class and the caller doesn't need to know anything about the `SysInfo` child classes. As the `SysInfo` class is a singleton, access will be easier for all widgets.

Let's begin by creating the `SysInfo` class. On Qt Creator, you can create a new C++ class from the contextual menu, accessible with a right-click on the project name in the hierarchy view. Then click on the **Add new** option, or from the menu, go to **File** | **New file or project** | **Files and classes**. Then perform the following steps:

1. Go to **C++ Class** | **Choose**.
2. Set the **Class name** field to `SysInfo`. As this class does not inherit from another class, we do not need to use the `Base` class field.

3. Click on **Next**, then **Finish** to generate an empty C++ class.

We will now specify our interface by adding three pure virtual functions: `init()`, `cpuLoadAverage()`, and `memoryUsed()`:

```
// In SysInfo.h
class SysInfo
{
public:
    SysInfo();
    virtual ~SysInfo();

    virtual void init() = 0;
    virtual double cpuLoadAverage() = 0;
    virtual double memoryUsed() = 0;
};

// In SysInfo.cpp
#include "SysInfo.h"

SysInfo::SysInfo()
{
}

SysInfo::~SysInfo()
{
}
```

Each of these functions has specific roles:

- `init()`: This function allows the derived class to perform any initialization process depending on the OS platform
- `cpuLoadAverage()`: This function calls some OS-specific code to retrieve the average CPU load and returns it as a percentage value
- `memoryUsed()`: This function calls some OS-specific code to retrieve the memory used and returns it as a percentage value

The `virtual` keyword indicates that the function can be overridden in a derived class. The `= 0` syntax means that this function is purely virtual and must be overridden in any concrete derived class. Moreover, this makes `SysInfo` an abstract class that cannot be instantiated.

We also added an empty virtual destructor. This destructor must be virtual to ensure that any deletion of an instance of a derived class—from a base class pointer—will call the derived class destructor and not only the base class destructor.

Now that our `SysInfo` class is an abstract class and ready to be derived, we will describe three implementations: Windows, macOS, and Linux. You can also perform only one implementation if you would rather not use the other two. We will not make any judgment on this. The `SysInfo` class will be transformed into a singleton after adding the implementations.

Adding the Windows implementation

Remember the UML diagram at the beginning of this chapter? The `SysInfoWindowsImpl` class is one of the classes derived from the `SysInfo` class. The main purpose of this class is to encapsulate the Windows-specific code to retrieve CPU and memory usage.

It's time to create the `SysInfoWindowsImpl` class. To do that, you need to perform the following steps:

1. Right click on the `ch02-sysinfo` project name in the hierarchy view
2. Click on **Add New | C++ Class | Choose**
3. Set the **Class name** field to `SysInfoWindowsImpl`
4. Set the **Base class** field to **<Custom>** and write under the `SysInfo` class
5. Click on **Next** then **Finish** to generate an empty C++ class

These generated files are a good starting point, but we must tune them:

```
#include "SysInfo.h"

class SysInfoWindowsImpl : public SysInfo
{
public:
    SysInfoWindowsImpl();

    void init() override;
    double cpuLoadAverage() override;
    double memoryUsed() override;
};
```

First, we need to add the `include` directive to our parent class, `SysInfo`. You can now override virtual functions defined in the base class.

Put your cursor on a derived class name (after the `class` keyword) and press *Alt* + *Enter* (Windows/Linux) or *Command* + *Enter* (Mac) to automatically insert virtual functions of the base class.

The `override` keyword comes from C++11. It ensures that the function is declared as virtual in the base class. If the function signature marked as `override` does not match any parent class' `virtual` function, a compile-time error will be displayed.

Retrieving the current memory used on Windows is easy. We will begin with this feature in the `SysInfoWindowsImpl.cpp` file:

```
#include "SysInfoWindowsImpl.h"

#include <windows.h>

SysInfoWindowsImpl::SysInfoWindowsImpl() :
    SysInfo()
{
}

double SysInfoWindowsImpl::memoryUsed()
{
    MEMORYSTATUSEX memoryStatus;
    memoryStatus.dwLength = sizeof(MEMORYSTATUSEX);
    GlobalMemoryStatusEx(&memoryStatus);
    qulonglong memoryPhysicalUsed =
        memoryStatus.ullTotalPhys - memoryStatus.ullAvailPhys;
    return (double)memoryPhysicalUsed /
        (double)memoryStatus.ullTotalPhys * 100.0;
}
```

Don't forget to include the `windows.h` file so that we can use the Windows API! Actually, this function retrieves the total and the available physical memory. A simple subtraction gives us the amount of memory used. As required by the `SysInfo` base class, this implementation will return the value as a `double` type; for example, a value of `23.0` for 23% memory used on a Windows OS.

Retrieving the total memory used is a good start, but we cannot stop now. Our class must also retrieve the CPU load. The Windows API can be messy sometimes. To make our code more readable, we will create two private helper functions. Update your `SysInfoWindowsImpl.h` file to match the following snippet:

```
#include <QtGlobal>
#include <QVector>

#include "SysInfo.h"

typedef struct _FILETIME FILETIME;

class SysInfoWindowsImpl : public SysInfo
{
public:
    SysInfoWindowsImpl();

    void init() override;
    double cpuLoadAverage() override;
    double memoryUsed() override;

private:
    QVector<qulonglong> cpuRawData();
    qulonglong convertFileTime(const FILETIME& filetime) const;

private:
    QVector<qulonglong> mCpuLoadLastValues;
};
```

Let's analyze these changes:

- `cpuRawData()` is the function that will perform the Windows API call to retrieve system-timing information and return values in a generic format. We will retrieve and return three values: the amount of time that the system has spent in idle, in Kernel, and in User mode.
- The `convertFileTime()` function is our second helper. It will convert a Windows `FILETIME struct` syntax to a `qulonglong` type. `qulonglong` is Qt type definition for `unsigned long long int`. This type is guaranteed by Qt to be 64-bit on all platforms. You can also use the `quint64 typedef`.
- `mCpuLoadLastValues` is a variable that will store system timing (idle, Kernel, and User) at a given moment.

- Don't forget to include the `<QtGlobal>` tag to use the `qulonglong` type and the `<QVector>` tag to use the `QVector` class.
- The `typedef struct _FILETIME FILETIME` syntax is a kind of forward-declaration for the `FILENAME` syntax. As we only use a reference, we can avoid including the `<windows.h>` tag in our `SysInfoWindowsImpl.h` file and keep it in the CPP file.

We can now switch to the `SysInfoWindowsImpl.cpp` file and implement these functions to finish the CPU load average feature on Windows:

```
#include "SysInfoWindowsImpl.h"

#include <windows.h>

SysInfoWindowsImpl::SysInfoWindowsImpl() :
    SysInfo(),
    mCpuLoadLastValues()
{
}

void SysInfoWindowsImpl::init()
{
    mCpuLoadLastValues = cpuRawData();
}
```

When the `init()` function is called, we store the return value from the `cpuRawData()` function in our `mCpuLoadLastValues` class variable. It will be helpful for the `cpuLoadAverage()` function process.

You may be wondering why we do not perform this task in the initialization list of the constructor. This is because when you call a function from the initialization list, the object is not yet fully constructed! In some circumstances, it may be unsafe because the function can try to access a member variable that has not been constructed yet. However, in this `ch02-sysinfo` project, the `cpuRawData` function does not use any member variables, so you are safe. If you really want to do it, add the `cpuRawData()` function to the `SysInfoWindowsImpl.cpp` file:

```
QVector<qulonglong> SysInfoWindowsImpl::cpuRawData()
{
    FILETIME idleTime;
    FILETIME kernelTime;
    FILETIME userTime;

    GetSystemTimes(&idleTime, &kernelTime, &userTime);
```

```
    QVector<qulonglong> rawData;

    rawData.append(convertFileTime(idleTime));
    rawData.append(convertFileTime(kernelTime));
    rawData.append(convertFileTime(userTime));
    return rawData;
}
```

Here we are: `GetSystemTimes()` is from the Windows API! This function will give us the amount of time that the system has spent idle and in the Kernel and User modes. Before filling the `QVector` class, we convert each value with our `convertFileTime()` helper described in the following code:

```
qulonglong SysInfoWindowsImpl::convertFileTime(const FILETIME& filetime)
const
{
    ULARGE_INTEGER largeInteger;
    largeInteger.LowPart = filetime.dwLowDateTime;
    largeInteger.HighPart = filetime.dwHighDateTime;
    return largeInteger.QuadPart;
}
```

The Windows `FILETIME` structure stores 64-bit information on two 32-bit parts (low and high). Our `convertFileTime()` function uses the Windows `ULARGE_INTEGER` structure to correctly build a 64-bit value in a single part before returning it as a `qulonglong` type. Last but not least, the `cpuLoadAverage()` implementation:

```
double SysInfoWindowsImpl::cpuLoadAverage()
{
    QVector<qulonglong> firstSample = mCpuLoadLastValues;
    QVector<qulonglong> secondSample = cpuRawData();
    mCpuLoadLastValues = secondSample;

    qulonglong currentIdle = secondSample[0] - firstSample[0];
    qulonglong currentKernel = secondSample[1] - firstSample[1];
    qulonglong currentUser = secondSample[2] - firstSample[2];
    qulonglong currentSystem = currentKernel + currentUser;

    double percent = (currentSystem - currentIdle) * 100.0 /
        currentSystem ;
    return qBound(0.0, percent, 100.0);
}
```

There are three important points to note here:

- Keep in mind that a sample is an absolute amount of time, so subtracting two different samples will give us instantaneous values that can be processed to get the current CPU load.
- The first sample comes from our `mCpuLoadLastValues` member variable, probed the first time by the `init()` function. The second one is retrieved when the `cpuRawData()` function is called. After initializing the samples, the `mCpuLoadLastValues` variable can store the new sample that will be used for the next call.
- The `percent` equation can be a little tricky because the Kernel value retrieved from the Windows API also contains the idle value.

If you want to learn more about the Windows API, take a look at the MSDN documentation at `https://msdn.microsoft.com/library`.

The final step to finish the Windows implementation is to edit the `ch02-sysinfo.pro` file so that it resembles the following snippet:

```
QT       += core gui charts
CONFIG   += C++14

greaterThan(QT_MAJOR_VERSION, 4): QT += widgets

TARGET = ch02-sysinfo
TEMPLATE = app

SOURCES += main.cpp \
    MainWindow.cpp \
    SysInfo.cpp

HEADERS += MainWindow.h \
    SysInfo.h

windows {
    SOURCES += SysInfoWindowsImpl.cpp
    HEADERS += SysInfoWindowsImpl.h
}

FORMS    += MainWindow.ui
```

Like we did in the `ch01-todo` project, we also use C++14 with the `ch02-sysinfo` project. The real new point here is that we removed the `SysInfoWindowsImpl.cpp` and `SysInfoWindowsImpl.h` files from the common `SOURCES` and `HEADERS` variables. Indeed, we added them into a `windows` platform scope. When building for other platforms, those files will not be processed by qmake. That is why we can safely include a specific header, such as `windows.h`, in the source `SysInfoWindowsImpl.cpp` file without harming the compilation on other platforms.

Adding the Linux implementation

Let's make the Linux implementation of our `ch02-sysinfo` project. If you have already done the Windows implementation, it will be a piece of cake! If you have not, you should take a look at it. Some information and tips will not be repeated in this part, such as how to create a `SysInfo` implementation class, keyboard shortcuts, and details about the `SysInfo` interface.

Create a new C++ class, called `SysInfoLinuxImpl`, that inherits from the `SysInfo` class and insert virtual functions from the base class:

```
#include <QtGlobal>

#include "SysInfo.h"

class SysInfoLinuxImpl : public SysInfo
{
public:
    SysInfoLinuxImpl();

    void init() override;
    double cpuLoadAverage() override;
    double memoryUsed() override;
};
```

We will start by implementing the `memoryUsed()` function in the `SysInfoLinuxImpl.cpp` file:

```
#include "SysInfoLinuxImpl.h"

#include <sys/types.h>
#include <sys/sysinfo.h>

SysInfoLinuxImpl::SysInfoLinuxImpl() :
    SysInfo()
{
```

```
}

double SysInfoLinuxImpl::memoryUsed()
{
    struct sysinfo memInfo;
    sysinfo(&memInfo);

    qulonglong totalMemory = memInfo.totalram;
    totalMemory += memInfo.totalswap;
    totalMemory *= memInfo.mem_unit;

    qulonglong totalMemoryUsed = memInfo.totalram - memInfo.freeram;
    totalMemoryUsed += memInfo.totalswap - memInfo.freeswap;
    totalMemoryUsed *= memInfo.mem_unit;

    double percent = (double)totalMemoryUsed /
        (double)totalMemory * 100.0;
    return qBound(0.0, percent, 100.0);
}
```

This function uses a Linux-specific API. After adding the required `includes`, you will be able to use the Linux `sysinfo()` function that returns information on the overall system statistics. With the two values: "total memory" and the "total memory used", we can easily return the `percent` value. Note that swap memory has been taken into account.

The CPU-load feature is a little more complex than the memory feature. Indeed, we will retrieve the total amount of time the CPU spent performing different kinds of work from Linux. That is not exactly what we want. We must return the instantaneous CPU load. A common way to get it is to retrieve two sample values in a short period of time and use the difference to get the instantaneous CPU load:

```
#include <QtGlobal>
#include <QVector>

#include "SysInfo.h"

class SysInfoLinuxImpl : public SysInfo
{
public:
    SysInfoLinuxImpl();

    void init() override;
    double cpuLoadAverage() override;
    double memoryUsed() override;
```

```
private:
    QVector<qulonglong> cpuRawData();
    QVector<qulonglong> mCpuLoadLastValues;
};
```

In this implementation, we will only add one helper function and one member variable:

- `cpuRawData()` is a function that will perform the Linux API call to retrieve system-timing information and return values in a `QVector` class of the `qulonglong` type. We retrieve and return four values containing the time the CPU has spent on the following: normal processes in User mode, nice processes in User mode, processes in Kernel mode, and idle.
- `mCpuLoadLastValues` is a variable that will store a sample of system-timing at a given moment.

Let's go to the `SysInfoLinuxImpl.cpp` file to update it:

```
#include "SysInfoLinuxImpl.h"

#include <sys/types.h>
#include <sys/sysinfo.h>

#include <QFile>

SysInfoLinuxImpl::SysInfoLinuxImpl() :
    SysInfo(),
    mCpuLoadLastValues()
{
}

void SysInfoLinuxImpl::init()
{
    mCpuLoadLastValues = cpuRawData();
}
```

As discussed previously, the `cpuLoadAverage` function will need two samples to be able to compute an instantaneous CPU load average. Calling the `init()` function allows us to set `mCpuLoadLastValues` for the first time:

```
QVector<qulonglong> SysInfoLinuxImpl::cpuRawData()
{
    QFile file("/proc/stat");
    file.open(QIODevice::ReadOnly);

    QByteArray line = file.readLine();
    file.close();
```

```
    qulonglong totalUser = 0, totalUserNice = 0,
        totalSystem = 0, totalIdle = 0;
    std::sscanf(line.data(), "cpu %llu %llu %llu %llu",
        &totalUser, &totalUserNice, &totalSystem,
        &totalIdle);

    QVector<qulonglong> rawData;
    rawData.append(totalUser);
    rawData.append(totalUserNice);
    rawData.append(totalSystem);
    rawData.append(totalIdle);

    return rawData;
}
```

To retrieve the CPU raw information on a Linux system, we will choose to parse the information available in the `/proc/stat` file. All we need is available on the first line, so a single `readLine()` is enough. Even though Qt provides some useful features, sometimes the C standard library functions are simpler. This is the case here: we are using `std::sscanf` to extract variables from a string. Now let's look at the `cpuLoadAvearge()` body:

```
double SysInfoLinuxImpl::cpuLoadAverage()
{
    QVector<qulonglong> firstSample = mCpuLoadLastValues;
    QVector<qulonglong> secondSample = cpuRawData();
    mCpuLoadLastValues = secondSample;

    double overall = (secondSample[0] - firstSample[0])
        + (secondSample[1] - firstSample[1])
        + (secondSample[2] - firstSample[2]);

    double total = overall + (secondSample[3] - firstSample[3]);
    double percent = (overall / total) * 100.0;
    return qBound(0.0, percent, 100.0);
}
```

This is where the magic happens. In this last function, we put all the puzzle pieces together. This function uses two samples of the CPU raw data. The first sample comes from our `mCpuLoadLastValues` member variable, which is set the first time by the `init()` function. The second sample is requested by the `cpuLoadAverage()` function. Then the `mCpuLoadLastValues` variable will store the new sample, which will be used as the first sample on the next `cpuLoadAverage()` function call.

The `percent` equation should be easy to understand:

- `overall` is equal to user + nice + kernel
- `total` is equal to overall + idle

You can find more information about `/proc/stat` in the Linux Kernel documentation at `https://www.kernel.org/doc/Documentation/filesystems/proc.txt`.

Like the other implementations, the last thing to do is edit the `ch02-sysinfo.pro` file, like this:

```
QT       += core gui charts
CONFIG   += C++14

greaterThan(QT_MAJOR_VERSION, 4): QT += widgets

TARGET = ch02-sysinfo
TEMPLATE = app

SOURCES += main.cpp \
    MainWindow.cpp \
    SysInfo.cpp \
    CpuWidget.cpp \
    MemoryWidget.cpp \
    SysInfoWidget.cpp

HEADERS += MainWindow.h \
    SysInfo.h \
    CpuWidget.h \
    MemoryWidget.h \
    SysInfoWidget.h

windows {
    SOURCES += SysInfoWindowsImpl.cpp
    HEADERS += SysInfoWindowsImpl.h
}

linux {
    SOURCES += SysInfoLinuxImpl.cpp
    HEADERS += SysInfoLinuxImpl.h
}

FORMS    += MainWindow.ui
```

With this Linux scope condition in the `ch02-sysinfo.pro` file, our Linux-specific files will not be processed by the `qmake` command on other platforms.

Adding the macOS implementation

Let's take a look at the Mac implementation of the `SysInfo` class. Start by creating a new C++ class named `SysInfoMacImpl`, which inherits from the `SysInfo` class. Override the `SysInfo` virtual functions and you should have a `SysInfoMacImpl.h` file, such as this:

```
#include "SysInfo.h"

#include <QtGlobal>
#include <QVector>

class SysInfoMacImpl : public SysInfo
{
public:
    SysInfoMacImpl();

    void init() override;
    double cpuLoadAverage() override;
    double memoryUsed() override;
};
```

The first implementation we will do is the `memoryUsed()` function, in the `SysInfoMacImpl.cpp` file:

```
#include "SysInfoMacImpl.h"

#include <mach/vm_statistics.h>
#include <mach/mach_types.h>
#include <mach/mach_init.h>
#include <mach/mach_host.h>
#include <mach/vm_map.h>

SysInfoMacImpl::SysInfoMacImpl() :
    SysInfo()
{

}

double SysInfoMacImpl::memoryUsed()
{
    vm_size_t pageSize;
    vm_statistics64_data_t vmStats;
```

```
        mach_port_t machPort = mach_host_self();
        mach_msg_type_number_t count = sizeof(vmStats)
                                / sizeof(natural_t);
        host_page_size(machPort, &pageSize);

        host_statistics64(machPort,
                          HOST_VM_INFO,
                          (host_info64_t)&vmStats,
                          &count);

        qulonglong freeMemory = (int64_t)vmStats.free_count
                              * (int64_t)pageSize;

        qulonglong totalMemoryUsed = ((int64_t)vmStats.active_count +
                              (int64_t)vmStats.inactive_count +
                              (int64_t)vmStats.wire_count)
                              * (int64_t)pageSize;

        qulonglong totalMemory = freeMemory + totalMemoryUsed;

        double percent = (double)totalMemoryUsed
                       / (double)totalMemory * 100.0;
        return qBound(0.0, percent, 100.0);
    }
```

We start by including the different headers for the macOS kernel. Then we initialize `machPort` with the call to the `mach_host_self()` function. `machPort` is a kind of special connection to the kernel that enables us to request information about the system. We then proceed to prepare other variables so that we can retrieve virtual memory statistics with `host_statistics64()`.

When the `vmStats` class is filled with the information needed, we extract the relevant data: `freeMemory` and `totalMemoryUsed`.

Note that macOS has a peculiar way of managing its memory: it keeps a lot of memory in cache, ready to be flushed when needed. This implies that our statistics can be misleading: we see the memory as used, whereas it was simply kept "just in case."

The percentage calculation is straightforward: we still return a min/max clamped value to avoid any crazy values in our future graph.

Next comes the `cpuLoadAverage()` implementation. The pattern is always the same: take samples at regular intervals and compute the growth on this interval. Therefore, we have to store intermediate values to be able to calculate the difference with the next sample:

```
    // In SysInfoMacImpl.h
```

```
#include "SysInfo.h"

#include <QtGlobal>
#include <QVector>

...

private:
    QVector<qulonglong> cpuRawData();
    QVector<qulonglong> mCpuLoadLastValues;
};

// In SysInfoMacImpl.cpp
void SysInfoMacImpl::init()
{
    mCpuLoadLastValues =  cpuRawData();
}

QVector<qulonglong> SysInfoMacImpl::cpuRawData()
{
    host_cpu_load_info_data_t cpuInfo;
    mach_msg_type_number_t cpuCount = HOST_CPU_LOAD_INFO_COUNT;
    QVector<qulonglong> rawData;
    qulonglong totalUser = 0, totalUserNice = 0, totalSystem = 0,
totalIdle = 0;
    host_statistics(mach_host_self(),
                    HOST_CPU_LOAD_INFO,
                    (host_info_t)&cpuInfo,
                    &cpuCount);

    for(unsigned int i = 0; i < cpuCount; i++) {
        unsigned int maxTicks = CPU_STATE_MAX * i;
        totalUser += cpuInfo.cpu_ticks[maxTicks + CPU_STATE_USER];
        totalUserNice += cpuInfo.cpu_ticks[maxTicks
                                           + CPU_STATE_SYSTEM];

        totalSystem += cpuInfo.cpu_ticks[maxTicks
                                           + CPU_STATE_NICE];

        totalIdle += cpuInfo.cpu_ticks[maxTicks + CPU_STATE_IDLE];
    }

    rawData.append(totalUser);
    rawData.append(totalUserNice);
    rawData.append(totalSystem);
    rawData.append(totalIdle);
    return rawData;
}
```

As you can see, the pattern used is strictly equivalent to the Linux implementation. You can even copy and paste the body of the `cpuLoadAverage()` function from the `SysInfoLinuxImpl.cpp` file. They do exactly the same thing.

Now, the implementation is different for the `cpuRawData()` function. We load `cpuInfo` and `cpuCount` with `host_statistics()` and then we loop through each CPU to have the `totalUser`, `totalUserNice`, `totalSystem`, and `totalIdle` functions filled. Finally, we append all this data to the `rawData` object before returning it.

The very last part is to compile the `SysInfoMacImpl` class only on macOS. Modify the `.pro` file to have the following body:

```
...

linux {
    SOURCES += SysInfoLinuxImpl.cpp
    HEADERS += SysInfoLinuxImpl.h
}

macx {
    SOURCES += SysInfoMacImpl.cpp
    HEADERS += SysInfoMacImpl.h
}

FORMS    += MainWindow.ui
```

Transforming SysInfo into a singleton

Promises are made to be kept: we will now transform the `SysInfo` class into a singleton. C++ offers many ways to implement the singleton design pattern. We will explain one of them here. Open the `SysInfo.h` file and make the following changes:

```
class SysInfo
{
public:
    static SysInfo& instance();
    virtual ~SysInfo();

    virtual void init() = 0;
    virtual double cpuLoadAverage() = 0;
    virtual double memoryUsed() = 0;

protected:
    explicit SysInfo();
```

```
private:
    SysInfo(const SysInfo& rhs);
    SysInfo& operator=(const SysInfo& rhs);
};
```

The singleton must guarantee that there will be only one instance of the class and that this instance will be easily accessible from a single access point.

So the first thing to do is to change the visibility of the constructor to `protected`. This way, only this class and the child classes will be allowed to call the constructor.

Since only one instance of the object must exist, allowing the copy constructor and the assignment operator is nonsense. One way to solve the problem is to make them `private`.

To disable the use of the copy constructors and assignment operator on a `QObject` class, you can also use the `Q_DISABLE_COPY` Qt macro. Moreover, since C++11, you can define a function as deleted with the `myFunction() = delete` syntax void. Any use of a deleted function will display a compile-time error. There are other ways to prevent the use of the copy constructor and the assignment operator with a singleton.

The last change is the "unique access point" with a `static` function instance that will return a reference of the `SysInfo` class.

It is now time to commit singleton changes to the `SysInfo.cpp` file:

```
#include <QtGlobal>

#ifdef Q_OS_WIN
    #include "SysInfoWindowsImpl.h"
#elif defined(Q_OS_MAC)
    #include "SysInfoMacImpl.h"
#elif defined(Q_OS_LINUX)
    #include "SysInfoLinuxImpl.h"
#endif

SysInfo& SysInfo::instance()
{
    #ifdef Q_OS_WIN
        static SysInfoWindowsImpl singleton;
    #elif defined(Q_OS_MAC)
        static SysInfoMacImpl singleton;
    #elif defined(Q_OS_LINUX)
        static SysInfoLinuxImpl singleton;
    #endif
```

```
        return singleton;
    }

    SysInfo::SysInfo()
    {
    }

    SysInfo::~SysInfo()
    {
    }
```

Here you can see another Qt cross-OS trick. Qt provides some macros: `Q_OS_WIN`, `Q_OS_LINUX`, or `Q_OS_MAC`. A Qt OS macro will be defined only on the corresponding OS. By combining these macros with an `#ifdef` conditional preprocessor directive, we can always include and instantiate the correct `SysInfo` implementation on all OSes.

Declaring the `singleton` variable as a static variable in the `instance()` function is a way to make a singleton in C++. We tend to prefer this version because you do not need to worry about the singleton memory management. The compiler will handle the instantiation the first time this function is called, as well as the destruction. Moreover, since C++11, this method is thread-safe.

Exploring Qt Charts

The core part is ready. It's now time to create a UI for this project and Qt Charts can help us with this task. Qt Charts is a module that provides a set of easy-to-use chart components, such as line chart, area chart, spline chart, and pie chart.

Qt Charts was previously a commercial-only Qt module. Since Qt 5.7, the module is now included in Qt on GPLv3 license for open source users. If you are stuck on Qt 5.6, you can build the module by yourself from sources. More information can be found at `https://github.com/qtproject/qtcharts`.

The aim now is to create two Qt widgets, `CpuWidget` and `MemoryWidget`, to display nice Qt charts of the CPU and the memory used. These two widgets will share a lot of common tasks, so we will first create an abstract class, `SysInfoWidget`:

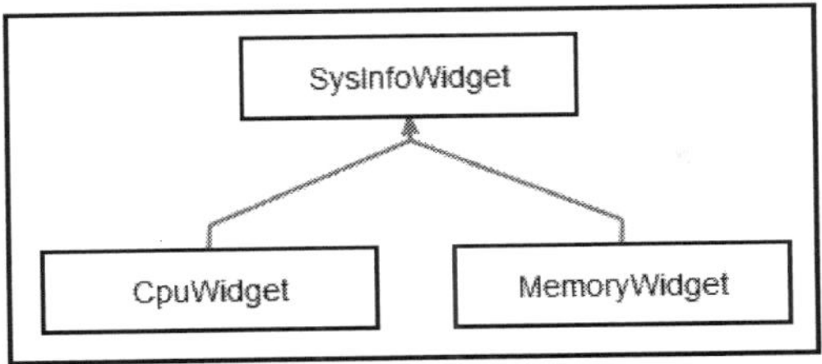

Then the two actual widgets will inherit from the `SysInfoWidget` class and perform their specific tasks.

First, add the `charts` module in your `.pro` file:

```
QT += charts
```

Then, create a new C++ class called `SysInfoWidget` with `QWidget` as a base class. Some enhancements must be processed in the `SysInfoWidget.h` file:

```
#include <QWidget>
#include <QTimer>
#include <QtCharts/QChartView>

class SysInfoWidget : public QWidget
{
    Q_OBJECT
public:
    explicit SysInfoWidget(QWidget *parent = 0,
                           int startDelayMs = 500,
                           int updateSeriesDelayMs = 500);

protected:
    QtCharts::QChartView& chartView();

protected slots:
    virtual void updateSeries() = 0;

private:
    QTimer mRefreshTimer;
    QtCharts::QChartView mChartView;
};
```

QChartView is the generic widget that can display many types of charts. This class will handle the layout and display QChartView. QTimer will call the updateSeries() slot function regularly. As you can see, this is a purely virtual slot. That is the reason why the SysInfoWidget class is abstract. The updateSeries() slot will be overridden by its child classes to retrieve a system value and define how the chart should be drawn. Note that the startDelayMs and updateSeriesDelayMs parameters have default values that can be customized by the caller if required.

We can now proceed to the SysInfoWidget.cpp file to correctly prepare this SysInfoWidget class before creating the child widgets:

```
#include <QVBoxLayout>

using namespace QtCharts;

SysInfoWidget::SysInfoWidget(QWidget *parent,
                             int startDelayMs,
                             int updateSeriesDelayMs) :
    QWidget(parent),
    mChartView(this)
{
    mRefreshTimer.setInterval(updateSeriesDelayMs);
    connect(&mRefreshTimer, &QTimer::timeout,
            this, &SysInfoWidget::updateSeries);
    mRefreshTimer.start(startDelayMs);

    mChartView.setRenderHint(QPainter::Antialiasing);
    mChartView.chart()->legend()->setVisible(false);

    QVBoxLayout* layout = new QVBoxLayout(this);
    layout->addWidget(&mChartView);
    setLayout(layout);
}

QChartView& SysInfoWidget::chartView()
{
    return mChartView;
}
```

All tasks in the SysInfoWidget constructor are common tasks required by the child widgets, CpuWidget and MemoryWidget. The first step is the mRefreshTimer initialization to define the timer interval and the slot to call whenever a timeout signal is triggered. Then, we start the timer after a delay defined by startDelayMs.

The next part enables the antialiasing to smooth the chart drawing. We hide the chart's legend to get a minimalist display. The last part handles the layout to display the `QChartView` widget in our `SysInfoWidget` class.

CpuWidget using QCharts

Now that the `SysInfoWidget` base class is ready, let's implement its first child class: `CpuWidget`. We will now use the Qt Charts API to display a good-looking widget. The average CPU load will be displayed in a pie graph with a hole in the center, like a partly-eaten donut where the eaten part is the percentage of the CPU used. The first step is to add a new C++ class, named `CpuWidget`, and make it inherit `SysInfoWidget`:

```
#include "SysInfoWidget.h"

class CpuWidget : public SysInfoWidget
{
public:
    explicit CpuWidget(QWidget* parent = 0);
};
```

In the constructor, the only parameter needed is `QWidget* parent`. Since we provided default values for the `startDelayMs` and `updateSeriesDelayMs` variables in the `SysInfoWidget` class, we get the best possible behavior; there is no need to remember it when subclassing `SysInfoWidget`, but it is still easy to override it if you need to.

The next step is to override the `updateSeries()` function from the `SysInfoWidget` class and start using the Qt Charts API:

```
#include <QtCharts/QPieSeries>

#include "SysInfoWidget.h"

class CpuWidget : public SysInfoWidget
{
    Q_OBJECT
public:
    explicit CpuWidget(QWidget* parent = 0);

protected slots:
    void updateSeries() override;

private:
    QtCharts::QPieSeries* mSeries;
};
```

Since we overrode the `SysInfoWidget::updateSeries()` slot, we have to include the `Q_OBJECT` macro to allow `CpuWidget` to respond to the `SysInfoWidgetmRefreshTimer::timeout()` signal.

We include `QPieSeries` from the Qt Charts module so that we can create a `QPieSeries*` member named `mSeries`. `QPieSeries` is a subclass of `QAbstractSeries`, which is the base class of all Qt Charts series (`QLineSeries`, `QAreaSeries`, `QPieSeries`, and so on). In Qt Charts, a `QAbstractSeries` subclass holds the data you want to display and defines how it should be drawn, but it does not define where the data should be displayed inside your layout.

We can now move on to `CpuWidget.cpp` to investigate how we can tell Qt where the drawing takes place:

```
using namespace QtCharts;

CpuWidget::CpuWidget(QWidget* parent) :
    SysInfoWidget(parent),
    mSeries(new QPieSeries(this))
{
    mSeries->setHoleSize(0.35);
    mSeries->append("CPU Load", 30.0);
    mSeries->append("CPU Free", 70.0);

    QChart* chart = chartView().chart();
    chart->addSeries(mSeries);
    chart->setTitle("CPU average load");
}
```

All Qt Charts classes are defined in the `QtCharts` namespace. This is why we start with `using namespace QtCharts`.

First, we initialize `mSeries` in the constructor initializer list. We then proceed to configure it. We carve the donut with `mSeries->setHoleSize(0.35)` and we append two data sets to `mSeries`: a fake `CPU Load` and `Cpu Free`, which are expressed in percentages (30% and 70%). These values are only here for your development phase. You should initialize these values to `0.0` when your application is finished. The `mSeries` function is now ready to be linked to the class managing its drawing: `QChart`.

The `QChart` class is retrieved from the `SysInfoWidget::chartView()` function. When calling `chart->addSeries(mSeries)`, `chart` takes the ownership of `mSeries` and will draw it according to the series type; in our case, `QPieSeries`.

QChart is not a QWidget—it is a subclass of QGraphicsWidget. QGraphicsWidget is similar to QWidget with some differences (its coordinates and geometry are defined with doubles or floats instead of integers, a subset of QWidget attributes are supported: custom drag, and drop framework).

The QGraphicsWidget class is designed to be added in a QGraphicsScene class, a high-performance Qt component used to draw hundreds of items onscreen at the same time.

In our SysInfo application, QChart has to be displayed in QVBoxLayout in SysInfoWidget. Here, the QChartView class comes in very handy. It lets us add chart in a QWidget layout.

So far, QPieSeries has seemed rather abstract. Let's add it to the MainWindow file to see how it looks:

```
// In MainWindow.h
#include "CpuWidget.h"

...

private:
    Ui::MainWindow *ui;
    CpuWidget mCpuWidget;
};

// In MainWindow.cpp
#include <QHBoxLayout>
#include "SysInfo.h"
MainWindow::MainWindow(QWidget *parent) :
    QMainWindow(parent),
    ui(new Ui::MainWindow),
    mCpuWidget(this)
{
    ui->setupUi(this);
    ui->centralWidget->setLayout(new QHBoxLayout());
    ui->centralWidget->layout()->addWidget(&mCpuWidget);
}
```

We simply declare mCpuWidget in the MainWindow.h file, initialize it, then add it to MainWindow->centralWidget->layout. The central widget is initialized as QHBoxLayout.

You should also initialize our singleton on the `main.cpp` file:

```
#include "MainWindow.h"
#include <QApplication>

#include "SysInfo.h"

int main(int argc, char *argv[])
{
    QApplication a(argc, argv);
    SysInfo::instance().init();
    MainWindow w;
    w.show();
    return a.exec();
}
```

Thanks to the architecture we built with the `SysInfo` and `SysInfoWidget` classes, the remaining part will be implemented swiftly.

Switch back to the `CpuWidget.cpp` file and implement the `updateSeries()` function with the following body:

```
void CpuWidget::updateSeries()
{
    double cpuLoadAverage = SysInfo::instance().cpuLoadAverage();
    mSeries->clear();
    mSeries->append("Load", cpuLoadAverage);
    mSeries->append("Free", 100.0 - cpuLoadAverage);
}
```

First, we get a reference to our `SysInfo` singleton. We then retrieve the current average CPU load in the `cpuLoadAverage` variable. We have to feed this data to our `mSeries`. The `mSeries` object is a `QPieSeries`, which implies that we just want a snapshot of the current CPU average load. Past history is not meaningful with this kind of graph. That's why we clear the `mSeries` data with the `mSeries->clear()` syntax, and append the `cpuLoadAverage` variable and then the free part (`100.0 - cpuLoadAverage`).

The nice thing to note is that, in the `CpuWidget` class, we don't have to worry about refreshing. All the work is done in the `SysInfoWidget` subclass with all the bells and whistles of the `QTimer` class. In a `SysInfoWidget` subclass, we only have to concentrate on the valuable specific code: what data should be displayed and what kind of graph is used to display it. If you look at the whole `CpuWidget` class, it is very short. The next `SysInfoWidget` subclass, `MemoryWidget`, will also be very concise and quick to implement.

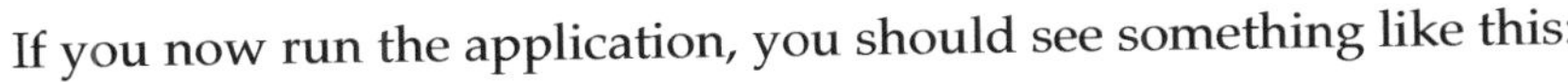

If you now run the application, you should see something like this:

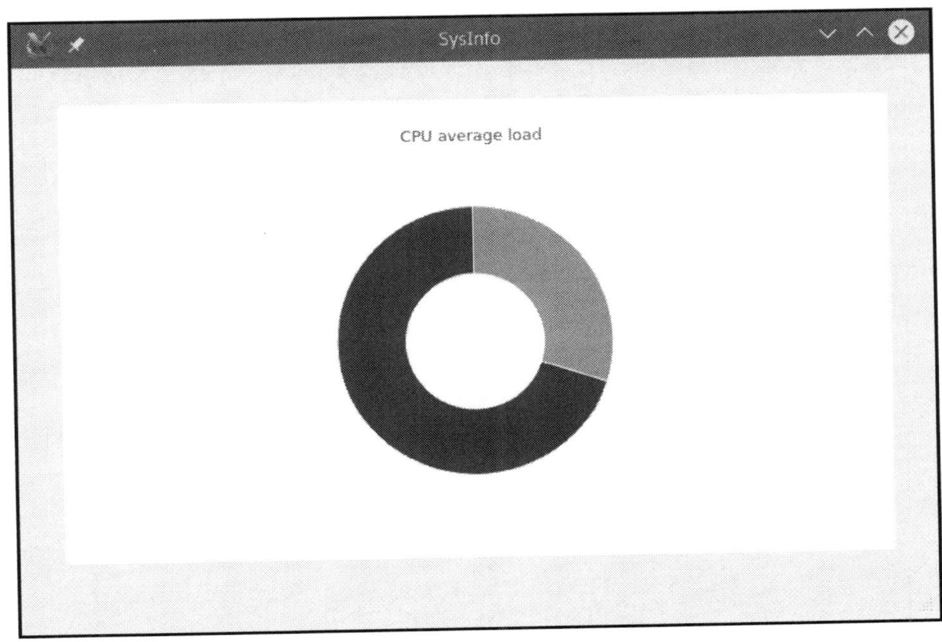

Memory using Qcharts

Our second `SysInfoWidget` is a `MemoryWidget` class. This widget will display a history of the data so that we can see how the memory consumption evolves over time. To display this data, we will use a `QLineSeries` class from the Qt Chart module. Create the `MemoryWidget` class and follow the same pattern we used for `CpuWidget`:

```
#include <QtCharts/QLineSeries>

#include "SysInfoWidget.h"

class MemoryWidget : public SysInfoWidget
{
    Q_OBJECT
public:
    explicit MemoryWidget(QWidget *parent = 0);

protected slots:
    void updateSeries() override;
```

```
private:
    QtCharts::QLineSeries* mSeries;
    qint64 mPointPositionX;
};
```

Instead of a being `QPieSeries*`, `mSeries` is a type of `QLineSeries*` that will be linked to the `chart` object in a very similar fashion to `MemoryWidget.cpp`:

```
#include "MemoryWidget.h"
#include <QtCharts/QAreaSeries>

using namespace QtCharts;

const int CHART_X_RANGE_COUNT = 50;
const int CHART_X_RANGE_MAX = CHART_X_RANGE_COUNT - 1;

MemoryWidget::MemoryWidget(QWidget *parent) :
    SysInfoWidget(parent),
    mSeries(new QLineSeries(this)),
    mPointPositionX(0)
{
    QAreaSeries* areaSeries = new QAreaSeries(mSeries);

    QChart* chart = chartView().chart();
    chart->addSeries(areaSeries);
    chart->setTitle("Memory used");
    chart->createDefaultAxes();
    chart->axisX()->setVisible(false);
    chart->axisX()->setRange(0, CHART_X_RANGE_MAX);
    chart->axisY()->setRange(0, 100);
}

void MemoryWidget::updateSeries()
{
}
```

The `mSeries` data is, as usual, initialized in the initializer list. `mPointPositionX` is an `unsigned long long` variable (using the `qint64` Qt notation) that will track the last X position of our dataset. This huge value is used to make sure that `mPointPositionX` never overflows.

We then use an intermediate `areaSeries` that takes ownership of `mSeries` upon its initialization in `QAreaSeries* areaSeries = new QareaSeries(mSeries)`. `areaSeries` is then added to the `chart` object at `chart->addSeries(areaSeries)`.

We do not want to display a single line in our `QChart`. Instead, we want to display an area that represents the used memory percentage. That is why we use an `areaSeries` type. Nonetheless, we will still update the `mSeries` data when adding new points to the dataset in the `updateSeries()` function. The `areaSeries` type will automatically handle them and deliver them to the `chart` object.

After `chart->addSeries(areaSeries)`, we configure the chart display:

- The `chart->createDefaultAxes()` function creates an *X* and *Y* axis based on the `areaSeries` type. If we used a 3D series, the `createDefaultAxes()` function would have added a *Z* axis.
- We hide the *X* axis tick values with `chart->axisX()->setVisible(false)` (intermediate values displayed at the bottom of the axis). In our `MemoryWidget` class, this information is not relevant.
- To define the number of points, we want to display the size of the display history. We call `chart->axisX()->setRange(0, CHART_X_RANGE_MAX)`. Here we use a constant to make it easier to modify this value afterward. Seeing the value at the top of the file, we avoid having to skim through `MemoryWidget.cpp`, searching for where this value is used to update it.
- `chart->axisY()->setRange(0, 100)` defines the maximum range of the *Y* axis, which is a percentage, based on the value returned by the `SysInfo::memoryUsed()` function.

The chart is now properly configured. We have to feed it by filling the `updateSeries()` body:

```
void MemoryWidget::updateSeries()
{
    double memoryUsed = SysInfo::instance().memoryUsed();
    mSeries->append(mPointPositionX++, memoryUsed);
    if (mSeries->count() > CHART_X_RANGE_COUNT) {
        QChart* chart = chartView().chart();
        chart->scroll(chart->plotArea().width()
                      / CHART_X_RANGE_MAX, 0);
        mSeries->remove(0);
    }
}
```

We first retrieve the latest memory percentage used and append it to `mSeries` at the `mPointPositionX` *X* coordinate (we post-increment it for the next `updateSeries()` call) and the `memoryUsed` *Y* coordinate. Since we want to keep a history of `mSeries`, we will never call the `mSeries->clear()` function. However, what will happen when we add more than just `CHART_X_RANGE_COUNT` points? The visible "window" on the chart is static and the points will be added outside. This means that we will see the memory usage only for the first `CHART_X_RANGE_MAX` points and then, nothing.

Fortunately, `QChart` provides a function to scroll inside the view to move the visible window. We start to handle this case only when the dataset is bigger than the visible window, translated by the `if (mSeries->count() > CHART_X_RANGE_COUNT)` code line. We then remove the point at the 0 index with `mSeries->remove(0)` to ensure that the widget will not store an infinite dataset. A `SysInfo` application that monitors the memory usage and has a memory leak is a bit sad.

The `chart->scroll(chart->plotArea().width() / CHART_X_RANGE_MAX, 0)` syntax will then scroll to the latest point on the *X* axis and nothing on *Y*. `chart->scroll(dx, dy)` expects coordinates expressed in our series coordinates. That is why we have to retrieve `char->plotArea()` divided by `CHART_X_RANGE_MAX`, the *X* axis unit.

We can now add the `MemoryWidget` class in `MainWindow`:

```
// In MainWindow.h
#include "CpuWidget.h"
#include "MemoryWidget.h"

...

private:
    Ui::MainWindow *ui;
    CpuWidget mCpuWidget;
    MemoryWidget mMemoryWidget;
};

// In MainWindow.cpp
MainWindow::MainWindow(QWidget *parent) :
    QMainWindow(parent),
    ui(new Ui::MainWindow),
    mCpuWidget(this),
    mMemoryWidget(this)
{
    ui->setupUi(this);
    SysInfo::instance().init();
    ui->centralWidget->setLayout(new QHBoxLayout());
```

```
        ui->centralWidget->layout()->addWidget(&mCpuWidget);
        ui->centralWidget->layout()->addWidget(&mMemoryWidget);
    }
```

Just like we did for `CpuWidget`, add a new member named `mMemoryWidget` to `MainWindow` and add it to the `centralWidget` layout with the `ui->centralWidget->layout()->addWidget(&mMemoryWidget)` syntax.

Compile, run the application, and wait for a few seconds. You should see something close to this:

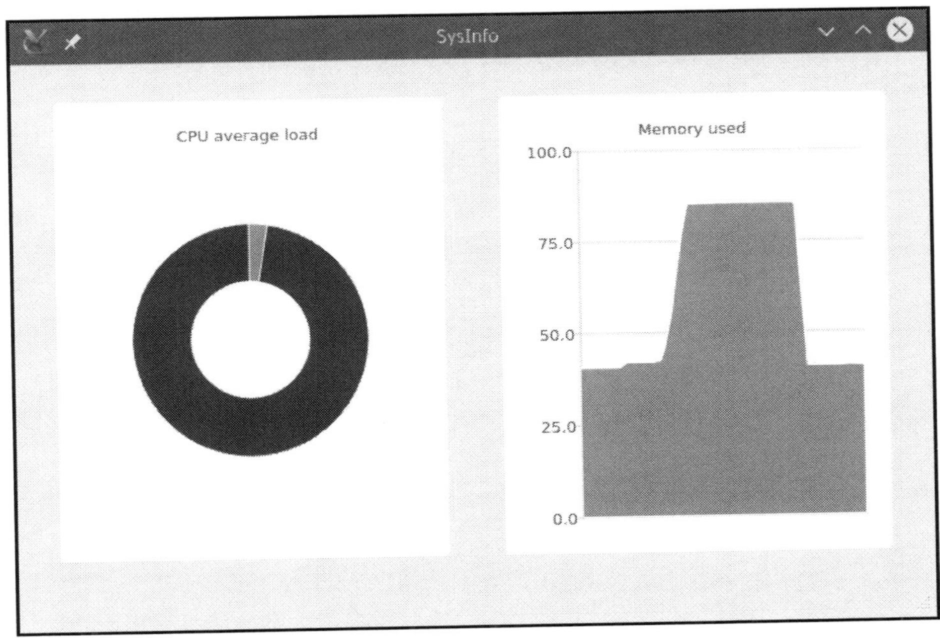

The `MemoryWidget` class works fine, but it looks a bit dull. We can customize it very easily with Qt. The goal is to have a bold line at the top of the memory area and a nice gradient from the top to the bottom. We just have to modify the `areaSeries` class in the `MemoryWidget.cpp` file:

```
#include <QtCharts/QAreaSeries>
#include <QLinearGradient>
#include <QPen>

#include "SysInfo.h"

using namespace QtCharts;
```

```
const int CHART_X_RANGE_COUNT = 50;
const int CHART_X_RANGE_MAX = CHART_X_RANGE_COUNT - 1;
const int COLOR_DARK_BLUE = 0x209fdf;
const int COLOR_LIGHT_BLUE = 0xbfdfef;
const int PEN_WIDTH = 3;

MemoryWidget::MemoryWidget(QWidget *parent) :
    SysInfoWidget(parent),
    mSeries(new QLineSeries(this))
{
    QPen pen(COLOR_DARK_BLUE);
    pen.setWidth(PEN_WIDTH);

    QLinearGradient gradient(QPointF(0, 0), QPointF(0, 1));
    gradient.setColorAt(1.0, COLOR_DARK_BLUE);
    gradient.setColorAt(0.0, COLOR_LIGHT_BLUE);
    gradient.setCoordinateMode(QGradient::ObjectBoundingMode);

    QAreaSeries* areaSeries = new QAreaSeries(mSeries);
    areaSeries->setPen(pen);
    areaSeries->setBrush(gradient);

    QChart* chart = chartView().chart();
    ...
}
```

The `QPen pen` function is part of the `QPainter` API. It is the foundation that Qt relies on to do most of the GUI drawing. This includes the whole `QWidget` API (`QLabel`, `QPushButton`, `QLayout`, and so on). For `pen`, we just have to specify its color and width and then apply it to the `areaSeries` class with `areaSeries->setPen(pen)`.

The principle is the same for the gradient. We define the starting point (`QPointF(0, 0)`) and the final point (`QPointF(0, 1)`) before specifying the color at each end of the vertical gradient. The `QGradient::ObjectBoundingMode` parameter defines how the start/final coordinates are mapped to the object. With the `QAreaSeries` class, we want the gradient coordinates to match the whole `QareaSeries` class. These coordinates are normalized coordinates, meaning that `0` is the start and `1` is the end of the shape:

- The `[0.0]` coordinates will point to the top-left corner of the `QAreaSeries` class
- The `[1.0]` coordinates will point to the bottom-left corner of the `QAreaSeries` class

One last build and run, and the `SysInfo` application will look like this:

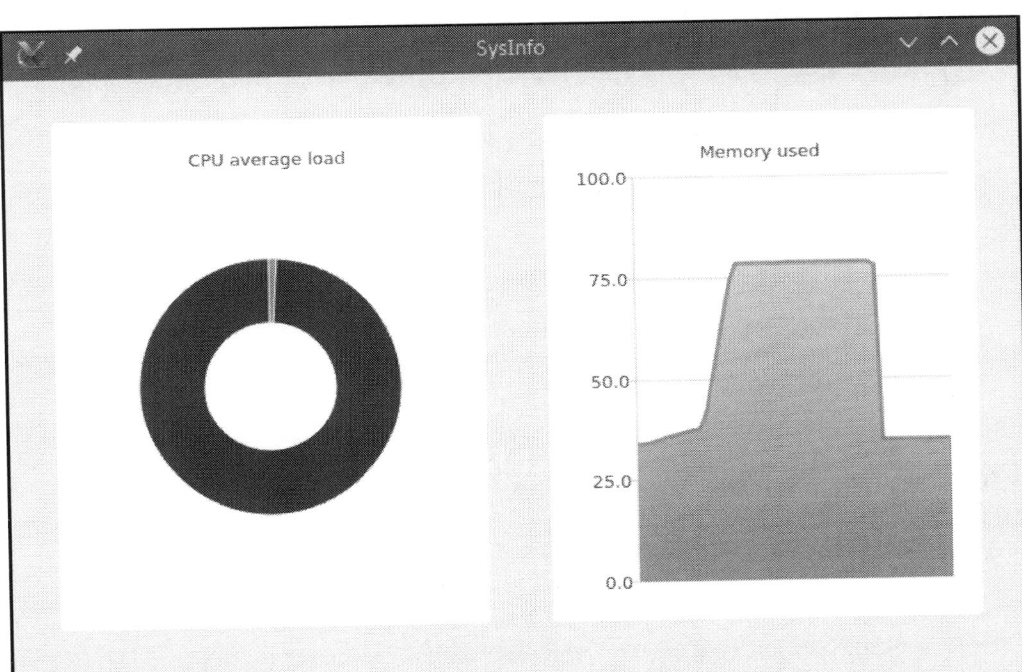

Generating memory leak or starting a virtual machine is a great way to make your memory go crazy. The `SysInfo` application is now finished and we even added some visual polish. You can explore the `QGradient` classes and the `QPainter` API if you want to further customize the widget.

The .pro file in depth

When you click on the **Build** button, what exactly is Qt Creator doing? How does Qt handle the compilation of the different platforms with a single `.pro` file? What does the `Q_OBJECT` macro imply, exactly? We will dig into each of these questions in the following sections. Our example case will be the `SysInfo` application we just completed and we will study what Qt is doing under the hood.

We can start this study by digging into the `.pro` file. It is the main entry point for compiling any Qt project. Basically, a `.pro` file is a `qmake` project file that describes the sources and headers used by the project. It is a platform-agnostic definition of a `Makefile`. First, we can cover the different `qmake` keywords used in the `ch02-sysinfo` application:

```
#-------------------------------------------------
#
# Project created by QtCreator 2016-03-24T16:25:01
#
#-------------------------------------------------
QT += core gui charts
CONFIG += C++14

greaterThan(QT_MAJOR_VERSION, 4): QT += widgets

TARGET = ch02-sysinfo
TEMPLATE = app
```

Each of these `qmake` variables has a specific role:

- `#`: The prefix needed to comment on a line. Yes, we generated the project on March 24, 2016 – crazy, huh?
- `QT`: A list of the Qt modules used in the project. In the platform-specific Makefile, each of the values will include the module headers and the corresponding library link.
- `CONFIG`: A list of configuration options for the project. Here, we configure the support of C++14 in the Makefile.
- `TARGET`: The name of the target output file.
- `TEMPLATE`: The project template used when generating the `Makefile`. The app tells `qmake` to generate a Makefile targeted for a binary. If you are building a library, use the `lib` value.

In the `ch02-sysinfo` application, we started to employ platform-specific compilation rules using the intuitive scope mechanism:

```
windows {
    SOURCES += SysInfoWindowsImpl.cpp
    HEADERS += SysInfoWindowsImpl.h
}
```

If you had to do this with a `Makefile`, you would probably lose some hair before getting it right (being bald is not an excuse). This syntax is simple yet powerful, and is also used for conditional statements. Let's say you wanted to build some files on debug only. You would have written the following:

```
windows {
    SOURCES += SysInfoWindowsImpl.cpp
    HEADERS += SysInfoWindowsImpl.h
    debug {
        SOURCES += DebugClass.cpp
        HEADERS += DebugClass.h
    }
}
```

Nesting the `debug` scope inside `windows` is the equivalent of `if (windows && debug)`. The scoping mechanism is even more flexible. You can have the OR Boolean operator condition with this syntax:

```
windows|unix {
  SOURCES += SysInfoWindowsAndLinux.cpp
}
```

You can even have `else if/else` statements:

```
windows|unix {
  SOURCES += SysInfoWindowsAndLinux.cpp
} else:macx {
  SOURCES += SysInfoMacImpl.cpp
} else {
  SOURCES += UltimateGenericSources.cpp
}
```

In this code snippet, we also see the use of the `+=` operator. The qmake tool provides a wide range of operators to modify the behavior of variables:

- `=`: This operator sets the variable to the value. The `SOURCES = SysInfoWindowsImpl.cpp` syntax would have assigned the single `SysInfoWindowsImpl.cpp` value to the `SOURCES` variable.
- `+=`: This operator adds the value to a list of values. This is what we commonly use in `HEADERS`, `SOURCES`, `CONFIG`, and so on.
- `-=`: This operator removes the value from the list. You can, for example, add a `DEFINE = DEBUG_FLAG` syntax in the common section, and in a platform-specific scope (say, a Windows release), remove it with the `DEFINE -= DEBUG_FLAG` syntax.

- `*=`: This operator adds the value to the list only if it is not already present. The `DEFINE *= DEBUG_FLAG` syntax adds the `DEBUG_FLAG` value only once.
- `~=`: This operator replaces any value that matches a regular expression with the specified value, `DEFINE ~= s/DEBUG_FLAG/debug`.

You can also define variables in the `.pro` file and reuse them in different places. We can simplify this with the use of the qmake `message()` function:

```
COMPILE_MSG = "Compiling on"

windows {
    SOURCES += SysInfoWindowsImpl.cpp
    HEADERS += SysInfoWindowsImpl.h
    message($$COMPILE_MSG windows)
}

linux {
    SOURCES += SysInfoLinuxImpl.cpp
    HEADERS += SysInfoLinuxImpl.h
    message($$COMPILE_MSG linux)
}

macx {
    SOURCES += SysInfoMacImpl.cpp
    HEADERS += SysInfoMacImpl.h
    message($$COMPILE_MSG mac)
}
```

If you build the project, you will see your platform-specific message each time you build the project in the **Compile Output** tab (you can access this tab from **Window** | **Output Panes** | **Compile Output**). Here, we defined a `COMPILE_MSG` variable and referenced it when calling `message($$COMPILE_MSG windows)`. This offers interesting possibilities when you need to compile external libraries from your `.pro` file. You can then aggregate all the sources in a variable, combine it with the call to a specific compiler, and so on.

If your scope-specific statement is a single line, you can use the following syntax to describe it:

`windows:message($$COMPILE_MSG windows).`

Besides `message()`, there are a few other helpful functions:

- `error(string)`: Displays the string and exits the compilation immediately.
- `exists(filename)`: Tests the existence of the `filename`. qmake also provides the `!` operator, which means you can write `!exist(myfile) { ... }`.
- `include(filename)`: Includes the content of another `.pro` file. It gives you the ability to slice your `.pro` files into more modular components. This will prove very useful when you have multiple `.pro` files for a single big project.

All the built-in functions are described at `http://doc.qt.io/qt-5/qmake-test-function-reference.html`.

Under the hood of qmake

As we said earlier, qmake is the foundation of the Qt framework compilation system. In Qt Creator, when you click on the **Build** button, qmake is invoked. Let's study what qmake is doing by calling it ourselves on the **command-line interface (CLI)**.

Create a temporary directory where you will store the generated files. We are working on a Linux box, but this is transposable on any OS. We will choose `/tmp/sysinfo`. Using the CLI, navigate to this new directory and execute the following command:

```
/path/to/qt/installation/5.7/gcc_64/bin/qmake -makefile -o Makefile
/path/to/sysinfoproject/ch02-sysinfo.pro
```

This command will execute qmake in the `-makefile` mode to generate a Makefile based on your `sysinfo.pro` file. If you skim through the Makefile content, you will see many things we covered earlier in the `.pro` section, such as the link to Qt modules, headers of different modules, and the inclusion of the headers and sources files of your project.

Now, let's build this Makefile by simply typing the `make` command.

This command will generate the `ch02-sysinfo` binary (based on the `TARGET` value of the `.pro` file). Here is the list of files now present in `/tmp/sysinfo`:

```
$ ls -1
ch02-sysinfo
CpuWidget.o
main.o
MainWindow.o
Makefile
MemoryWidget.o
moc_CpuWidget.cpp
moc_CpuWidget.o
moc_MainWindow.cpp
moc_MainWindow.o
moc_MemoryWidget.cpp
moc_MemoryWidget.o
moc_SysInfoWidget.cpp
moc_SysInfoWidget.o
SysInfoLinuxImpl.o
SysInfo.o
SysInfoWidget.o
ui_MainWindow.h
```

Now this is very interesting, we find all our sources compiled in the usual `.o` extension (`SysInfo.o`, `SysInfoWidget.o`, and so on), but there are also a lot of files prefixed with `moc_`. Here lies another keystone of the Qt framework: the Meta Object Compiler.

Every time you create a new class that inherits `QObject`, you have to include the macro `Q_OBJECT` in your header. Each time you emit a signal or receive one in a slot and you did not write any specific code to handle it, Qt took care of it. This is done by generating an intermediate implementation of your class (the `moc_*.cpp` file), which contains everything Qt needs to properly handle your signals and slots.

A picture is worth a thousand words. Here is the complete compilation pipeline for a standard qmake project:

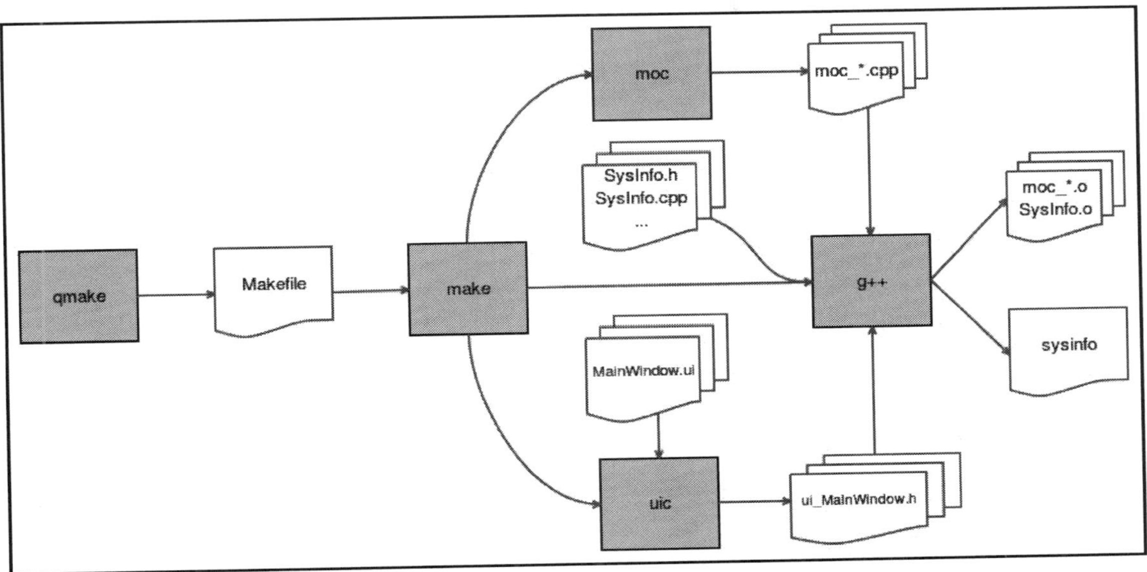

The blue boxes refer to commands and the wavy boxes are documents (sources or final binary). Let's walk through the steps:

1. The `qmake` command is executed with the project `.pro` file. It generates a Makefile based on the project file.
2. The `make` command is executed, which will call other commands to generate intermediate files.
3. The `uic` command stands for User-Interface Compiler. It takes all the `.ui` files (which are basically an XML description of your interface) and generates the corresponding `ui_*.h` header that you include in your own `.cpp` (in our `ch02-sysinfo` project, it is in `MainWindow.cpp`).
4. The `moc` command takes every class containing the `Q_OBJECT` macro (paired with the superclass `QObject`) and generates the intermediate `moc_*.cpp` files, which include everything needed to make the signal/slot framework work.

5. The `g++` command is executed, compiling all your source files and intermediate `moc` files into `.o` files before finally linking everything in the `ch02-sysinfo` binary.

Note that if you add a `Q_OBJECT` macro after the creation of a class, sometimes the compiler will complain about your signals and slots. To fix this, simply run the `qmake` command from **Build | Run qmake**. You can now see that this stems from the fact that the Makefile has to be regenerated to include the generation of the new intermediate `moc` file.

Generally, source-code generation is regarded as bad practice in the developer community. Qt has been criticized for this for a long time. We always fear that the machine does some kind of voodoo behind our back. Unfortunately, C++ does not offer any practical way of doing code introspection (namely reflection), and the signal and slots mechanism needs some kind of metadata about your class to be resolved. This could have been done partly with the C++ template system, but this solution seemed to be much less readable, portable, usable, and robust for Qt. You also need an excellent compiler support for templates. This cannot be assumed in the wild world of C++ compilers.

The `moc` system is now fully mature. There are some very specific edge cases where it could bring trouble (some people have reported problems in very specific situations with Visual Studio), but even so, we think that the gain of this feature largely outweighs any possible issues. The signal/slot system is a marvel to work with and if you look at the beginnings of Qt, the system has been present from the very first releases. Adding the functor notation in Qt 5 (which gives a compile time check of the validity of your `connect()` function), combined with C++11 `lambas`, makes it a real delight.

Beneath Q_OBJECT and signals/slots

The Qt building system should be clearer now. Still, the `Q_OBJECT` macro and the signal/slot/emit keywords are still black boxes. Let's dive into `Q_OBJECT`. You can *Ctrl* + click on the macro name, or select it and press *F2* to go to its declaration.

The truth lies in the source code; `Q_OBJECT` is defined in the `qobjectdefs.h` file (in Qt 5.7):

```
#define Q_OBJECT \
public: \
    // skipped details
    static const QMetaObject staticMetaObject; \
    virtual const QMetaObject *metaObject() const; \
```

```
        virtual void *qt_metacast(const char *); \
        virtual int qt_metacall(QMetaObject::Call, int, void **); \
        QT_TR_FUNCTIONS \
    private: \
        // skipped details
    qt_static_metacall(QObject *, QMetaObject::Call, int, void **);
```

This macro defines some static functions and `static QMetaObject`. The body of these static functions is implemented in the generated `moc` file. We will not drown you in the gory details of the `QMetaObject` class. The role of this class is to store all the meta-information for the `QObject` subclass. It also maintains a correspondence table between the signals and slots of your class and to the signals and slots of any connected class. Each signal and each slot is assigned with a unique index:

- The `metaObject()` function returns `&staticMetaObject` for a normal Qt class and `dynamicMetaObject` when working with QML objects.
- The `qt_metacast()` function performs a dynamic cast using the name of the class. This function is required because Qt does not rely on standard C++ **Runtime Type Information (RTTI)** to retrieve metadata about an object or a class.
- `qt_metacall()` directly calls an internal signal or slot by its index. Because an index is used rather than a pointer, there is no pointer dereferencing and the generated `switch case` can be heavily optimized by the compiler (the compiler can directly include the `jump` instruction to the specific case very early on, avoiding a lot of branch evaluation). Thus, the execution of the signal/slot mechanism is quite fast.

Qt also adds non-standard C++ keywords to manage the signal/slot mechanism, namely `signals`, `slots`, and `emit`. Let's see what's behind each one and how everything fits inside a `connect()` function.

The `slots` and `signals` keywords are also defined in `qobjectdefs.h`:

```
#     define slots
#     define signals public
```

That is right: `slots` points to nothing and the `signals` keyword is just a placeholder for the `public` keyword. All your `signals`/`slots` are just functions. The `signals` keyword is forced to be `public` to make sure that your signal functions are visible outside of your class (what is the point of a `private signal` anyway?). The Qt magic is simply the ability to emit a `signal` function to any connected `slot` function without knowing the details of the class implementing this `slot`. Everything is done through the `QMetaObject` class implementation in the `moc` file. When a signal is emitted, the `QMetaObject::activate()` function is called with the changed value and the signals index.

The last definition to study is `emit`:

```
# define emit
```

So many definitions of nothing, it is almost absurd! The `emit` keyword is completely useless from a code perspective: `moc` plainly ignores it and nothing particular happens with it afterwards. It is merely a hint for the developer to notice they are working with signals/slots rather than plain functions.

To trigger `slot`, you must connect your `signal` to it using the `QObject::connect()` function. This function creates a new `Connection` instance, which is defined in `qobject_p.h`:

```
struct Connection
    {
        QObject *sender;
        QObject *receiver;
        union {
            StaticMetaCallFunction callFunction;
            QtPrivate::QSlotObjectBase *slotObj;
        };
        // The next pointer for the singly-linked ConnectionList
        Connection *nextConnectionList;
        //senders linked list
        Connection *next;
        Connection **prev;
        ...
    };
```

The `Connection` instance stores a pointer to the signal emitter class (`sender`), the slot-receiver class (`receiver`), and the indexes of the connected `signal` and `slot` keywords. When a signal is emitted, every connected slot must be called. To be able to do this, every `QObject` has a linked list of `Connection` instances for each `signal` and the same linked list of `Connection` for each of its `slot` keywords.

This pair of linked lists allows Qt to properly walk through each dependent `slot/signal` couple to trigger the right functions using the indexes. The same reasoning is used to handle the `receiver` destruction. Qt walks through the double-linked list and removes the object from where it was connected.

This walk happens in the famous UI thread, where the whole message loop is processed and every connected signal/slot is triggered according to the possible events (mouse, keyboard, network, and so on). Because the `QThread` class inherits `QObject`, any `QThread` can use the signal/slot mechanism. Additionally, the `signals` keyword can be posted to other threads where they will be processed in the receiving threads' event loop.

Summary

In this chapter, we created a cross-platform `SysInfo` application. We covered the singleton and the strategy pattern to have neat code organization with platform-specific code. You learned to use the Qt Charts module to display system information in real time. Finally, we took a deep dive into the `qmake` command to see how Qt implements the signal/slot mechanism and to see what is hidden behind Qt-specific keywords (`emit`, `signals`, and `slots`).

By now, you should have a clear picture of how Qt works and how you can tackle a cross-platform application. In the next chapter, we will look at how you can split a bigger project in order to keep your sanity as a maintainer. We will study a fundamental pattern in Qt—the Model/View—and discover how to use a database with Qt.

3

Dividing Your Project and Ruling Your Code

The last chapter delved into qmake to study what lies beneath the signal/slot system and covered a reasonable approach to implementing platform-specific code. This chapter will show you how a project can be properly divided to enjoy the maximum leverage from the Qt framework.

To do this, you will create a gallery application that handles albums and pictures. You will be able to create, read, update, and delete any album and display the pictures in a grid of thumbnails or in full resolution. All of this will be persisted in a SQL database.

This chapter lays the foundations of the gallery by creating a core library that will be used in the following two chapters: `Chapter 4`, *Conquering the Desktop UI*, and `Chapter 5`, *Dominating the Mobile UI*.

This chapter covers the following topics:

- Designing a maintainable project
- Storing your data in a database
- Protecting your code with a smart pointer
- Implementing the model

Designing a maintainable project

The first step in designing a maintainable project is to properly split it in clearly defined modules. A common approach is to separate the engine from the user interface. This separation forces you to reduce coupling between the different parts of your code and make it more modular.

This is exactly the approach we will take with the gallery application. The project will be divided into three sub-projects:

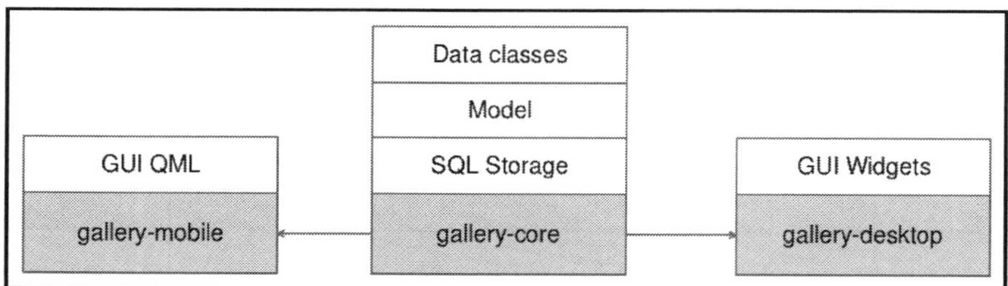

The sub-projects are as follows:

- **gallery-core**: This is a library containing the core of the application logic: the data classes (or business classes), persistent storage (in SQL), and the model that makes the storage available to the UI through a single entry point.
- **gallery-desktop**: This is a Qt widget application that will depend on the `gallery-core` library to retrieve data and display it to the user. This project will be covered in `Chapter 4`, *Conquering the Desktop UI.*
- **gallery-mobile**: This is a QML application targeted at mobile platforms (Android and iOS). It will also rely on `gallery-core`. This project will be covered in `Chapter 5`, *Dominating the Mobile UI.*

As you can see, each layer has a single responsibility. This principle is applied to both the project structure and the code organization. Throughout these three projects, we will endeavor to live up to the motto of the chapter: *Dividing Your Project and Ruling Your Code.*

To separate your Qt project this way, we will create a different kind of project, a **Subdirs** project:

1. Click on **File** | **New File or Project**
2. In the **Projects** types, select **Other Project** | **Subdirs Project** | **Choose**

3. Name it `ch03-gallery-core` and then click on **Next**
4. Select your latest **Qt Desktop Kit**, and then click on **Next** | **Finish & Add Subproject**

Here, Qt Creator created the parent project, `ch03-gallery-core`, which will host our three sub-projects (`gallery-core`, `gallery-desktop`, and `gallery-mobile`). The parent project has neither code nor a compilation unit in itself, it is simply a convenient way to group multiple `.pro` projects and express the dependencies between them.

The next step is to create the first `subdir` project, which Qt Creator proposed immediately when you clicked on **Finish & Add Subproject**. We will start with `gallery-core`:

1. Select **Library** in the **Projects** tab.
2. Select **C++ Library**.
3. Choose the **Shared Library** type, name it `gallery-core`, and click on **Next**.
4. Select the modules, `QtCore`, and `QtSql`, and then click on **Next**.
5. Type `Album` in the **Class name** field, and click on **Next**. Qt Creator will generate the basic skeleton of a library with this class as an example.
6. Check that the project is properly added as a sub-project of `ch03-gallery-core.pro` and click on **Finish**.

Before delving into the `gallery-core` code, let's study what Qt Creator just made for us. Open the parent `.pro` file, `ch03-gallery-core.pro`:

```
TEMPLATE = subdirs

SUBDIRS += \
    gallery-core
```

So far, we've used the `TEMPLATE = app` syntax in our `.pro` files. The `subdirs` project template indicates to Qt that it should search for sub-projects to compile. When we added the `gallery-core` project to `ch03-gallery-core.pro`, Qt Creator added it to the `SUBDIRS` variable. As you can see, `SUBDIRS` is a list, so you can add as many sub-projects as you want.

When compiling `ch03-gallery-core.pro`, Qt will scan each `SUBDIRS` value to compile them. We can now switch to `gallery-core.pro`:

```
QT       += sql
QT       -= gui

TARGET = gallery-core
TEMPLATE = lib

DEFINES += GALLERYCORE_LIBRARY
SOURCES += Album.cpp
HEADERS += Album.h\
        gallery-core_global.h

unix {
    target.path = /usr/lib
    INSTALLS += target
}
```

Let's see how this works:

- `QT` has appended the `sql` module and removed the `gui` module. By default, `QtGui` is always included and has to be removed explicitly.
- The `TEMPLATE` value is different, again. We use `lib` to tell qmake to generate a Makefile that will output a shared library, named `gallery-core` (as specified by the `TARGET` variable).
- The `DEFINES += GALLERY_CORE_LIBRARY` syntax is a compilation flag that lets the compiler know when it should import or export library symbols. We will come back to this soon.
- `HEADERS` contains our first class, `Album.h`, but also another generated header: `gallery-core_global.h`. This file is syntactic sugar provided by Qt to ease the pain of a cross-platform library.
- The `unix { ... }` scope specifies the installation destination of the library. This platform scope is generated because we created the project on Linux. By default, it will try to install the library in the system library path (`/usr/lib`).

Please remove the `unix` scope altogether, we don't need to make the library available across the system.

To have a better understanding of the cross-platform shared object issue, you can open `gallery-core_global.h`:

```
#include <QtCore/qglobal.h>

#if defined(GALLERYCORE_LIBRARY)
#  define GALLERYCORESHARED_EXPORT Q_DECL_EXPORT
#else
#  define GALLERYCORESHARED_EXPORT Q_DECL_IMPORT
#endif
```

We encounter `GALLERYCORE_LIBRARY`, defined in the `gallery-core.pro` file, again. Qt Creator generated a useful piece of code for us: the cross-platform way to handle symbol-visibility in a shared library.

When your application links to a shared library, symbol functions, variables, and classes must be marked in a special way to be visible by the application using the shared library. The default visibility of a symbol depends on the platform. Some platforms will hide symbols by default, other platforms will make them public. Of course, each platform and compiler has its own macros to express this public/private notion.

To obviate the whole `#ifdef windows #else` boilerplate code, Qt provides `Q_DECL_EXPORT` (if we are compiling the library) and `Q_DECL_IMPORT` (if we are compiling your application using the shared library). Thus, throughout the symbols you want to mark as public, you just have to use the `GALLERYCORESHARED_EXPORT` macro.

An example is available in the `Album.h` file:

```
#ifndef ALBUM_H
#define ALBUM_H

#include "gallery-core_global.h"

class GALLERYCORESHARED_EXPORT Album
{

public:
    Album();
};

#endif // ALBUM_H
```

You include the proper `gallery-core_global.h` file to have access to the macro and you use it just after the `class` keyword. It does not pollute your code too much and will still be cross-platform.

Another possibility is to make a Statically Linked Library. This path is interesting if you want fewer dependencies to handle (a single binary is always easier to deploy). There are several downsides:

Increased compilation time: Each time you modify the library, the application will have to be recompiled as well.

Tighter coupling: Multiple applications cannot link to your library. Each one of them must embed it.

Defining data classes

We are building our gallery from the ground up. We will start with the implementation of our data classes to be able to properly write the database layer. The application aims to organize pictures into albums. Hence, the two obvious classes are `Album` and `Picture`. In our example, an album simply has a name. A `Picture` class must belong to an `Album` class and have a file path (the path on your filesystem where the original file is located).

The `Album` class has already been created on project creation. Open the `Album.h` file and update it to include the following implementation:

```
#include <QString>

#include "gallery-core_global.h"

class GALLERYCORESHARED_EXPORT Album
{
public:
    explicit Album(const QString& name = "");

    int id() const;
    void setId(int id);
    QString name() const;
    void setName(const QString& name);

private:
    int mId;
    QString mName;
};
```

As you can see, the `Album` class contains only an `mId` variable (the database ID) and an `mName` variable. In a typical **Object-Oriented Paradigm (OOP)**, the `Album` class would have had a `QVector<Picture>mPictures` field. We did not do it on purpose. By decoupling these two objects, we will have more flexibility when we want to load an album without pulling the potential thousands of associated pictures. The other problem in having `mPictures` in the `Album` class is that the developer (you or anybody else) using this code will ask themself: when is `mPictures` loaded? Should I do a partial load of `Album` and have an incomplete `Album` or should I always load `Album` with every picture in it?

By completely removing the field, the question ceases to exist, and the code is simpler to grasp. The developer knows intuitively that they will have to explicitly load the pictures if they want them. Otherwise, they can continue with this simple `Album` class.

The getters and setters are obvious enough; we will let you implement them without showing them to you. We will only take a look at the `Album` class' constructor in `Album.cpp`:

```
Album::Album(const QString& name) :
    mId(-1),
    mName(name)
{
}
```

The `mId` variable is initialized to `-1` to be sure that, by default, an invalid ID is used and the `mName` variable is assigned a `name` value.

We can now proceed to the `Picture` class. Create a new C++ class named `Picture` and open `Picture.h` to modify it like so:

```
#include <QUrl>
#include <QString>

#include "gallery-core_global.h"

class GALLERYCORESHARED_EXPORT Picture
{
public:
    Picture(const QString& filePath = "");
    Picture(const QUrl& fileUrl);

    int id() const;
    void setId(int id);

    int albumId() const;
    void setAlbumId(int albumId);
```

```
    QUrl fileUrl() const;
    void setFileUrl(const QUrl& fileUrl);
private:
    int mId;
    int mAlbumId;
    QUrl mFileUrl;
};
```

Don't forget to add the `GALLERYCORESHARED_EXPORT` macro right before the `class` keyword to export the class from the library. As a data structure, `Picture` has an `mId` variable, belongs to an `mAlbumId` variable, and has an `mFileUrl` value. We use the `QUrl` type to make path manipulation easier to use depending on the platform (desktop or mobile).

Let's take a look at `Picture.cpp`:

```
#include "Picture.h"
Picture::Picture(const QString& filePath) :
    Picture(QUrl::fromLocalFile(filePath))
{
}

Picture::Picture(const QUrl& fileUrl) :
    mId(-1),
    mAlbumId(-1),
    mFileUrl(fileUrl)
{
}

QUrl Picture::fileUrl() const
{
    return mFileUrl;
}

void Picture::setFileUrl(const QUrl& fileUrl)
{
    mFileUrl = fileUrl;
}
```

In the first constructor, the static function, `QUrl::fromLocalFile`, is called to provide a `QUrl` object to the other constructor, which takes a `QUrl` parameter.

The ability to call other constructors is a nice addition in C++11.

Storing your data in a database

Now that the data classes are ready, we can implement the database layer. Qt provides a ready-to-use `sql` module. Various databases are supported in Qt using SQL database drivers. In `gallery-desktop`, we will use the `SQLITE` driver, which is included in the `sql` module and perfectly fits the use case:

- **A very simple database schema**: No need for complex queries
- **Very few or no concurrent transactions**: No need for a complex transaction model
- **A single-purpose database**: No need to spawn a system service, the database is stored in a single file and does not need to be accessed by multiple applications

The database will be accessed from multiple locations; we need to have a single entry point for it. Create a new C++ class named `DatabaseManager` and modify `DatabaseManager.h` to look like this:

```
#include <QString>

class QSqlDatabase;

const QString DATABASE_FILENAME = "gallery.db";

class DatabaseManager
{
public:
    static DatabaseManager& instance();
    ~DatabaseManager();

protected:
    DatabaseManager(const QString& path = DATABASE_FILENAME);
    DatabaseManager& operator=(const DatabaseManager& rhs);

private:
    QSqlDatabase* mDatabase;
};
```

The first thing to notice is that we implement the singleton pattern in the `DatabaseManager` class, like we did in the *Transforming SysInfo in a singleton* section from `Chapter 2`, *Discovering qmake Secrets*. The `DatabaseManager` class will open the connection in the `mDatabase` field and lend it to other possible classes.

Also, QSqlDatabase is forward-declared and used as a pointer for the mDatabase field. We could have included the QSqlDatabase header, but we would have had a undesired side-effect: every file, which includes DatabaseManager, must also include QSqlDatabase. Thus, if we ever have some transitive inclusion in our application (which links to the gallery-core library), the application is forced to enable the sql module. As a consequence, the storage layer leaks through the library. The application should not have any knowledge about the storage-layer implementation. For all the application cares, it could be in SQL, XML, or anything else; the library is a black box that should honor the contract and persist the data.

Let's switch to DatabaseManager.cpp and open the database connection:

```
#include "DatabaseManager.h"

#include <QSqlDatabase>

DatabaseManager& DatabaseManager::instance()
{
    static DatabaseManager singleton;
    return singleton;
}

DatabaseManager::DatabaseManager(const QString& path) :
    mDatabase(new QSqlDatabase(QSqlDatabase::addDatabase("QSQLITE")))
{
    mDatabase->setDatabaseName(path);
    mDatabase->open();
}

DatabaseManager::~DatabaseManager()
{
    mDatabase->close();
    delete mDatabase;
}
```

The correct database driver is selected on the mDatabase field initialization with the QSqlDatabase::addDatabase("QSQLITE") function call. The following steps are just a matter of configuring the database name (which is incidentally the file path in SQLITE) and opening the connection with the mDatabase->open() function. In the DatabaseManager destructor, the connection is closed and the mDatabase pointer is properly deleted.

The database link is now opened. All we have to do is to execute our Album and Picture queries.

Implementing the **CRUD (Create/Read/Update/Delete)** for both our data classes in `DatabaseManager` would quickly push `DatabaseManager.cpp` to be several hundreds lines long. Add a few more tables and you can already see what a monster `DatabaseManager` would turn into.

For this reason, each of our data classes will have a dedicated database class, responsible for all the database CRUD operations. We will start with the `Album` class. Create a new C++ class named `AlbumDao` (data access object), and update `AlbumDao.h`:

```
class QSqlDatabase;

class AlbumDao
{
public:
    AlbumDao(QSqlDatabase& database);
    void init() const;

private:
    QSqlDatabase& mDatabase;
};
```

The `AlbumDao` class' constructor takes a `QSqlDatabase&` parameter. This parameter is the database connection that will be used for all the SQL queries done by the `AlbumDao` class. The `init()` function aims to create the `albums` table and should be called when `mDatabase` is opened.

Let's see the implementation of `AlbumDao.cpp`:

```
#include <QSqlDatabase>
#include <QSqlQuery>

#include "DatabaseManager.h"

AlbumDao::AlbumDao(QSqlDatabase& database) :
    mDatabase(database)
{
}

void AlbumDao::init() const
{
    if (!mDatabase.tables().contains("albums")) {
        QSqlQuery query(mDatabase);
        query.exec("CREATE TABLE albums (id INTEGER PRIMARY KEY
AUTOINCREMENT, name TEXT)");
    }
}
```

As usual, the `mDatabase` field is initialized with the database parameter. In the `init()` function, we can see a real SQL request in action. If the `albums` table class does not exist, a `QSqlQuery` query is created that will use the `mDatabase` connection to be executed. If you omit `mDatabase`, the query will use a default anonymous connection.
The `query.exec()` function is the simplest manner of executing a query: you simply pass your query as a `QString` object. Here, we create the `albums` table with the fields matching the `Album` data class (`id` and `name`).

The `QSqlQuery::exec()` function returns a `bool` value that indicates whether the request has been successful. In your production code, always check this value. You can further investigate the error with `QSqlQuery::lastError()`. An example is available in this chapter's source code in `DatabaseManager::debugQuery()`.

The skeleton of the `AlbumDao` class is done. The next step is to link it to the `DatabaseManager` class. Update the `DatabaseManager` class like so:

```
// In DatabaseManager.h
#include "AlbumDao.h"

...

private:
    QSqlDatabase* mDatabase;

public:
    const AlbumDao albumDao;
};

// In DatabaseManager.cpp
DatabaseManager::DatabaseManager(const QString& path) :
    mDatabase(new QSqlDatabase(QSqlDatabase::addDatabase("QSQLITE"))),
    albumDao(*mDatabase)
{
    mDatabase->setDatabaseName(path);
    mDatabase->open();

    albumDao.init();
}
```

The `albumDao` field is declared as a `public const AlbumDao` in the `DatabaseManager.h` file. This needs some explanation:

- The `public` visibility is to give `DatabaseManager` clients access to the `albumDao` field. The API becomes intuitive enough; if you want to make a database operation on an `album`, just call `DatabaseManager::instance().albumDao`.
- The `const` keyword is to make sure that nobody can modify `albumDao`. Because it is `public`, we cannot guarantee the safety of the object (anybody could modify the object). As a side-effect, we force every public function of `AlbumDao` to be `const`. This makes sense; after all, the `AlbumDao` field could have been a namespace with a bunch of functions. It is more convenient for it to be a class because we can keep the reference to the database connection with the `mDatabase` field.

In the `DatabaseManager` constructor, the `albumDao` class is initialized with the `mDatabase` dereferenced pointer. The `albumDao.init()` function is called after the database connection has opened.

We can now implement more interesting SQL queries. We can start with the creation of a new album in the `AlbumDao` class:

```
// In AlbumDao.h
class QSqlDatabase;
class Album;

class AlbumDao
{
public:
    AlbumDao(QSqlDatabase& database);
    void init() const;
    void addAlbum(Album& album) const;
    ...
};

// In AlbumDao.cpp
#include "AlbumDao.h"

#include <QSqlDatabase>
#include <QSqlQuery>
#include <QVariant>

...

void AlbumDao::addAlbum(Album& album) const
```

```
{
    QSqlQuery query(mDatabase);
    query.prepare("INSERT INTO albums (name) VALUES (:name)");
    query.bindValue(":name", album.name());
    query.exec();
    album.setId(query.lastInsertId().toInt());
}
```

The `addAlbum()` function takes an `album` parameter to extract its information and execute the corresponding query. Here, we approach the prepared query notion: the `query.prepare()` function takes a `query` parameter that contains placeholders for parameters provided later. We will provide the `name` parameter with the `:name` syntax. Two syntaxes are supported: Oracle style with a colon-name (for example, `:name`) or ODBC style with a question mark (for example, `?name`).

We then use the bind `:name` syntax to the value of the `album.name()` function. Because `QSqlQuery::bind()` expects a `QVariant` as a parameter value, we have to add the `include` directive to this class.

In a nutshell, a `QVariant` is a generic data-holder that accepts a wide range of primitive types (`char`, `int`, `double`, and so on) and complex types (`QString`, `QByteArray`, `QUrl`, and so on).

When the `query.exec()` function is executed, the bound values are properly replaced. The `prepare()` statement technique makes the code more robust to SQL injection (injecting a hidden request would fail) and be more readable.

The execution of the query modifies the state of the query object itself. The `QSqlQuery` query is not simply a SQL query-executor, it also contains the state of the active query. We can retrieve information about the query with the `query.lastInsertId()` function, which returns a `QVariant` value containing the ID of the album row we just inserted. This `id` is given to the `album` provided in the `addAlbum()` parameter. Because we modify `album`, we cannot mark the parameter as `const`. Being strict about the `const` correctness of your code is a good hint for a fellow developer, who can deduce that your function may or may not modify the passed parameter.

The remaining update and delete operations follow strictly the same pattern used for `addAlbum()`. We will just provide the expected function signatures in the next code snippet. Please refer to the source code of the chapter for the complete implementation. However, we need to implement the request to retrieve all the albums in the database. This one deserves a closer look:

```
// In AlbumDao.h
```

```
#include <QVector>

    ...
    void addAlbum(Album& album) const;
    void updateAlbum(const Album& album) const;
    void removeAlbum(int id) const;
    QVector<Album*> albums() const;
    ...
};

// In AlbumDao.cpp
QVector<Album*> AlbumDao::albums() const
{
    QSqlQuery query("SELECT * FROM albums", mDatabase);
    query.exec();
    QVector<Album*> list;
    while(query.next()) {
        Album* album = new Album();
        album->setId(query.value("id").toInt());
        album->setName(query.value("name").toString());
        list.append(album);
    }
    return list;
}
```

The `albums()` function must return a `QVector<Album*>` value. If we take a look at the body of the function, we see yet another property of `QSqlQuery`. To walk through multiple rows for a given request, `query` handles an internal cursor pointing to the current row. We can then proceed to create a `new Album*()` function and fill it with the row data given by the `query.value()` statement, which takes a column name parameter and returns a `QVariant` value that is casted to the proper type. This new `album` parameter is appended to the `list` and, finally, this `list` is returned to the caller.

The `PictureDao` class is very similar to the `AlbumDao` class, both in usage and implementation. The main difference is that a picture has a foreign key to an album. The `PictureDao` function must be conditioned by an `albumId` parameter. The following code snippet shows the `PictureDao` header and the `init()` function:

```
// In PictureDao.h
#include <QVector>

class QSqlDatabase;
class Picture;

class PictureDao
{
```

```
public:
    explicit PictureDao(QSqlDatabase& database);
    void init() const;

    void addPictureInAlbum(int albumId, Picture& picture) const;
    void removePicture(int id) const;
    void removePicturesForAlbum(int albumId) const;
    QVector<Picture*> picturesForAlbum(int albumId) const;

private:
    QSqlDatabase& mDatabase;
};

// In PictureDao.cpp
void PictureDao::init() const
{
    if (!mDatabase.tables().contains("pictures")) {
        QSqlQuery query(mDatabase);
        query.exec(QString("CREATE TABLE pictures")
        + " (id INTEGER PRIMARY KEY AUTOINCREMENT, "
        + "album_id INTEGER, "
        + "url TEXT)");
    }
}
```

As you can see, multiple functions take an `albumId` parameter to make the link between the picture and the owning `album` parameter. In the `init()` function, the foreign key is expressed in the `album_id INTEGER` syntax. SQLite 3 does not have a proper foreign key type. It is a very simple database and there is no strict constraint for this type of field; a simple integer is used.

Finally, the `PictureDao` function is added in the `DatabaseManager` class just like we did for `albumDao`. One could argue that, if there are a lot of `Dao` classes, adding a `const Dao` member in the `DatabaseManager` class and calling the `init()` function quickly becomes cumbersome.

A possible solution could be to make an abstract `Dao` class, with a pure, virtual `init()` function. The `DatabaseManager` class would have a `Dao` registry, which maps each `Dao` to a `QString` key with `QHash<QString, const Dao> mDaos`. The `init()` function call would then be called in a `for` loop and a `Dao` object would be accessed using the `QString` key. This is outside the scope of this project, but is nevertheless an interesting approach.

Protecting your code with a smart pointer

The code we just described is fully functional. But it can be strengthened, specifically with the `AlbumDao::albums()` function. In this function, we iterate through the database rows and create a new `Album` to fill a list. We can zoom in on this specific code section:

```
QVector<Album*> list;
while(query.next()) {
    Album* album = new Album();
    album->setId(query.value("id").toInt());
    album->setName(query.value("name").toString());
    list.append(album);
}
return list;
```

Let's say that the `name` column has been renamed to `title`. If you forget to update `query.value("name")`, you might run into trouble. The Qt framework does not rely on exceptions, but this cannot be said for every API available in the wild. An exception here would cause a memory leak: the `Album* album` function has been allocated on the heap but not released. To handle this, you would have to surround the risky code with a `try/catch` statement and deallocate the `album` parameter if an exception has been thrown. Maybe this error should bubble up; hence, your `try/catch` statement is only there to handle the potential memory leak. Can you picture the spaghetti code weaving in front of you?

The real issue with pointers is the uncertainty of their ownership. Once it has been allocated, who is the owner of a pointer? Who is responsible for deallocating the object? When you pass a pointer as a parameter, when does the caller retain the ownership or release it to the callee?

Since C++11, a major milestone has been reached in memory management: the smart pointer feature has been stabilized and can greatly improve the safety of your code. The goal is to explicitly indicate the ownership of a pointer through simple template semantics. There are three types of smart pointer:

- The `unique_ptr` pointer indicates that only one client has the ownership at one time
- The `shared_ptr` pointer indicates that the pointer's ownership is shared among several clients
- The `weak_ptr` pointer indicates that the pointer does not belong to the client

For now, we will focus on the `unique_ptr` pointer to understand the smart pointer's mechanics.

A `unique_ptr` pointer is simply a variable allocated on the stack that takes the ownership of the pointer you provide with it. Let's allocate an `Album` with this semantic:

```
#include <memory>
void foo()
{
    Album* albumPointer = new Album();
    std::unique_ptr<Album> album(albumPointer);
    album->setName("Unique Album");
}
```

The whole smart pointer API is available in the `memory` header. When we declared `album` as a `unique_ptr`, we did two things:

- We allocated `unique_ptr<Album>` on the stack. The `unique_ptr` pointer relies on templates to check the validity of the pointer type at compile-time.
- We granted the ownership of the `albumPointer` memory to `album`. From this point on, `album` is the owner of the pointer.

This simple line has important ramifications. First and foremost, you no longer have to worry about the pointer's life cycle. Because a `unique_ptr` pointer is allocated on the stack, it will be destroyed as soon as it goes out of scope. In this example, when we exit `foo()`, `album` will be removed from the stack. The `unique_ptr` implementation will take care of calling the `Album` destructor and deallocating the memory.

Secondly, you explicitly indicate the ownership of your pointer at compile-time. Nobody can deallocate the `albumPointer` content if they do not voluntarily fiddle with your `unique_ptr` pointer. Your fellow developers will also know at first glance who the owner of your pointer is.

Note that even though `album` is a type of `unique_ptr<Album>`, you can still call `Album` functions (for example, `album->setName()`) using the `->` operator. This is possible thanks to the overload of this operator. The usage of the `unique_ptr` pointer becomes transparent.

Well, this use case is nice, but the purpose of a pointer is to be able to allocate a chunk of memory and share it. Let's say the `foo()` function allocates the `album unique_ptr` pointer and then transfers the ownership to `bar()`. That would look like this:

```
void bar(std::unique_ptr<Album> barAlbum)
{
   qDebug() << "Album name" << barAlbum->name();
}

void foo()
```

```
{
    std::unique_ptr<Album> album(new Album());
    bar(std::move(album));
}
```

Here, we introduce the `std::move()` function: its goal is to transfer the ownership of a `unique_ptr` function. Once `bar(std::move(album))` has been called, `album` becomes invalid. You can test it with a simple `if` statement: `if (album) { ... }`.

From now on, the `bar()` function becomes the owner of the pointer (through `barAlbum`) by allocating a new `unique_ptr` on the stack and it will deallocate the pointer on its exit. You do not have to worry about the cost of a `unique_ptr` pointer, as these objects are very lightweight and it is unlikely that they will affect the performance of your application.

Again, the signature of `bar()` tells the developer that this function expects to take the ownership of the passed `Album`. Trying to pass around `unique_ptr` without the `move()` function will lead to a compile error.

Another thing to note is the different meanings of the `.` (dot) and the `->` (arrow) when working with a `unique_ptr` pointer:

- The `->` operator dereferences to the pointer members and lets your call function on your real object
- The `.` operator gives you access to the `unique_ptr` object functions

The `unique_ptr` pointer provides various functions. Among them, the most important are:

- The `get()` function returns the raw pointer. `album.get()` returns an `Album*` value.
- The `release()` function releases the ownership of the pointer and returns the raw pointer. The `album.release()` function returns an `Album*` value.
- The `reset(pointer p = pointer())` function destroys the currently-managed pointer and takes ownership of the given parameter. An example would be the `barAlbum.reset()` function, which destroys the currently owned `Album*`. With a parameter, `barAlbum.reset(new Album())` also destroys the owned object and takes the ownership of the provided parameter.

Finally, you can dereference the object with the * operation, meaning *album will return an Album& value. This dereferencing is convenient, but you will see that the more a smart pointer is used, the less you will need it. Most of the time, you will replace a raw pointer with the following syntax:

```
void bar(std::unique_ptr<Album>& barAlbum);
```

Because we pass unique_ptr by reference, bar() does not take ownership of the pointer and will not try to deallocate it upon its exit. With this, there is no need to use move(album) in foo(); the bar() function will just do operations on the album parameter but will not take its ownership.

Now, let's consider shared_ptr. A shared_ptr pointer keeps a reference counter on a pointer. Each time a shared_ptr pointer references the same object, the counter is incremented. When this shared_ptr pointer goes out of scope, the counter is decremented. When the counter reaches zero, the object is deallocated.

Let's rewrite our foo()/bar() example with a shared_ptr pointer:

```
#include <memory>

void bar(std::shared_ptr<Album> barAlbum)
{
   qDebug() << "Album name" << barAlbum->name();
} // ref counter = 1
void foo()
{
    std::shared_ptr<Album> album(new Album()); // ref counter = 1
    bar(album); // ref counter = 2
} // ref counter = 0
```

As you can see, the syntax is very similar to the unique_ptr pointer. The reference counter is incremented each time a new shared_ptr pointer is allocated and points to the same data, and is decremented on the function exit. You can check the current count by calling the album.use_count() function.

The last smart pointer we will cover is the weak_ptr pointer. As the name suggests, it does not take any ownership or increment the reference counter. When a function specifies weak_ptr, it indicates to the callers that it is just a client and not an owner of the pointer. If we re-implement bar() with a weak_ptr pointer, we get:

```
#include <memory>

void bar(std::weak_ptr<Album> barAlbum)
{
```

```
    qDebug() << "Album name" << barAlbum->name();
} // ref counter = 1

void foo()
{
    std::shared_ptr<Album> album(new Album()); // ref counter = 1
    bar(std::weak_ptr<Album>(album)); // ref counter = 1
} // ref counter = 0
```

If the story stopped here, there would not be any interest in using `weak_ptr` versus a raw pointer. `weak_ptr` has a major advantage for the dangling pointer issue. If you are building a cache, you typically do not want to keep strong references to your object. On the other hand, you want to know whether the objects are still valid. By using `weak_ptr`, you know when an object has been deallocated. Now, consider the raw pointer approach: your pointer might be invalid but you do not know the state of the memory.

There is another semantic introduced in C++14 that we have to cover: `make_unique`. This keyword aims to replace the `new` keyword and construct a `unique_ptr` object in an exception-safe manner. This is how it is used:

```
unique_ptr<Album> album = std::make_unique<Album>();
```

The `make_unique` keyword wraps the `new` keyword to make it exception-safe, specifically in this situation:

```
foo(new Album(), new Picture())
```

This code will be executed in the following order:

1. Allocate and construct the `Album` function
2. Allocate and construct the `Picture` function
3. Execute the `foo()` function

If `new Picture()` throws an exception, the memory allocated by `new Album()` will be leaked. This is fixed by using the `make_unique` keyword:

```
foo(make_unique<Album>(), make_unique<Picture>())
```

The `make_unique` keyword returns a `unique_ptr` pointer; the C++ standard committee also provided an equivalent for `shared_ptr` in the form of `make_shared`, which follows the same principle.

All these new C++ semantics try very hard to get rid of `new` and `delete`. Yet, it may be cumbersome to write all the `unique_ptr` and `make_unique` stuff. The `auto` keyword comes to the rescue in our `album` creation:

```
auto album = std::make_unique<Album>();
```

This is a radical departure from the common C++ syntax. The variable type is deduced, there is no explicit pointer, and the memory is automatically managed. After some time with smart pointers, you will see fewer and fewer raw pointers in your code (and even fewer `delete`, which is such a relief). The remaining raw pointers will simply indicate that a client is using the pointer but does not own it.

Overall, C++11 and C++14 smart pointers are a real step up in C++ code writing. Before them, the bigger the code base, the more insecure we felt about memory management. Our brain is bad at properly grasping complexity at such a level. Smart pointers simply make you feel safe about what you write. On the other hand, you retain full control of the memory. For performance-critical code, you can always handle the memory yourself. For everything else, smart pointers are an elegant way of explicitly indicating your object's ownership and freeing your mind.

We are now equipped to rewrite the little insecure snippet in the `AlbumDao::albums()` function. Update `AlbumDao::albums()` like so:

```
// In AlbumDao.h
std::unique_ptr<std::vector<std::unique_ptr<Album>>> albums() const;

// In AlbumDao.cpp
std::unique_ptr<vector<unique_ptr<Album>>> AlbumDao::albums() const
{
    QSqlQuery query("SELECT * FROM albums", mDatabase);
    query.exec();
    unique_ptr<vector<unique_ptr<Album>>> list(new
vector<unique_ptr<Album>>());
    while(query.next()) {
        unique_ptr<Album> album(new Album());
        album->setId(query.value("id").toInt());
        album->setName(query.value("name").toString());
        list->push_back(move(album));
    }
    return list;
}
```

Wow! The signature of the `album()` function has turned into something very peculiar. Smart pointers are supposed to make your life easier, right? Let's break it down to understand a major point of smart pointers with Qt: container behavior.

The initial goal of the rewrite was to secure the creation of `album`. We want `list` to be the explicit owner of `album`. This would have changed our `list` type (that is, the `albums()` return type) to `QVector<unique_ptr<Album>>`. However, when the `list` type is returned, its elements will be copied (remember, we previously defined the return type to `QVector<Album>`). A natural way out of this would be to return a `QVector<unique_ptr<Album>>*` type to retain the uniqueness of our `Album` elements.

Behold, here lies a major pain: the `QVector` class overloads the copy operator. Hence, when the `list` type is returned, the uniqueness of our `unique_ptr` elements cannot be guaranteed by the compiler and it will throw a compile error. This is why we have to resort to a `vector` object coming from the standard library and write the long type: `unique_ptr<vector<unique_ptr<Album>>>`.

Take a look at the official response for the support of the `unique_ptr` pointer in the Qt container. It is clear beyond any possible doubt: `http://lists.qt-project.org/pipermail/interest/2013-July/007776.html`. The short answer is: no, it will never be done. Do not even mention it. Ever.

If we translate this new `albums()` signature into plain English, it will read: the `album()` function returns a vector of `Album`. This vector is the owner of the `Album` elements it contains and you will be the owner of the vector.

To finish covering this implementation of `albums()`, you may notice that we did not use the `auto` and `make_unique` keywords for the `list` declaration. Our library will be used on a mobile in `Chapter 5`, *Dominating the Mobile UI*, and C++14 is not yet supported on this platform. Therefore, we have to restrain our code to C++11.

We also encounter the use of the `move` function in the `list->push_back(move(album))` instruction. Until that line, `album` is "owned" by the `while` scope, the move gives the ownership to the list. At the last instruction, `return list`, we should have written `move(list)`, but C++11 accepts the direct return and will automatically make the `move()` function for us.

What we covered in this section is that the `AlbumDao` class is completely matched in `PictureDao`. Please refer to the source code of the chapter to see the full `PictureDao` class implementation.

Implementing the model

The data is ready to be exposed to potential clients (the applications that will display and edit its content). However, a direct connection between the client and the database will make a very strong coupling. If we decide to switch to another storage type, the view would have to be rewritten, partially at least.

This is where the model comes to our rescue. It is an abstract layer that communicates with the data (our database) and exposes this data to the client in a data-specific, implementation-agnostic form. This approach is a direct offspring of the **Model View Controller** (**MVC**) concept. Let's recapitulate how MVC works:

- The Model manages the data. It is responsible for requesting data and updating it.
- The View displays data to the user.
- The Controller interacts with both the Model and the View. It is responsible for feeding the View with the correct data and sending commands to the Model based on the user interaction received from the View.

This paradigm enables swapping various parts without disturbing the others. Multiple views can display the same data, the data layer can be changed, and the upper parts will not be aware of it.

Qt combines the View and the Controller to form the Model/View architecture. The separation of the storage and the presentation is retained while being simpler to implement than a full MVC approach. To allow editing and view customization, Qt introduces the concept of Delegate, which is connected to both the Model and the View:

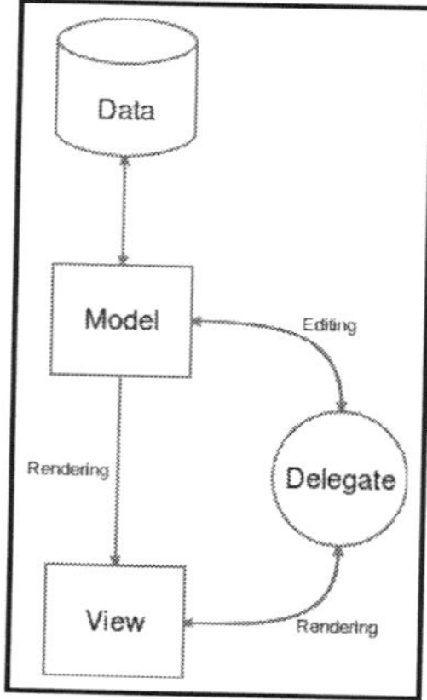

The Qt documentation about Model/View is truly plethoric. It is nevertheless easy to get lost in the details; it can feel a bit overwhelming. We will try to clear things up by implementing the `AlbumModel` class and see how it works.

Qt offers various Model sub-classes that all extend from `QAbstractItemModel`. Before starting the implementation, we have to carefully choose which base class will be extended. Keep in mind that our data is in lists: we will have a list of albums, and each album will have a list of pictures. Let's see what Qt offers us:

- `QAbstractItemModel`: This class is the most abstract, and therefore, the most complex, to implement. We will have to redefine a lot of functions to properly use it.
- `QStringListModel`: This class is a model that supplies strings to views. It is too simple. Our model is more complex (we have custom objects).
- `QSqlTableModel` (or `QSqLQueryModel`): This class is a very interesting contender. It automatically handles multiple SQL queries. On the other hand, it works only for very simple table schemas. In the `pictures` table, for example, the `album_id` foreign key makes it very hard to fit this model. You might save some lines of code, but if feels like trying to shoehorn a round peg into a square hole.
- `QAbstractListModel`: This class provides a model that offers one-dimensional lists. This fits nicely with our requirements, saves a lot of key strokes, and is still flexible enough.

We will go with the `QAbstractListModel` class and create a new C++ class, named `AlbumModel`. Update the `AlbumModel.h` file to look like this:

```
#include <QAbstractListModel>
#include <QHash>
#include <vector>
#include <memory>

#include "gallery-core_global.h"
#include "Album.h"
#include "DatabaseManager.h"

class GALLERYCORESHARED_EXPORT AlbumModel : public QAbstractListModel
{
    Q_OBJECT
public:

    enum Roles {
        IdRole = Qt::UserRole + 1,
        NameRole,
```

```
    };

    AlbumModel(QObject* parent = 0);

    QModelIndex addAlbum(const Album& album);

    int rowCount(const QModelIndex& parent = QModelIndex()) const override;
    QVariant data(const QModelIndex& index, int role = Qt::DisplayRole)
const override;
    bool setData(const QModelIndex& index, const QVariant& value, int role)
override;
    bool removeRows(int row, int count, const QModelIndex& parent)
override;
    QHash<int, QByteArray> roleNames() const override;

private:
    bool isIndexValid(const QModelIndex& index) const;

private:
    DatabaseManager& mDb;
    std::unique_ptr<std::vector<std::unique_ptr<Album>>> mAlbums;
};
```

The `AlbumModel` class extends the `QAbstractListModel` class and has only two members:

- `mDb`: This is the link to the database. In the Model/View schema, the model will communicate with the data layer through `mDb`.
- `mAlbums`: This acts as a buffer that will avoid hitting the database too much. The type should remind you of what we wrote for `AlbumDao::albums()` with the smart pointers.

The only specific functions the `AlbumModel` class has are `addAlbum()` and `isIndexValid()`. The rest are overrides of `QAbstractListModel` functions. We will go through each of these functions to understand how a model works.

First, let's see how the `AlbumModel` class is constructed in the `AlbumModel.cpp` file:

```
AlbumModel::AlbumModel(QObject* parent) :
    QAbstractListModel(parent),
    mDb(DatabaseManager::instance()),
    mAlbums(mDb.albumDao.albums())
{
}
```

The `mDb` file is initialized with the `DatabaseManager` singleton address, and, after that, we see the now-famous `AlbumDao::albums()` in action.

The `vector` type is returned and initializes `mAlbums`. This syntax makes the ownership transfer automatic without any need for an explicit call to the `std::move()` function. If there are any stored albums in the database, `mAlbums` is immediately filled with those.

Each time the model interacts with the view (to notify us about changes or to serve data), `mAlbums` will be used. Because it is in memory only, reading will be very fast. Of course, we have to be careful about maintaining `mAlbum` coherently with the database state, but everything will stay inside the `AlbumModel` inner mechanics.

As we said earlier, the model aims to be the central point to interact with the data. Each time the data changes, the model will emit a signal to notify the view; each time the view wants to display data, it will request the model for it. The `AlbumModel` class overrides everything needed for read and write access. The read functions are:

- `rowCount()`: used to get the list size.
- `data()`: used to get a specific piece of information about the data to display.
- `roleNames()`: This function is used to indicate the name for each "role" to the framework. We will explain in a few paragraphs what a role is.

The editing functions are:

- `setData()`: used to update data.
- `removeRows()`: used to delete data.

We will start with the read part, where the view asks the model for the data.

Because we will display a list of albums, the first thing the view should know is how many items are available. This is done in the `rowCount()` function:

```
int AlbumModel::rowCount(const QModelIndex& parent) const
{
    Q_UNUSED(parent);
    return mAlbums->size();
}
```

Being our buffer object, using `mAlbums->size()` is perfect. There is no need to query the database, as `mAlbums` is already filled with all the albums of the database. The `rowCount()` function has an unknown parameter: `const QModelIndex& parent`. Here, it is not used, but we have to explain what lies beneath this type before continuing our journey in the `AlbumModel` class.

The `QModelIndex` class is a central concept of the Model/View framework in Qt. It is a lightweight object used to locate data within a model. We use a simple `QAbstractListModel` class, but Qt is able to handle three representation types. There is no better explanation than an official Qt diagram:

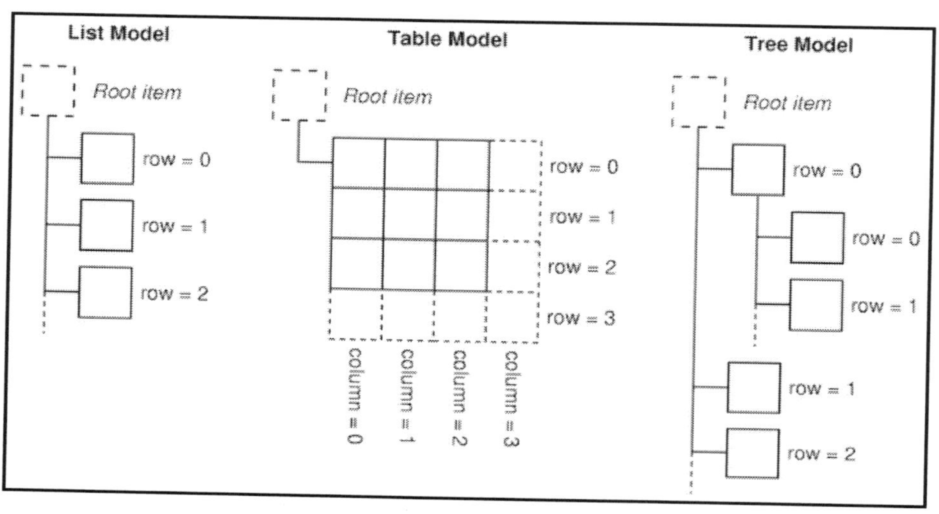

Let's now see the models in detail:

- **List Model**: Data is stored in a one-dimensional array (rows)
- **Table Model**: Data is stored in a two-dimensional array (rows and columns)
- **Tree Model**: Data is stored in a hierarchical relationship (parent/children)

To handle all these model types, Qt came up with the `QModelIndex` class, which is an abstract way of dealing with them. The `QModelIndex` class has the functions for each of the use cases: `row()`, `column()`, and `parent()/child()`. Each instance of `QModelIndex` is meant to be short-lived: the model might be updated and thus the index will become invalid.

The model will produce indexes according to its data type and will provide these indexes to the view. The view will then use them to query back the new data to the model without needing to know whether an `index.row()` function corresponds to a database row or a `vector` index.

We can see the `index` parameter in action with the implementation of `data()`:

```
QVariant AlbumModel::data(const QModelIndex& index, int role) const
{
    if (!isIndexValid(index)) {
        return QVariant();
    }
    const Album& album = *mAlbums->at(index.row());

    switch (role) {
        case Roles::IdRole:
            return album.id();

        case Roles::NameRole:
        case Qt::DisplayRole:
            return album.name();

        default:
            return QVariant();
    }
}
```

The view will ask for data with two parameters: `index` and `role`. As we have already covered `index`, we can focus on the `role` responsibility.

When the data is displayed, it will probably be an aggregation of multiple information. For example, displaying the picture will consist of a thumbnail and the picture name. Each one of these data elements needs to be retrieved by the view. The `role` parameter fills this need, it associates each data element with a tag for the view to know what category of data is shown.

Qt provides various default roles (`DisplayRole`, `DecorationRole`, `EditRole`, and so on) and you can define your own if needed. This is what we did in the `AlbumModel.h` file with `enum Roles`: we added `IdRole` and `NameRole`.

The body of the `data()` function is now within our reach! We first test the validity of the `index` with a helper function, `isIndexValid()`. Take a look at the source code of the chapter to see what it does in detail. The view asked for data at a specific `index`: we retrieve the `album` row at the given `index` with `*mAlbums->at(index.row())`.

This returns a `unique_ptr<Album>` value at the `index.row()` index, and we dereference it to have an `Album&`. The `const` modifier is interesting here because we are in a read function, and it makes no sense to modify the `album` row. The `const` modifier adds this check at compile-time.

The `switch` on the `role` parameter tells us what data category should be returned. The `data()` function returns a `QVariant` value, which is the Swiss Army Knife of types in Qt. We can safely return `album.id()`, `album.name()`, or a default `QVariant()` if we do not handle the specified role.

The last read function to cover is `roleNames()`:

```
QHash<int, QByteArray> AlbumModel::roleNames() const
{
    QHash<int, QByteArray> roles;
    roles[Roles::IdRole] = "id";
    roles[Roles::NameRole] = "name";
    return roles;
}
```

At this level of abstraction, we do not know what type of view will be used to display our data. If the views are written in QML, they will need some meta-information about the data structure. The `roleNames()` function provides this information so the role names can be accessed via QML. If you are writing for a desktop widget view only, you can safely ignore this function. The library we are currently building will be used for QML, which is why we override this function.

The reading part of the model is now over. The client view has everything it needs to properly query and display the data. We shall now investigate the editing part of `AlbumModel`.

We will start with the creation of a new album. The view will build a new `Album` object and pass it to `Album::addAlbum()` to be properly persisted:

```
QModelIndex AlbumModel::addAlbum(const Album& album)
{
    int rowIndex = rowCount();
    beginInsertRows(QModelIndex(), rowIndex, rowIndex);
    unique_ptr<Album> newAlbum(new Album(album));
    mDb.albumDao.addAlbum(*newAlbum);
    mAlbums->push_back(move(newAlbum));
    endInsertRows();
    return index(rowIndex, 0);
}
```

Indexes are a way to navigate within the model data. This first thing we do is determinate the index of this new album by getting the `mAlbums` size with `rowCount()`.

From here, we start to use specific model functions: `beginInsertRows()` and `endInsertRows()`. These functions wrap real data modifications. Their purpose is to automatically trigger signals for whoever might be interested:

- `beginInsertRows()`: Notify the view that new rows will be inserted for the given indexes
- `endInsertRows()`: Notify the view that new rows have been inserted

The first parameter of the `beginInsertRows()` function is the `parent` for this new element. The root for a model is always a default-constructed `QModelIndex()` value. Because we do not handle any hierarchical relationship in `AlbumModel`, it is safe to always add the new element to the root.

The following parameters are the first and last modified indexes. We insert a single element per call, so we provide `rowIndex` twice. In this way, the user selection will correctly be managed by your Qt application even if you insert new rows.

This may look strange at first, but it enables Qt to automatically handle a lot of signaling for us and in a generic way. You will see very soon how well this works when designing the UI of the application in `Chapter 4`, *Conquering the Desktop UI*.

The real insertion begins after the `beginInsertRows()` instruction. We start by creating a copy of the `album` row with `unique_ptr<Album> newAlbum`. This object is then inserted in the database with `mDb.albumDao.addAlbum(*newAlbum)`. Do not forget that the `AlbumDao::addAlbum()` function also modifies the passed album by setting its `mId` to the last SQLite-3-inserted ID.

Finally, `newAlbum` is added to `mAlbums` and its ownership is transferred with `std::move()`. The return gives the index object of this new album, which is simply the row wrapped in a `QModelIndex` object.

Let's continue the editing functions with `setData()`:

```
bool AlbumModel::setData(const QModelIndex& index, const QVariant& value,
int role)
{
    if (!isIndexValid(index)
            || role != Roles::NameRole) {
        return false;
    }
    Album& album = *mAlbums->at(index.row());
```

```
        album.setName(value.toString());
        mDb.albumDao.updateAlbum(album);
        emit dataChanged(index, index);
        return true;
    }
```

This function is called when the view wants to update the data. The signature is very similar to `data()`, with the additional parameter value.

The body also follows the same logic. Here, the `album` row is an `Album&`, without the `const` keyword. The only possible value to edit is the name, which is done on the object and then updated into the database.

We have to emit ourselves the `dataChanged()` signal to notify whoever is interested that a row changed for the given indexes (the start index and end index). This powerful mechanism centralizes all the states of the data, enabling possible views (album list and current album detail, for example) to be automatically refreshed.

The return of the function simply indicates whether the data update was successful. In a production application, you should test the database's processing success and return the relevant value.

Finally, the last editing function we will cover is `removeRows()`:

```
bool AlbumModel::removeRows(int row, int count, const QModelIndex& parent)
{
    if (row < 0
            || row >= rowCount()
            || count < 0
            || (row + count) > rowCount()) {
        return false;
    }
    beginRemoveRows(parent, row, row + count - 1);
    int countLeft = count;
    while (countLeft--) {
        const Album& album = *mAlbums->at(row + countLeft);
        mDb.albumDao.removeAlbum(album.id());
    }
    mAlbums->erase(mAlbums->begin() + row,
                   mAlbums->begin() + row + count);
    endRemoveRows();
    return true;
}
```

The function signature should start to look familiar by now. When a view wants to remove rows, it has to provide the starting row, the number of rows to delete, and the parent of the row.

After that, just as we did for `addAlbum()`, we wrap the effective removal with two functions:

- The `beginRemoveRows()` function, triggers a signal in the model framework. It expects the parent, the starting index, and the last index.
- The `endRemoveRows()` function, which simply triggers signal.

The rest of the function is not very hard to follow. We loop on the rows left to delete and, for each one, we delete it from the database and remove it from `mAlbums`. We simply retrieve the album from our in-memory `mAlbums` vector and process the real database deletion with `mDb.albumDao.removeAlbum(album.id())`.

The `AlbumModel` class is now completely covered. You can now create a new C++ class and name it `PictureModel`.

We will not cover the `PictureModel` class in so much detail. The major parts are the same (you simply swap the `Album` data class for `Picture`). There is, however, one main difference: `PictureModel` always handles pictures for a given album. This design choice illustrates how two models can be linked with a few simple signals.

Here is the updated version of `PictureModel.h`:

```
#include <memory>
#include <vector>

#include <QAbstractListModel>

#include "gallery-core_global.h"
#include "Picture.h"

class Album;
class DatabaseManager;
class AlbumModel;

class GALLERYCORESHARED_EXPORT PictureModel : public QAbstractListModel
{
    Q_OBJECT
public:

    enum PictureRole {
        FilePathRole = Qt::UserRole + 1
```

```
    };
    PictureModel(const AlbumModel& albumModel, QObject* parent = 0);

    QModelIndex addPicture(const Picture& picture);

    int rowCount(const QModelIndex& parent = QModelIndex()) const override;
    QVariant data(const QModelIndex& index, int role) const override;
    bool removeRows(int row, int count, const QModelIndex& parent)
override;

    void setAlbumId(int albumId);
    void clearAlbum();

public slots:
    void deletePicturesForAlbum();

private:
    void loadPictures(int albumId);
    bool isIndexValid(const QModelIndex& index) const;

private:
    DatabaseManager& mDb;
    int mAlbumId;
    std::unique_ptr<std::vector<std::unique_ptr<Picture>>> mPictures;
};
```

The interesting parts are those concerning the album. As you can see, the constructor expects `AlbumModel`. This class also stores the current `mAlbumId` to be able to request the pictures for a given album only. Let's see what the constructor really does:

```
PictureModel::PictureModel(const AlbumModel& albumModel, QObject* parent) :
    QAbstractListModel(parent),
    mDb(DatabaseManager::instance()),
    mAlbumId(-1),
    mPictures(new vector<unique_ptr<Picture>>())
{
    connect(&albumModel, &AlbumModel::rowsRemoved,
            this, &PictureModel::deletePicturesForAlbum);
}
```

As you can see, the `albumModel` class is used only to connect a signal to our `deletePicturesForAlbum()` slot, which is self-explanatory. This makes sure that the database is always valid: a picture should be deleted if the owning album is deleted. This will be done automatically when `AlbumModel` emits the `rowsRemoved` signal.

Now, `mPictures` is not initialized with all the pictures of the database. Because we chose to restrict `PictureModel` to work on the pictures for a given album, we do not know which album to choose at the construction of `PictureModel`. The loading can only be done when the album is selected, in `setAlbumId()`:

```
void PictureModel::setAlbumId(int albumId)
{
    beginResetModel();
    mAlbumId = albumId;
    loadPictures(mAlbumId);
    endResetModel();
}
```

When the album changes, we completely reload `PictureModel`. The reloading phase is wrapped with the `beginResetModel()` and `endResetModel()` functions. They notify any attached views that their state should be reset as well. Any previous data (for example, `QModelIndex`) reported from the model becomes invalid.

The `loadPictures()` function is quite straightforward:

```
void PictureModel::loadPictures(int albumId)
{
    if (albumId <= 0) {
        mPictures.reset(new vector<unique_ptr<Picture>>());
        return;
    }
    mPictures = mDb.pictureDao.picturesForAlbum(albumId);
}
```

By convention, we decided that if a negative `album id` is provided, we have to clear the pictures. To do it, we reinitialize `mPictures` with the `mPictures.reset(new vector<unique_ptr<Picture>>())` call. This will call the destructor on the owned vector, which in turn will do the same for the `Picture` elements. We force `mPictures` to always have a valid vector object to avoid any possible null reference (in `PictureModel::rowCount()`, for example).

After that, we simply assign the database pictures for the given `albumId` to `mPictures`. Because we work with smart pointers at every level, we do not even see any specific semantics here. Still, `mPicture` is `unique_ptr<vector<unique_ptr<Picture>>>`. When the `=` operator is called, the `unique_ptr` pointer overloads it and two things happen:

- The ownership of the right-hand side (the pictures retrieved from the database) is transferred to `mPictures`
- The old content of `mPictures` is automatically deleted

It is effectively the same as calling `mPictures.reset()` and then `mPictures = move(mDb.pictureDao.picturesForAlbum(albumId))`. With the = overload, everything is streamlined and much more pleasant to read.

`PictureModel` shows you how flexible the model paradigm can be. You can easily adapt it to your own use case without making any strong coupling. After all, `albumModel` is only used to connect to a single signal; there are no retained references. The remainder of the class is available in the source code of this chapter.

Summary

This chapter was a journey to create a well-defined `gallery-core` library. We studied advanced techniques with `.pro` files to split your project into sub-modules, persisted data in a SQLite 3 database with the help of smart pointers, and finally, studied how the Model/View architecture works in Qt.

From now on, a project organization with Qt should hold no terror for you. The next chapter will continue right where we stopped; the library is ready, now let's make great QWidgets to have a stunning gallery application and look at the other side of the model: the View layer.

4
Conquering the Desktop UI

In the previous chapter, we built the brain of our gallery using Qt models. It is now time to build a desktop application using this engine. This software will use all the features offered by the `gallery-core` library, leading to a completely usable gallery on your computer.

The first task will be to link your project-shared library to this new application. Then you will learn how to create custom widgets, when to use Qt views, and how to synchronize them with the model.

The following topics will be covered in this chapter:

- Creating a GUI linked to a core shared library
- Listing your albums with AlbumListWidget
- Creating a ThumbnailProxyModel
- Displaying a picture with PictureWidget

Creating a GUI linked to a core shared library

The `gallery-core` shared library is now ready. Let's see how to create the desktop GUI project. We will create a Qt Widgets application sub-project called `gallery-desktop`. But the first steps differ slightly from a classic Qt Widgets application. Right-click on the main project, and select **ch04-gallery-desktop** | **New subproject** | **Application** | **Qt Widgets Application** | **Choose**.

You will get a nice multi-projects hierarchy:

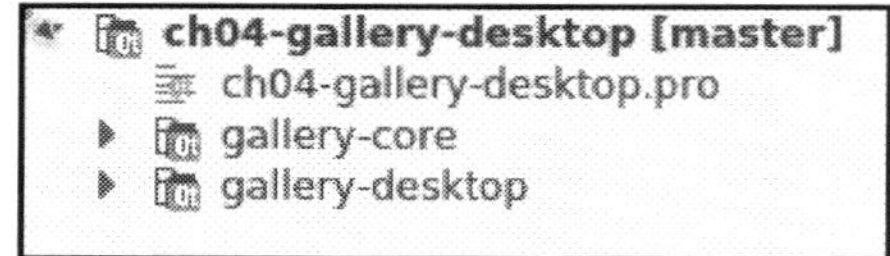

It is now time to link this `gallery-desktop` application to `gallery-core`. You can edit the `gallery-desktop.pro` file yourself, or use the Qt Creator wizard: right-click on the project and select **gallery-desktop** | **Add library** | **Internal library** | **gallery-core** | **Next** | **Finish**. Here is the updated `gallery-desktop.pro`:

```
QT       += core gui

TARGET = desktop-gallery
TEMPLATE = app

SOURCES += main.cpp\
        MainWindow.cpp

HEADERS  += MainWindow.h

FORMS    += MainWindow.ui

win32:CONFIG(release, debug|release): LIBS += -L$$OUT_PWD/../gallery-
core/release/ -lgallery-core
else:win32:CONFIG(debug, debug|release): LIBS += -L$$OUT_PWD/../gallery-
core/debug/ -lgallery-core
else:unix: LIBS += -L$$OUT_PWD/../gallery-core/ -lgallery-core

INCLUDEPATH += $$PWD/../gallery-core
DEPENDPATH += $$PWD/../gallery-core
```

The `LIBS` variable specifies the libraries to link in this project. The syntax is very simple: you can provide library paths with the `-L` prefix and library names with the `-l` prefix:

```
LIBS += -L<pathToLibrary> -l<libraryName>
```

By default, compiling a Qt project on Windows will create a `debug` and `release` sub-directory. That is why a different `LIBS` edition is created depending on the platform.

Now that the application is linked to the `gallery-core` library and knows where to find it, we must indicate where the library header files are located. That is why we must add the `gallery-core` source path to `INCLUDEPATH` and `DEPENDPATH`.

To complete all those tasks successfully, qmake offers some useful variables:

- `$$OUT_PWD`: The absolute path to the output directory
- `$$PWD`: The absolute path of the current `.pro` file

To ensure that qmake will compile the shared library before the desktop application, we must update the `ch04-gallery-desktop.pro` file according to the following snippet:

```
TEMPLATE = subdirs

SUBDIRS += \
    gallery-core \
    gallery-desktop

gallery-desktop.depends = gallery-core
```

The `depends` attribute explicitly indicates that `gallery-core` must be built before `gallery-desktop`.

Try to always use the `depends` attribute instead of relying on `CONFIG += ordered`, which only specifies a simple list order. The `depends` attribute helps qmake process your projects in parallel, if it can be done.

Instead of rushing into coding blindly, we will take some time to think about the UI architecture. We have a lot of features to implement from the `gallery-core` library. We should split these features into independent QWidgets:

The final application will look like this:

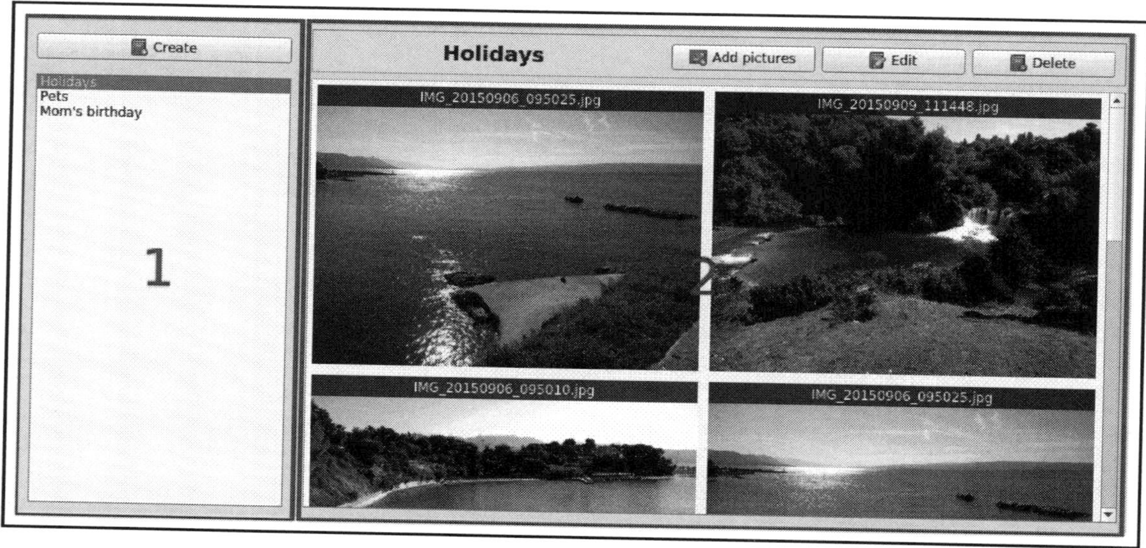

The expanded view of a photo will look like this—double-click on a thumbnail to display it in full size:

Here are the main UI components:

- `AlbumListWidget`: Lists all existing albums
- `AlbumWidget`: Shows the selected album and its thumbnails
- `PictureWidget`: Displays the picture in full size

This is how we will organize it:

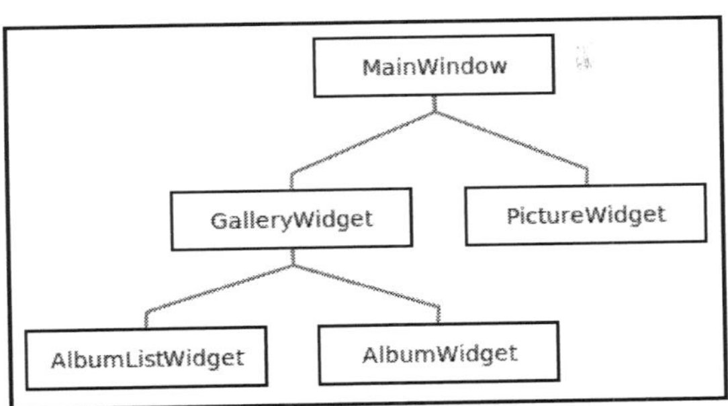

Each widget has a defined role and will handle specific features:

Class name	**Features**
`MainWindow`	• Handles the switch between the gallery and the current picture
`GalleryWidget`	• Displays existing albums • Album-selection • Album-creation
`AlbumListWidget`	• Displays existing albums • Album-selection • Album-creation
`AlbumWidget`	• Displays existing pictures as thumbnails • Adds pictures in the album • Album-rename • Album-deletion • Picture-selection
`PictureWidget`	• Displays the selected picture • Picture-selection • Picture-deletion

In the core shared library, we used smart pointers with standard containers (`vector`). Generally, in Qt GUI projects, we tend to only use Qt containers. This approach seems more appropriate to us. That is why we will rely on Qt containers for the GUI (and won't use smart pointers) in this chapter.

We can now safely begin to create our widgets; all of them are created from **Qt Designer Form Class**. If you have a memory lapse, you can check the *Custom QWidget* section in `Chapter 1`, *Get Your Qt Feet Wet*.

Listing your albums with AlbumListWidget

This widget must offer a way to create a new album and display existing ones. Selecting an album must also trigger an event that will be used by other widgets to display the proper data. The `AlbumListWidget` component is the simplest widget in this project using the Qt View mechanism. Take the time to fully understand `AlbumListWidget` before jumping to the next widget.

The following screenshot shows the **Form Editor** view of the file, `AlbumListWidget.ui`:

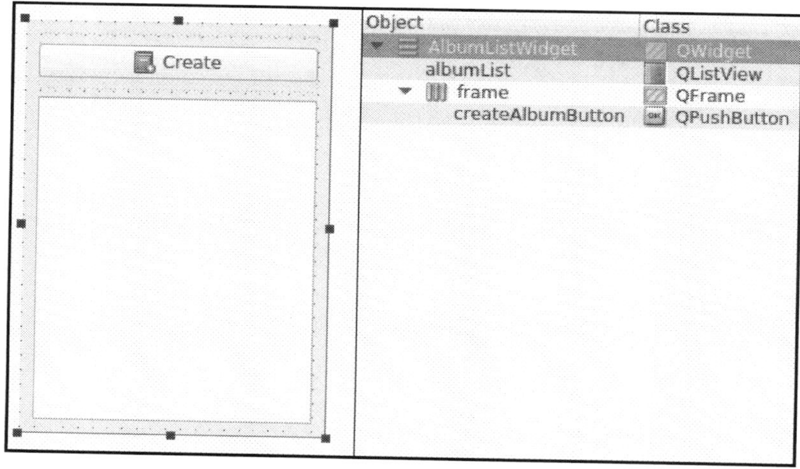

The layout is very simple. The components are described as follows:

- The `AlbumListWidget` component uses a vertical layout to display the **Create** button above the list
- The `frame` component contains an attractive button
- The `createAlbumButton` component handles album-creation
- The `albumList` component displays the album list

You should recognize most of the types used here. Let's talk about the real new one: `QListView`. As we already saw in the previous chapter, Qt provides a Model/View architecture. This system relies on specific interfaces that you must implement to provide generic data access via your model classes. That is what we did in the `gallery-core` project with the `AlbumModel` and `PictureModel` classes.

It's now time to deal with the view part. The view is in charge of the presentation of the data. It will also handle user interactions, such as selection, drag and drop, or item editing. Fortunately, to achieve these tasks, the view is helped by other Qt classes such as `QItemSelectionModel`, `QModelIndex`, or `QStyledItemDelegate`, which we will use in this chapter.

We can now enjoy one of the ready-to-use views offered by Qt:

- `QListView`: This view displays items from a model as a simple list
- `QTableView`: This view displays items from a model as a two-dimensional table
- `QTreeView`: This view displays items from a hierarchy of lists

Here, the choice is rather obvious because we want to display a list of album names. But in a more complex situation, a rule of thumb for choosing the proper view is to look for the model type: here we want to add a view for `AlbumModel` of the `QAbstractListModel` type, so the `QListView` class seems correct.

A **Qt resource** file is a collection of files for embedding binary files in your application. You can store any type of file, but we commonly use it to store pictures, sounds, or translation files. To create a resource file, right-click on the project name and then follow **Add New** | **Qt** | **Qt Resource File**. Qt Creator will create a default file, `resource.qrc`, and add this line in your `gallery-desktop.pro` file:

```
RESOURCES += resource.qrc
```

The resource file can be mainly displayed in two ways: **Resource Editor** and **Plain Text Editor**. You can choose an editor by right-clicking on the resource file and selecting **Open With**.

The **Resource Editor** is a visual editor that helps you to easily add and remove files in your resource file, as shown in the following screenshot:

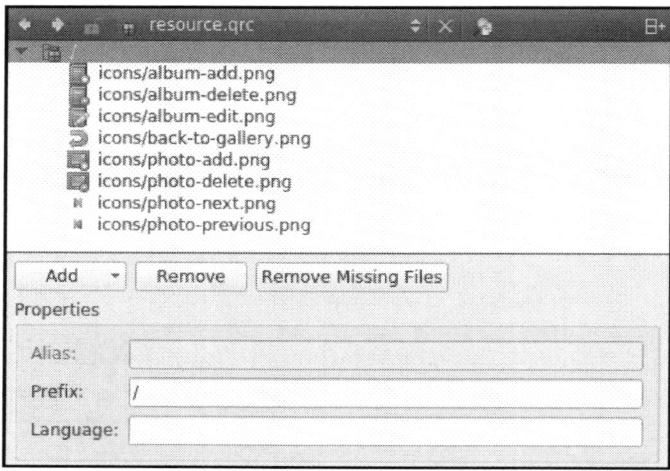

The **Plain Text Editor** will display this XML-based file `resource.qrc` in this way:

```
<RCC>
    <qresource prefix="/">
        <file>icons/album-add.png</file>
        <file>icons/album-delete.png</file>
        <file>icons/album-edit.png</file>
        <file>icons/back-to-gallery.png</file>
        <file>icons/photo-add.png</file>
        <file>icons/photo-delete.png</file>
        <file>icons/photo-next.png</file>
        <file>icons/photo-previous.png</file>
    </qresource>
</RCC>
```

At build time, qmake and RCC (Qt Resource Compiler) embed your resources into the application binary.

The `createAlbumButton` object has an icon. You can add one to a `QPushButton` class by selecting the widget. Then in the **Property Editor**, select **icon** | **Choose resource**. You can now choose a picture from the `resource.qrc` file.

Now that the form part is clear, we can analyze the `AlbumListWidget.h` file:

```
#include <QWidget>
#include <QItemSelectionModel>
```

```
namespace Ui {
class AlbumListWidget;
}

class AlbumModel;

class AlbumListWidget : public QWidget
{
    Q_OBJECT

public:
    explicit AlbumListWidget(QWidget *parent = 0);
    ~AlbumListWidget();

    void setModel(AlbumModel* model);
    void setSelectionModel(QItemSelectionModel* selectionModel);

private slots:
    void createAlbum();

private:
    Ui::AlbumListWidget* ui;
    AlbumModel* mAlbumModel;
};
```

The `setModel()` and `setSelectionModel()` functions are the most important lines in this snippet. This widget requires two things to work correctly:

- `AlbumModel`: This is the model class that provides access to data. We already created this class in the `gallery-core` project.
- `QItemSelectionModel`: This is a Qt class that handles the selection in a view. By default, views use their own selection model. Sharing the same selection model with different views or widgets will help us to synchronize album-selection more easily.

This is the main part of `AlbumListWidget.cpp`:

```
#include "AlbumListWidget.h"
#include "ui_AlbumListWidget.h"

#include <QInputDialog>

#include "AlbumModel.h"

AlbumListWidget::AlbumListWidget(QWidget *parent) :
    QWidget(parent),
    ui(new Ui::AlbumListWidget),
```

```
    mAlbumModel(nullptr)
{
    ui->setupUi(this);

    connect(ui->createAlbumButton, &QPushButton::clicked,
            this, &AlbumListWidget::createAlbum);
}

AlbumListWidget::~AlbumListWidget()
{
    delete ui;
}

void AlbumListWidget::setModel(AlbumModel* model)
{
    mAlbumModel = model;
    ui->albumList->setModel(mAlbumModel);
}

void AlbumListWidget::setSelectionModel(QItemSelectionModel*
selectionModel)
{
    ui->albumList->setSelectionModel(selectionModel);
}
```

The two setters will mainly be used to set the model and the selection model of `albumList`. Our `QListView` class will then automatically request the model (`AlbumModel`) to get the row count and `Qt::DisplayRole` (the album's name) for each one of them.

Let's now see the last part of the `AlbumListWidget.cpp` file, which handles album-creation:

```
void AlbumListWidget::createAlbum()
{
    if(!mAlbumModel) {
        return;
    }

    bool ok;
    QString albumName = QInputDialog::getText(this,
                            "Create a new Album",
                            "Choose an name",
                            QLineEdit::Normal,
                            "New album",
                            &ok);

    if (ok && !albumName.isEmpty()) {
```

```
            Album album(albumName);
            QModelIndex createdIndex = mAlbumModel->addAlbum(album);
            ui->albumList->setCurrentIndex(createdIndex);
        }
    }
```

We already worked with the `QInputDialog` class in `Chapter 1`, *Get Your Qt Feet Wet*. This time we are using it to ask the user to enter an album's name. Then we create an `Album` class with the requested name. This object is just a data holder; `addAlbum()` will use it to create and store the real object with a unique ID.

The `addAlbum()` function returns the `QModelIndex` value corresponding to the created album. From here, we can request the list view to select this new album.

Creating ThumbnailProxyModel

The future `AlbumWidget` view will display a grid of thumbnails with the pictures attached to the selected `Album`. In `Chapter 3`, *Dividing Your Project and Ruling Your Code*, we designed the `gallery-core` library to be agnostic of how a picture should be displayed: a `Picture` class contains only a `mUrl` field.

In other words, the generation of the thumbnails has to be done in `gallery-desktop` rather than `gallery-core`. We already have the `PictureModel` class, which is responsible for retrieving the `Picture` information, so it would be great to be able to extend its behavior with the thumbnail data.

This is possible in Qt with the use of the `QAbstractProxyModel` class and its subclasses. The goal of this class is to process data from a `QAbstractItemModel` base (sorting, filtering, adding data, and so on) and present it to the view by proxying the original model. To take a database analogy, you can view it as a projection over a table.

The `QAbstractProxyModel` class has two subclasses:

- The `QIdentityProxyModel` subclass proxies its source model without any modification (all the indexes match). This class is suitable if you want to transform the `data()` function.
- The `QSortFilterProxyModel` subclass proxies its source model with the ability to sort and filter the passing data.

QIdentityProxyModel fits our requirements. The only thing we need to do is extend the data() function with the thumbnail-generation content. Create a new class named ThumbnailProxyModel. Here is the ThumbnailProxyModel.h file:

```
#include <QIdentityProxyModel>
#include <QHash>
#include <QPixmap>

class PictureModel;

class ThumbnailProxyModel : public QIdentityProxyModel
{
    Q_OBJECT

public:
    ThumbnailProxyModel(QObject* parent = 0);

    QVariant data(const QModelIndex& index, int role) const override;
    void setSourceModel(QAbstractItemModel* sourceModel) override;
    PictureModel* pictureModel() const;

private:
    void generateThumbnails(const QModelIndex& startIndex, int count);
    void reloadThumbnails();

private:
   QHash<QString, QPixmap*> mThumbnails;

};
```

This class extends QIdentityProxyModel and overrides a couple of functions:

- The data() function to provide the thumbnail data to the client of ThumbnailProxyModel
- The setSourceModel() function to register to signals emitted by sourceModel

The remaining custom functions have the following goals:

- pictureModel() is a helper function that casts sourceModel to PictureModel*
- The generateThumbnails() function takes care of generating the QPixmap thumbnails for a given set of pictures
- reloadThumbnails() is a helper function that clears the stored thumbnails before calling generateThumbnails()

As you might have guessed, the `mThumbnails` class stores the `QPixmap*` thumbnails using the `filepath` for the key.

We now switch to the `ThumbnailProxyModel.cpp` file and build it from the ground up. Let's focus on `generateThumbnails()`:

```
const unsigned int THUMBNAIL_SIZE = 350;
...
void ThumbnailProxyModel::generateThumbnails(const QModelIndex& startIndex,
int count)
{
    if (!startIndex.isValid()) {
        return;
    }

    const QAbstractItemModel* model = startIndex.model();
    int lastIndex = startIndex.row() + count;
    for(int row = startIndex.row(); row < lastIndex; row++) {
        QString filepath = model->data(
                  model->index(row, 0),
                  PictureModel::Roles::FilePathRole).toString();
        QPixmap pixmap(filepath);
        auto thumbnail = new QPixmap(pixmap
                              .scaled(THUMBNAIL_SIZE, THUMBNAIL_SIZE,
                                  Qt::KeepAspectRatio,
                                  Qt::SmoothTransformation));
        mThumbnails.insert(filepath, thumbnail);
    }
}
```

This function generates the thumbnails for a given range indicated by the parameters (`startIndex` and `count`). For each picture, we retrieve the `filepath` from the original model, using `model->data()`, and we generate a downsized `QPixmap` that is inserted in the `mThumbnails` QHash. Note that we arbitrarily set the thumbnail size using `const THUMBNAIL_SIZE`. The picture is scaled down to this size and respects the aspect ratio of the original picture.

Each time that an album is loaded, we should clear the content of the `mThumbnails` class and load the new pictures. This work is done by the `reloadThumbnails()` function:

```
void ThumbnailProxyModel::reloadThumbnails()
{
    qDeleteAll(mThumbnails);
    mThumbnails.clear();
    generateThumbnails(index(0, 0), rowCount());
}
```

In this function, we simply delete all the pointers using `qDeleteAll()`, and then clear the content of `mThumbnails`. The last call to the `generateThumbnails()` function with these parameters indicating that all the thumbnails should be generated. Let's see when these two functions will be used in `setSourceModel()`:

```
void ThumbnailProxyModel::setSourceModel(QAbstractItemModel* sourceModel)
{
    QIdentityProxyModel::setSourceModel(sourceModel);
    if (!sourceModel) {
        return;
    }

    connect(sourceModel, &QAbstractItemModel::modelReset,
                [this] {
        reloadThumbnails();
    });

    connect(sourceModel, &QAbstractItemModel::rowsInserted,
                [this] (const QModelIndex& parent, int first, int last) {
        generateThumbnails(index(first, 0), last - first + 1);
    });
}
```

When the `setSourceModel()` function is called, the `ThumbnailProxyModel` class is configured to know which base model should be proxied. In this function, we register lambdas to two signals emitted by the original model:

- The `modelReset` signal is triggered when pictures should be loaded for a given album. In this case, we have to completely reload the thumbnails.
- The `rowsInserted` signal is triggered each time new pictures are added. At this point, `generateThumbnails` should be called to update `mThumbnails` with these newcomers.

Finally, we have to cover the `data()` function:

```
QVariant ThumbnailProxyModel::data(const QModelIndex& index, int role)
const
{
    if (role != Qt::DecorationRole) {
        return QIdentityProxyModel::data(index, role);
    }

    QString filepath = sourceModel()->data(index,
PictureModel::Roles::FilePathRole).toString();
    return *mThumbnails[filepath];
}
```

For any role that is not `Qt::DecorationRole`, the `data()` parent class is called. In our case, this triggers the `data()` function from the original model, `PictureModel`. After that, when `data()` must return a thumbnail, the `filepath` of the picture referenced by the `index` is retrieved and used to return the `QPixmap` object of `mThumbnails`. Luckily for us, `QPixmap` can be implicitly cast to `QVariant`, so we do not have anything special to do here.

The last function to cover in the `ThumbnailProxyModel` class is the `pictureModel()` function:

```
PictureModel* ThumbnailProxyModel::pictureModel() const
{
    return static_cast<PictureModel*>(sourceModel());
}
```

Classes that will interact with `ThumbnailProxyModel` will need to call some functions specific to `PictureModel` to create or delete pictures. This function is a helper to centralize the cast of `sourceModel` to `PictureModel*`.

As you can see, `QIdentityProxyModel`, and more generally `QAbstractProxyModel`, are valuable tools to add behavior to an existing model without breaking it. In our case, this is enforced by design insofar as the `PictureModel` class is defined in `gallery-core` rather than `gallery-desktop`. Modifying `PictureModel` implies modifying `gallery-core`, and potentially breaking its behavior for other users of the library. This approach lets us keep things cleanly separated.

Displaying the selected album with AlbumWidget

This widget will display the data of the selected album from `AlbumListWidget`. Some buttons will allow us to interact with this album.

Try now to create the layout of the `AlbumWidget.ui` file. Here is the final result:

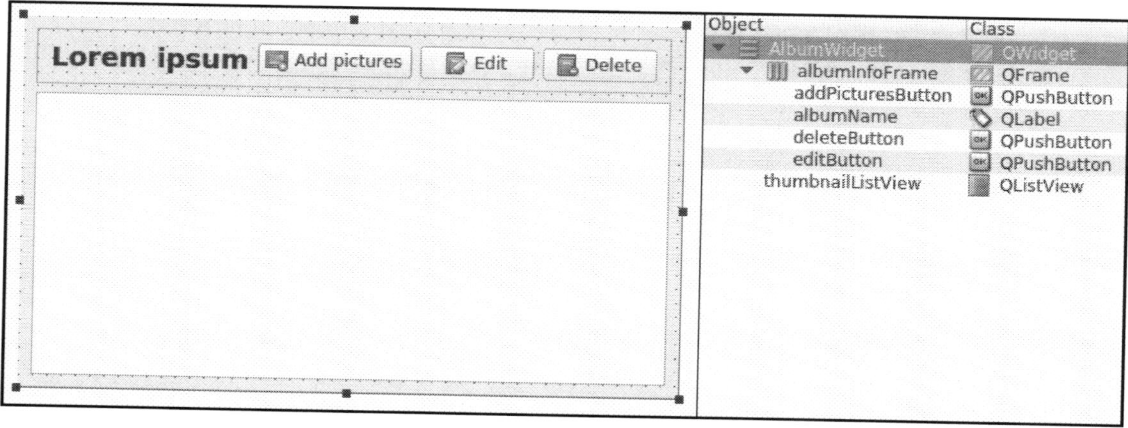

The top frame, `albumInfoFrame`, with a horizontal layout contains:

- `albumName`: displays the album's name (**Lorem ipsum** in the designer).
- `addPicturesButton`: allows the user to add picture files.
- `editButton`: used to rename the album.
- `deleteButton`: Used to delete the album.

The bottom element, `thumbnailListView`, is a `QListView`. This list view represents items from `PictureModel`. By default, `QListView` is able to display a picture next to a text requesting `Qt::DisplayRole` and `Qt::DecorationRole` from the model.

Take a look at the `AlbumWidget.h` header file:

```
#include <QWidget>
#include <QModelIndex>

namespace Ui {
class AlbumWidget;
}

class AlbumModel;
class PictureModel;
class QItemSelectionModel;
class ThumbnailProxyModel;

class AlbumWidget : public QWidget
{
    Q_OBJECT
```

```
public:
    explicit AlbumWidget(QWidget *parent = 0);
    ~AlbumWidget();

    void setAlbumModel(AlbumModel* albumModel);
    void setAlbumSelectionModel(QItemSelectionModel* albumSelectionModel);
    void setPictureModel(ThumbnailProxyModel* pictureModel);
    void setPictureSelectionModel(QItemSelectionModel* selectionModel);

signals:
    void pictureActivated(const QModelIndex& index);

private slots:
    void deleteAlbum();
    void editAlbum();
    void addPictures();

private:
    void clearUi();
    void loadAlbum(const QModelIndex& albumIndex);

private:
    Ui::AlbumWidget* ui;
    AlbumModel* mAlbumModel;
    QItemSelectionModel* mAlbumSelectionModel;

    ThumbnailProxyModel* mPictureModel;
    QItemSelectionModel* mPictureSelectionModel;
};
```

As this widget needs to deal with `Album` and `Picture` data, this class has `AlbumModel` and `ThumbnailProxyModel` setters. We also want to know and share the model selection with other widgets and views (that is, `AlbumListWidget`). That is why we also have `Album` and `Picture` model-selection setters.

The `pictureActivated()` signal will be triggered when the user double-clicks on a thumbnail. We will see later how `MainWindow` will connect to this signal to display the picture at full size.

The private slots, `deleteAlbum()`, `editAlbum()`, and `addPictures()`, will be called when the user clicks on one of these buttons.

Finally, the `loadAlbum()` function will be called to update the UI for a specific album. The `clearUi()` function will be useful for clearing all information displayed by this widget UI.

Take a look at the beginning of the implementation in the `AlbumWidget.cpp` file:

```
#include "AlbumWidget.h"
#include "ui_AlbumWidget.h"

#include <QInputDialog>
#include <QFileDialog>

#include "AlbumModel.h"
#include "PictureModel.h"

AlbumWidget::AlbumWidget(QWidget *parent) :
    QWidget(parent),
    ui(new Ui::AlbumWidget),
    mAlbumModel(nullptr),
    mAlbumSelectionModel(nullptr),
    mPictureModel(nullptr),
    mPictureSelectionModel(nullptr)
{
    ui->setupUi(this);
    clearUi();

    ui->thumbnailListView->setSpacing(5);
    ui->thumbnailListView->setResizeMode(QListView::Adjust);
    ui->thumbnailListView->setFlow(QListView::LeftToRight);
    ui->thumbnailListView->setWrapping(true);

    connect(ui->thumbnailListView, &QListView::doubleClicked,
            this, &AlbumWidget::pictureActivated);

    connect(ui->deleteButton, &QPushButton::clicked,
            this, &AlbumWidget::deleteAlbum);

    connect(ui->editButton, &QPushButton::clicked,
            this, &AlbumWidget::editAlbum);

    connect(ui->addPicturesButton, &QPushButton::clicked,
            this, &AlbumWidget::addPictures);
}

AlbumWidget::~AlbumWidget()
{
    delete ui;
}
```

The constructor configures `thumbnailListView`, our `QListView` that will display thumbnails of the current selected album. Here, we set various parameters:

- `setSpacing()`: By default, items are glued to each other. You can add spacing between them.
- `setResizeMode()`: This parameter dynamically lays out items when the view is resized. By default, items keep their original placement even if the view is resized.
- `setFlow()`: This parameter specifies the list direction. Here, we want to display items from left to right. By default, the direction is `TopToBottom`.
- `setWrapping()`: This parameter allows an item to wrap when there is not enough space to display it in the visible area. By default, wrapping is not allowed and scrollbars will be displayed.

The end of the constructor performs all the signal connections related to the UI. The first one is a good example of signal relaying, explained in `Chapter 1`, *Get Your Qt Feet Wet*. We connect the `QListView::doubleClicked` signal to our class signal, `AlbumWidget::pictureActivated`. Other connections are common: we want to call a specific slot when the user clicks on a button. As always in the **Qt Designer Form Class**, the destructor will delete the `ui` member variable.

Let's see the `AlbumModel` setter implementation:

```
void AlbumWidget::setAlbumModel(AlbumModel* albumModel)
{
    mAlbumModel = albumModel;

    connect(mAlbumModel, &QAbstractItemModel::dataChanged,
        [this] (const QModelIndex &topLeft) {
            if (topLeft == mAlbumSelectionModel->currentIndex()) {
                loadAlbum(topLeft);
            }
    });
}

void AlbumWidget::setAlbumSelectionModel(QItemSelectionModel*
albumSelectionModel)
{
    mAlbumSelectionModel = albumSelectionModel;

    connect(mAlbumSelectionModel,
            &QItemSelectionModel::selectionChanged,
            [this] (const QItemSelection &selected) {
                if (selected.isEmpty()) {
```

```
                        clearUi();
                        return;
                    }
                    loadAlbum(selected.indexes().first());
        });
    }
```

If the selected album's data changes, we need to update the UI with the `loadAlbum()` function. A test is performed to ensure that the updated album is the currently-selected one. Notice that the `QAbstractItemModel::dataChanged()` function has three parameters but the lambda slot syntax allows us to omit unused parameters.

Our `AlbumWidget` component must update its UI according to the currently-selected album. As we share the same selection model, each time the user selects an album from `AlbumListWidget`, the `QItemSelectionModel::selectionChanged` signal is triggered. In this case, we update the UI by calling the `loadAlbum()` function. As we do not support album multi-selection, we can restrict the process to the first selected element. If the selection is empty, we simply clear the UI.

It is now the turn of the `PictureModel` setter implementation:

```
#include "ThumbnailProxyModel.h"

void AlbumWidget::setPictureModel(ThumbnailProxyModel* pictureModel)
{
    mPictureModel = pictureModel;
    ui->thumbnailListView->setModel(mPictureModel);
}

void AlbumWidget::setPictureSelectionModel(QItemSelectionModel*
selectionModel)
{
    ui->thumbnailListView->setSelectionModel(selectionModel);
}
```

It is very simple here. We set the model and the selection model of `thumbnailListView`, our `QListView` that will display the selected album's thumbnails. We also keep the picture model to manipulate the data later on.

We can now cover the features one by one. Let's start with album deletion:

```
void AlbumWidget::deleteAlbum()
{
    if (mAlbumSelectionModel->selectedIndexes().isEmpty()) {
        return;
    }
```

```
    int row = mAlbumSelectionModel->currentIndex().row();
    mAlbumModel->removeRow(row);

    // Try to select the previous album
    QModelIndex previousModelIndex = mAlbumModel->index(row - 1,
        0);
    if(previousModelIndex.isValid()) {
        mAlbumSelectionModel->setCurrentIndex(previousModelIndex,
             QItemSelectionModel::SelectCurrent);
        return;
    }

    // Try to select the next album
    QModelIndex nextModelIndex = mAlbumModel->index(row, 0);
    if(nextModelIndex.isValid()) {
        mAlbumSelectionModel->setCurrentIndex(nextModelIndex,
            QItemSelectionModel::SelectCurrent);
        return;
    }
}
```

The most important task in the `deleteAlbum()` function is to retrieve the current row index from `mAlbumSelectionModel`. Then, we can request `mAlbumModel` to delete this row. The rest of the function will only try to automatically select the previous or the next album. Once again, as we shared the same selection model, `AlbumListWidget` will automatically update its album selection.

The following snippet shows the album rename feature:

```
void AlbumWidget::editAlbum()
{
    if (mAlbumSelectionModel->selectedIndexes().isEmpty()) {
        return;
    }

    QModelIndex currentAlbumIndex =
        mAlbumSelectionModel->selectedIndexes().first();

    QString oldAlbumName = mAlbumModel->data(currentAlbumIndex,
        AlbumModel::Roles::NameRole).toString();

    bool ok;
    QString newName = QInputDialog::getText(this,
                                            "Album's name",
                                            "Change Album name",
                                            QLineEdit::Normal,
                                            oldAlbumName,
```

```
                                                        &ok);

        if (ok && !newName.isEmpty()) {
            mAlbumModel->setData(currentAlbumIndex,
                                 newName,
                                 AlbumModel::Roles::NameRole);
        }
    }
```

Here, the `QInputDialog` class will help us to implement a feature. You should be comfortable with its behavior now. This function performs three steps:

1. Retrieve the current name from album model
2. Generate a great input dialog
3. Request the album model to update the name

As you can see, the generic `data()` and `setData()` functions from the models are very powerful when combined with `ItemDataRole`. As already explained, we do not directly update our UI; this will be automatically performed because `setData()` emits a signal, `dataChanged()`, which `AlbumWidget` handles.

The last feature allows us to add some new picture files in the current album:

```
void AlbumWidget::addPictures()
{
    QStringList filenames =
        QFileDialog::getOpenFileNames(this,
            "Add pictures",
             QDir::homePath(),
            "Picture files (*.jpg *.png)");

    if (!filenames.isEmpty()) {
        QModelIndex lastModelIndex;
        for (auto filename : filenames) {
            Picture picture(filename);
            lastModelIndex = mPictureModel->pictureModel()
                ->addPicture(picture);
        }
        ui->thumbnailListView->setCurrentIndex(lastModelIndex);
    }
}
```

The `QFileDialog` class is employed here to help the user select several picture files. For each filename, we create a `Picture` data holder, like we have already seen in this chapter for album-creation. Then we can request `mPictureModel` to add this picture in the current album. Note that, because `mPictureModel` is a `ThumbnailProxyModel` class, we have to retrieve the real `PictureModel` using the helper function, `pictureModel()`. As the `addPicture()` function returns the corresponding `QModelIndex`, we select the most recently-added picture in `thumbnailListView`.

Let's complete `AlbumWidget.cpp`:

```
void AlbumWidget::clearUi()
{
    ui->albumName->setText("");
    ui->deleteButton->setVisible(false);
    ui->editButton->setVisible(false);
    ui->addPicturesButton->setVisible(false);
}

void AlbumWidget::loadAlbum(const QModelIndex& albumIndex)
{
    mPictureModel->pictureModel()->setAlbumId(mAlbumModel->data(albumIndex,
        AlbumModel::Roles::IdRole).toInt());

    ui->albumName->setText(mAlbumModel->data(albumIndex,
        Qt::DisplayRole).toString());

    ui->deleteButton->setVisible(true);
    ui->editButton->setVisible(true);
    ui->addPicturesButton->setVisible(true);
}
```

The `clearUi()` function clears the album's name and hides the buttons, while the `loadAlbum()` function retrieves `Qt::DisplayRole` (the album's name) and displays the buttons.

Enhancing thumbnails with PictureDelegate

By default, a `QListView` class will request `Qt::DisplayRole` and `Qt::DecorationRole` to display text and a picture for each item. Thus, we already have a visual result, for free, that looks like this:

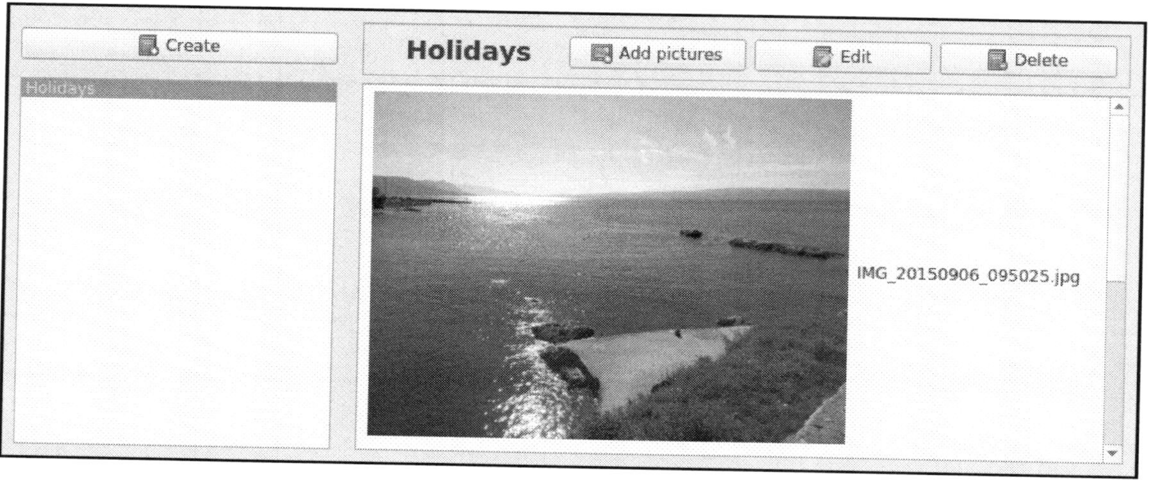

However, our **Gallery** application deserves better thumbnail rendering. Hopefully, we can easily customize it using the view's delegate concept. A `QListView` class provides a default item rendering. We can do our own item rendering by creating a class that inherits `QStyledItemDelegate`. The aim is to paint your dream thumbnails with a name banner, like in the following screenshot:

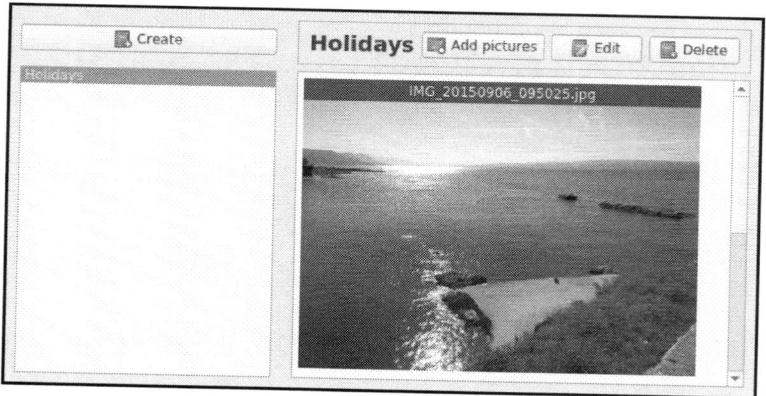

Let's take a look at PictureDelegate.h:

```
#include <QStyledItemDelegate>

class PictureDelegate : public QStyledItemDelegate
{
    Q_OBJECT
public:
    PictureDelegate(QObject* parent = 0);

    void paint(QPainter* painter, const QStyleOptionViewItem&
        option, const QModelIndex& index) const override;

    QSize sizeHint(const QStyleOptionViewItem& option,
        const QModelIndex& index) const override;
};
```

That's right, we only have to override two functions. The most important function, paint(), will allow us to paint the item the way we want. The sizeHint() function will be used to specify the item's size.

We can now see the painter work in PictureDelegate.cpp:

```
#include "PictureDelegate.h"

#include <QPainter>

const unsigned int BANNER_HEIGHT = 20;
const unsigned int BANNER_COLOR = 0x303030;
const unsigned int BANNER_ALPHA = 200;
const unsigned int BANNER_TEXT_COLOR = 0xffffff;
const unsigned int HIGHLIGHT_ALPHA = 100;

PictureDelegate::PictureDelegate(QObject* parent) :
    QStyledItemDelegate(parent)
{
}

void PictureDelegate::paint(QPainter* painter, const QStyleOptionViewItem&
option, const QModelIndex& index) const
{
    painter->save();

    QPixmap pixmap = index.model()->data(index,
        Qt::DecorationRole).value<QPixmap>();
    painter->drawPixmap(option.rect.x(), option.rect.y(), pixmap);

    QRect bannerRect = QRect(option.rect.x(), option.rect.y(),
```

```
        pixmap.width(), BANNER_HEIGHT);
    QColor bannerColor = QColor(BANNER_COLOR);
    bannerColor.setAlpha(BANNER_ALPHA);
    painter->fillRect(bannerRect, bannerColor);

    QString filename = index.model()->data(index,
        Qt::DisplayRole).toString();
    painter->setPen(BANNER_TEXT_COLOR);
    painter->drawText(bannerRect, Qt::AlignCenter, filename);

    if (option.state.testFlag(QStyle::State_Selected)) {
        QColor selectedColor = option.palette.highlight().color();
        selectedColor.setAlpha(HIGHLIGHT_ALPHA);
        painter->fillRect(option.rect, selectedColor);
    }

    painter->restore();
}
```

Each time `QListView` needs to display an item, this delegate's `paint()` function will be called. The paint system can be seen as layers that you paint one on top of each other. The `QPainter` class allows us to paint anything we want: circles, pies, rectangles, text, and so on. The item area can be retrieved with `option.rect()`. Here are the steps:

1. It is easy to break the `painter` state passed in the parameter list, thus we must save the painter state with `painter->save()` before doing anything. We will be able to restore it when we have finished our drawing.
2. Retrieve the item thumbnail and draw it with the `QPainter::drawPixmap()` function.
3. Paint a translucent gray banner on top of the thumbnail with the `QPainter::fillRect()` function.
4. Retrieve the item display name and draw it on the banner using the `QPainter::drawText()` function.
5. If the item is selected, we paint a translucent rectangle on the top using the highlight color from the item.
6. We restore the painter state to its original state.

If you want to learn how to draw a more complex item, check out the `QPainter` official documentation at `doc.qt.io/qt-5/qpainter.html`.

This is the `sizeHint()` function's implementation:

```
QSize PictureDelegate::sizeHint(const QStyleOptionViewItem& /*option*/,
const QModelIndex& index) const
{
    const QPixmap& pixmap = index.model()->data(index,
        Qt::DecorationRole).value<QPixmap>();
    return pixmap.size();
}
```

This one is easier. We want the item's size to be equal to the thumbnail's size. As we kept the aspect ratio of the thumbnail during its creation in `Picture::setFilePath()`, thumbnails can have a different width and height. Hence, we basically retrieve the thumbnail and return its size.

When you create an item delegate, avoid directly inheriting the `QItemDelegate` class and instead inherit `QStyledItemDelegate`. This last one supports Qt style sheets, allowing you to easily customize the rendering.

Now that `PictureDelegate` is ready, we can configure `thumbnailListView` to use it, updating the `AlbumWidget.cpp` file like this:

```
AlbumWidget::AlbumWidget(QWidget *parent) :
    QWidget(parent),
    ui(new Ui::AlbumWidget),
    mAlbumModel(nullptr),
    mAlbumSelectionModel(nullptr),
    mPictureModel(nullptr),
    mPictureSelectionModel(nullptr)
{
    ui->setupUi(this);
    clearUi();

    ui->thumbnailListView->setSpacing(5);
    ui->thumbnailListView->setResizeMode(QListView::Adjust);
    ui->thumbnailListView->setFlow(QListView::LeftToRight);
    ui->thumbnailListView->setWrapping(true);
    ui->thumbnailListView->setItemDelegate(
        new PictureDelegate(this));
    ...
}
```

An item delegate can also manage the editing process with the `QStyledItemDelegate::createEditor()` function.

Displaying a picture with PictureWidget

This widget will be called to display a picture at its full size. We also add some buttons to go to the previous/next picture or delete the current one.

Let's start to analyze the `PictureWidget.ui` form, here is the design view:

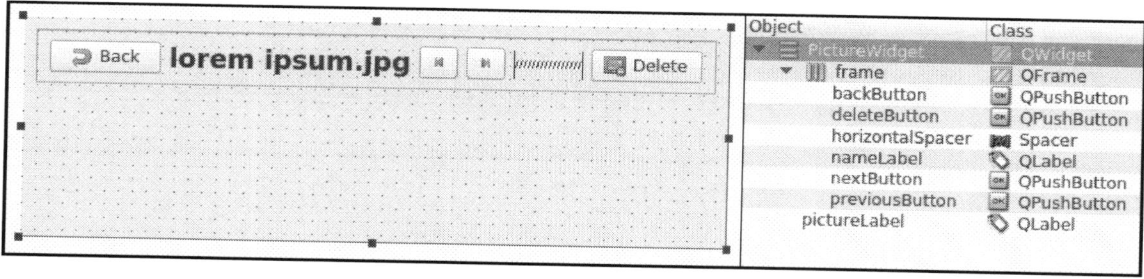

Here are the details:

- `backButton`: Requests to display the gallery
- `deleteButton`: Removes the picture from the album
- `nameLabel`: Displays the picture name
- `nextButton`: Selects the next picture in the album
- `previousButton`: Selects the previous picture in the album
- `pictureLabel`: Displays the picture

We can now take a look at the `PictureWidget.h` header:

```
#include <QWidget>
#include <QItemSelection>

namespace Ui {
class PictureWidget;
}

class PictureModel;
class QItemSelectionModel;
```

```
class ThumbnailProxyModel;

class PictureWidget : public QWidget
{
    Q_OBJECT

public:
    explicit PictureWidget(QWidget *parent = 0);
    ~PictureWidget();
    void setModel(ThumbnailProxyModel* model);
    void setSelectionModel(QItemSelectionModel* selectionModel);

signals:
    void backToGallery();

protected:
    void resizeEvent(QResizeEvent* event) override;

private slots:
    void deletePicture();
    void loadPicture(const QItemSelection& selected);

private:
    void updatePicturePixmap();

private:
    Ui::PictureWidget* ui;
    ThumbnailProxyModel* mModel;
    QItemSelectionModel* mSelectionModel;
    QPixmap mPixmap;
};
```

No surprises here, we have the `ThumbnailProxyModel*` and `QItemSelectionModel*` setters in the `PictureWidget` class. The `backToGallery()` signal is triggered when the user clicks on the `backButton` object. It will be handled by `MainWindow` to display the gallery. We override `resizeEvent()` to ensure that we always use all the visible area to display the picture. The `deletePicture()` slot will process the deletion when the user clicks on the corresponding button. The `loadPicture()` function will be called to update the UI with the specified picture. Finally, `updatePicturePixmap()` is a helper function to display the picture according to the current widget size.

This widget is really similar to the others. As a result, we will not put the full implementation code of `PictureWidget.cpp` here. You can check the full source code example if needed.

Let's see how this widget is able to always display the picture at its full size in `PictureWidget.cpp`:

```
void PictureWidget::resizeEvent(QResizeEvent* event)
{
    QWidget::resizeEvent(event);
    updatePicturePixmap();
}

void PictureWidget::updatePicturePixmap()
{
    if (mPixmap.isNull()) {
        return;
    }
    ui->pictureLabel->setPixmap(mPixmap.scaled(ui->pictureLabel->size(),
Qt::KeepAspectRatio));
}
```

So, every time the widget is resized, we call `updatePicturePixmap()`. The `mPixmap` variable is the full-size picture from `PictureModel`. This function will scale the picture to the `pictureLabel` size, keeping the aspect ratio. You can freely resize the window and enjoy your picture with the biggest possible size.

Composing your Gallery app

Alright, we completed `AlbumListWidget`, `AlbumWidget`, and `PictureWidget`. If you remember correctly, `AlbumListWidget` and `AlbumWidget` are contained in a widget called `GalleryWidget`.

Let's take a look at the `GalleryWidget.ui` file:

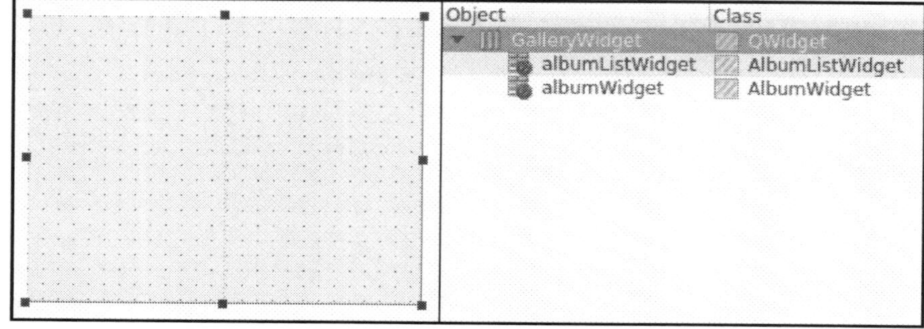

This widget does not contain any standard Qt widgets, only our created widgets. Qt provides two ways to use your own widgets in the Qt designer:

- **Promoting widgets**: This is the fastest and easiest way
- **Creating widget plugin for Qt designer**: This is more powerful but more complex

In this chapter, we will use the first way, which consists of placing a generic `QWidget` as a placeholder and then promoting it to our custom widget class. You can follow these steps to add the `albumListWidget` and `albumWidget` objects to the `GalleryWidget.ui` file from the Qt designer:

1. Drag and drop a **Widget** from **Containers** to your form
2. Set the **objectName** (for example, `albumListWidget`) from the **Property Editor**
3. Select **Promote to...** from the widget contextual menu
4. Set the promoted class name (for example, `AlbumWidget`)
5. Check that header file is correct (for example, `AlbumWidget.h`)
6. Click on the **Add** button and then click on **Promote**

If you fail your widget promotion, you can always reverse it with **Demote to QWidget** from the contextual menu.

There is nothing really exciting in the header and implementation of `GalleryWidget`. We only provide setters for the model and model selection of `Album` and `Picture` to forward them to `albumListWidget` and `albumWidget`. This class also relays the `pictureActivated` signal from `albumWidget`. Please check the full source code if needed.

This is the final part of this chapter. We will now analyze `MainWindow`. Nothing is done in `MainWindow.ui` because everything is handled in the code. This is `MainWindow.h`:

```
#include <QMainWindow>
#include <QStackedWidget>

namespace Ui {
class MainWindow;
}

class GalleryWidget;
class PictureWidget;

class MainWindow : public QMainWindow
{
```

```
    Q_OBJECT

public:
    explicit MainWindow(QWidget *parent = 0);
    ~MainWindow();

public slots:
    void displayGallery();
    void displayPicture(const QModelIndex& index);

private:
    Ui::MainWindow *ui;
    GalleryWidget* mGalleryWidget;
    PictureWidget* mPictureWidget;
    QStackedWidget* mStackedWidget;
};
```

The two slots, `displayGallery()` and `displayPicture()`, will be used to switch the display between the gallery (album list with the album and thumbnail) and the picture (full-size). The `QStackedWidget` class can contain various widgets but display only one at a time.

Let's take a look at the beginning of the constructor in the `MainWindow.cpp` file:

Here is the constructor initialization list:

```
MainWindow::MainWindow(QWidget *parent) :
    QMainWindow(parent),
    ui(new Ui::MainWindow),
    mGalleryWidget(new GalleryWidget(this)),
    mPictureWidget(new PictureWidget(this)),
    mStackedWidget(new QStackedWidget(this))
{
   ...
}
```

Then we can start the body constructor:

```
ui->setupUi(this);

AlbumModel* albumModel = new AlbumModel(this);
QItemSelectionModel* albumSelectionModel =
    new QItemSelectionModel(albumModel, this);
mGalleryWidget->setAlbumModel(albumModel);
mGalleryWidget->setAlbumSelectionModel(albumSelectionModel);
```

First, we initialize the UI by calling `ui->setupUi()`. Then we create `AlbumModel` and its `QItemSelectionModel`. Finally, we call the setters of `GalleryWidget`, which will dispatch them to the `AlbumListWidget` and `AlbumWidget` objects.

Let's continue our analysis of this constructor:

```
PictureModel* pictureModel = new PictureModel(*albumModel, this);
ThumbnailProxyModel* thumbnailModel = new ThumbnailProxyModel(this);
thumbnailModel->setSourceModel(pictureModel);

QItemSelectionModel* pictureSelectionModel =
    new QItemSelectionModel(thumbnailModel, this);

mGalleryWidget->setPictureModel(thumbnailModel);
mGalleryWidget->setPictureSelectionModel(pictureSelectionModel);
mPictureWidget->setModel(thumbnailModel);
mPictureWidget->setSelectionModel(pictureSelectionModel);
```

The behavior with `Picture` is close to the previous one with `Album`. But we also share `ThumbnailProxyModel`, which is initialized from `PictureModel` and its `QItemSelectionModel` with `PictureWidget`.

The constructor now performs the signal/slot connections:

```
connect(mGalleryWidget, &GalleryWidget::pictureActivated,
        this, &MainWindow::displayPicture);

connect(mPictureWidget, &PictureWidget::backToGallery,
        this, &MainWindow::displayGallery);
```

Do you remember the `pictureActivated()` function? This signal is emitted when you double-click on a thumbnail in `albumWidget`. We can now connect it to our `displayPicture` slot, which will switch the display with the picture at its full size. Do not forget to also connect the `backToGallery` signal emitted when the user clicks on the `backButton` from `PictureWidget`. It will switch again to display the gallery.

The last part of the constructor is easy:

```
mStackedWidget->addWidget(mGalleryWidget);
mStackedWidget->addWidget(mPictureWidget);
displayGallery();

setCentralWidget(mStackedWidget);
```

We add our two widgets, `mGalleryWidget` and `mPictureWidget`, to the `mStackedWidget` class. When the application starts, we want to display the gallery, so we call our own `displayGallery()` slot. Finally, we define `mStackedWidget` as the main window's central widget.

To finish this chapter, let's see what happens in these two magic slots that allows us to switch the display when the user requests it:

```
void MainWindow::displayGallery()
{
    mStackedWidget->setCurrentWidget(mGalleryWidget);
}

void MainWindow::displayPicture(const QModelIndex& /*index*/)
{
    mStackedWidget->setCurrentWidget(mPictureWidget);
}
```

That seems ridiculously easy. We just request `mStackedWidget` to select the corresponding widget. As `PictureWidget` shares the same selection model with other views, we can even ignore the `index` variable.

You can now compile the project and enjoy your desktop gallery project!

Summary

The real separation between data and representation is not always an easy task. Learning to divide the core and the GUI into two different projects is good practice; it will force you to design separated layers in your application. At first sight, the Qt model/view system can appear complex. But this chapter taught you how powerful it can be and how easy it is to use. Thanks to the Qt framework, we can persist data in a database without headaches.

This chapter built on top of the foundations we laid with the `gallery-core` library. In the next chapter, we will reuse the same core library and create a mobile UI with Qt Quick in QML.

5
Dominating the Mobile UI

In `Chapter 3`, *Dividing Your Project and Ruling Your Code,* we created a strong core library to handle an image gallery. We will now use this `gallery-core` library to create a mobile application.

We will teach you how to create a Qt Quick project from scratch. You will create custom Qt Quick views with QML. This chapter will also cover how your QML views can communicate with the C++ library.

At the end of this chapter, your gallery application will run on your mobile (Android or iOS) with a dedicated GUI compliant with touch devices. This application will offer the same features as the desktop application.

This chapter covers the following topics:

- Starting with Qt Quick and QML
- Creating a Qt Quick project
- Displaying albums with ListView
- Loading a database on mobile
- Loading images with an ImageProvider
- Displaying thumbnails in a GridView

Starting with Qt Quick and QML

Qt Quick is another way of creating complete application in place of Qt Widgets. The Qt Quick module provides transitions, animations, and visual effects. You can also customize graphical effects with shaders. This module is especially efficient at making software for devices using touchscreens. Qt Quick uses a dedicated language – the Qt Modeling Language (QML). It is a declarative language, with a syntax similar to that of JSON (JavaScript Object Notation). Furthermore, QML also supports JavaScript expressions inline or in a separate file.

Let's begin with a simple example of a **Qt Quick application** using QML. Create a new file called `main.qml` with this code snippet:

```
import QtQuick 2.5
import QtQuick.Window 2.2

Window {
    visible: true
    width: 640; height: 480

    // A nice red rectangle
    Rectangle {
        width: 200; height: 200
        color: "red"
    }
}
```

Qt 5 provides a nice tool called `qmlscene` to prototype a QML user interface. You can find the binary file in your Qt installation folder, for example: `Qt/5.7/gcc_64/bin/qmlscene`. To load your `main.qml` file, you can run the tool and select the file, or use the CLI with the `.qml` file in an argument: `qmlscene main.qml`. You should see something like this:

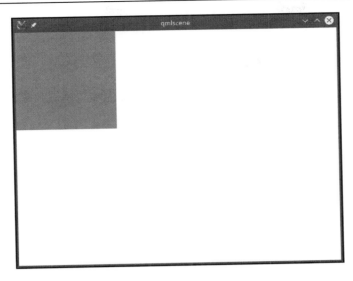

To use a Qt Quick module, you need to import it. The syntax is straightforward:

```
import <moduleName> <moduleVersion>
```

In this example, we import `QtQuick`, which is the common module that will provide basic components (`Rectangle`, `Image`, and `Text`) and we also import the `QtQuick.Window` module, which will provide the main application window (`Window`).

A QML component can have properties. For example, we set the `width` property of the `Window` class to a value of `640`. The generic syntax is as follows:

```
<ObjectType> {
    <PropertyName>: <PropertyValue>
}
```

We can now update the `main.qml` file with new rectangles:

```
import QtQuick 2.5
import QtQuick.Window 2.2

Window {
    visible: true
    width: 640; height: 480

    Rectangle {
        width: 200; height: 200
        color: "red"
    }

    Rectangle {
        width: 200; height: 200
        color: "green"
        x: 100; y: 100

        Rectangle {
            width: 50; height: 50
            color: "blue"
            x: 100; y: 100
        }
    }
}
```

The visual result is as follows:

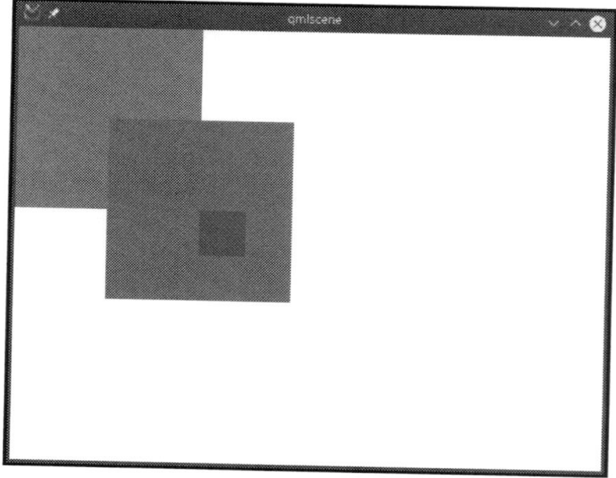

Your QML file describes the UI as a hierarchy of components. The hierarchy beneath the `Window` element is as follows:

- Red `Rectangle`
- Green `Rectangle`
- Blue `Rectangle`

Each nested item will always have its `x` and `y` coordinates relative to its parent.

To structure your application, you can build reusable QML components. You can easily create a new component. All QML components must have a single root item. Let's build a new `MyToolbar` component by creating a new file called `MyToolbar.qml`:

```
import QtQuick 2.5

Rectangle {
    color: "gray"
    height: 50

    Rectangle {
        id: purpleRectangle
        width: 50; height: parent.height
        color: "purple"
        radius: 10
    }

    Text {
        anchors.left: purpleRectangle.right
        anchors.right: parent.right
        text: "Dominate the Mobile UI"
        font.pointSize: 30
    }
}
```

The gray `Rectangle` element will be our root item used as the background. We also created two items:

- A purple `Rectangle` element that can be identified with the ID `purpleRectangle`. The height of this item will be the height of its parent, that is, the gray `Rectangle` element.

- A `Text` item. In this case, we use anchors. It will help us to set out items without using hardcoded coordinates. The left-hand side of the `Text` item will be aligned with the right-hand side of `purpleRectangle`, and the right-hand side of the `Text` item will be aligned with the right-hand side of the parent (the gray `Rectangle` element).

Qt Quick provides many anchors: `left`, `horizontalCenter`, `right`, `top`, `verticalCenter`, `baseline`, and `bottom`. You can also use convenience anchors such as `fill` or `centerIn`. For more information on anchors, refer to `http://doc.qt.io/qt-5/qtquick-positioning-anchors.html`.

You can use `MyToolbar` in your window by updating your `main.qml`:

```
Window {
    ...
    MyToolbar {
        width: parent.width
    }
}
```

We set the width to the width of the parent. This is how the toolbar fills the width of the window. The result is as follows:

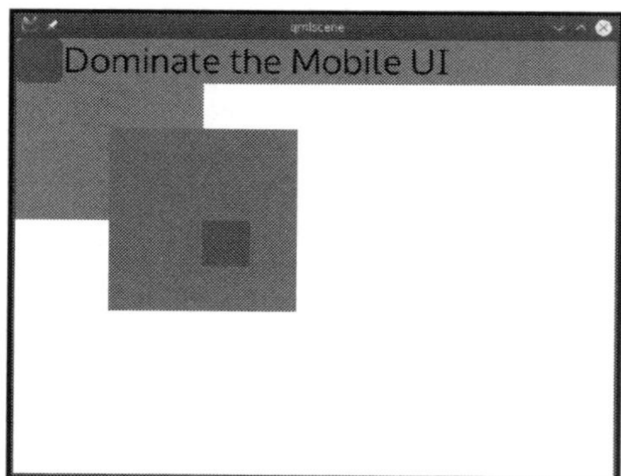

Anchors are great for aligning specific items, but, if you want to set out several items in grid, row, or column fashion, you can use the `QtQuick.Layouts` module. Here is an example of the updated `main.qml` file:

```
import QtQuick 2.5
import QtQuick.Window 2.2
import QtQuick.Layouts 1.3
```

```
Window {
    visible: true
    width: 640; height: 480

    MyToolbar {
        id: myToolbar
        width: parent.width
    }

    RowLayout {
        anchors.top: myToolbar.bottom
        anchors.left: parent.left
        anchors.right: parent.right
        anchors.bottom: parent.bottom

        Rectangle { width: 200; height: 200; color: "red" }
        Rectangle { width: 200; height: 200; color: "green" }
        Rectangle { width: 50; height: 50; color: "blue" }
    }
}
```

You should get something like this:

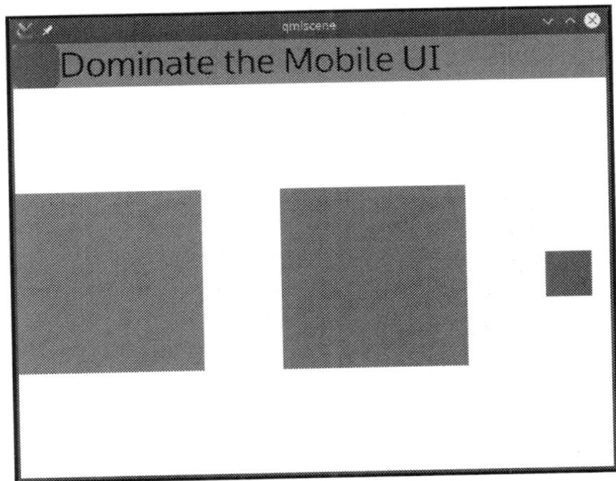

As you can see, we use a `RowLayout` element that fits under the `myToolbar` and its parent, a `Window` element. This item provides a way of dynamically laying out items in a row. Qt Quick also provides other layouts: `ColumnLayout`, `GridLayout`, and `StackLayout`.

Your custom component may also expose custom properties that can be modified outside of the component itself. You can do this by adding the `property` attribute. Let's update `MyToolbar.qml`:

```
import QtQuick 2.5

Rectangle {

    property color iconColor: "purple"
    property alias title: label.text

    color: "gray"
    height: 50

    Rectangle {
        id: purpleRectangle
        width: 50; height: parent.height
        color: iconColor
        radius: 10
    }

    Text {
        id: label
        anchors.left: purpleRectangle.right
        anchors.right: parent.right
        text: "Dominate the Mobile UI"
        font.pointSize: 30
    }
}
```

`iconColor` is a new property that is a fully fledged variable. We also update the `Rectangle` attribute to use this property as `color`. The `title` property is only an `alias`; you can see it as a pointer to update the `label.text` property.

From outside, you can use these attributes with the same syntax; please update the `main.qml` file with the following snippet:

```
import QtQuick 2.5
import QtQuick.Window 2.2
import QtQuick.Layouts 1.3

Window {
    visible: true
    width: 640; height: 480

    MyToolbar {
        id: myToolbar
```

```
        width: parent.width

        title: "Dominate Qt Quick"
        iconColor: "yellow"
    }
    ...
}
```

You should get a nice updated toolbar as follows:

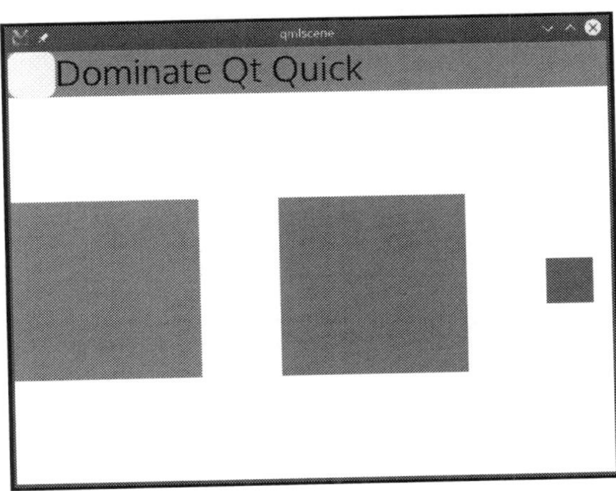

We have covered the basics of QML. Now, we are going to proceed to mobile application development using QML.

Checking your development environment

To be able to create a Qt application for Android, you must have the following:

- A device with Android v2.3.3 (API 10) or later
- Android SDK (version 25.2.5 or earlier)
- Android NDK (version 10e is recommended)
- JDK (version 6 or later)
- Qt Prebuilt components for Android x86 (from the Qt maintenance tool)
- Qt Prebuilt components for Android ARMv7 (from the Qt maintenance tool)

To be able to create a Qt application for iOS, you must have the following:

- A device with iOS 5.0 or later

- A macOS desktop computer
- Xcode
- Qt for iOS (from the Qt maintenance tool)

When starting, Qt Creator will detect and create Android and iOS Qt kits. You can check your existing kits under **Tools** | **Options** | **Build & Run** | **Kits**, as shown in the following screenshot:

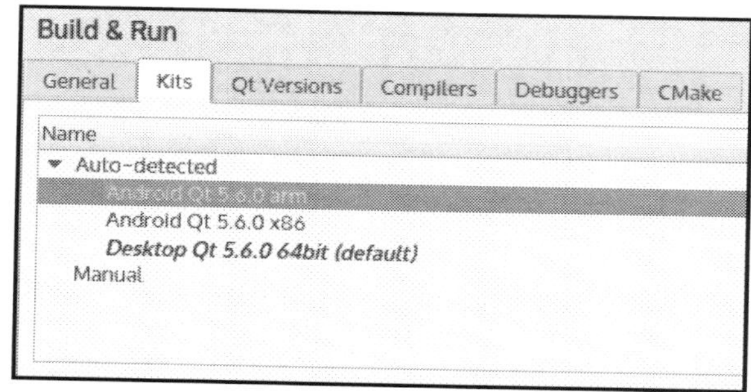

Creating a Qt Quick project

This chapter will follow the same project structure we covered in `Chapter 4`, *Conquering the Desktop UI*: a parent project `ch05-gallery-mobile.pro` will host our two subprojects, `gallery-core` and the new `gallery-mobile`.

In Qt creator, you can create a Qt Quick subproject from **File** | **New File or Project** | **Application** | **Qt Quick Application – Empty** | **Choose**.

The Wizard will allow you to customize your project creation:

- Location
    - Choose a project name (`gallery-mobile`) and a location
- Kits
    - Select your desktop kit
    - Select at least one mobile kit
- Summary
    - Be sure to add `gallery-mobile` as a subproject of `ch05-gallery-mobile.pro`

Let's take time to explain why we created our project with these options.

The first thing to analyze is the application template. By default, Qt Quick only provides basic QML components (`Rectangle`, `Image`, `Text`, and so on). Advanced components will be handled by Qt Quick modules. For this project, we will use Qt Quick Controls (`ApplicationWindow`, `Button`, `TextField`, and so on). That is why we chose to begin with a **Qt Quick Controls application**. Bear in mind that you can always import and use Qt Quick modules later.

In this chapter, we will not use Qt Quick Designer. As a consequence, `.ui.qml` files are not required. Even if the designer can help a lot, it is good to understand and write QML files yourself.

Finally, we select at least two kits. The first one is our desktop kit. The other kits are the mobile platforms you target. We usually use the following development workflow:

- Fast iterations on desktop
- Check and fix behavior on a mobile emulator/simulator
- Perform actual tests on the mobile device

Deployment on a real device is generally longer, so you can do most of the development with the desktop kit. The mobile kits will allow you to check your application's behavior on a real mobile device or on an emulator (for example, with a Qt Android x86 kit).

Let's talk about the files automatically generated by the wizard. Here is the `main.cpp` file:

```
#include <QGuiApplication>
#include <QQmlApplicationEngine>

int main(int argc, char *argv[])
{
    QCoreApplication::setAttribute(Qt::AA_EnableHighDpiScaling);

    QGuiApplication app(argc, argv);

    QQmlApplicationEngine engine;
    engine.load(QUrl(QStringLiteral("qrc:/main.qml")));
    if (engine.rootObjects().isEmpty())
        return -1;

    return app.exec();
}
```

Here, we use `QGuiApplication` and not `QApplication` because we do not use Qt Widgets in this project. Then, we create the QML engine and load `qrc:/main.qml`. As you may have guessed (with the `qrc:/` prefix), this QML file is in a Qt resource file.

You can open the qml.qrc file to find the main.qmlfile:

```
import QtQuick 2.11
import QtQuick.Window 2.11

Window {
    visible: true
    width: 640
    height: 480
    title: qsTr("Hello World")
}
```

The first thing to do is to import the types used in the file. Notice the module version at the end of each import. The QtQuick module will import basic QML elements (Rectangle, Image, and so on).

Before proceeding, check that this sample runs correctly on your desktop and on your mobile.

Preparing your Qt Quick gallery entry point

First of all, you need to link this project to our gallery-core library. We already covered how to link an internal library in Chapter 4, *Conquering the Desktop UI*. This is the updated gallery-mobile.pro file:

```
TEMPLATE = app

QT += qml quick sql svg

CONFIG += c++11

SOURCES += main.cpp

RESOURCES += gallery.qrc

LIBS += -L$$OUT_PWD/../gallery-core/ -lgallery-core
INCLUDEPATH += $$PWD/../gallery-core
DEPENDPATH += $$PWD/../gallery-core

contains(ANDROID_TARGET_ARCH,x86) {
    ANDROID_EXTRA_LIBS = \
        $$[QT_INSTALL_LIBS]/libQt5Sql.so
}
```

Please be aware that we made several changes here:

- We added the `sql` module to deploy the dependency on your mobile device.
- We added the `svg` module for the button icons.
- The `qml.qrc` file has been renamed in `gallery.qrc`.
- We linked the `gallery-core` library.
- By default, the `sql` shared object (`libQt5Sql.so`) will not be deployed on your Android x86 device. You have to explicitly include it in your `.pro` file.

You can now use classes from the `gallery-core` library in our `gallery-mobile` application. Let's see how to bind C++ models using QML. This is the updated `main.cpp`file:

```
#include <QGuiApplication>
#include <QQmlApplicationEngine>
#include <QQmlContext>
#include <QQuickView>

#include "AlbumModel.h"
#include "PictureModel.h"

int main(int argc, char *argv[])
{
    QGuiApplication app(argc, argv);

    AlbumModel albumModel;
    PictureModel pictureModel(albumModel);

    QQmlApplicationEngine engine;

    QQmlContext* context = engine.rootContext();
    context->setContextProperty("albumModel", &albumModel);
    context->setContextProperty("pictureModel", &pictureModel);

    engine.load(QUrl(QStringLiteral("qrc:/qml/main.qml")));

    return app.exec();
}
```

Notice that the `main.qml` file is in a `qml` sub-directory. Our models will be instantiated in C++ and exposed to QML using the root `QQmlContext` object.
The `setContextProperty()` function allows us to bind a C++ `QObject` to a QML property. The first argument will be the QML property name. We are only binding a C++ object to a QML property; the `context` object does not take ownership of this object.

Let's now talk about the mobile application itself. We will define three pages with specific roles:

- `AlbumListPage`
    - Displays existing albums
    - Album creation
    - Album selection
- `AlbumPage`
    - Displays existing images as thumbnails
    - Adds images to albums
    - Album rename
    - Album deletion
    - Image selection
- `PicturePage`
    - Displays selected images
    - Image selection
    - Image deletion

To handle the navigation, we will use a `StackView` component from Qt Quick Controls. This QML component implements stack-based navigation. You can push a page when you want to display it. When the user requests to go back, you can pop it. Here is the workflow using a `StackView` component for our gallery mobile application. The page with the solid border is the page currently displayed on screen:

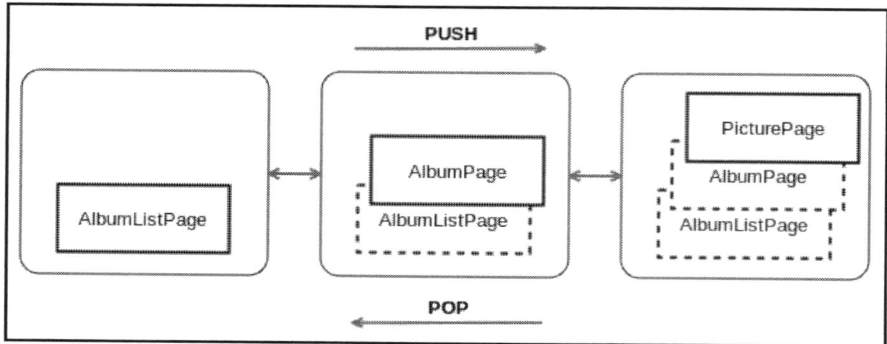

This is the implementation of `main.qml`:

```
import QtQuick 2.6
```

```
import QtQuick.Controls 2.0

ApplicationWindow {

    readonly property alias pageStack: stackView

    id: app
    visible: true
    width: 768
    height: 1280

    StackView {
        id: stackView
        anchors.fill: parent
        initialItem: AlbumListPage {}
    }

    onClosing: {
        if (Qt.platform.os == "android") {
            if (stackView.depth > 1) {
                close.accepted = false
                stackView.pop()
            }
        }
    }
}
```

This main file is really simple. The application is constructed around the `StackView` component. We set the `id` property to allow our `StackView` to be identified and referred to by other QML objects. The `anchors` property will set `stackView` to fill its parent, the `ApplicationWindow` type. Finally, we set the `initialItem` property to a page, `AlbumListPage`, that will be implemented soon.

On Android, `onClosing` will be executed each time the user presses the Back button. To mimic a native Android application, we will first pop the last stacked page before actually closing the application.

At the top of the file, we define a `property alias` for `stackView`. A `property alias` is a simple reference to another existing property. This alias will be useful to access `stackView` from other QML components. To prevent a QML component from crushing the `stackView`, we use the `readonly` keyword. After initialization, the components can access the property but not change its value.

Displaying albums with ListView

Now let's make our first page for this mobile application! Create a file in `gallery.qrc` called `AlbumListPage.qml`. Here is the page header implementation:

```
import QtQuick 2.0
import QtQuick.Layouts 1.3

import QtQuick.Controls 2.0

Page {

    header: ToolBar {
        Label {
            Layout.fillWidth: true
            text: "Albums"
            font.pointSize: 30
        }
    }
...
}
```

A `Page` is a container control with a header and footer. In this application, we will only use the header item. We assign a `ToolBar` to the `header` property. The height of this toolbar will be handled by Qt and will be adjusted depending on the target platform. In this first simple implementation, we only put a `Label` displaying the text `Albums`.

Now, you can add a `ListView` element to this page after the `header` initialization:

```
ListView {
    id: albumList
    model: albumModel
    spacing: 5
    anchors.fill: parent

    delegate: Rectangle {
        width: parent.width
        height: 120
        color: "#d0d1d2"

        Text {
            text: name
            font.pointSize: 16
            color: "#000000"
            anchors.verticalCenter: parent.verticalCenter
        }
```

```
        }
    }
```

The Qt Quick `ListView` is the Qt Widget `QListView` equivalent. It displays a list of items from a model provided. We set the `model` property to the value `albumModel`. This refers to the C++ model from the `main.cpp` file accessible from QML because we used the `setContextProperty()` function. In Qt Quick, you must provide a delegate to describe how a row will be displayed. In this case, a row will only display the album's name with a `Text` item. Accessing the album's name in QML is straightforward because our `AlbumModel` exposes its role list to QML. Let's refresh your memory regarding the overridden `roleNames()` function of `AlbumModel`:

```
QHash<int, QByteArray> AlbumModel::roleNames() const
{
    QHash<int, QByteArray> roles;
    roles[Roles::IdRole] = "id";
    roles[Roles::NameRole] = "name";
    return roles;
}
```

So, each time your delegate from Qt Quick uses the `name` role, it will call the `AlbumModel` function `data()` with the correct role integer and return the correct album name string.

To handle the mouse, click on a row and add a `MouseArea` element to the delegate:

```
ListView {
    ...
    delegate: Rectangle {
        ...
        MouseArea {
            anchors.fill: parent
            onClicked: {
                albumList.currentIndex = index
                pictureModel.setAlbumId(id)
                pageStack.push("qrc:/qml/AlbumPage.qml",
                        { albumName: name, albumRowIndex: index })
            }
        }
    }
}
```

The `MouseArea` is an invisible item that can be used with any visible item to handle mouse events. This also applies to a simple touch on a phone's touchscreen. Here, we tell the `MouseArea` element to take the full area of the parent `Rectangle`.

In our case, we only perform tasks on the clicked signal. We update the currentIndex of the ListView with index. This index is a special role containing the index of the item in the model.

When the user clicks, we tell pictureModel to load the selected album with the pictureModel.setAlbumId(id) call. We will soon discover how QML can call C++ methods.

Finally, we push AlbumPage on the pageStack property. The push() function allows us to set a list of QML properties using a {key: value, ... } syntax. Each property will be copied into the pushed item. Here, the name and the index will be copied in the albumName and albumRowIndex properties of AlbumPage. It is a simple, yet powerful, way to instantiate a QML page with property arguments.

From your QML code, you can only call some specific C++ code using the following:

- Properties (using Q_PROPERTY)
- Public slots
- Functions decorated as invokable (using Q_INVOKABLE)

In this case, we will decorate PictureModel::setAlbumId() as Q_INVOKABLE; please update the PictureModel.h file:

```
class GALLERYCORESHARED_EXPORT PictureModel : public QAbstractListModel
{
    Q_OBJECT
public:
    ...
    Q_INVOKABLE void setAlbumId(int albumId);
    ...
};
```

Theming the application with a QML singleton

Styling and theming a QML application can be executed in various ways. In this chapter, we will declare a QML singleton with the theme data used by custom components. Moreover, we will also create a custom Page component to handle the toolbar and its default item (the **Back** button and the page's title).

Please create a new `Style.qml` file:

```
pragma Singleton
import QtQuick 2.0

QtObject {
    property color text: "#000000"

    property color windowBackground: "#eff0f1"
    property color toolbarBackground: "#eff0f1"
    property color pageBackground: "#fcfcfc"
    property color buttonBackground: "#d0d1d2"

    property color itemHighlight: "#3daee9"
}
```

We declare a `QtObject` component that will only contain our theme properties. A `QtObject` is a non-visual QML component.

Declaring a singleton type in QML requires two steps: First, you need to use the `pragma singleton`, which will indicate the use of a single instance of the component. The second step is to register it. This can be done in C++, or by creating a `qmldir` file.

Let's look at the second step. Create a new plain text file called `qmldir`:

```
singleton Style 1.0 Style.qml
```

This `qmldir` file must be in the resource file, like the QML files. This simple line will declare a QML `singleton` type named `Style`, with the version 1.0 from the file named `Style.qml`.

It's now time to use these theme properties in custom components. Let's look at a simple example by creating a new QML file called `ToolBarTheme.qml`:

```
import QtQuick 2.0
import QtQuick.Controls 2.0

import "."

ToolBar {
     background: Rectangle {
         color: Style.toolbarBackground
     }

}
```

This QML object describes a customized `ToolBar`. Here, the `background` element is a simple `Rectangle` with our color. We can easily access our singleton `Style` and its theme property using `Style.toolbarBackground`.

QML singletons require an explicit import to load the `qmldir` file. `import "."` is a workaround for this Qt bug. For more information, please check `https://bugreports.qt.io/browse/QTBUG-34418`.

We will now create a QML file, `PageTheme.qml`, with the aim of containing all the code related to the page's toolbar and theme:

```
import QtQuick 2.0

import QtQuick.Layouts 1.3
import QtQuick.Controls 2.0
import "."

Page {

    property alias toolbarButtons: buttonsLoader.sourceComponent
    property alias toolbarTitle: titleLabel.text

    header: ToolBarTheme {
        RowLayout {
            anchors.fill: parent
            ToolButton {
                background: Image {
                    source: "qrc:/res/icons/back.svg"
                }
                onClicked: {
                    if (stackView.depth > 1) {
                        stackView.pop()
                    }
                }
            }

            Label {
                id: titleLabel
                Layout.fillWidth: true
                color: Style.text
                elide: Text.ElideRight
                font.pointSize: 30
            }

            Loader {
                Layout.alignment: Qt.AlignRight
```

```
                    id: buttonsLoader
                }
            }
        }

        Rectangle {
            color: Style.pageBackground
            anchors.fill: parent
        }
    }
```

This `PageTheme` element will customize the page's header. We use our previously created `ToolBarTheme`. This toolbar only contains a `RowLayout` element to display items horizontally in a single row. This layout contains three elements:

- `ToolButton`: the "back" that displays an image from `gallery.qrc` and pops the current page if clicked
- `Label`: an element that displays the page title
- `Loader`: an element that allows a page to dynamically add specific items in this generic toolbar

The `Loader` element has a `sourceComponent` property. In this application, this property can be assigned by `PageTheme` pages to add specific buttons. Like everything in QML, these buttons will be instantiated at runtime.

The `PageTheme` pages also contain a `Rectangle` element that fits the parent and configures the page background color using the `Style.pageBackground`.

Now that our `Style.qml` and `PageTheme.qml` files are ready, we can update the `AlbumListPage.qml` file to use it:

```
import QtQuick 2.6
import QtQuick.Controls 2.0
import "."

PageTheme {

    toolbarTitle: "Albums"

    ListView {
        id: albumList
        model: albumModel
        spacing: 5
        anchors.fill: parent
```

```
            delegate: Rectangle {
                width: parent.width
                height: 120
                color: Style.buttonBackground

                Text {
                    text: name
                    font.pointSize: 16
                    color: Style.text
                    anchors.verticalCenter: parent.verticalCenter
                }
                ...
            }
        }
    }
```

Now that `AlbumListPage` is a `PageTheme` element, we do not manipulate `header` directly. We only need to set the `toolbarTitle` property to display a nice "Albums" text in the toolbar. We can also utilize attractive colors using properties from the `Style` singleton.

By centralizing the theme properties in a single file, you can easily change the look and feel of your application. The source code for the project also contains a dark theme.

Loading a database on mobile devices

Before continuing the UI implementation, we have to handle database deployment on mobile devices (spoiler alert: this will not be fun!).

We have to jump back to `DatabaseManager.cpp` in the `gallery-core` project:

```
DatabaseManager& DatabaseManager::instance()
{
    return singleton;
}

DatabaseManager::DatabaseManager(const QString& path) :
    mDatabase(new QSqlDatabase(QSqlDatabase::addDatabase("QSQLITE"))),
    albumDao(*mDatabase),
    pictureDao(*mDatabase)
{
    mDatabase->setDatabaseName(path);
    ...
}
```

Although, on desktop devices, the SQLite3 database is created with the instruction `mDatabase->setDatabaseName()`, on mobile devices, it does not work at all. This is due to the fact that the filesystem is very specific on each mobile platform (Android and iOS). An application only has access to a narrow sandbox where it cannot interfere with the rest of the filesystem. All the files inside the application directory must have specific file permissions. If we let SQLite3 create the database file, it will not have the correct permission and the OS will prevent the database from opening.

As a consequence, the database will not be created properly and your data won't be persisted. When using the native API, this is not a problem since the OS takes care of the proper configuration of the database. Since we are developing with Qt, we do not have easy access to this API (except by using JNI or other black magic). A workaround is to include a "ready-to-use" database in the application's package and copy it to the correct filesystem path with the correct rights.

This database should contain an empty database created without any content. The database is available in the source code of the chapter (you can also generate it from the source code of `Chapter 4`, *Conquering the Desktop UI*). You can add it to the `gallery.qrc` file.

Because our layers are clearly defined, we just have to modify the `DatabaseManager::instance()` implementation to handle this case:

```
DatabaseManager& DatabaseManager::instance()
{
#if defined(Q_OS_ANDROID) || defined(Q_OS_IOS)
    QFile assetDbFile(":/database/" + DATABASE_FILENAME);
    QString destinationDbFile =
QStandardPaths::writableLocation(QStandardPaths::AppLocalDataLocation)
          .append("/" + DATABASE_FILENAME);

    qDebug() << "Assets file" << assetDbFile.fileName();
    qDebug() << "Database file" << destinationDbFile;
    if (assetDbFile.exists()) {
        if (!QFile::exists(destinationDbFile)) {
            assetDbFile.copy(destinationDbFile);
            QFile::setPermissions(destinationDbFile,
                QFile::WriteOwner | QFile::ReadOwner);
            qDebug() << "Setted permissions on copied file";
        }
    }
    static DatabaseManager singleton(destinationDbFile);
#else
    static DatabaseManager singleton;
#endif
    return singleton;
}
```

We first retrieve the platform-specific path of the application with a nifty Qt class: `QStandardPaths`. This class returns paths for multiple types (`AppLocalDataLocation`, `DocumentsLocation`, `PicturesLocation`, and so on). The database should be stored in the application's data directory. If the file does not exist, we copy it from our assets.

Finally, the file permissions are modified to ensure that the OS does not block the opening of the database (due to permissions not being restrictive enough).

When everything is done, the `DatabaseManager singleton` is instantiated with the correct database file path and the constructor can open this database transparently.

In the iOS simulator, the `QStandardPaths::writableLocation()` function will not return the proper path. Since iOS 8, the simulator's storage path on the host has changed and Qt does not reflect this. For more information, please check out `https://bugreports.qt.io/browse/QTCREATORBUG-13655`.

These workarounds were not trivial. This shows the limitations of a cross-platform application on mobile devices. Each platform has its own very specific way of handling the filesystem and deploying its content. Even if we manage to write platform-agnostic code in QML, we still have to deal with differences between the OSes.

Creating a new album from a custom InputDialog

The `AlbumListPage` needs some data to display. The next step is to be able to add a new album. To do this, at some point, we will have to call an `AlbumModel` function from QML in order to add this new album. Before building the UI, we have to make a small modification to `gallery-core`.

The `AlbumModel` function is already available in QML. However, we cannot directly call `AlbumModel::addAlbum(const Album& album)` from the QML code: the QML engine will not recognize the function and will throw an error: TypeError: Property 'addAlbum' of object AlbumModel(...) is not a function. This can be fixed by simply decorating the desired function with the `Q_INVOKABLE` macro (as we did for `PictureModel::setAlbumId()`).

Nonetheless, there is a second issue here: `Album` is a C++ class that is not recognized in QML. If we wanted to have full access to `Album` in QML, it would involve important modifications to the class:

- Force the `Album` class to inherit from the `QObject` class.
- Add a `Q_PROPERTY` macro to specify which property of the class should be accessible from QML.
- Add a specific constructor.
- Force the `AlbumModel::addAlbum()` function to take an `Album*` rather than an `Album&`. For complex objects (that is, not primitive types), QML can only handle pointers. This is not a major issue, but using references instead of pointers tends to make the code safer.

These modifications are perfectly reasonable if the class is heavily manipulated in QML. Our use case is very limited: we only want to create a new album. Throughout the application, we will rely on the native Model/View API to display the album data and nothing specific to `Album` will be used.

For all these reasons, we will simply add a wrapper function in `AlbumModel`:

```
// In AlbumModel.h
...
QModelIndex addAlbum(const Album& album);
Q_INVOKABLE void addAlbumFromName(const QString& name);
...

// In AlbumModel.cpp
void AlbumModel::addAlbumFromName(const QString& name)
{
    addAlbum(Album(name));
}
```

The new `addAlbumFromName()` function just wraps the call to `addAlbum()` with the desired album `name` parameter. The `Q_INVOKABLE` macro makes the function available to the Qt meta-object system.

We can now switch back to the UI in the `gallery-mobile` project. We will add this album using a QML `Dialog`. Qt Quick provides various default implementations of dialogs:

- `ColorDialog`: This is used to choose a color
- `Dialog`: This uses the generic dialog with standard buttons (the equivalent of a `QDialog`)
- `FileDialog`: This is used to choose a file from the local filesystem

- `FolderDialog`: This is used to choose a folder from the local filesystem
- `FontDialog`: This is used to choose a font
- `MessageDialog`: This is used to display a message

You would have expected to see an `InputDialog` in this list (as we used the `QInputDialog` widget in `Chapter 4`, *Conquering the Desktop UI*), but Qt Quick does not have it. Create a new **QML File (Qt Quick 2)** and name it `InputDialog.qml`.

The content should appear as follows:

```
import QtQuick 2.6
import QtQuick.Layouts 1.3
import QtQuick.Dialogs 1.2
import QtQuick.Window 2.2
import "."

Dialog {

    property string label: "New item"
    property string hint: ""
    property alias editText : editTextItem

    standardButtons: StandardButton.Ok | StandardButton.Cancel
    onVisibleChanged: {
        editTextItem.focus = true
        editTextItem.selectAll()
    }
    onButtonClicked: {
        Qt.inputMethod.hide();
    }
    Rectangle {

        implicitWidth: parent.width
        implicitHeight: 100

        ColumnLayout {
            Text {
                id: labelItem
                text: label
                color: Style.text
            }

            TextInput {
                id: editTextItem
                inputMethodHints: Qt.ImhPreferUppercase
                text: hint
                color: Style.text
```

```
            }
        }
    }
}
```

In this custom `InputDialog`, we take the generic Qt Quick `Dialog` and modify it to contain our `TextInput` item referenced by the ID `editTextItem`. We also added a `labelItem` just above `editTextItem` to describe the expected input. There are several things to note in this dialog: First, because we want this dialog to be generic, it has to be configurable. The caller should be able to provide parameters to display its specific data. This is done with the three properties at the top of the `Dialog` element:

- `label`: Configures the displayed text in `labelItem`.
- `hint`: The default text displayed in `editTextItem`.
- `editText`: References the "local" `editTextItem` element. This will let the caller retrieve the value when the dialog is closed.

We also configure the `Dialog` element to automatically use the platform buttons to validate or cancel the dialog with `standardButtons: StandardButton.Ok | StandardButton.Cancel` syntax.

Finally, to make the dialog a bit more user friendly, `editTextItem` has the input focus when the `Dialog` element becomes visible and the text is selected. These two steps are undertaken in the `onVisibleChanged()` callback function. When the dialog is hidden (that is, **Ok** or **Cancel** has been clicked), we hide the virtual keyboard with `Qt.InputMethod.hide()`.

`InputDialog` is now ready to be used! Open `AlbumListPage.qml` and modify it as follows:

```
PageTheme {

    toolbarTitle: "Albums"
    toolbarButtons: ToolButton {
        background: Image {
            source: "qrc:/res/icons/album-add.svg"
        }
        onClicked: {
            newAlbumDialog.open()
        }
    }

    InputDialog {
        id: newAlbumDialog
```

```
            title: "New album"
            label: "Album name:"
            hint: "My Album"

            onAccepted: {
                editText.focus = false;
                albumModel.addAlbumFromName(editText.text)
            }
        }
    ...
    }
```

We add `InputDialog` with the ID `newAlbumDialog` inside the `PageTheme` element. We define all our custom properties: `title`, `label` and `hint`. When the user clicks on the **OK** button, the `onAccepted()` function is called. Here, it is a simple matter of calling the wrapper function `addAlbumFromName()` in the `AlbumModel` element with the text entered.

This `Dialog` element is not visible by default, we open it by adding a `ToolButton` in `toolbarButtons`. This `ToolButton` will be added at the far right of the header as we specified in the `PageTheme.qml` file. To comply with mobile standards, we simply use a custom icon inside that button rather than text.

On some Android devices, you must close the onscreen keyboard beforehand in order to retrieve the `editText` string from `InputDialog`. Otherwise, you will get an empty `string`. One way to fix that is to set the `focus` to `false` before reading the `string` text.

Here, you can see that it is possible to reference images stored in the `.qrc` file with the syntax `qrc:/res/icons/album-add.svg`. We use SVG files to have scalable icons, but you are free to use your own icons for the `gallery-mobile` application.

When the user clicks on the `ToolButton`, the `onClicked()` function is called, where we open `newAlbumDialog`.

Don't forget to select the root `ch05-gallery-mobile` project as the active project. On our reference device, a Nexus 5X, this is how it appears:

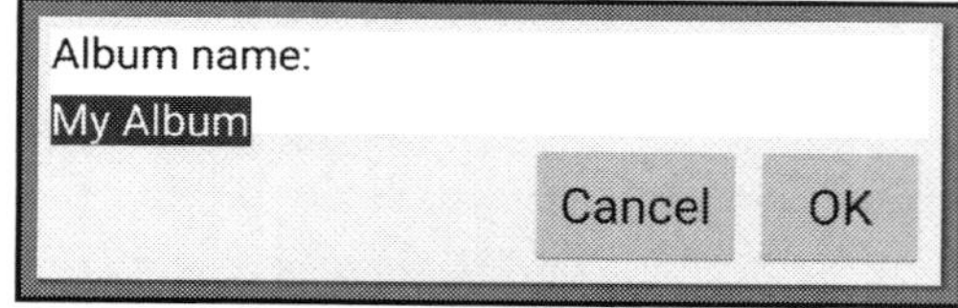

When the user clicks on the **OK** button, the whole Model/View pipeline starts to work. This new album is persisted, the AlbumModel element emits the correct signals to notify our ListView, and albumList, to refresh itself. We are starting to leverage the power of our gallery-core, which can be used in a desktop application and a mobile application without rewriting a significant portion of the engine code.

Loading images with an ImageProvider

It is now time to display the thumbnails for our freshly persisted album. These thumbnails have to be loaded somehow. Because our application is targeted at mobile devices, we cannot afford to freeze the UI thread while loading thumbnails. We would either hog the CPU or be killed by the OS, neither of which are desirable destinies for gallery-mobile. Qt provides a very handy class for handling image loading: QQuickImageProvider.

The QQuickImageProvider class provides an interface to load the QPixmap class in your QML code in an asynchronous manner. This class automatically spawns threads to load the QPixmap class and you simply have to implement the requestPixmap() function. In addition, QQuickImageProvider caches the requested pixmap by default to avoid hitting the data source too much.

Our thumbnails must be loaded from the PictureModel element, which gives access to the fileUrl of a given Picture. Our implementation of QQuickImageProvider will have to get the QPixmap class for a row index in PicturelModel. Create a new C++ class named PictureImageProvider, and modify PictureImageProvider.h as follows:

```
#include <QQuickImageProvider>

class PictureModel;

class PictureImageProvider : public QQuickImageProvider
{
public:

    PictureImageProvider(PictureModel* pictureModel);

    QPixmap requestPixmap(const QString& id, QSize* size,
            const QSize& requestedSize) override;

private:
    PictureModel* mPictureModel;
};
```

A pointer to the `PictureModel` element has to be provided in the constructor in order to be able to retrieve the `fileUrl`. We override `requestPixmap()`, which takes an `id` parameter in its parameters list (the `size` and `requestedSize` can be safely ignored for now). This `id` parameter will be provided in the QML code when we want to load an image. For a given `Image` in QML, the `PictureImageProvider` class will be called as follows:

```
Image { source: "image://pictures/" + index }
```

Let's break it down:

- `image`: This is the scheme for the URL source of the image. This tells Qt to work with an image provider to load the image.
- `pictures`: This is the image provider identifier. We will link the `PictureImageProvider` class and this identifier at the initialization of `QmlEngine` in `main.cpp`.
- `index`: This is the ID of the image. Here, it is the row index of the image. This corresponds to the `id` parameter in `requestPixmap()`.

We already know that we want to display an image in two modes: thumbnail and full resolution. In both cases, a `QQuickImageProvider` class will be used. These two modes have a very similar behavior: they will request `PictureModel` for `fileUrl` and return the loaded `QPixmap`.

There is a pattern here. We can easily encapsulate these two modes in `PictureImageProvider`. The only thing we have to know is whether the caller wants a thumbnail or a full resolution `QPixmap`. This can be easily done by making the `id` parameter more explicit.

We are going to implement the `requestPixmap()` function to be able to be called in two ways:

- `images://pictures/<index>/full`: this syntax is used to retrieve the full resolution image.
- `images://pictures/<index>/thumbnail`: this syntax is used to retrieve the thumbnail version of the image.

If the `index` value was `0`, these two calls would set the ID to `0/full` or `0/thumbnail` in `requestPixmap()`. Let's see the implementation in `PictureImageProvider.cpp`:

```
#include "PictureModel.h"

PictureImageProvider::PictureImageProvider(PictureModel* pictureModel) :
```

```
    QQuickImageProvider(QQuickImageProvider::Pixmap),
    mPictureModel(pictureModel)
{
}

QPixmap PictureImageProvider::requestPixmap(const QString& id, QSize*
/*size*/, const QSize& /*requestedSize*/)
{
    QStringList query = id.split('/');
    if (!mPictureModel || query.size() < 2) {
        return QPixmap();
    }

    int row = query[0].toInt();
    QString pictureSize = query[1];

    QUrl fileUrl = mPictureModel->data(mPictureModel->index(row, 0),
PictureModel::Roles::UrlRole).toUrl();
    return ?? // Patience, the mystery will be soon unraveled
}
```

We start by calling the `QQuickImageProvider` constructor with the `QQuickImageProvider::Pixmap` parameter to configure `QQuickImageProvider` in order to call `requestPixmap()`. The `QQuickImageProvider` constructor supports various image types (`QImage`, `QPixmap`, `QSGTexture`, `QQuickImageResponse`) and each one has its specific `requestXXX()` function.

In the `requestPixmap()` function, we start by splitting this ID with the `/` separator. From here, we retrieve the `row` values and the desired `pictureSize`. The `fileUrl` is loaded by simply calling the `mPictureModel::data()` function with the correct parameters. We used the exact same call in `Chapter 4`, *Conquering the Desktop UI*.

Great! We know which `fileUrl` should be loaded and what the desired dimension is. However, we have one last thing to sort out. Because we manipulate a row and not a database ID, we will have the same request URL for two different images that are in different albums. Remember that `PictureModel` loads a list of images for a given `Album`.

We should picture (pun intended) the situation. For an album called `Holidays`, the request URL for loading the first image will be `images://pictures/0/thumbnail`. It will be the same URL for another album, `Pets`, which will load the first image with `images://pictures/0/thumbnail`. As we said earlier, `QQuickImageProvider` automatically generates a cache that will avoid subsequent calls to `requestPixmap()` for the same URL. Thus, we will always serve the same image, irrespective of which album is selected.

This constraint forces us to disable the cache in `PictureImageProvider` and to roll out our own cache. This is an interesting thing to do; here is one possible implementation:

```
// In PictureImageProvider.h

#include <QQuickImageProvider>
#include <QCache>

...
public:
    static const QSize THUMBNAIL_SIZE;

    QPixmap requestPixmap(const QString& id, QSize* size, const QSize&
requestedSize) override;

    QPixmap* pictureFromCache(const QString& filepath, const QString&
pictureSize);

private:
    PictureModel* mPictureModel;
    QCache<QString, QPixmap> mPicturesCache;
};

// In PictureImageProvider.cpp
const QString PICTURE_SIZE_FULL = "full";
const QString PICTURE_SIZE_THUMBNAIL = "thumbnail";
const QSize PictureImageProvider::THUMBNAIL_SIZE = QSize(350, 350);

QPixmap PictureImageProvider::requestPixmap(const QString& id, QSize*
/*size*/, const QSize& /*requestedSize*/)
{
    ...
    return *pictureFromCache(fileUrl.toLocalFile(), pictureSize);
}

QPixmap* PictureImageProvider::pictureFromCache(const QString& filepath,
const QString& pictureSize)
{
    QString key = pictureSize + "-" + filepath;

        QPixmap* cachePicture = nullptr;
    if (!mPicturesCache.contains(key)) {
        QPixmap originalPicture(filepath);
        if (pictureSize == PICTURE_SIZE_THUMBNAIL) {
            cachePicture = new QPixmap(originalPicture
                                .scaled(THUMBNAIL_SIZE,
                                        Qt::KeepAspectRatio,
```

```
                                Qt::SmoothTransformation));
        } else if (pictureSize == PICTURE_SIZE_FULL) {
            cachePicture = new QPixmap(originalPicture);
        }
        mPicturesCache.insert(key, cachePicture);
    } else {
        cachePicture = mPicturesCache[key];
    }

    return cachePicture;
}
```

This new `pictureFromCache()` function aims to store the generated `QPixmap` in `mPicturesCache` and return the proper `QPixmap`. The `mPicturesCache` class relies on a `QCache`; this class allows us to store data in a key/value fashion with the possibility of assigning a cost for each entry. This cost should roughly correspond to the memory cost of the object (by default, `cost = 1`). When `QCache` is instantiated, it is initialized with a `maxCost` value (by default `100`). When the cost of the sum of all the objects exceeds the `maxCost`, `QCache` starts deleting objects to make room for new objects, starting with those objects accessed further back.

In the `pictureFromCache()` function, we first generate a key composed of the `fileUrl` and the `pictureSize` before trying to retrieve the `QPixmap` from the cache. If it is not present, the proper `QPixmap` (scaled to the `THUMBNAIL_SIZE` constant if needed) will be generated and stored inside the cache. The `mPicturesCache` object becomes the owner of this `QPixmap`.

The final step for completing the `PictureImageProvider` class is to make it available in the QML context. This is done in `main.cpp`:

```
#include "AlbumModel.h"
#include "PictureModel.h"
#include "PictureImageProvider.h"

int main(int argc, char *argv[])
{
    QGuiApplication app(argc, argv);
    ...

    QQmlContext* context = engine.rootContext();
    context->setContextProperty("thumbnailSize",
PictureImageProvider::THUMBNAIL_SIZE.width());
    context->setContextProperty("albumModel", &albumModel);
    context->setContextProperty("pictureModel", &pictureModel);
```

```
    engine.addImageProvider("pictures", new
                            PictureImageProvider(&pictureModel));
    ...
}
```

The `PictureImageProvider` class is added to the QML engine with `engine.addImageProvider()`. The first argument will be the provider identifier in QML. Note that the engine takes ownership of the passed `PictureImageProvider`. One final thing to mention is the fact that the `thumbnailSize` parameter is also passed to `engine`; it will constrain the thumbnails to be displayed with the specified size in the QML code.

Displaying thumbnails in GridView

The next step is to display these thumbnails. Create a new QML file named `AlbumPage.qml`:

```
import QtQuick 2.6
import QtQuick.Layouts 1.3
import QtQuick.Controls 2.0
import "."

PageTheme {

    property string albumName
    property int albumRowIndex

    toolbarTitle: albumName

    GridView {
        id: thumbnailList
        model: pictureModel
        anchors.fill: parent
        anchors.leftMargin: 10
        anchors.rightMargin: 10
        cellWidth : thumbnailSize
        cellHeight: thumbnailSize

        delegate: Rectangle {
            width: thumbnailList.cellWidth - 10
            height: thumbnailList.cellHeight - 10
            color: "transparent"

            Image {
                id: thumbnail
```

```
                    anchors.fill: parent
                    fillMode: Image.PreserveAspectFit
                    cache: false
                    source: "image://pictures/" + index + "/thumbnail"
                }
            }
        }
    }
```

This new `PageTheme` element defines two properties: `albumName` and `albumRowIndex`. The `albumName` property is used to update the title in `toolbarTitle`; `albumRowIndex` will be used to interact with `AlbumModel` in order to rename or delete the album from the current page.

To display thumbnails, we rely on a `GridView` element that will lay out the thumbnails in a grid of cells. This `thumbnailList` item uses the `pictureModel` to request its data:

- The delegate is simply a `Rectangle` element with a single `Image` inside.
- This `Rectangle` element is slightly smaller than the `thumbnailList.cellWidth` or `thumbnailList.cellHeight`.
- The `GridView` element does not provide a `spacing` property (like `ListView`) to establish some room between each item. Thus, we simulate it by using a smaller area to display the content.
- The `Image` item will try to take all the available space with `anchors.fill: parent`, but will still keep the aspect ratio of the image provided with `fillMode: Image.PreserveAspectFit`. You recognize the `source` attribute where the current delegate `index` is provided to retrieve the thumbnail.
- Finally, the `cache: false` attribute ensures that the `PictureImageProvider` class will not try to use the native cache.

To display `AlbumPage.qml`, we have to update the `stackView` (located in `main.qml`). Remember that `stackView` has been declared as a property (`pageStack`); it is therefore accessible from any QML file.

The `AlbumPage` element will be displayed when the user clicks on the `MouseArea` element for a given `Album` value in `AlbumListPage.qml`.

We will now give the user the ability to add a new image. To do this, we will rely on a Qt Quick Dialog: `FileDialog`. Here is the updated version of `AlbumPage.qml`:

```
import QtQuick 2.6
import QtQuick.Layouts 1.3
import QtQuick.Controls 2.0
```

```
import QtQuick.Dialogs 1.2
import "."

PageTheme {

    property string albumName
    property int albumRowIndex

    toolbarTitle: albumName
    toolbarButtons: RowLayout {
        ToolButton {
            background: Image {
                source: "qrc:/res/icons/photo-add.svg"
            }
            onClicked: {
                dialog.open()
            }
        }
    }

    FileDialog {
        id: dialog
        title: "Open file"
        folder: shortcuts.pictures
        onAccepted: {
            var pictureUrl = dialog.fileUrl
            pictureModel.addPictureFromUrl(pictureUrl)
            dialog.close()
        }
    }

    GridView {
        ...
}
```

The `FileDialog` element is straightforward to implement. By using the `folder: shortcuts.pictures` property, Qt Quick will automatically position the `FileDialog` element in the platform-specific images' directory. Even better, on iOS, it will open the native photo application where you can select your own image.

When the user validates his image choice, the path is available in the `onAccepted()` function with the `dialog.fileUrl` field, which we stored in the `pictureUrl` variable. This `pictureUrl` variable is then passed to a new wrapper function of `PictureModel: addPictureFromUrl()`. The pattern used is exactly the same as we did for `AlbumModel::addAlbumFromName()`: a `Q_INVOKABLE` wrapper function around `PictureModel::addPicture()`.

The only missing parts of `AlbumPage` are the **Delete album** and **Rename album** features. They follow patterns that we have already covered. Deletion will be effected using a wrapper function in `AlbumModel`, and the rename reuses the `InputDialog` we created for `AlbumListPage.qml`. Please refer to the source code of the chapter to see the implementation for these features. This is how the thumbnails will look on an Android device:

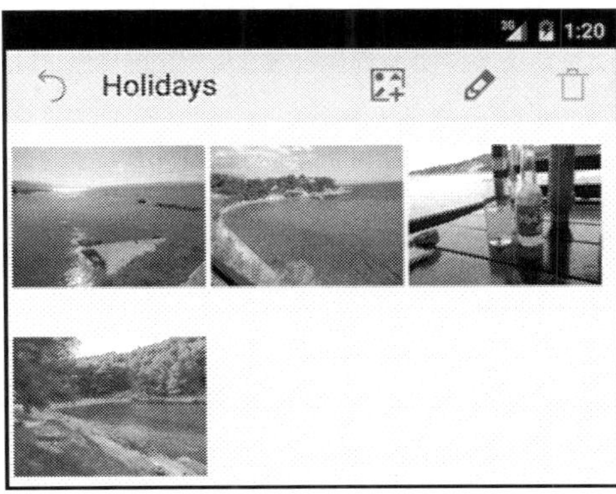

Swiping through full resolution images

The last page we have to implement in `gallery-mobile` is the full resolution image page. In `Chapter 4`, *Conquering the Desktop UI*, we navigated through the images using previous/next buttons. In this chapter, we target the mobile platform. Therefore, navigation should be effected using a touch-based gesture: a fling.

Here is the implementation of this new `PicturePage.qml` file:

```
import QtQuick 2.0
import QtQuick.Layouts 1.3
import QtQuick.Controls 2.0
import "."

PageTheme {

    property string pictureName
    property int pictureIndex

    toolbarTitle: pictureName

    ListView {
        id: pictureListView
```

```
            model: pictureModel
            anchors.fill: parent
            spacing: 5
            orientation: Qt.Horizontal
            snapMode: ListView.SnapOneItem
            currentIndex: pictureIndex

            Component.onCompleted: {
                positionViewAtIndex(currentIndex,
                                    ListView.SnapPosition)
            }

            delegate: Rectangle {
                property int itemIndex: index
                property string itemName: name

                width: ListView.view.width === 0 ?
                       parent.width : ListView.view.width
                height: pictureListView.height
                color: "transparent"

                Image {
                    fillMode: Image.PreserveAspectFit
                    cache: false
                    width: parent.width
                    height: parent.height
                    source: "image://pictures/" + index + "/full"
                }
            }
        }
    }
```

We first define two properties, `pictureName` and `pictureIndex`. The current `pictureName` property is displayed in the `toolbarTitle` and `pictureIndex` is used to initialize the correct `currentIndex` in `ListView`, `currentIndex: pictureIndex`.

To be able to swipe through the images, we again use a `ListView`. Here, each item (a simple `Image` element) will take the full size of its parent. When the component is loaded, even if `currentIndex` is correctly set, the view has to be updated to be positioned at the correct index. This is what we do with this in `pictureListView`:

```
Component.onCompleted: {
    positionViewAtIndex(currentIndex, ListView.SnapPosition)
}
```

This will update the position of the current visible item to `currentIndex`. So far, so good. Nonetheless, when a `ListView` is created, the first thing it does is to initialize its delegate. A `ListView` provides a `ListView.view` attached property, which is available in delegates. The `ListView.view` attached property does not have any width in `Component.onCompleted()`. As a consequence, the `positionViewAtIndex()` function does absolutely nothing! To prevent this behavior, we have to provide a default initial width to the delegate with the ternary expression `ListView.view.width === 0 ? parent.width : ListView.view.width`. The view will then have a default width on the first load and the `positionViewAtIndex()` function can happily move until `ListView.view` is properly loaded.

To swipe through each image, we set the `snapMode` value of the `ListView` to `ListView.SnapOneItem`. Each fling will snap to the following, or the previous, image without continuing the motion.

The `Image` item of the delegate looks very much like the thumbnail version. The sole difference is the source property, where we request the `PictureImageProvider` class with `full` resolution.

When `PicturePage` opens, the correct `pictureName` property is displayed in the header. However, when the user flings to another image, the name is not updated. To handle this, we have to detect the motion state. Add the following callbacks in `pictureListView`:

```
onMovementEnded: {
    currentIndex = itemAt(contentX, contentY).itemIndex
}

onCurrentItemChanged: {
    toolbarTitle = currentItem.itemName
}
```

The `onMovementEnded()` class is triggered when the motion started by the swipe has ended. In this function, we update the `ListViewcurrentIndex` with the `itemIndex` of the visible item at the `contentX` and `contentY` coordinates.

The second function, `onCurrentItemChanged()`, is called upon the `currentIndex` update. It will simply update the `toolbarTitle` with the image name of the current item.

To display `PicturePage.qml`, the same `MouseArea` pattern is used in the `thumbnailList` delegate of `AlbumPage.qml`:

```
MouseArea {
    anchors.fill: parent
    onClicked: {
```

```
            thumbnailList.currentIndex = index
            pageStack.push("qrc:/qml/PicturePage.qml",
        { pictureName: name, pictureIndex: index })
        }
    }
```

Again, the `PicturePage.qml` file is pushed on the `pageStack` and the requisite parameters (`pictureName` and `pictureIndex`) are provided in the same manner.

Summary

This chapter brings closure to the development of the gallery application. We built a strong foundation with `gallery-core`, created a UI widget with `gallery-desktop`, and finally crafted a QML UI with `gallery-mobile`.

QML facilitates a very fast approach to UI development. Unfortunately, the technology is still in its infancy and changing rapidly. The integration with mobile OSes (Android, iOS) is under heavy development and we hope that it will lead to excellent mobile applications with Qt. For now, the inherent limits of a mobile cross-platform toolkit are still hard to overcome.

The next chapter will take QML technology to new shores: the development of a snake game running on a Raspberry Pi.

6

Even Qt Deserves a Slice of Raspberry Pi

In the previous chapter, we created a QML UI targeted at Android and iOS. We will continue our journey in the embedded world by discovering how we can deploy a Qt application on a Raspberry Pi. The example project to illustrate this topic will be a snake game using the Qt3D modules. The player will control a snaketrying to eat apples to get as big as possible.

In this chapter, you will learn:

- Discovering Qt3D
- Configuring Qt for your Raspberry Pi
- Crafting entities from the factory
- Building a snake engine in JavaScript
- Profiling your QML application

Discovering Qt3D

The example project of this chapter will rely on 3D rendering. For this, we will use Qt3D. This part of the framework is divided into various Qt modules that enable the application to have a near-real time simulation of a 3D environment. Built on OpenGL, Qt3D offers a high-level API to describe complex scenes without having to resort to writing low-level OpenGL instructions. Qt3D supports the following basic features:

- 2D and 3D rendering for C++ and Qt Quick
- Meshes
- Materials
- GLSL shaders
- Shadow mapping

- Deferred rendering
- Instance rendering
- Uniform Buffer Object

All these features are implemented in the **entity component system** (**ECS**) architecture. Each mesh, material, or shader that you define is a component. The aggregation of these components makes an entity. If you wanted to draw a 3D red apple, you would need the following components:

- A mesh component, holding the vertices of your apple
- A material component, applying a texture on the mesh or coloring it

These two components will then be regrouped to define the entity Apple. You see here the two parts of the ECS, the entities and components. The overall architecture looks like this:

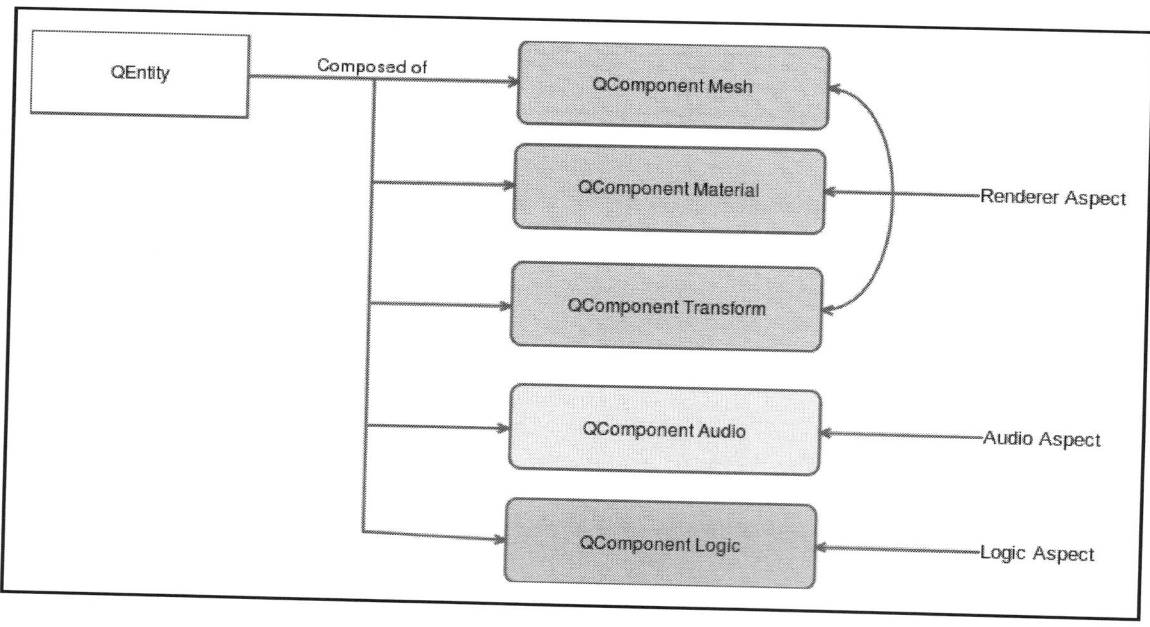

Each of these components can be regrouped into aspects. An aspect is a "slice" of multiple components working on the same part (rendering, positioned 3D audio, and logic). When the graph of all your entities is processed by the Qt3D engine, each layer of aspects is processed sequentially.

The underlying approach is to favor composition over inheritance. In a game, an entity (an apple, a player, an enemy) can have various states during its life cycle, such as spawning, animating for a given state, a dying animation, and so on. Using inheritance to describe these states will lead to a nerve-wracking tree of `AppleSpawn`, `AppleAnimationShiny`, `AppleDeath`, and so on. It would become quickly unmaintainable. Any modification to a class could have huge impact on many other classes and the number of possible combinations of states would get out of hand. Saying that a state is simply a component for a given entity gives the flexibility to easily swap components and still keep the entity abstraction; an apple `Entity` element is still an apple, even though it is using the `AnimationShiny` component instead of the `AnimationSpawn` component.

Let's see how to define a basic `Entity` element in QML. Imagine that this is the apple we have been talking about. The `Apple.qml` file would look like this:

```
import Qt3D.Core 2.0
import Qt3D.Render 2.0
import Qt3D.Extras 2.0

Entity {

    property alias position: transform.translation
    PhongMaterial {
        id: material
        diffuse: "red"
    }

    SphereMesh {
        id: mesh
    }

    Transform {
        id: transform
    }

    components: [material, mesh, transform]
}
```

In very few lines, you describe every aspect of the `Entity` element:

- `Entity`: This is the root object of the file; it follows the same QML pattern we studied in `Chapter 5`, *Dominating the Mobile UI*.
- `PhongMaterial`: This defines how the surface will be rendered. Here, it uses the Phong shading technique to achieve smooth surfaces. It inherits `QMaterial`, which is the base class for all the material classes.

- `SphereMesh`: This defines what type of mesh will be used. It inherits `QGeometryRenderer`, which also gives the ability to load custom models (exported from 3D modeling software).
- `Transform`: This defines the transformation matrix of the component. It can customize the translation, scale, and position of the `Entity` element.
- `position`: This is a property to expose `transform.translation` for a given caller/parent. This might quickly become handy if we want to move the apple around.
- `components`: This is the array containing all the IDs of all the components for the `Entity` element.

If we want to make this `Apple` a child of another `Entity`, it is simply a matter of defining the Apple inside this new `Entity` element. Let's call it `World.qml`:

```
import Qt3D.Core 2.0
import Qt3D.Render 2.0
import Qt3D.Extras 2.0

Entity {
    id: sceneRoot
     RenderSettings {
        id: renderSettings
        activeFrameGraph: ForwardRenderer {
            clearColor: Qt.rgba(0, 0, 0, 1)
        }
    }

    Apple {
        id: apple
        position: Qt.vector3d(3.0, 0.0, 2.0)
    }

    components: [frameGraph]
}
```

Here, the `World Entity` has no visual representation; we want it to be the root of our 3D scene. It only contains the `Apple` we defined earlier. The *x*, *y*, *z* coordinates of the apple are relative to the parent. When the parent makes a translation, the same translation will be applied to the apple.

This is how the hierarchy of entities/components is defined. If you write your Qt3D code in C++, the same logic applies to the equivalent C++ classes (`QEntity`, `QComponent`, and so on).

Because we decided to use the `World.qml` file as the root of our scene, it has to define how the scene will be rendered. The Qt3D rendering algorithm is data-driven. In other words, there is a clear separation between what should be rendered (the tree of entities and components) and how it should be rendered.

The *how* relies on a similar tree structure called a frame graph. In Qt Quick, a single method of rendering is used, which covers the 2D drawing. On the other hand, in 3D, the need for flexible rendering makes it necessary to decouple the rendering techniques.

Consider this example; you play a game where you control your avatar and you encounter a mirror. The same 3D scene must be rendered from multiple viewports. If the rendering technique is fixed, this poses multiple problems; which viewport should be drawn first? Is it possible to parallelize the rendering of the viewports in the GPU? What if we need to make multiple passes for the rendering?

In this code snippet, we use the traditional OpenGL rendering technique with the `ForwardRenderer` tree, where each object is rendered directly on the back buffer, one at a time. Qt3D offers the possibility to choose the renderer (Forward Renderer, Deferred Renderer, and so on) and configure how the scene should be rendered.

OpenGL typically uses the double-buffering technique to render its content. The front-buffer is what is displayed on the screen and the back-buffer is where the scene is being rendered. When the back-buffer is ready, the two buffers are swapped.

One last thing to notice at the top of each `Entity` element is that we specified the following:

```
import Qt3D.Core 2.0
import Qt3D.Render 2.0
import Qt3D.Extras 2.0
```

There are the only Qt3D modules in the import section. Qt3D classes do not inherit `Item` so cannot be directly mixed with QML components. This inheritance tree of the basic Qt3D building blocks is as follows:

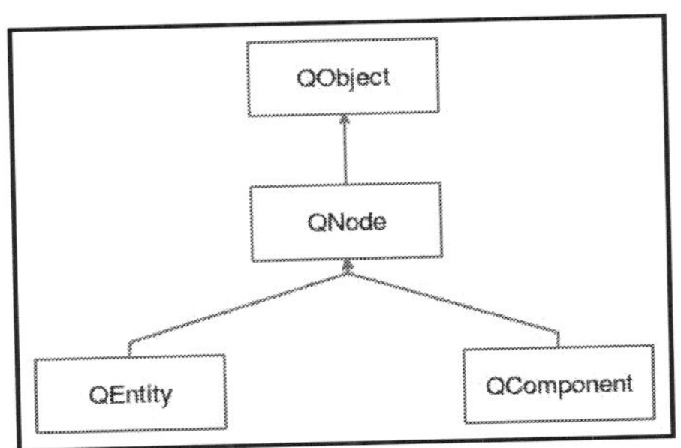

The `QNode` class is the base class of all Qt3D node classes. It relies on the `QObject` class to define the parenting relationship. Each `QNode` class instance also adds a unique `id` variable, which allows it to be recognized from other instances.

Even though `QNode` cannot be mixed with Qt Quick types, they can be added to a `Q3DScene` element (or `Scene3D` in QML), which serves as the canvas for Qt3D content and can be added to a Qt Quick `Item`. Adding `World.qml` to a scene is as simple as this:

```
Rectangle {

    Scene3D {
        id: scene
        anchors.fill: parent
        focus: true

        World { }
    }
}
```

The `Scene3D` element includes a `World` instance and defines common Qt Quick properties (`anchors`, `focus`).

Configuring Qt for your Raspberry Pi

This project targets a new embedded platform, the Raspberry Pi. Qt officially supports the Raspberry Pi 2, but we got the project running without any trouble on a Raspberry Pi 3. If you do not have one of these devices, it might be nonetheless interesting to read this section to know how the cross-compilation works and how to configure your own kit in Qt Creator. The rest of the chapter will work on a desktop platform anyway.

Before diving into the Raspberry Pi's configuration, let's take a step back to understand our aim. Your computer is probably running on an x86 CPU architecture. This means that every program you run will be executed with the x86 instructions set of your CPU. In Qt Creator, this translates to your available kits. A kit must match your target platform. On startup, Qt Creator searches for available kits in your computer and loads them for you.

In `Chapter 5`, *Dominating the Mobile UI*, we targeted different platforms, Android and iOS. These platforms are running on a different CPU instruction set, ARM. Luckily, the people behind Qt automatically configured for us the necessary nuts and bolts to make it work.

The Raspberry Pi also runs on ARM but it is not ready for Qt by default. We have to prepare it before playing with it in Qt Creator. Note that the following commands are run from a Linux box, but you should be able to run them from Mac or Windows with Cygwin.

Please follow the complete guide to prepare your Raspberry Pi for Qt at `https://wiki.qt.io/RaspberryPi2EGLFS`, or simply download a precompiled bundle from `https://github.com/neuronalmotion/qtrpi`.

The complete Raspberry Pi installation guide is outside the scope of the book. It is interesting nonetheless to sum up the main steps:

1. Install a Linux OS on the Raspberry Pi (for example, Raspbian)
2. Add development packages to the Raspberry Pi
3. Retrieve the complete toolchain, including the cross-compiler that will be executed from your machine
4. Create a `sysroot` folder on your machine that will mirror the necessary directories from the Raspberry Pi
5. Compile Qt with the cross-compiler in the `sysroot` folder
6. Synchronize this `sysroot` with the Raspberry Pi

A `sysroot` is simply a directory that contains a minimal filesystem for a given platform. It typically contains the `/usr/lib` and `/usr/include` directories. Having this directory on your machine enables the cross-compiler to properly compile and link the output binary without being executed from the Raspberry Pi.

All these steps are done to avoid compiling anything directly on the Raspberry Pi. Being a low-powered device, the execution of any compilation task would take a very, very long time. It easily takes more than 40 hours. Knowing this, the time spent on configuring the cross-compiler seems much easier to bear.

The `qopenglwidget` example mentioned in the wiki should be properly running before proceeding. Once this has been done, we have to cross-compile a few more Qt modules to have our project running:

- `qtdeclarative`: Used to access Qt Quick
- `qt3d`: Used to construct a 3D world
- `qtquickcontrols`: Used to include interesting controls (Label)
- `qtquickcontrols2`: Used to make some new layouts available

For each of these modules, execute the following commands (from your `~/raspi` directory):

```
git clone git://code.qt.io/qt/<modulename>.git -b 5.11
cd <modulename>
~/raspi/qt5/bin/qmake -r
```

```
make
make install
```

You can speed up the compilation by adding the parameter `-j` (or `--jobs`) to the `make` command. It will try to parallelize the compilations jobs over your CPU cores; if you have four cores, use `make -j 4`, eight cores, `make -j 8`, and so on.

When everything has been compiled, synchronize your `sysroot` directory again with the following command:

```
rsync -avz qt5pi pi@IP:/usr/local
```

In the preceding command, you must replace the `IP` with the real Raspberry Pi address.

The Raspberry Pi is ready to execute our Qt code. However, we have to create our own kit in Qt Creator to be able to compile and deploy our program on it. A kit is composed of the following parts:

- A **compiler** that will compile your code using the CPU instruction set of the target platform
- A **debugger** that will know the instruction set of the target platform, to properly break and read the memory's content
- A **Qt version** compiled for the targeted platform, to compile and link your binary to the target platform's shared objects
- A **device** to which Qt Creator can connect to deploy and execute your program

We will start with the compiler. In Qt Creator:

1. Go to **Tools** | **Options** | **Build & Run** | **Compilers**
2. Click on **Add** |**GCC** | **C++**
3. Click on the **Browse** button near **Compiler path** and select `~/raspi/tools/arm-bcm2708/gcc-linaro-arm-linux-gnueabihf-raspbian/bin/arm-linux-gnueabihf-g++`
4. Rename the compiler to `Rpi GCC`

This strange binary name makes it easier for Qt to parse the **application binary interface** (**ABI**) to find out the platform architecture, file format, and so on. It should look like this:

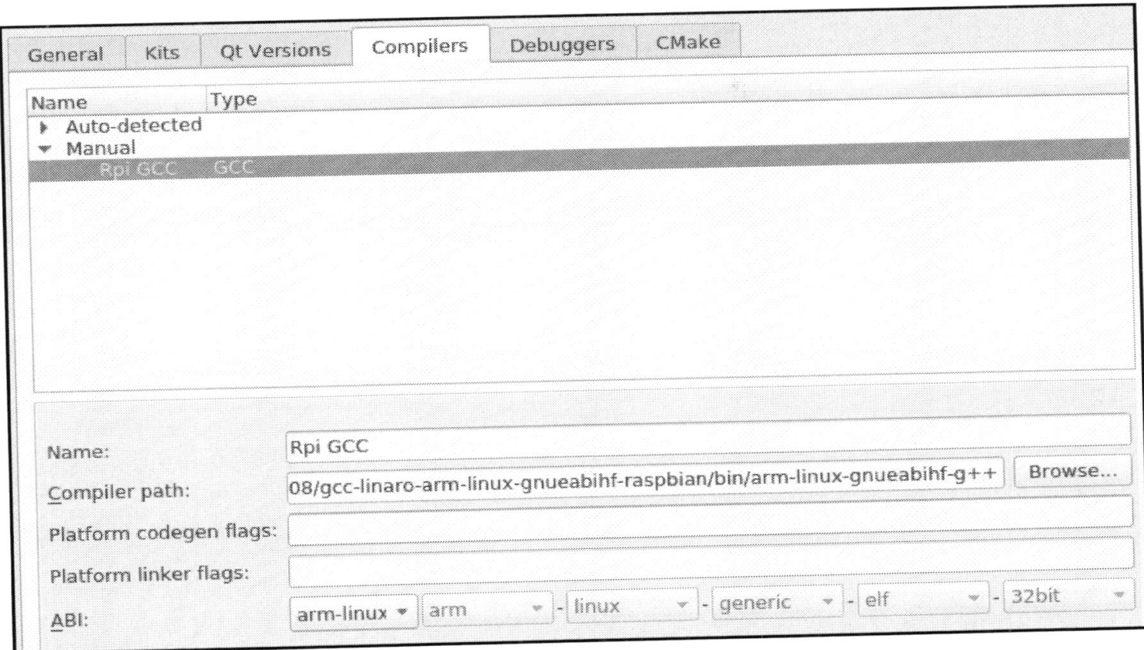

Now for the debugger. As we said earlier, we are building this project from a Linux box (Ubuntu). Cross-compilation and embedded development tend to be easier on Linux but you should be able to do the same on Windows or a Mac with a few additional steps.

On Ubuntu Linux, just install a multi-architecture `gdb` with the command `sudo apt-get install gdb-multiarch`. In Qt Creator, add this new debugger in the **Debuggers** tab:

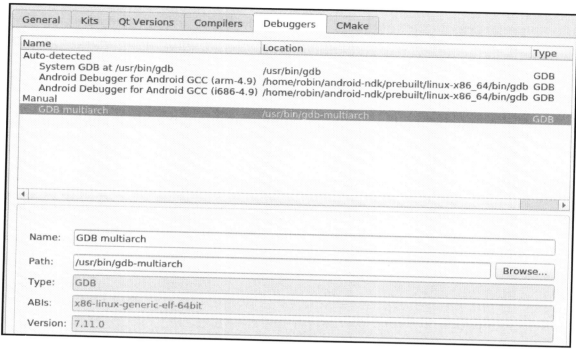

Next, add the cross-compiled Qt explained on the wiki page in the **Qt Versions** tab. Click on **Add** and browse to `~/raspi/qt5/bin/qmake`. This is the resulting Qt Version:

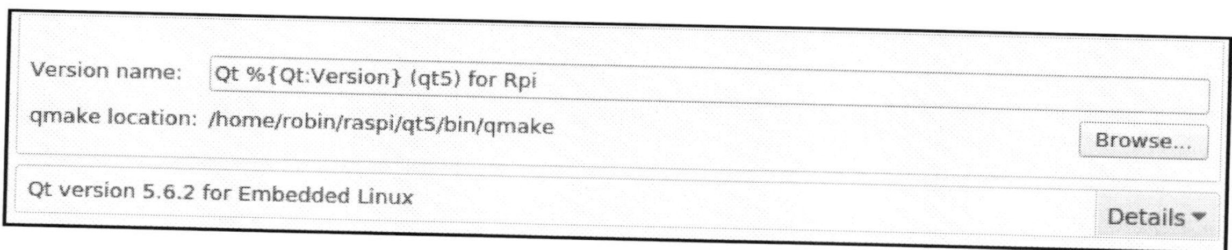

We are almost there! Before building the kit, we simply have to configure Raspberry Pi device access. In **Options** | **Devices**, follow this procedure:

1. Click on **Add..** | **Generic Linux Device** | **Start Wizard**
2. The name will be `Rpi 2` (or 3 if you have one)

3. Enter the IP address of your device (indeed, you have to be connected to your local network!)
4. The default username is **pi**
5. The default password is "raspberry"
6. Click on **Next** to test the connection to the device

If everything went well, this is your new device:

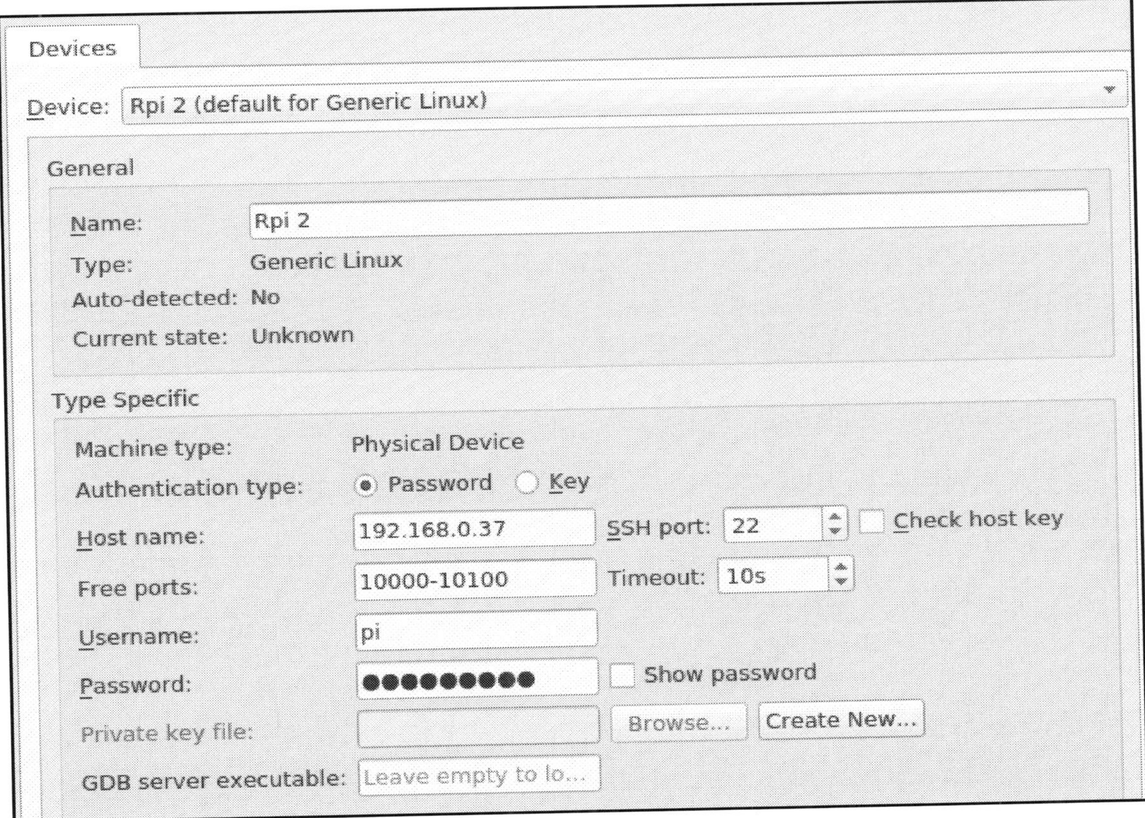

Finally, the kit will compose all these parts into a valid Qt Creator platform. Go back to **Build & Run** | **Kits**. From here you simply have to point to each of the parts we built previously. Here is the resulting kit:

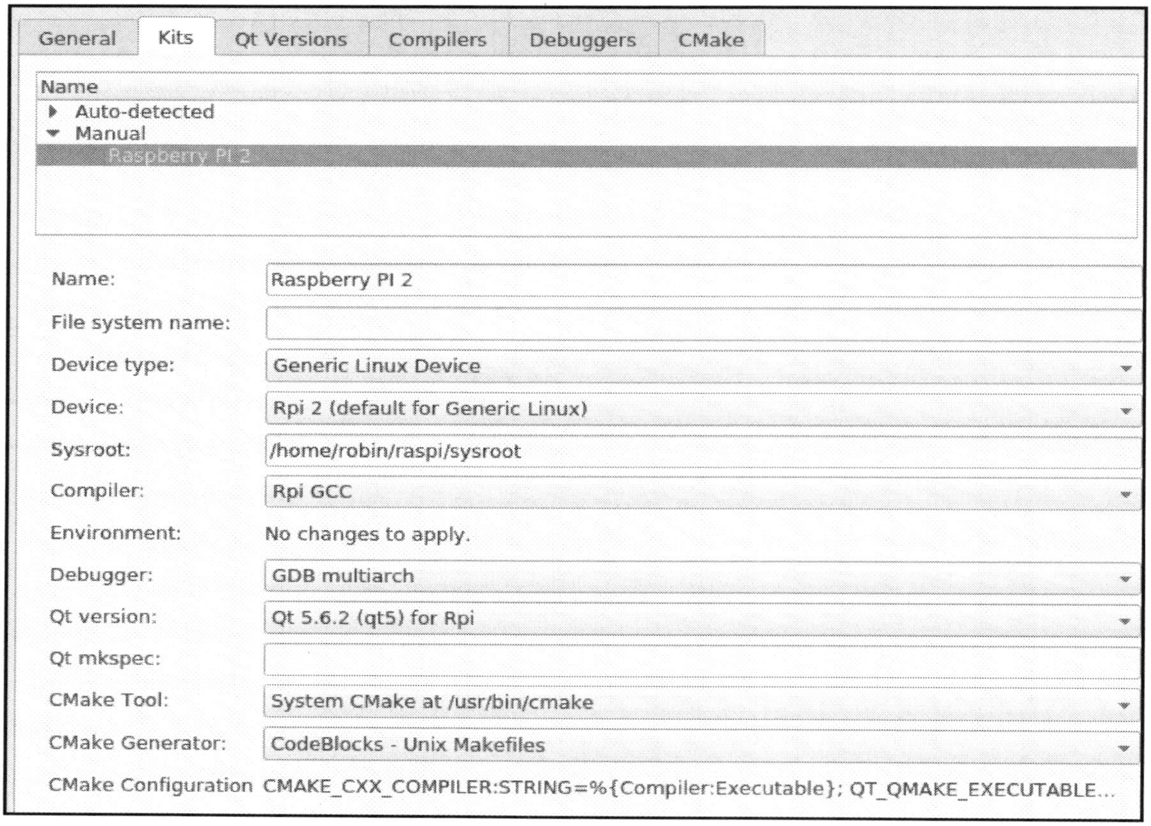

General | Kits | Qt Versions | Compilers | Debuggers | CMake

Name
Auto-detected
Manual
Raspberry PI 2

Name:	Raspberry PI 2
File system name:	
Device type:	Generic Linux Device
Device:	Rpi 2 (default for Generic Linux)
Sysroot:	/home/robin/raspi/sysroot
Compiler:	Rpi GCC
Environment:	No changes to apply.
Debugger:	GDB multiarch
Qt version:	Qt 5.6.2 (qt5) for Rpi
Qt mkspec:	
CMake Tool:	System CMake at /usr/bin/cmake
CMake Generator:	CodeBlocks - Unix Makefiles
CMake Configuration	CMAKE_CXX_COMPILER:STRING=%{Compiler:Executable}; QT_QMAKE_EXECUTABLE...

Note that the `Sysroot` file should point to the `sysroot` folder we previously created at `~/raspi/sysroot`.

If you click on the button to the right of **Name**, you can choose a custom picture for a kit, such as the Raspberry Pi logo.

Everything is now ready to make an awesome snake game.

Creating an entry point for your Qt3D code

For those who did not play the snake game in their youth, here is a quick reminder of the gameplay:

- You control a snake moving in an empty area.
- This area is surrounded by walls.
- An apple spawns randomly in the game area.
- If the snake eats the apple, the snake grows and you gain a point. Right after, another apple spawns in the game area.
- If the snake touches a wall or a part of its own body, you lose.

The goal is to eat as many apples as possible to have the highest score. The longer the snake, the harder it will become to avoid the wall and its own tail. Oh, and the snake goes faster and faster each time it eats an apple. The architecture of the game will be the following:

- All the game items will be defined using Qt3D in QML
- All the game logic will be done in JavaScript, which will communicate with the QML elements

We will keep the 2D feel of the original snake game by placing the camera above the game area, but we will spice things up with 3D models and some shaders.

Alright, we spent an awful lot of pages preparing for this moment. It is now time to begin the snake project. Create a new **Qt Quick Application - Empty** named `ch06-snake`. In the project details:

1. Select **Qt 5.11** for the **minimal required Qt version** field
2. Click on **Next** and select the following kits:
   - **RaspberryPi 2**
   - **Desktop**
3. Click on **Next** | **Finish**

We have to add the Qt3D modules. Modify `ch06-snake.pro` like this:

```
TEMPLATE = app

QT += qml quick 3dcore 3drender 3dquick 3dinput 3dextras
CONFIG += c++11

SOURCES += main.cpp
```

```
RESOURCES += \
    snake.qrc

HEADERS +=

target.files = ch06-snake
target.path = /home/pi
INSTALLS += target
```

We have to prepare the entry point of the application to have a proper OpenGL context with which Qt3D can work. Open and update `main.cpp` like so:

```
#include <QGuiApplication>
#include <QtGui/QOpenGLContext>
#include <QtQuick/QQuickView>
#include <QtQml/QQmlEngine>

int main(int argc, char *argv[])
{
    QGuiApplication app(argc, argv);

    qputenv("QT3D_GLSL100_WORKAROUND", "");

    QSurfaceFormat format;
    if (QOpenGLContext::openGLModuleType() ==
        QOpenGLContext::LibGL) {
        format.setVersion(3, 2);
        format.setProfile(QSurfaceFormat::CoreProfile);
    }
    format.setDepthBufferSize(24);
    format.setStencilBufferSize(8);

    QQuickView view;
    view.setFormat(format);
    view.setResizeMode(QQuickView::SizeRootObjectToView);
    QObject::connect(view.engine(), &QQmlEngine::quit,
                     &app, &QGuiApplication::quit);
    view.setSource(QUrl("qrc:/main.qml"));
    view.show();

    return app.exec();
}
```

The idea is to configure a `QSurfaceFormat` to properly handle OpenGL and to give it to a custom `QQuickView view`. This `view` will use this format to paint itself.

The `qputenv("QT3D_GLSL100_WORKAROUND", "")` instruction is a workaround related to Qt3D shaders on some embedded Linux devices, such as the Raspberry Pi. It will enable a separate GLSL 1.00 snippet for the lights required by some embedded devices. If you do not use this workaround, you will get a black screen and will not be able to properly run the project on the Raspberry Pi.

The details of the Qt3d lights workaround are here: `https://codereview.qt-project.org/#/c/143136/`.

Note that `view` from the `main.cpp` file tries to load a `main.qml` file. You can see it coming; here is the `main.qml`:

```
import QtQuick 2.6
import QtQuick.Controls 1.4

Item {
    id: mainView

    property int score: 0
    readonly property alias window: mainView

    width: 1280; height: 768
    visible: true

    Keys.onEscapePressed: {
        Qt.quit()
    }

    Rectangle {
        id: hud

        color: "#31363b"
        anchors.left: parent.left
        anchors.right: parent.right
        anchors.top : parent.top
        height: 60

        Label {
            id: snakeSizeText
            anchors.centerIn: parent
            font.pointSize: 25
            color: "white"
            text: "Score: " + score
        }
    }
```

```
}
```

Here we define the **heads up display (HUD)** at the top of the screen, where the score (the number of apples eaten) will be displayed. Note that we bound the Escape key to the `Qt.quit()` signal. This signal is connected in `main.cpp` to the `QGuiApplication::quit()` signal to quit the application.

The QML context is now ready to welcome Qt3D content. Modify `main.qml` like so:

```
import QtQuick 2.6
import QtQuick.Controls 1.4
import QtQuick.Scene3D 2.0

Item {
    ...

    Rectangle {
        id: hud
        ...
    }

    Scene3D {
        id: scene
        anchors.top: hud.bottom
        anchors.bottom: parent.bottom
        anchors.left: parent.left
        anchors.right: parent.right
        focus: true
        aspects: "input"
    }
}
```

The `Scene3D` element takes all the available space below the `hud` object. It takes the focus of the window to be able to intercept keyboard events. It also enables the input aspect to let the Qt3D engine process keyboard events in its graph traversal.

Setting up the scene

We can now start writing Qt3D code. The first step is to define the root of the scene. Create a new file named `GameArea.qml`:

```
import Qt3D.Core 2.0
import Qt3D.Render 2.0
import Qt3D.Extras 2.0
```

```
Entity {
    id: root

    property alias gameRoot: root

    Camera {
        id: camera
        property real x: 24.5
        property real y: 14.0

        projectionType: CameraLens.PerspectiveProjection
        fieldOfView: 45
        aspectRatio: 16/9
        nearPlane : 0.1
        farPlane : 1000.0
        position: Qt.vector3d(x, y, 33.0)
        upVector: Qt.vector3d(0.0, 1.0, 0.0)
        viewCenter: Qt.vector3d(x, y, 0.0)
    }



    RenderSettings {
        id: frameFraph
        activeFrameGraph: ForwardRenderer {
            clearColor: Qt.rgba(0, 0, 0, 1)
            camera: camera
        }
    }

    components: [frameFraph]
}
```

The first thing we do is create a camera and position it. Remember that, in OpenGL, the coordinate system is right-handed:

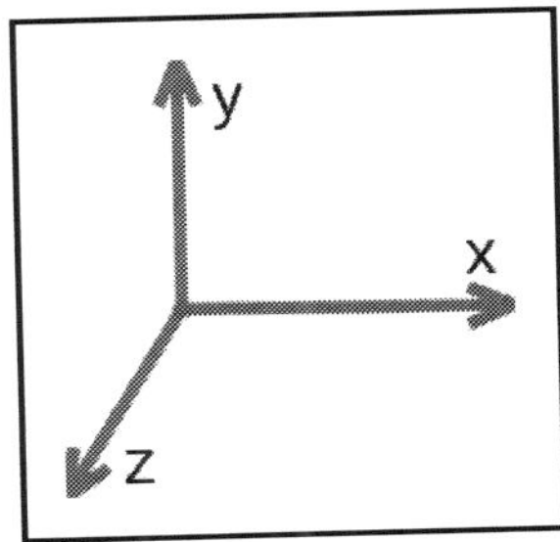

By placing the camera at `Qt.vector3d(x, y, 33)`, we make it come "out of the screen" to be able to express our yet-to-be-created entity's coordinates with the simple *x*, *y* axes. The `upVector: Qt.vector3d(0.0, 1.0, 0.0)` specifies the up vector of the camera; in our case it is the *Y* axis. Finally, we point at `Qt.vector(x, y, 0)`, meaning the center of the screen.

The overall goal is to simplify coordinate expressions. By positioning the camera this way, placing an object at the coordinate {0, 0} will put it in the bottom-left part of the window, whereas the coordinates {50, 28} mean the top-right part of the window.

We also configure `RenderSettings` with a `ForwardRendered` that defines two properties:

- `clearColor`: This value `Qt.rgba(0, 0, 0, 1)` means that the background will be pitch-black
- `camera`: Determines what we are seeing in the viewport

The scene is ready to be rendered, but we need to handle user input, namely the keyboard. To capture keyboard events, modify `GameArea.qml` to look like this:

```
import Qt3D.Core 2.0
import Qt3D.Render 2.0
import Qt3D.Input 2.0
import Qt3D.Extras 2.0

Entity {
    ...
    RenderSettings {
        ...
    }

    KeyboardDevice {
        id: keyboardController
    }

    InputSettings { id: inputSettings }

    KeyboardHandler {
        id: input
        sourceDevice: keyboardController
        focus: true
        onPressed: { }
    }

    components: [frameFraph, input]
}
```

The `KeyboardDevice` element is in charge of dispatching key events to the active `KeyboardHandler`, namely `input`. The `KeyboardHandler` component is attached to the controller and the `onPressed()` function will be called each time a key is pressed. The `KeyboardHandler` is a component; therefore it needs to be added to the list of components for `GameArea`.

The last missing part of `GameArea` is preparing the engine's execution (initialization and update):

```
import Qt3D.Core 2.0
import Qt3D.Render 2.0
import Qt3D.Input 2.0
import Qt3D.Extras 2.0
import QtQuick 2.6 as QQ2

Entity {
    id: root

    property alias gameRoot: root
    property alias timerInterval: timer.interval
    property int initialTimeInterval: 80
    property int initialSnakeSize: 5
    property string state: ""
    ...

    KeyboardDevice {
        id: keyboardController
    }

    QQ2.Component.onCompleted: {
        console.log("Start game...");
        timer.start()
    }

    QQ2.Timer {
        id: timer
        interval: initialTimeInterval
        repeat: true
        onTriggered: {}
    }

    components: [frameFraph, input]
}
```

Here we mix Qt Quick elements with Qt3D. Due to possible name conflicts, we have to import the module using the alias `QQ2`. We already met `Component.onCompleted` in `Chapter 5`, *Dominating the Mobile UI*. Its job will be to start the game engine and start the `timer` defined right after.

This `timer` variable will repeat every 80 milliseconds (as defined in the `initialTimeInterval` property) and call the engine's `update()` function. This function will be covered when we build the engine code, later in this chapter. The goal is to emulate the original snake game as closely as possible. The whole game logic will be updated at this interval and not at the normal frame refresh interval. After each call to `update()`, the snake will advance. As a result, the snake's movement will not be smooth but rather jerky. This is clearly a design choice we made to have a retro-gaming feeling.

Each time the snake eats an apple, two things happen:

- The `interval` of the timer will be reduced by the engine (accessed by the `timerInterval` property)
- The snake will grow. Its initial size is defined in the `intialSnakeSize` property

Reducing the timer interval will make the snake advance faster until it becomes very hard to manage its direction.

Assembling your Qt3D entities

We will now proceed to create the building blocks of the game, each in the form of an `Entity` element:

- `Wall`: This represents the limit of where the snake can go
- `SnakePart`: This represents a part of the snake's body
- `Apple`: This represents the apple (no way!) spawned at a random location
- `Background`: This represents a good-looking background behind the snake and the apple

Each entity will be placed on a grid handled by the engine and will have a type identifier to make it easier to find. To factorize these properties, let's create a parent QML file named `GameEntity.qml`:

```
import Qt3D.Core 2.0

Entity {
    property int type: 0
```

```
    property vector2d gridPosition: Qt.vector2d(0, 0)
}
```

This Entity element only defines a type property and a gridPosition property, which will be used by the engine to lay out the content on the grid.

The first item we will build is the Wall.qml file:

```
import Qt3D.Core 2.0

GameEntity {
    id: root

    property alias position: transform.translation

    Transform {
        id: transform
    }

    components: [transform]
}
```

As you can see, the Wall type does not have any visual representation. Because we target a Raspberry Pi device, we have to be very careful with the CPU/GPU consumption. The game area will be a grid where each cell contains an instance of one of our entities. The snake will be surrounded by Wall instances. The Raspberry Pi is much slower than your average computer, to the extent that the game would become unbearably slow if we displayed all the walls.

To address this issue, the walls are invisible. They will be placed outside the visible viewport and the borders of the window will act as the visual limit of the snake. Of course, if you do not target the Raspberry Pi, but rather your computer, it is fine to display the walls and make them look fancier than just nothing.

The next Entity element we will implement is SnakePart.qml:

```
import Qt3D.Core 2.0
import Qt3D.Render 2.0
import Qt3D.Extras 2.0

GameEntity {
    id: root

    property alias position: transform.translation

    PhongMaterial {
        id: material
```

```
            diffuse: "green"
        }

        CuboidMesh {
            id: mesh
        }

        Transform {
            id: transform
        }

        components: [material, mesh, transform]
    }
```

If added to the GameArea scene, the SnakePart block will display a single green cube. The SnakePart block is not the complete snake, but rather a part of its body. Remember that the snake grows each time it eats an apple. Growing means adding a new instance of SnakePart to a list of SnakePart.

Let's proceed with the Apple.qml:

```
import Qt3D.Core 2.0
import Qt3D.Render 2.0
import Qt3D.Extras 2.0

GameEntity {
    id: root

    property alias position: transform.translation
    property alias color: material.diffuse

    Transform {
        id: transform
        scale: 0.5
    }

    Mesh {
        id: mesh
        source: "models/apple.obj"
    }

    DiffuseMapMaterial {
        id: material
        diffuse:  TextureLoader { source: "qrc:/models/apple-texture.png" }
    }

    components: [material, mesh, transform]
```

```
}
```

This snippet starts by introducing more complex yet easy-to-use features of Qt3D, namely a custom mesh and a texture applied to it. Qt3D supports the Wavefront `obj` format to load custom meshes. Here, we added a home-cooked apple to the `.qrc` file of the application, and we just have to provide the path to this resource to load it.

The same principle is applied for the `DiffuseMapMaterial` element. We added a custom texture and added it as a source of the component.

As you can see, the `Entity` definition and its components look very much the same. Yet we effortlessly traded a Qt3D `CuboidMesh` with a custom model.

We will push things even further with `Background.qml`:

```
import Qt3D.Core 2.0
import Qt3D.Render 2.0
import Qt3D.Extras 2.0

Entity {
    id: root

    property alias position: transform.translation
    property alias scale3D: transform.scale3D

    MaterialBackground {
        id: material
    }

    CuboidMesh {
        id: mesh
    }

    Transform {
        id: transform
    }

    components: [material, mesh, transform]
}
```

The `Background` block will be displayed behind the snake and the apple. At first sight, this entity looks very much like `SnakePart`. However, `Material` is not a Qt3D class. It is a custom defined `Material` that relies on shaders. Let's see `MaterialBackground.qml`:

```
import Qt3D.Core 2.0
import Qt3D.Render 2.0
```

```
Material {
    id: material

    effect: Effect {
        FilterKey {
            id: forward
            name: "renderingStyle"
            value: "forward"
        }
        techniques: [
            Technique {
                filterKeys: [forward]
                graphicsApiFilter {
                    api: GraphicsApiFilter.OpenGL
                    profile: GraphicsApiFilter.CoreProfile
                    majorVersion: 3
                    minorVersion: 2
                }
                renderPasses: RenderPass {
                    shaderProgram: ShaderProgram {
                        vertexShaderCode:
                        loadSource("qrc:/shaders/gl3/grass.vert")
                        fragmentShaderCode:
                        loadSource("qrc:/shaders/gl3/grass.frag")
                    }
                }
            }
        ]
    }
}
```

If you are not familiar with shaders, we can summarize them in the following statement; shaders are computer programs written in a C-style syntax that are executed by the GPU. Data from your logic will be fed by the CPU and made available to the GPU memory where your shaders will run. Here, we manipulate two types of shader:

- **Vertex shader,** which is executed on each vertex of the source of your mesh
- **Fragment shader,** which is executed on each pixel to produce the final rendering

By being executed on the GPU, these shaders utilize the huge parallelization power of the GPU (which is orders of magnitude higher than your CPU's). It enables modern games to have such stunning visual rendering. Covering shaders and the OpenGL pipeline is beyond the scope of this book (you can fill several bookshelves on this subject alone). We will limit ourselves to showing you how you can use shaders in Qt3D.

If you want to delve into OpenGL or sharpen your skills with shaders, we recommend the *OpenGL SuperBible*, by Graham Sellers, Richard S Wright Jr., and Nicholas Haemel.

Qt3D supports shaders in a very convenient way. Simply add your shader file to the `.qrc` resource file and load it in the `effect` property of a given `Material`.

In this snippet, we specify that this shader `Technique` should be run only on OpenGL 3.2. This is indicated in the `graphicsApiFilter` block. This version of OpenGL targets your desktop machine. Because the performance gap between your desktop and your Raspberry Pi is very marked, we have the ability to execute different shaders depending on the platform.

Thus, here is the Raspberry Pi-compatible technique:

```
Technique {
    filterKeys: [forward]
    graphicsApiFilter {
        api: GraphicsApiFilter.OpenGLES
        profile: GraphicsApiFilter.CoreProfile
        majorVersion: 2
        minorVersion: 0
    }

    renderPasses: RenderPass {
        shaderProgram: ShaderProgram {
            vertexShaderCode:
                loadSource("qrc:/shaders/es2/grass.vert")
            fragmentShaderCode:
                loadSource("qrc:/shaders/es2/grass.frag")
        }
    }
}
```

You just have to add it to the `techniques` property of the `Material`. Note that the targeted OpenGL version is OpenGLES 2.0, which will run fine on your Raspberry Pi and even your iOS/Android phone.

A last thing to cover is how parameters can be passed to shaders. Here is an example:

```
Material {
    id: material

    parameters:  [
        Parameter {
```

```
                name: "score"; value: score
            }
        ]
        ...
    }
```

The `score` variable will be accessible in the shader with this simple section. Please take a look at the source code for the chapter to see the complete content of this `Material` element. We had the fun of writing a shader displaying a moving and glowing wave over a grass texture.

The only fixed element of the game is the background. We can directly add it to `GameArea.qml`:

```
Entity {
    id: root
    ...

    Background {
        position: Qt.vector3d(camera.x, camera.y, 0)
        scale3D: Qt.vector3d(camera.x * 2, camera.y * 2, 0)
    }

    components: [frameFraph, input]
}
```

The `Background` element is positioned to cover the whole visible area behind the snake and the apple. Being defined inside `GameArea`, it will be automatically added to the entity/component tree and will be drawn right away.

Preparing the board game

Even if our game has a 3D representation, we will implement 2D gameplay like the original snake game. Our game items are born, will live, and die in a 2D area. Like chess, this board will be composed of rows and columns. But in our snake game, each square can be:

- An apple
- A snake
- A wall
- Empty

Here is an example of a board representation from the point of view of the engine:

W	W	W	W	W	W	W	W	W	W
W									W
W							A		W
W									W
W			S	S	S				W
W					S				W
W									W
W	W	W	W	W	W	W	W	W	W

This is a small 10x8 board; even if size does not matter, you will be able to define a bigger one. Your game, your rules! We have walls (**W**) surrounding the game area. An apple (**A**) is spawned at (7; 2). Finally, we have a snake (**S**) beginning at (3; 4) and ending at (5; 5).

It is time to create our board class. Please create a JS file called `board.js`:

```
function Board(columnCount, rowCount, blockSize) {
    this.columnCount = columnCount;
    this.rowCount = rowCount;
    this.blockSize = blockSize;
    this.maxIndex = columnCount * rowCount;
    this.data = new Array(this.maxIndex);
}
```

This object constructor function required three parameters. The `columnCount` and `rowCount` parameters will help you to choose the board dimensions. The last parameter, `blockSize`, is the size of a board square in the OpenGL world. For example, we can set `blockSize` to 10. In this case, the apple in (7; 2) on the board will be displayed with `x = 70` and `y = 20` in the OpenGL world. In this chapter, we will use a `blockSize` of 1, so the board coordinates match OpenGL coordinates.

Let's add some utility functions to `board.js`:

```
Board.prototype.init = function() {
    for (var i = 0; i < this.data.length; i++) {
        this.data[i] = null;
    }
}

Board.prototype.index = function(column, row) {
```

```
        return column + (row * this.columnCount);
    }

    Board.prototype.setData = function(data, column, row) {
        this.data[this.index(column, row)] = data;
    }

    Board.prototype.at = function(column, row) {
        return this.data[this.index(column, row)];
    }
```

Defining a class in JavaScript can be disturbing for a C++ developer. Every JavaScript object has a prototype object to which you can add functions. We are using it to add class methods to `Board`.

Here is a summary of the purpose of each function of the `Board` class:

- `init()`: initializes all array values to the `null` value.
- `index()`: returns the array index from column/row coordinates.
- `setData()`: assigns the `data` value on the board from column/row coordinates.
- `at()`: retrieves the `data` value in an array from column/row coordinates.

Please note that, in our case, a `null` square means an empty square.

Crafting entities from the factory

Now that we have a board to receive items, we will create the game items' factory. The factory is a design pattern that allows us to create an object without exposing the creation logic to the caller. This factory can be seen as a helper class that will handle all the dirty tasks required when you want to create a new game item from JavaScript. Do you remember `GameEntity.qml`? It is the parent component of `Apple.qml`, `Snake.qml`, and `Wall.qml`. The factory will be able to create a specific entity for a given a type and coordinates. We will use the property type to identify an entity kind. Here is the factory pattern schema used in our snake game:

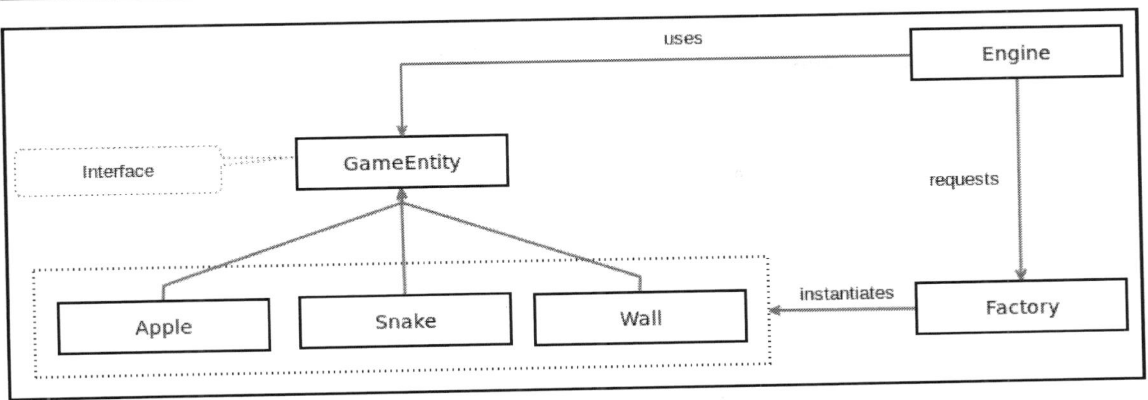

We can now create the `factory.js` file, which begins like this:

```
var SNAKE_TYPE = 1;
var WALL_TYPE  = 2;
var APPLE_TYPE = 3;

var snakeComponent = Qt.createComponent("SnakePart.qml");
var wallComponent = Qt.createComponent("Wall.qml");
var appleComponent = Qt.createComponent("Apple.qml");
```

First of all, we define all the game entity types. In our case we have apple, snake, and wall types. Then, we create game item components from QML files. These components will be used by the factory to dynamically create new game entities.

We can now add the constructor and a `removeAllEntities()` utility function to remove all instantiated entities:

```
function GameFactory() {

    this.board = null;
    this.parentEntity = null;
    this.entities = [];
}

GameFactory.prototype.removeAllEntities = function() {
    for(var i = 0; i < this.entities.length; i++) {
        this.entities[i].setParent(null);
    }
    this.entities = [];
}
```

This factory has three member variables:

- A reference to the game `board` described in the previous section
- A reference to the `parentEntity` variable; that is, the game area
- An `entities` array that keeps a reference to created items

The `removeAllEntities()` function will remove the items from their parent (that is, the game area) and create a new empty entities array. This ensures that old entities are deleted by the garbage collector.

Let's add the core function `createGameEnity()` in the factory:

```
GameFactory.prototype.createGameEntity = function(type, column, row) {
    var component;
    switch(type) {
    case SNAKE_TYPE:
        component = snakeComponent;
        break;

    case WALL_TYPE:
        component = wallComponent;
        break;

    case APPLE_TYPE:
        component = appleComponent;
        break;
    }
    var gameEntity = component.createObject(this.parentEntity);
    gameEntity.setParent(this.parentEntity);

    this.board.setData(gameEntity, column, row);
    gameEntity.gridPosition = Qt.vector2d(column, row);
    gameEntity.position.x = column * this.board.blockSize;
    gameEntity.position.y = row * this.board.blockSize;

    this.entities.push(gameEntity);
    return gameEntity;
}
```

As you can see, the caller provides an entity `type` and board coordinates (`column` and `row`). The first part is a switch to select the correct QML component. Once we have the component, we can call `component.createObject()` to create an instance of this component. The parent of this new component will be `this.parentEntity`; in our case, `GameArea`. Then, we can update the board, update the entity position, and add this new entity in the `entities` array.

The last thing to do is to update our QML game entities with the proper factory type. Please open `Apple.qml` and update the file like this:

```
import "factory.js" as Factory

GameEntity {

    id: root
    type: Factory.APPLE_TYPE
    ...
}
```

You can now update `Snake.qml` with the `Factory.SNAKE_TYPE` type and `Wall.qml` with the `Factory.WALL_TYPE` type.

Building a snake engine in JavaScript

It is time to get your hands dirty. Let's see how to create an engine in JavaScript to manage a snake game using our board, our factory, and the power of QML.

Please create a new `engine.js` file with the following snippet:

```
.import "factory.js" as Factory
.import "board.js" as Board

var COLUMN_COUNT = 50;
var ROW_COUNT = 29;
var BLOCK_SIZE = 1;

var factory = new Factory.GameFactory();
var board = new Board.Board(COLUMN_COUNT, ROW_COUNT, BLOCK_SIZE);

var snake = [];
var direction;
```

The first lines are the Qt way to import a JavaScript file from another JavaScript file. Then, we can easily instantiate a `factory` variable and a 50x29 `board` variable. The `snake` array contains all the snake game items instantiated. This array will be useful to move our snake. Finally, the `direction` variable is a 2D vector handling the current snake's direction.

This is the first function of our engine:

```
function start() {
    initEngine();

    createSnake();
    createWalls();

    spawnApple();
    gameRoot.state = "PLAY";
}
```

This gives you a summary of what is done when we start the engine:

1. Initialize the engine
2. Create the initial snake
3. Create walls surrounding the game area
4. Spawn the first apple
5. Switch the `GameArea` state to `PLAY`

Let's begin with the `initEngine()` function:

```
function initEngine() {
    timer.interval = initialTimeInterval;
    score = 0;

    factory.board = board;
    factory.parentEntity = gameRoot;
    factory.removeAllEntities();

    board.init();
    direction = Qt.vector2d(-1, 0);
}
```

This function initializes and resets all the variables. The first task is to set the `GameArea` timer interval to its initial value. Each time the snake eats an apple, this interval is reduced, increasing the game speed and thus the snake's movement speed. Logically, we reset the score of the player to `0`. Then we initialize the factory, giving the board and `gameRoot` references. The `gameRoot` refers to the `GameArea`; this entity will be the parent of all items instantiated by the factory. Then, we remove all the existing entities from the factory and call the board's `init()` function to clear the board. Finally, we set a default direction for the snake. The vector `-1,0` means that the snake will begin moving to the left. If you want the snake to start moving up, you can set the vector to `0, 1`.

The next function is creating the snake:

```
function createSnake() {
    snake = [];
    var initialPosition = Qt.vector2d(25, 12);
    for (var i = 0; i < initialSnakeSize; i++) {
        snake.push(factory.createGameEntity(Factory.SNAKE_TYPE,
                                            initialPosition.x + i,
                                            initialPosition.y));

    }
}
```

No big deal here, we reset and initialize the `snake` array. The first snake item will be created at (25; 12). We then proceed to create as many snake items as we need to spawn a snake with the correct initial size. Please note that other snake items will be created to the right of the first item; (26; 12), (27,12), and so on. You can see how easy it is to call our factory and request a new snake item instance.

Let's add the `createWalls()` function to `engine.js`:

```
function createWalls() {
    for (var x = 0; x < board.columnCount; x++) {
        factory.createGameEntity(Factory.WALL_TYPE, x, 0);
        factory.createGameEntity(Factory.WALL_TYPE, x, board.rowCount - 1);
    }
    for (var y = 1; y < board.rowCount - 1; y++) {
        factory.createGameEntity(Factory.WALL_TYPE, 0, y);
        factory.createGameEntity(Factory.WALL_TYPE, board.columnCount - 1,
y);
    }
}
```

The first loop creates the top and bottom walls. The second loop creates the left and right walls. The indexes of the second loop are different from the first one to avoid creating the corners twice.

Let's see now how to implement the `spawnApple()` function in `engine.js`:

```
function spawnApple() {
    var isFound = false;
    var position;
    while (!isFound) {
        position = Qt.vector2d(Math.floor(Math.random()
                                    * board.columnCount),
                              Math.floor(Math.random()
                                    * board.rowCount));
        if (board.at(position.x, position.y) === null) {
            isFound = true;
        }
    }
    factory.createGameEntity(Factory.APPLE_TYPE, position.x, position.y);

    if (timerInterval > 10) {
        timerInterval -= 2;
    }
}
```

The first step is to find an empty square. The while loop will generate a random board position and check whether a square is empty. As soon as an empty square is found, we request the factory to create an apple entity at this position. Finally, we reduce the `timerInverval` value of `GameArea` to speed up the game.

We will now add some utility functions related to the snake's position in `engine.js`:

```
function setPosition(item, column, row) {
    board.setData(item, column, row);
    item.gridPosition = Qt.vector2d(column, row);
    item.position.x = column * board.blockSize;
    item.position.y = row * board.blockSize;
}

function moveSnake(column, row) {
    var last = snake.pop();
    board.setData(null, last.gridPosition.x, last.gridPosition.y);
    setPosition(last, column, row);
    snake.unshift(last);
}
```

The `setPosition()` function handles all the necessary tasks when we want to move a game item. We first assign the game item to the correct board square, then we update the `gridPosition` property (from `GameEntity`) but also the OpenGL `position.x` and `position.y`.

The second function, `moveSnake()`, moves the snake to an adjacent square. Let's dissect all the steps performed by this function:

1. The `snake` is our global array containing all the snake items. The `pop()` method removes and returns the last element that we store in the `last` variable.
2. The `last` variable contains the snake's tail's grid position. We set this board square to `null`; that means an empty square for us.
3. The `last` variable is now put on the adjacent square requested by the caller.
4. The `last` variable is finally inserted at the beginning of the `snake` array.

The next schema illustrates the `moveSnake()` process when a snake is moving on the left. We also name snake items with a letter to visualize how the tail becomes the head, simulating a moving snake:

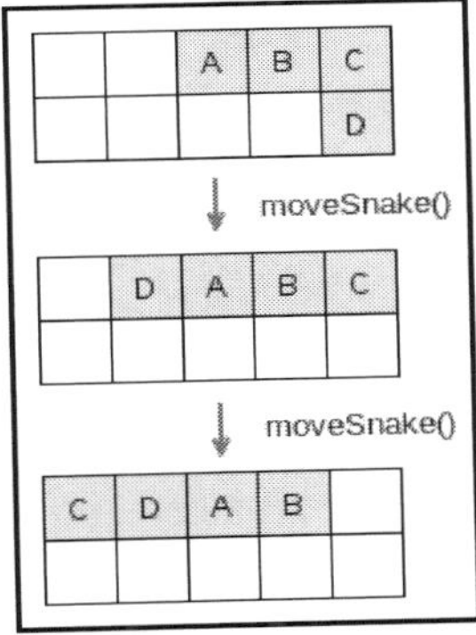

Now that we can move our snake, we must handle key events to move the snake in the correct direction. Please add this new function to `engine.js`:

```
function handleKeyEvent(event) {
    switch(event.key) {
        // restart game
        case Qt.Key_R:
            start();
            break;

        // direction UP
        case Qt.Key_I:
            if (direction != Qt.vector2d(0, -1)) {
                direction = Qt.vector2d(0, 1);
            }
            break;
```

```
            // direction RIGHT
            case Qt.Key_L:
                if (direction != Qt.vector2d(-1, 0)) {
                    direction = Qt.vector2d(1, 0);
                }
                break;

            // direction DOWN
            case Qt.Key_K:
                if (direction != Qt.vector2d(0, 1)) {
                    direction = Qt.vector2d(0, -1);
                }
                break;

            // direction LEFT
            case Qt.Key_J:
                if (direction != Qt.vector2d(1, 0)) {
                    direction = Qt.vector2d(-1, 0);
                }
                break;
        }
    }
```

In this game, we use the `I-J-K-L` keys to update the snake direction vector. Like the original snake game, you can't reverse your direction. A check is performed to avoid this behavior. Please notice that pressing the *R* key will call `start()` and so restart the game. We will see soon how to bind this function with the QML keyboard controller.

Here we are, the last (but not least) function, the `update()` function of `engine.js`:

```
function update() {
    if (gameRoot.state === "GAMEOVER") {
        return;
    }

    var headPosition = snake[0].gridPosition;
    var newPosition = Qt.vector2d(headPosition.x + direction.x,
                                  headPosition.y + direction.y);
    var itemOnNewPosition = board.at(newPosition.x,
                                     newPosition.y);

   ...
}
```

This function will be called at regular intervals by QML. As you can see, if the `gameRoot` (that is, `GameArea`) `state` variable equals `GAMEOVER`, this function does nothing and returns immediately. Then, three important steps are performed:

1. Retrieve the grid position of the snake's head in `headPosition`
2. Process where the snake goes using the `direction` vector in `newPosition`
3. Put the item where the snake is going in `itemOnNewPosition`

The second part of the `update()` function is the following snippet:

```
function update() {
    ...
    if(itemOnNewPosition === null) {
        moveSnake(newPosition.x, newPosition.y);
        return;
    }

    switch(itemOnNewPosition.type) {
        case Factory.SNAKE_TYPE:
        case Factory.WALL_TYPE:
            gameRoot.state = "GAMEOVER";
            break;

        case Factory.APPLE_TYPE:
            itemOnNewPosition.setParent(null);
            board.setData(null, newPosition.x, newPosition.y);
            snake.unshift(factory.createGameEntity(
                    Factory.SNAKE_TYPE,
                    newPosition.x,
                    newPosition.y));
            spawnApple();
            score++;
            break;
    }
}
```

If the snake is going to an empty square (`itemOnNewPosition` is `null`), it is alright and we only move the snake to `newPosition`.

If the square is not empty, we must apply the correct rule depending on the item type. If the next square is a snake part or a wall, we update the state to `GAMEOVER`. On the other hand, if the next square is an apple, several steps are performed:

1. Detach the apple item from `GameArea`, setting its parent to `null`
2. Remove the apple from the board, setting the board square to `null`

3. Grow the snake, creating a snake part at the beginning of the `snake` array
4. Spawn a new apple in a random empty square
5. Increment the score

Our snake engine is now complete. The last step is to call some engine functions from QML. Please update `GameArea.qml`:

```
...
import "engine.js" as Engine

Entity {
    ...
    QQ2.Component.onCompleted: {
        console.log("Start game...");
        Engine.start();
        timer.start()
    }

    QQ2.Timer {
        id: timer
        interval: initialTimeInterval
        repeat: true
        onTriggered: Engine.update()
    }

    KeyboardInput {
        id: input
        controller: keyboardController
        focus: true
        onPressed: Engine.handleKeyEvent(event)
    }
    ...
}
```

You can already play the game. If you eat an apple, the snake grows and you get one point. When you hit yourself or a wall, the game state switches to `GAMEOVER` and the game stops. Finally, if you press the `R` key, the game restarts. The game looks like the following screenshot on the Raspberry Pi:

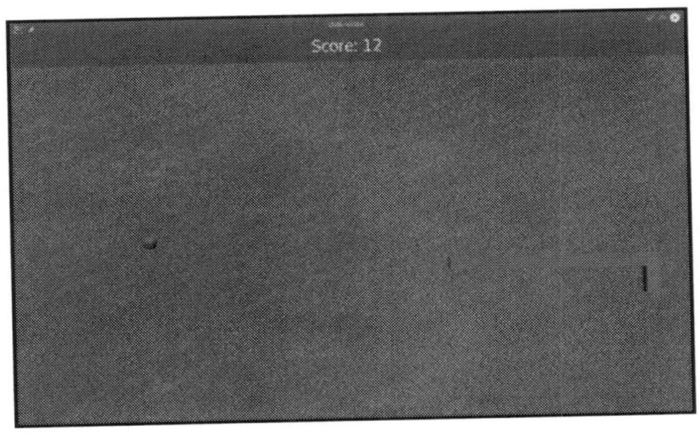

Varying the HUD with QML states

We will now create a "Game Over" HUD, displayed when you lose the game. Create a new file, `GameOverItem.qml`:

```
Item {
    id: root
    anchors.fill: parent

    onVisibleChanged: {
        scoreLabel.text = "Your score: " + score
    }

    Rectangle {
        anchors.fill: parent
        color: "black"
        opacity: 0.75
    }

    Label {
        id: gameOverLabel
        anchors.centerIn: parent
        color: "white"
        font.pointSize: 50
        text: "Game Over"
    }

    Label {
        id: scoreLabel
        width: parent.width
        anchors.top: gameOverLabel.bottom
```

```
            horizontalAlignment: "AlignHCenter"
            color: "white"
            font.pointSize: 20
        }

        Label {
            width: parent.width
            anchors.bottom: parent.bottom
            anchors.bottomMargin: 50
            horizontalAlignment: "AlignHCenter"
            color: "white"
            font.pointSize: 30
            text:"Press R to restart the game"
        }
    }
```

Let's examine the items of this Game Over screen:

- A black rectangle filling the entire screen with an `opacity` value of 75%. Therefore, the game area will still be visible at 25% behind the game over screen.
- A `gameOverLabel` label displaying the text "Game Over". This is a traditional video game message but you can edit this label with text such as "Loser!" or "Too bad!".
- A dynamic `scoreLabel` label that will display the final score.
- A label explaining to the player how he can restart the game.

Please notice that, when the visibility of the root item changes, the `scoreLabel` text is updated with the current `score` variable from `main.qml`.

Qt Quick provides an interesting feature related to UI states. You can define several states for an item and describe the behaviors for each state. We will now use this feature and our `GameOverItem` in a new file called `OverlayItem.qml`:

```
Item {
    id: root

    states: [
        State {
            name: "PLAY"
            PropertyChanges { target: root; visible: false }
        },
        State {
            name: "GAMEOVER"
            PropertyChanges { target: root; visible: true }
            PropertyChanges { target: gameOver; visible: true }
        }
```

```
        ]

        GameOverItem {
            id: gameOver
        }
    }
```

You can see that the `states` element is an `Item` property. By default, the `states` element contains an empty string state. Here, we are defining two `State` items named `PLAY` and `GAMEOVER`. We are using the same naming convention as in `engine.js`. Afterwards, we will be able to bind the property values to a state. In our case, when the state is `GAMEOVER`, we set the visibility to `true` for this `OverlayItem` and its `GameOverItem`. Otherwise, for the state `PLAY`, we hide it.

The overlay HUD and its "Game Over" screen are ready to be used. Please update your `main.qml` with the following snippet:

```
Item {
    id: mainView
    property int score: 0
    readonly property alias window: mainView
    ...

    Scene3D {
        id: scene
        anchors.top: hud.bottom
        anchors.bottom: parent.bottom
        anchors.left: parent.left
        anchors.right: parent.right
        focus: true
        aspects: "input"

        GameArea {
            id: gameArea
            initialSnakeSize: 5
        }
    }
    OverlayItem {
        id: overlayItem
        anchors.fill: mainView
        visible: false

        Connections {
            target: gameArea
            onStateChanged: {
                overlayItem.state = gameArea.state;
            }
```

```
            }
        }
    }
```

Our `OverlayItem` element fits the screen and is not visible by default. Like a C++ Qt Widgets signal/slot connection, you can perform a QML connection. The target property contains the item that will send the signal. Then you can use the QML slot syntax:

```
on<PropertyName>Changed
```

In our case, the target is `gameArea`. This item contains the `state` variable, so we can be notified when the state variable is updated using `onStateChanged`. Then, we switch the state of `OverlayItem`. This assignation will trigger all of the `ProperyChanged` items that are defined in the `OverlayItem` element, and display or hide our `GameOverItem`.

Notice that in this case, you could also avoid using a `Connections` block, adding a property binding:

```
OverlayItem {
    id: overlayItem
    anchors.fill: mainView
    visible: false
    state: gameArea.state
}
```

You can now lose the game and enjoy your Game Over overlay:

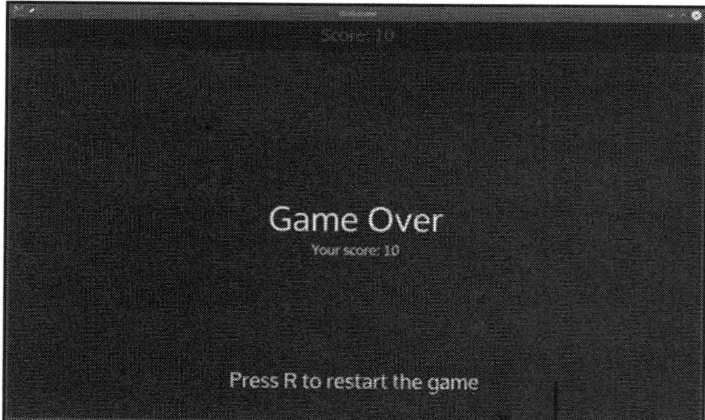

Profiling your QML application

Qt Creator provides a QML profiler to collect useful data on your application during the runtime. You can use it on a desktop and also on a remote target such as our Raspberry Pi. Let's check that your debug build configuration allows QML debugging and profiling. Click on **Projects** | **Rpi 2** | **Build**. Then, you can click on **Details** of **qmake** from **Build Steps**. You should also check it for your desktop kit:

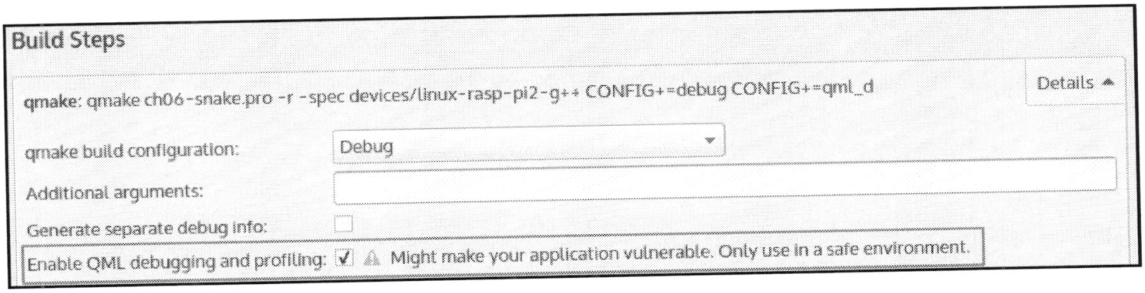

Build Steps
qmake: qmake ch06-snake.pro -r -spec devices/linux-rasp-pi2-g++ CONFIG+=debug CONFIG+=qml_d Details
qmake build configuration: Debug
Additional arguments:
Generate separate debug info:
Enable QML debugging and profiling: Might make your application vulnerable. Only use in a safe environment.

By default, data is only sent from target to host when you stop profiling. You can flush data periodically with **Tools** | **Options** | **Analyser** | **QML Profiler**.

Keep in mind that flushing data while profiling frees memory on the target device but takes time. Thus, it can affect your profiling result and analysis.

While we are using Qt Creator kits, we can start the QML profiler in the same way for desktops or remote devices. Switch to a kit and click on **Analyze** | **QML Profiler** to start the QML profiling. If you are profiling an application running on your desktop, Qt Creator starts your software with an argument like this:

```
-qmljsdebugger=file:/tmp/QtCreator.OU7985
```

If you're profiling an application on a remote device (such as a Raspberry Pi), Qt Creator uses a TCP socket to retrieve data, adding an argument such as this:

```
-qmljsdebugger=port:10000
```

For both targets, the QML profiler will afterwards try to connect to your application. Another way to start the QML profiler on a remote device is to start the application yourself with the `-qmljsdebugger` argument. For example:

```
./ch06-snake -qmljsdebugger=port:3768
```

Then, you can click on **Analyze** | **QML Profiler (External)**. Select your remote kit (such as Rpi 2), set the **port** to `3768`, and click on **OK**.

Great, the QML profiler is started, a new toolbar appears. You can play the game for a few seconds and click on the **Stop** button from the QML Profiler toolbar. Then, the QML profiler processes data and displays something like this:

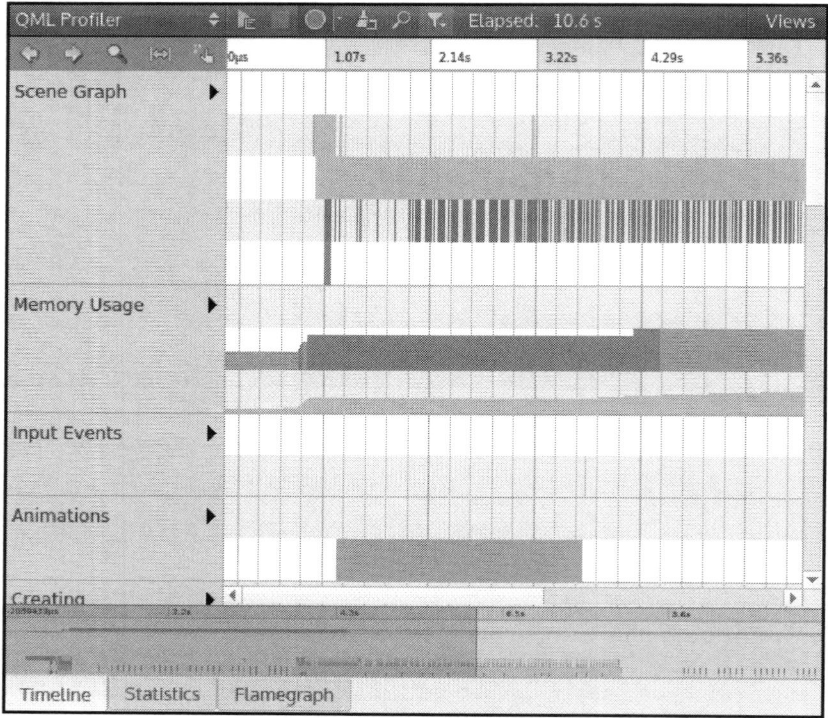

Let's begin analyzing the top buttons from left to right:

1. Start QML profiler.
2. Stop the application and the QML profiler.
3. Enable/disable profiling. You can also select an event to capture.
4. Discard data to clean your profiling session.
5. Search timeline event notes.
6. Hide or show event categories.
7. **Elapsed** indicates the session duration.
8. **Views** hides or shows the **Timeline**, **Statistics**, and **Flamegraph** tabs.

To learn to use the QML profiler, we will take a real case. Restarting the game is a little slow on the Raspberry Pi. Let's find, with the QML profiler, why it requires several seconds to restart the game!

Please follow this operational mode to gather data from the QML profiler:

1. Select the Raspberry Pi kit
2. Start the QML profiler
3. Wait for the snake to hit a wall
4. Press the *R* key to restart the game
5. Wait for the game to restart and the snake to move again
6. Stop the QML profiler

Let's begin our investigation using the **Timeline** tab. This view displays a chronological view of events, grouped by event type. The JavaScript row dissects your code and displays useful information. You can click on an item to get some details. Identify in the timeline when you restart the game. The JavaScript row can be read as a call stack, from the top to the bottom:

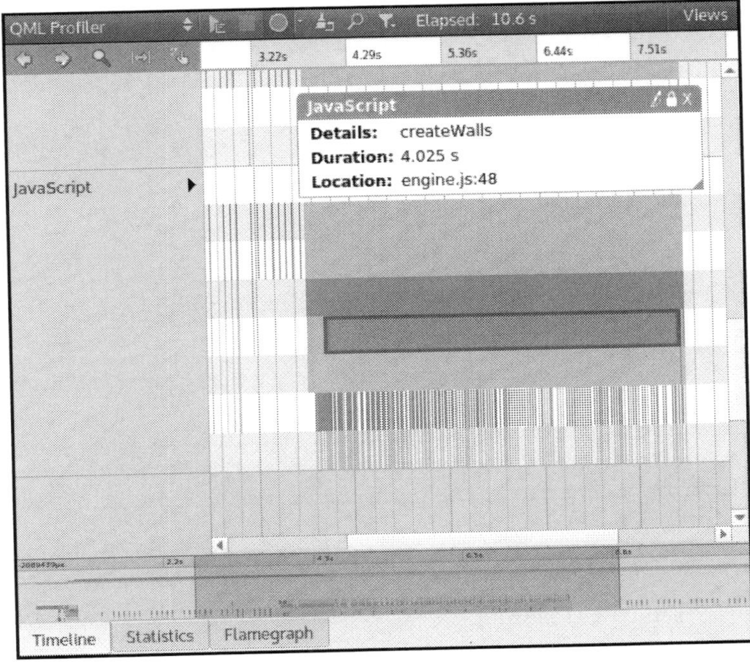

In our case, we restarted the game around 3.5 seconds after the application started. Here is the stack with durations provided by the QML profiler. Let's track all the functions that are called when we restart the game pressing the R key:

- The `onPressed()` function from `GameArea.qml`
- The `handleKetEvent()` function from `engine.js`
- The `start()` function from `engine.js` at 4.2 seconds:
    - `initEngine()` at 80 ms
    - `createSnake()` at 120 ms
    - `createWalls()` at 4.025 seconds!

Here we are, `createWalls()` takes ~4 seconds on the Raspberry Pi when we restart the game.

Let's switch to the **Statistics** view:

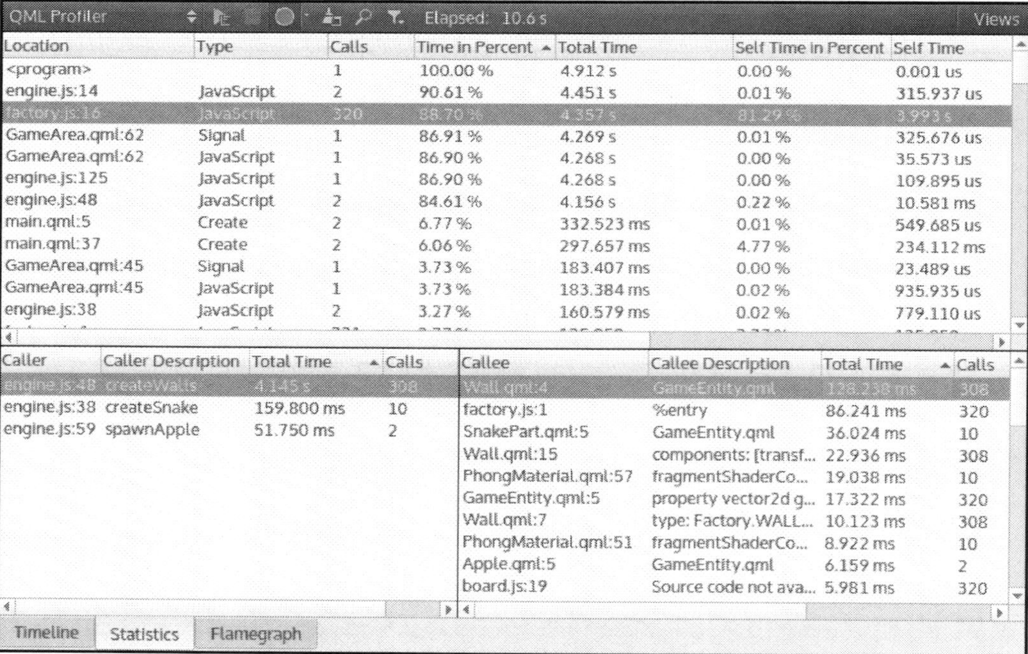

The **Statistics** view displays numbers concerning the call count of an event. An event can be a QML binding, creation, signal triggered, or a JavaScript function. The bottom part shows QML callers and callees.

A caller is the source of a change in a binding. For example, the JS function `createWalls()` is a caller.

A callee is the affected item that a binding triggers. For example, the QML item `Wall.qml` is a callee.

Once again, `createWalls()` requesting many factory item creation seems responsible for the slow restart of the game on the Raspberry Pi.

Take a look at the last view of the QML profiler, the **Flamegraph**:

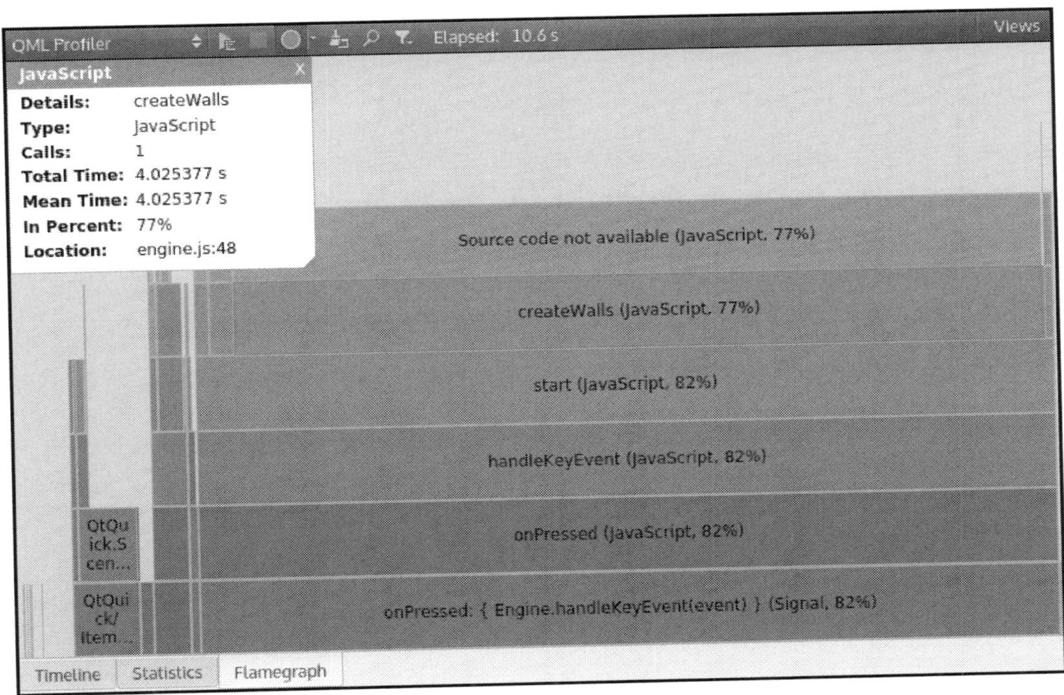

The **Flamegraph** view is a compact summary of your QML and JavaScript code while running the game. You can see the call count and the amount of time relative to the total duration. Like the **Timeline** view, you can see the call stack but from the bottom to the top!

Again, the profiler indicates `createWalls()` is a heavy function. On a profiling session of 10 seconds with one game restart, 77% of the time is spent in `engine.createWalls()`.

You will now be able to profile a QML application. You can try to edit the code to speed up the restart. Here are some hints:

- Create the walls only once at application's startup; do not delete and recreate them on each restart.
- Implement a common design pattern in video games, which is an object pool of preloaded items. Request a wall when needed, and return the wall to the pool when you do not use it.

Summary

In this chapter, we discovered how to use the Qt3D module. You also learned how to configure Qt Creator to create a new kit for an embedded Linux device. Your Raspberry Pi can now run your Qt applications. We created a snake game using QML views and an engine in JavaScript. We also covered the Factory design pattern to easily create new game items from the engine. Finally, you are now able to investigate the bad behavior of your QML software using the powerful QML profiler.

Even if Qt is a powerful framework, sometimes you need to use a third-party library. In the next chapter, we will see how to integrate the OpenCV library into your Qt application.

7
Third-Party Libraries without a Headache

In previous chapters, we used our own libraries or the ones provided by Qt. In this chapter, we will learn how to integrate the third-party library OpenCV with a Qt project. This library will give you an impressive image processing toolbox. For each platform, you will learn to use a specific compiler link configuration.

Qt Designer is a powerful WYSIWYG editor. This is why this chapter will also teach you to build a Qt Designer plugin that can be dragged and dropped from the **Widget Box** to the **Form Editor**, and then configured directly from Qt Creator.

In the example project, the user can load a picture, select a filter from thumbnail previews, and save the result. This application will rely on OpenCV's functions for image processing.

This chapter will cover the following topics:

- Creating your Qt Designer plugin
- Implementing your OpenCV filters
- Exposing your plugin to Qt Designer
- Using your Qt Designer plugin

Creating your Qt Designer plugin

In `Chapter 4`, *Conquering the Desktop UI*, we created a custom Qt widget in Qt Designer using the promoting technique. It is now time to learn how to create a custom Qt widget by building a plugin for Qt Designer. Your widget will be available from the **Design** mode in the **Widget Box**, alongside other regular Qt widgets. For this project example, we will create a `FilterWidget` class that processes an input image to apply a filter. The widget will also display the filter name and a dynamic thumbnail of the filtered picture.

This project is composed of two subprojects:

- `filter-plugin-designer`: This is a Qt Designer plugin containing the `FilterWidget` class and the image-processing code. This plugin is a dynamic library that will be used by the Qt Creator to offer our new `FilterWidget` in the **Form Editor**.
- `image-filter`: This is a Qt widget application using multiple `FilterWidget` classes. The user can open an image from their hard disk, select a filter (grayscale, blur, and so on), and save the filtered image.

Our `filter-plugin-designer` will use the third-party library **Open Source Computer Vision (OpenCV)**. It is a powerful, cross-platform open source library to manipulate images. The following diagram shows an overview schema:

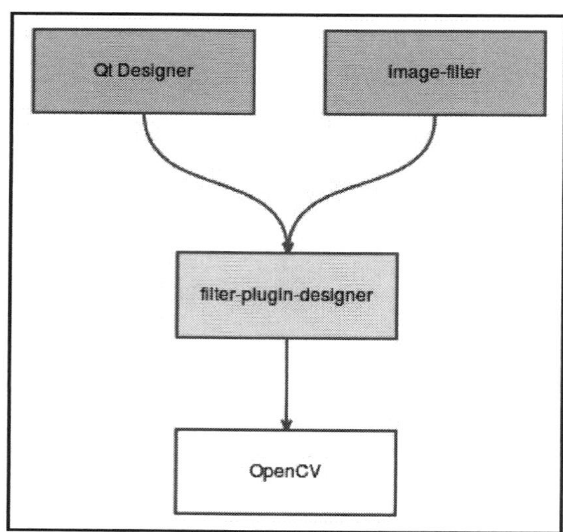

You can see a plugin as a kind of module, which can be easily added to an existing software. A plugin must respect a specific interface to be automatically called by the application. In our case, Qt Designer is the application that loads Qt plugins, so creating a plugin allows us to enhance the application without the need to modify the Qt Designer source code and recompile it. A plugin is usually a dynamic library (`.dll/.so`), so it will be loaded at runtime by the application.

Now that you have a clear idea about the Qt Designer plugins, let's build one! First, create a `Subdirs` project called `ch07-image-filter`. Then, you can add a subproject called `filter-plugin-designer`. You can use the **Empty qmake Project** template because we start this project from scratch. Here is the `filter-plugin-designer.pro` file:

```
QT += widgets uiplugin
CONFIG += plugin
CONFIG += c++14
TEMPLATE = lib
DEFINES += FILTERPLUGINDESIGNER_LIBRARY

TARGET = $$qtLibraryTarget($$TARGET)
INSTALLS += target
```

Please note the `uiplugin` and `plugin` keywords for `QT` and `CONFIG`. They are required to create a Qt Designer plugin. We set the `TEMPLATE` keyword to `lib` because we are creating a dynamic library. The `DEFINES`, called `FILTERPLUGINDESIGNER_LIBRARY`, will be used by the import/export mechanism of the library. We already covered this topic in `Chapter 3`, *Dividing Your Project and Ruling Your Code*. By default, our `TARGET` is `filter-plugin-designer`; the `$$qtLibraryTarget()` function will update it according to your platform. For example, the suffix `d` (standing for debug) will be appended on Windows. Finally, we append `target` to `INSTALLS`. Right now, this line does nothing, but we will describe a destination path for each platform soon. This way, executing the `make install` command will copy our target library file (`.dll/.so`) into the correct folder. To automatically perform this task on each compilation, you can add a new build step.

The deploy path is configured by `INSTALLS`, but it will not be done automatically. Open the **Projects** tab and do the following:

1. Open **Build Settings** | **Build Steps**
2. Click on **Add Build Step** | **Make**
3. In the **Make arguments** field, type `install`

You should get something like this:

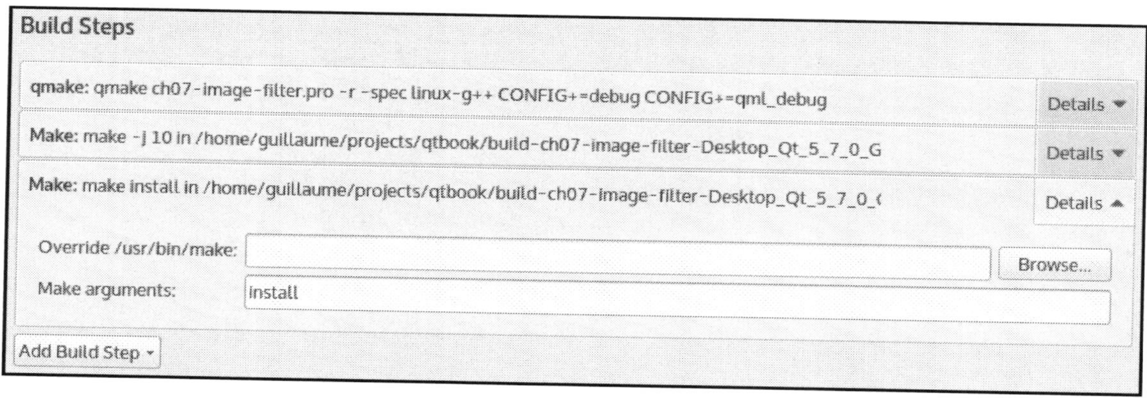

Each time you build the project, the `make install` command will be called and it will deploy the library in Qt Creator.

Configuring the project for Windows

Before preparing this project on Windows, let's talk about the available choices when you develop a Qt application on a Windows host. The official Qt website provides multiple binary packages. We are mainly interested in the following:

- Qt for Windows 32-bit (MinGW)
- Qt for Windows 32-bit (VS 2013)

You may already be using one of these versions. The first one comes with a MinGW GCC compiler and the Qt framework. The second only provides the Qt framework and relies on the Microsoft Visual C++ compiler that will be installed with Visual Studio.

Both versions are fine when you want to create a common Qt application for Windows. However, for this chapter, we want to link our `filter-plugin-designer` project with OpenCV libraries. Qt Designer must also be able to dynamically load `filter-plugin-designer`, so we must use a consistent compiler version at all stages.

Please note that Qt Creator on Windows is always based on MSVC, even in the MinGW binary package! So if you create a Qt Designer plugin using a MinGW compiler, your Qt Creator will not be able to load it. OpenCV for Windows provides only MSVC libraries, compile for MSVC11 (which is VS 2012), and MSVC12 (VS 2013).

The following table shows a summary of the different solutions for building our project example in Windows:

	MinGW GCC	MSVC
OpenCV	Binary not provided Recompilation required	Binary for msvc11 and msvc12 provided
Qt Designer	Binary not provided Recompilation required	Based on msvc12 32-bit

Keep in mind that you can always try to compile open source software, such as Qt Creator and OpenCV, from a source with a different compiler. So, if you absolutely want to use a MinGW compiler, you must recompile OpenCV and Qt Creator from their sources. Otherwise, we suggest that you use Qt for Windows 32-bit (VS 2013), as previously explained. Here are the steps to prepare your development environment:

1. Download and install Visual Studio Community Edition
2. Download and install Qt for Windows 32-bit (VS 2013)
3. Download and extract OpenCV for Windows (for example, `C:\lib\opencv`)
4. Create a new `OPENCV_HOME: C:\lib\opencv\build\x86\vc12` environment variable
5. Append to your system `Path` the following OpenCV path `C:\lib\opencv\build\x86\vc12\bin`

The `OPENCV_HOME` directory will be used in our `.pro` file. We will also add an OpenCV libraries folder to the `Path` directory to easily resolve the dependencies at runtime.

You can now add the following snippet to the `filter-plugin-designer.pro` file:

```
windows {
    target.path = $$(QTDIR)/../../Tools/QtCreator/bin/plugins/designer

    debug:target_lib.files = $$OUT_PWD/debug/$${TARGET}.lib
    release:target_lib.files = $$OUT_PWD/release/$${TARGET}.lib
    target_lib.path = $$(QTDIR)/../../Tools/QtCreator/bin/plugins/designer
    INSTALLS += target_lib

    INCLUDEPATH += $$(OPENCV_HOME)/../../include
    LIBS += -L$$(OPENCV_HOME)/lib
```

```
        -lopencv_core320
        -lopencv_imgproc320
}
```

The `target` path is set to the Qt Creator plugin folder. We also create a `target_lib` library to copy the `.lib` file generated by MSVC when we make a dynamic library (`.dll`). We add the OpenCV's headers folder to the `INCLUDEPATH` to easily include them in our code. Finally, we update the `LIBS` variable to link our plugin with the OpenCV's modules (`core` and `imgproc`) from the OpenCV `lib` folder.

Please note that the standalone Qt Designer application and the Qt Creator are different software. Both programs use a different plugin path. In our case, we only used the form editor from the Qt Creator, so we are targeting the Qt Creator plugin path.

Just as we appended `target` and `target_lib` to `INSTALLS`, both the `.dll` and `.lib` files will be copied in the Qt Creator's plugin path on a `make install` command. Qt Creator only requires the `.dll` file to load the plugin at runtime. The `.lib` file is only used to resolve the links with `filter-plugin-designer` when building our `image-filter` application. For simplicity, we are using the same directory.

Configuring the project for Linux

OpenCV binaries are certainly available in official software repositories. Depending on your distribution and your package manager, you can install it with commands such as the following:

```
# On Debian system
apt-get install libopencv-dev

# On Red Hat system
yum install opencv
```

When OpenCV is installed on your Linux, you can add this snippet to the `filter-plugin-designer.pro` file:

```
linux {
    target.path = $$(QTDIR)/../../Tools/QtCreator/lib/Qt/plugins/designer/
     CONFIG += link_pkgconfig
    PKGCONFIG += opencv
}
```

This time, we do not use the `LIBS` variable but `PKGCONFIG`, which relies on `pkg-config`.

It is a helper tool that will insert the correct options into the compile command line. In our case, we will request `pkg-config` to link our project with OpenCV.

You can list all the libs managed by `pkg-config` with the `pkg-config --list-all` command.

Configuring the project for Mac

The first step in making the project work on Mac OS is to install OpenCV. Fortunately, this is very easy using the `brew` command. If you develop on Mac OS and do not use it already, you should download it right now. In a nutshell, `brew` is an alternative package manager that gives you access to many packages (for developers and non-developers) that are not available in the Mac App Store.

You can download and install `brew` from `http://brew.sh/`.

In a Terminal, simply type the following command:

```
brew install opencv
```

This will download, compile, and install OpenCV on your machine. At the time of writing, the latest OpenCV version available on `brew` was version 3.2. Once this is done, open `filter-plugin-designer.pro` and add the following block:

```
macx {
    target.path =
"$$(QTDIR)/../../QtCreator.app/Contents/PlugIns/designer/"
    target_lib.files = $$OUT_PWD/lib$${TARGET}.dylib
    target_lib.path =
"$$(QTDIR)/../../QtCreator.app/Contents/PlugIns/designer/"
    INSTALLS += target_lib

    INCLUDEPATH += /usr/local/Cellar/opencv/3.2.0/include/

    LIBS += -L/usr/local/lib \
         -lopencv_core \
         -lopencv_imgproc
}
```

We add OpenCV headers and link the path with the INCLUDEPATH and LIBS variables. The target definition and INSTALLS are used to automatically deploy the output shared object to the Qt Creator's application plugins directory.

The last thing we have to do is to add an environment variable to let Qt Creator know where it will find the library that will link it to the final application. In the **Projects** tab, go through the following steps:

1. Open the **Details** window in **Build Environment**
2. Click on the **Add** button
3. Type DYLD_LIBRARY_PATH in the <VARIABLE> field
4. Type the path of the build directory in <VALUE> (you can copy and paste it from **General | Build directory**)

Implementing your OpenCV filters

Now that your development environment is ready, we can begin the fun part! We will implement three filters using OpenCV:

- FilterOriginal: Does nothing and returns the same picture (lazy!)
- FilterGrayscale: Converts a picture from color to grayscale
- FilterBlur: Smooths the picture

The parent class of all these filters is Filter. Here is the abstract class:

```
//Filter.h
class Filter
{
public:
    Filter();
    virtual ~Filter();

    virtual QImage process(const QImage& image) = 0;
};

//Filter.cpp
Filter::Filter() {}
Filter::~Filter() {}
```

As you can see, `process()` is a pure abstract method. All filters will implement a specific behavior with this function. Let's begin with the simple `FilterOriginal` class. Here is `FilterOriginal.h`:

```
class FilterOriginal : public Filter
{
public:
 FilterOriginal();
 ~FilterOriginal();

QImage process(const QImage& image) override;
};
```

This class inherits `Filter`, and we override the `process()` function. The implementation is also really simple. Fill `FilterOriginal.cpp` with the following:

```
FilterOriginal::FilterOriginal() :
Filter()
{
}

FilterOriginal::~FilterOriginal()
{
}

QImage FilterOriginal::process(const QImage& image)
{
    return image;
}
```

No modification is performed; we return the same picture. Now that the filter structure is clear, we can create `FilterGrayscale`. The `.h` and `.cpp` files are similar to `FilterOriginalFilter`, so let's jump to the `process()` function of `FilterGrayscale.cpp`:

```
QImage FilterGrayscale::process(const QImage& image)
{
    // QImage => cv::mat
    cv::Mat tmp(image.height(),
                image.width(),
                CV_8UC4,
                (uchar*)image.bits(),
                image.bytesPerLine());
    cv::Mat resultMat;
    cv::cvtColor(tmp, resultMat, CV_BGR2GRAY);
    // cv::mat => QImage
    QImage resultImage((const uchar *) resultMat.data,
```

```
                            resultMat.cols,
                            resultMat.rows,
                            resultMat.step,
                            QImage::Format_Grayscale8);
        return resultImage.copy();
    }
```

In the Qt framework, we use the `QImage` class to manipulate pictures. In the OpenCV world, we use the `Mat` class, so the first step is to create a correct `Mat` object from the `QImage` source. OpenCV and Qt both handle many image formats. An image format describes the data bytes' organization, with information such as the following:

- `Channel count`: A grayscale picture only needs one channel (white intensity), while a color picture requires three channels (red, green, and blue). You will need four channels to handle the opacity (alpha) pixel information.
- `Bit depth`: The number of bits used to store a pixel color.
- `Channel order`: The most common orders are RGB and BGR. Alpha can be placed before or after the color information.

For example, the OpenCV image format, `CV_8UC4`, means four channels of unsigned 8 bit, which is the perfect fit for an alpha color picture. In our case, we are using a compatible Qt and OpenCV image format to convert our `QImage` in `Mat`. The following table shows a small summary:

Qt		OpenCV	
Order	QImage	Order	cv::Mat
BGRX	Format_RGB32	BGRA	CV_8UC4
BGRA	Format_ARGB32		
RGBA	Format_RGBA8888		
RGB	Format_RGB888	BGR	CV_8UC3
Gray	Format_Grayscale8	Gray	CV_8UC1

Please note that some `QImage` class formats also depend on your platform's *endianness*. The preceding table is for a little endian system. For OpenCV, the order is always the same: `BGRA`. It is not required in our project example, but you can swap the blue and red channels if needed, as follows:

```
// with OpenCV
cv::cvtColor(mat, mat, CV_BGR2RGB);

// with Qt
QImage swapped = image.rgbSwapped();
```

The OpenCV `Mat` and Qt `QImage` classes perform shallow construction/copying by default. This means that only metadata is really copied; the pixel data is shared. To create a deep copy of a picture, you must call the `copy()` function:

```
// with OpenCV
mat.clone();

// with Qt
image.copy();
```

We created a `Mat` class called `tmp` from the `QImage` class. Note that `tmp` is not a deep copy of `image`; they share the same data pointer. Then, we can call the `OpenCV` function to convert the picture from color to grayscale using `cv::cvtColor()`. Finally, we create a `QImage` class from the grayscale `resultMat` element. In that case too, `resultMat` and `resultImage` share the same data pointer. Once we're done, we return a deep copy of `resultImage`.

It is now time to implement the last filter. The following code shows the `process()` function of `FilterBlur.cpp`:

```
QImage FilterBlur::process(const QImage& image)
{
    // QImage => cv::mat
    cv::Mat tmp(image.height(),
                image.width(),
                CV_8UC4,
                (uchar*)image.bits(),
                image.bytesPerLine());
    int blur = 17;
    cv::Mat resultMat;
    cv::GaussianBlur(tmp,
                     resultMat,
                     cv::Size(blur, blur),
                     0.0,
                     0.0);
    // cv::mat => QImage
    QImage resultImage((const uchar *) resultMat.data,
                       resultMat.cols,
                       resultMat.rows,
                       resultMat.step,
                       QImage::Format_RGB32);
    return resultImage.copy();
}
```

The conversion from `QImage` to `Mat` is the same. The processing differs because we use the `cv::GaussianBlur()` OpenCV function to smooth the picture. The `blur` is the kernel's size used by the Gaussian blur. You can increase this value to get a softer picture, but you must only use an odd and positive number. Finally, we convert the `Mat` to `QImage` and return a deep copy to the caller.

Designing the UI with FilterWidget

Fine. Our filter classes are implemented, and we can now create our custom widget. This widget will take as inputs: a source picture and a thumbnail picture. Then the thumbnail will be immediately processed to display a preview of the filter. If the user clicks on the widget, it will process the source picture and trigger a signal with the filtered picture. Keep in mind that this widget will later be dragged and dropped in the **Form Editor** of Qt Creator. That's why we will provide properties with getters and setters to select a filter from Qt Creator. Let's create a new widget called `FilterWidget` using the **Qt Designer Form Class** template. The `FilterWidget.ui` is really simple, as you can see in the following screenshot:

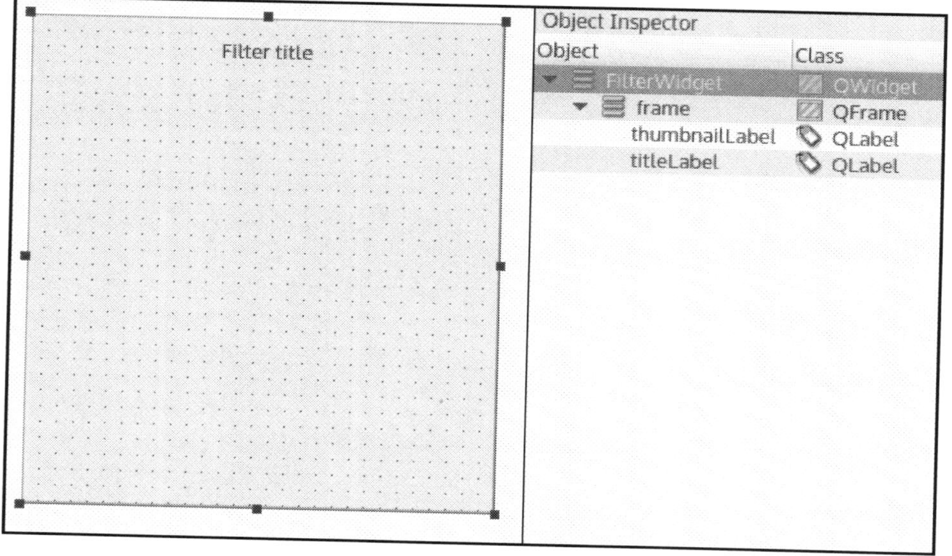

The `titleLabel` is a `QLabel` on top of the `QWidget`. In the following code, `thumbnailLabel` will display the filtered picture thumbnail. Let's switch to `FilterWidget.h`:

```
class FILTERPLUGINDESIGNERSHARED_EXPORT FilterWidget : public QWidget
{
    Q_OBJECT
public:
    enum FilterType { Original, Blur, Grayscale };
    Q_ENUM(FilterType)
    Q_PROPERTY(QString title READ title WRITE setTitle)
    Q_PROPERTY(FilterType filterType READ filterType WRITE setFilterType)

    explicit FilterWidget(QWidget *parent = 0);
    ~FilterWidget();
    void process();
    void setSourcePicture(const QImage& sourcePicture);
    void updateThumbnail(const QImage& sourceThumbnail);
    QString title() const;
    FilterType filterType() const;
public slots:
    void setTitle(const QString& tile);
    void setFilterType(FilterType filterType);
signals:
    void pictureProcessed(const QImage& picture);
protected:
    void mousePressEvent(QMouseEvent*) override;
private:
    Ui::FilterWidget *ui;
    std::unique_ptr<Filter> mFilter;
    FilterType mFilterType;
    QImage mDefaultSourcePicture;
    QImage mSourcePicture;
    QImage mSourceThumbnail;
    QImage mFilteredPicture;
    QImage mFilteredThumbnail;
};
```

The top part defines all the available filter types with the `enumFilterType`. We also use the Qt property system to expose the widget title and the current filter type in the **Property Editor** of Qt Creator. The syntax is shown in the following code:

```
Q_PROPERTY(<type> <name> READ <getter> WRITE <setter>)
```

Note that exposing an enumeration requires it to be registered using the `Q_ENUM()` macro, so the **Property Editor** will display a combo box that allows you to choose the filter type from Qt Creator. The `Q_ENUM()` macro must be placed after the `enum` definition.

The middle part lists all functions, slots, and signals. The most notable phrase is the `process()` function that will use the current filter to modify the source picture. The `pictureProcessed()` signal will notify the application with the filtered picture.

The bottom part lists the picture and thumbnail `QImage` variables used in this class. In both cases, we handle both the source and filtered pictures. The default source picture is an embedded picture in the plugin. This allows you to display a default preview when no thumbnail has been provided. The `mFilter` variable is a smart pointer to the current `Filter` class.

Let's switch to the implementation with `FilterWidget.cpp`:

```
FilterWidget::FilterWidget(QWidget *parent) :
    QWidget(parent),
    ui(new Ui::FilterWidget),
    mFilterType(Original),
    mDefaultSourcePicture(":/lenna.jpg"),
    mSourcePicture(),
    mSourceThumbnail(mDefaultSourcePicture.scaled(QSize(256, 256),
                     Qt::KeepAspectRatio,
                     Qt::SmoothTransformation)),
    mFilteredPicture(),
    mFilteredThumbnail()
{
    ui->setupUi(this);
    setFilterType(Original);
}
FilterWidget::~FilterWidget()
{
    delete ui;
}
```

The preceding code shows the constructor and the destructor. Note that the default source picture loads an embedded picture of the gorgeous Lenna often used in image-processing literature.

The picture is in the resource file called `filter-plugin-designer.qrc`. The `mSourceThumbnail` function is initialized with a scaled picture of Lenna. The constructor calls the `setFilterType()` function to initialize an `Original` filter by default. The following code shows the core `process()` function:

```
void FilterWidget::process()
{
    mFilteredPicture = mFilter->process(mSourcePicture);
    emitpictureProcessed(mFilteredPicture);
}
```

The `process()` function is powerful and really simple. We call the `process()` function of the current filter to update our filtered picture from the current source picture. Then we trigger the `pictureProcessed()` signal with the filtered picture. We can now add our `QImage` setters:

```
void FilterWidget::setSourcePicture(const QImage& sourcePicture)
{
    mSourcePicture = sourcePicture;
}

void FilterWidget::updateThumbnail(const QImage& sourceThumbnail)
{
    mSourceThumbnail = sourceThumbnail;
    mFilteredThumbnail = mFilter->process(mSourceThumbnail);
    QPixmappixmap = QPixmap::fromImage(mFilteredThumbnail);
    ui->thumbnailLabel->setPixmap(pixmap);
}
```

The `setSourcePicture()` function is a simple setter called by the application with a new source picture. The `updateThumbnail()` method will filter the new source thumbnail and display it. Let's add the setters used by `Q_PROPERTY`:

```
void FilterWidget::setTitle(const QString& tile)
{
    ui->titleLabel->setText(tile);
}
void FilterWidget::setFilterType(FilterWidget::FilterType filterType)
{
    if (filterType == mFilterType&&mFilter) {
        return;
    }
    mFilterType = filterType;

    switch (filterType) {
        case Original:
```

```
            mFilter = make_unique<FilterOriginal>();
            break;

        case Blur:
            mFilter = make_unique<FilterBlur>();
            break;

        case Grayscale:
            mFilter = make_unique<FilterGrayscale>();
            break;

        default:
            break;
    }

    updateThumbnail(mSourceThumbnail);
}
```

The `setTitle()` function is a simple setter that is used to customize the widget title. Let's look at the `setFilterType()` function. As you can see, this function does not just update the current filter type, `mFilterType`. Depending on the type, the corresponding filter will be created. Do you remember the smart pointer from `Chapter 3`, *Dividing Your Project and Ruling Your Code*? Here, we are using a `unique_ptr` pointer for the `mFilter` variable, so we can use `make_unique` instead of a `new` raw pointer. The `FilterWidget` class takes the ownership of the `Filter` class, and we do not need to worry about the memory management. Upon the `make_unique` instruction, the old owned pointer (if there is any) will be automatically deleted.

Finally, we call the `updateThumbnail()` function to display a filtered thumbnail corresponding to the selected filter type. The following code shows the getters and the mouse event handler:

```
QString FilterWidget::title() const
{
    returnui->titleLabel->text();
}

FilterWidget::FilterType FilterWidget::filterType() const
{
    returnmFilterType;
}

void FilterWidget::mousePressEvent(QMouseEvent*)
{
    process();
}
```

```
class FilterWidget;

class MainWindow : public QMainWindow
{
    Q_OBJECT

public:
    explicit MainWindow(QWidget *parent = 0);
    ~MainWindow();

    void loadPicture();

private slots:
    void displayPicture(const QImage& picture);

private:
    void initFilters();
    void updatePicturePixmap();

private:
    Ui::MainWindow *ui;
    QImage mFilteredPicture;
    QPixmap mCurrentPixmap;
    FilterWidget* mCurrentFilter;
    QVector<FilterWidget*> mFilters;
};
```

Let's look at the following elements in more detail:

- `mFilteredPicture`: Resulting image of the current filter.
- `mCurrentPixmap`: The current `QPixmap` in the `pictureLabel` widget.
- `mCurrentFilter`: The current applied filter. Each time the user clicks on a different `FilterWidget`, this pointer will be updated.
- `mFilters`: A `QVector` of the `FilterWidget` class that we added to `MainWindow.ui`. It is only a helper, introduced to easily apply the same instructions to each `FilterWidget` class.

Now for the functions. We will limit ourselves to a broad overview. The details will be covered when we look at the implementation of each function:

- `loadPicture()`: This function triggers the whole pipeline. It will be called when the user clicks on `actionOpenPicture`.
- `initFilters()`: This function is in charge of initializing `mFilters`.
- `displayPicture()`: This function is the slot called by `mCurrentWidget::pictureProcessed()` to display the filtered picture.
- `updatePicturePixmap()`: This function handles the display of `mCurrentPixmap` inside `pictureLabel`.

Let's look at the `MainWindow` class's constructor implementation in `MainWindow.cpp`:

```
#include <QFileDialog>
#include <QPixmap>
#include <QDir>

#include "FilterWidget.h"

MainWindow::MainWindow(QWidget *parent) :
    QMainWindow(parent),
    ui(new Ui::MainWindow),
    mFilteredPicture(),
    mCurrentPixmap(),
    mCurrentFilter(nullptr),
    mFilters()
{
    ui->setupUi(this);
    ui->pictureLabel->setMinimumSize(1, 1);

    connect(ui->actionOpenPicture, &QAction::triggered,
            this, &MainWindow::loadPicture);
    connect(ui->actionExit, &QAction::triggered,
            this, &QMainWindow::close);
    initFilters();
}
```

We connect the `actionOpenPicture::triggered()` signal to our yet-to-be-implemented `loadPicture()` function. The `actionExit` is straightforward: it is simply connected to the `QMainWindow::close()` slot. Finally, `initFilter()` is called. The following code shows its body:

```
void MainWindow::initFilters()
{
    mFilters.append(ui->filterWidgetOriginal);
```

```
    mFilters.append(ui->filterWidgetBlur);
    mFilters.append(ui->filterWidgetGrayscale);

    for (inti = 0; i<mFilters.size(); ++i) {
        connect(mFilters[i], &FilterWidget::pictureProcessed,
                this, &MainWindow::displayPicture);
    }
    mCurrentFilter = mFilters[0];
}
```

Each `FilterWidget` instance is added to `mFilters`. We then proceed to connect the `pictureProcessed()` signal to the `MainWindow::displayPicture` instruction and `mCurrentFilter` is initialized to the original filter.

The class is now ready to load some pictures! The following is the implementation of `loadPicture()`:

```
void MainWindow::loadPicture()
{
    QString filename = QFileDialog::getOpenFileName(this,
                        "Open Picture",
                        QDir::homePath(),
                        tr("Images (*.png *.jpg)"));
    if (filename.isEmpty()) {
        return;
    }
    QImage sourcePicture = QImage(filename);
    QImage sourceThumbnail = sourcePicture.scaled(QSize(256, 256),
                        Qt::KeepAspectRatio,
                        Qt::SmoothTransformation);
    for (inti = 0; i<mFilters.size(); ++i) {
        mFilters[i]->setSourcePicture(sourcePicture);
        mFilters[i]->updateThumbnail(sourceThumbnail);
    }

    mCurrentFilter->process();
}
```

The `sourcePicture` image is loaded using a `QFileDialog`, and `sourceThumbnail` is generated from this input. Every `FilterWidget` class is updated with this new data, and the `mCurrentFilter` element is triggered by calling its `process()` function.

When `FilterWidget::process()` is finished, it emits the `pictureProcessed()` signal, which is connected to our `displayPicture()` slot. Let's switch to this function:

```
void MainWindow::displayPicture(const QImage& picture)
{
    mCurrentPixmap = QPixmap::fromImage(picture);
    updatePicturePixmap();
}
```

Nothing very fancy here: `mCurrentPixmap` is updated from the given picture and the `updatePicturePixmap()` function is in charge of updating the `pictureLabel` element. The following is the implementation of `updatePicturePixmap()`:

```
void MainWindow::updatePicturePixmap()
{
    if (mCurrentPixmap.isNull()) {
        return;
    }
    ui->pictureLabel->setPixmap(
                mCurrentPixmap.scaled(ui->pictureLabel->size(),
                Qt::KeepAspectRatio,
                Qt::SmoothTransformation));
}
```

This function simply creates a scaled version of `mCurrentPixmap` that fits inside `pictureLabel`.

All of the picture loading/filter processing is completed. If you run the application, you should be able to load and modify your pictures. However, if you resize the window, you will see that the `pictureLabel` element does not scale very well.

To address this issue, we have to regenerate the scaled version of `mCurrentPixmap` each time the window is resized. Update `MainWindow` like so:

```
// In MainWindow.h
class MainWindow : public QMainWindow
{
    ...
    void loadPicture();

protected:
    void resizeEvent(QResizeEvent* event) override;
    ...
};

// In MainWindow.cpp
void MainWindow::resizeEvent(QResizeEvent* /*event*/)
```

```
{
    updatePicturePixmap();
}
```

Here, the separation of `mCurrentPixmap` and the `pictureLabel` element's pixmap makes sense. Because we always generate the scaled version from the full-resolution `mCurrentPixmap`, we are sure that the resulting pixmap will look good.

The image-filtering application would not be complete without the ability to save your filtered picture. This will not take much effort. The following is the updated version of `MainWindow.h`:

```
class MainWindow : public QMainWindow
{
    ...

private slots:
    void displayPicture(const QImage& picture);
    void saveAsPicture();
    ...

private:
    Ui::MainWindow *ui;
    QImage mFilteredPicture;
    ...
};
```

Here, we simply added a `saveAsPicture()` function that will take the `mFilteredPicture` image and save it to a file. The implementation in `MainWindow.cpp` should not blow your mind:

```
// In MainWindow.cpp
MainWindow::MainWindow(QWidget *parent) :
    QMainWindow(parent),
    ui(new Ui::MainWindow),
    mFilteredPicture(),
    mCurrentPixmap(),
    mCurrentFilter(nullptr),
    mFilters()
{
    ui->setupUi(this);
    ui->actionSaveAs->setEnabled(false);
    ui->pictureLabel->setMinimumSize(1, 1);

    connect(ui->actionOpenPicture, &QAction::triggered,
            this, &MainWindow::loadPicture);
    connect(ui->actionSaveAs, &QAction::triggered,
```

```
                this, &MainWindow::saveAsPicture);
    ...
}

void MainWindow::loadPicture()
{
    ...
    if (filename.isEmpty()) {
        return;
    }
    ui->actionSaveAs->setEnabled(true);
    ...
}

void MainWindow::displayPicture(const QImage& picture)
{
    mFilteredPicture = picture;
    mCurrentPixmap = QPixmap::fromImage(picture);
    updatePicturePixmap();
}

void MainWindow::saveAsPicture()
{
    QString filename = QFileDialog::getSaveFileName(this,
            "Save Picture",
            QDir::homePath(),
            tr("Images (*.png *.jpg)"));
    if (filename.isEmpty()) {
        return;
    }
    mFilteredPicture.save(filename);
}
```

The code snippet is long, but not very complex. The `actionSaveAs` function is enabled only when a picture is loaded. When the picture has been processed, `mFilteredPicture` is updated with the given picture.

Finally, the `saveAsPicture()` function asks the user for a path and saves it using the `QImage` API, which tries to deduce the picture type based on the file extension.

Summary

In this chapter, you learned how to integrate a third-party library with each desktop OS (Windows, Linux, and Mac OS). We chose the OpenCV library, which has been included in a custom Qt Designer plugin and which can display a live preview of your image processing result in Qt Designer. We created an image-filtering application that can open pictures, apply filters to them, and save the result on your machine.

We had a good look at how you can integrate third-party libraries and how you can make a Qt Designer plugin. In the next chapter, we will push things forward by making the `image-filter` application ready to load filter plugins that could be implemented by third-party developers. To make things even cooler, we will cover the Qt animation framework to make the `image-filter` more spectacular.

8
Animations - Its Alive, Alive!

In the previous chapter, you learned how to create a custom Qt Designer plugin. This chapter will push things further and teach you how to create a distributable **software development kit (SDK)** to third-party developers, how the plugin system works with Qt, and how to make your application more attractive using fancy animations.

The example project will be a reimplementation of the project from `Chapter 7`, *Third-Party Libraries Without a Headache*. You will build the same image-processing application, but with the ability to import the filters from plugins.

This chapter will cover the following topics:

- Creating an SDK using the Qt Plugin system
- Creating your plugins
- Loading your plugins dynamically
- Discovering the Animation Framework

Creating an SDK using the Qt Plugin system

Before diving into the code, we have to take a moment to decide how we are going to structure it. This chapter has two goals:

- Cover the Qt Plugin system in more depth
- Study and integrate the Qt Animation Framework

The first part of the chapter will focus on the plugin system. We aim to provide a way to build plugins that can be integrated in our application by third-party developers. These plugins should be dynamically loaded. The application will be a direct offspring of the example project from `Chapter 7`, *Third-Party Libraries Without a Headache*. The features will be exactly the same, except it will be using this new plugin system and will have fancy animations.

The structure of the project will be as follows:

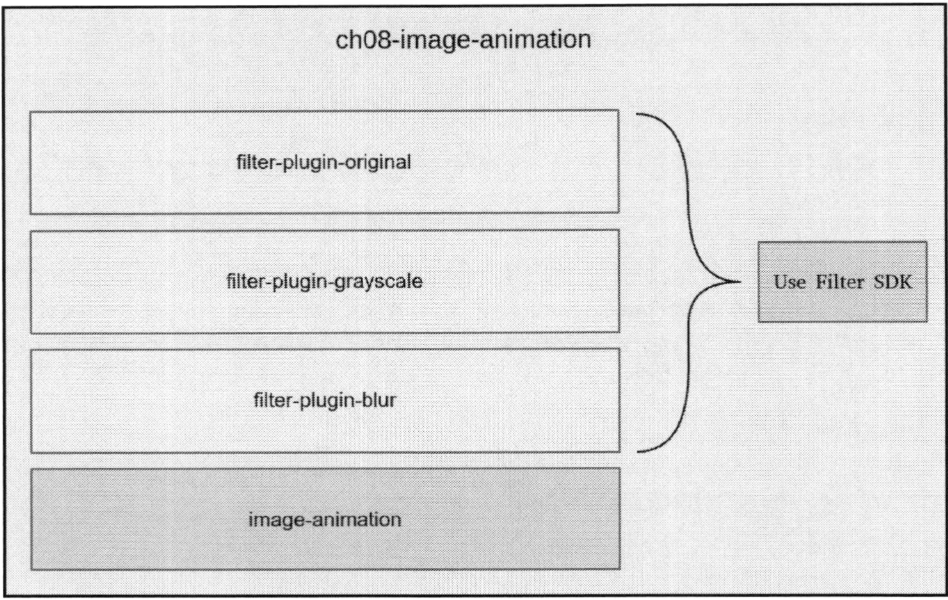

The parent project is `ch08-image-animation`, which is composed of the following:

- `filter-plugin-original`: A first library project, which is the implementation of the original filter
- `filter-plugin-grayscale`: A second library project, which is the implementation of the grayscale filter
- `filter-plugin-blur`: A third library project, which is the implementation of the blur filter
- `image-animation`: A Qt Widgets application, which will load the plugins needed to display them and make it possible to apply each one to a loaded picture

We will develop each one of these plugins, but keep in mind that they might have been created by a third-party developer. To achieve this openness, an SDK will be available for each plugin. This SDK relies on the Qt Plugin system.

It is crucial to think about what should be handled by the plugin. Our application is an image-processing piece of software. We chose to limit the responsibility of the plugin to the picture-processing part, but this is definitely a design choice.

Another approach could have been to let the plugin developer provide its own UI to configure the plugin (for example, to vary the intensity of the blur). In this chapter, we have kept it simple by focusing only on the plugin development itself. It is really up to you and how you want to design your application. By opening up the range of what the plugin can do, you also increase the burden for the plugin developer. There is always a trade-off; giving more choice tends to increase the complexity. It is a well-known fact that we developers are a bunch of lazy people. At least, we want to be lazy while the computer is working for us.

We will start by building the SDK that will be deployed in each plugin. Execute the following steps:

1. Create a **Subdirs project** named `ch08-image-animation` (do not add a subproject at the end of the wizard)
2. In your filesystem explorer, open the `ch08-image-animation` directory and create an `sdk` directory
3. Inside `sdk`, create an empty `Filter.h` file

Our SDK will consist of a single file, `Filter.h`, which is the interface (or header) that should be implemented with each plugin. Each plugin is responsible for returning the modified picture according to its desired features. Because this SDK is not linked to any particular project, we will simply display it in Qt Creator under the **Other files** special folder. To do so, update `ch08-image-animation.pro`:

```
TEMPLATE = subdirs

CONFIG += c++14

OTHER_FILES += \
            sdk/Filter.h
```

After `ch08-image-animation.pro` has been parsed by Qt Creator, you should see the following in the **Projects** tab:

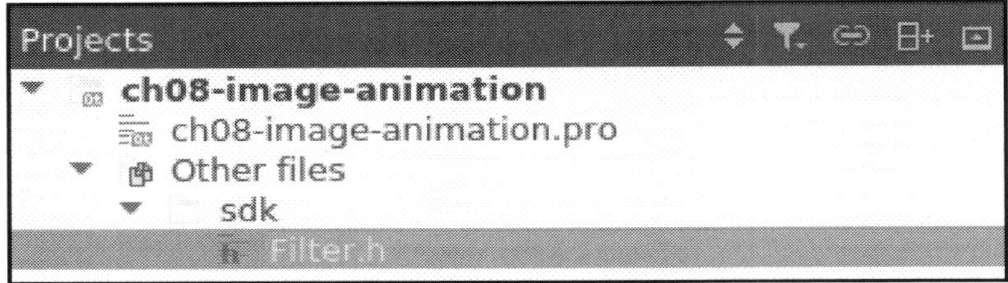

The `Filter.h` file is available at the parent-project level. As a result, it will be easier to factorize the SDK plumbing code between our various plugins. Let's implement `Filter.h`:

```
#include <QImage>

class Filter
{
public:
    virtual ~Filter() {}
    virtual QString name() const = 0;
    virtual QImage process(const QImage& image) = 0;
};

#define Filter_iid "org.masteringqt.imageanimation.filters.Filter"
Q_DECLARE_INTERFACE(Filter, Filter_iid)
```

Let's break down this interface: a `Filter` subclass must provide a name by implementing `name()` and returning a processed image when implementing `process()`. As you can see, `Filter.h` is indeed very close to the version seen in `Chapter 7`, *Third-Party Libraries Without a Headache*.

However, the really new stuff comes right after the class definition:

```
#define Filter_iid "org.masteringqt.imageanimation.filters.Filter"
Q_DECLARE_INTERFACE(Filter, Filter_iid)
```

`Filter_iid` is a unique identifier to let Qt know the interface name. This will be enforced on the implementer side, which will also have to state this identifier.

For a real-world use case, you should add a version number to this unique identifier. This will let you properly handle the versioning of your SDK and the attached plugins.

The `Q_DECLARE_INTERFACE` macro associates the class to the given identifier. It will give Qt the ability to check that the loaded plugin can be safely casted to the `Filter` type.

In production code, it is safer to declare your interfaces inside a namespace. You never know the code environment in which your SDK will be deployed. This way, you avoid potential name collision. If you do declare in a namespace, make sure that the `Q_DECLARE_INTERFACE` macro is outside the namespace scope.

Creating your plugins

The SDK was painless to create. We can now create our first plugin. We already know that all our plugins will include the SDK we just completed. Fortunately, this can be easily factorized in a `.pri` file (`Project Include`). A `.pri` file behaves exactly like a `.pro` file; the only difference is that it is intended to be included inside `.pro` files.

In the `ch08-image-animation` directory, create a file, named `plugins-common.pri`, that contains the following code:

```
INCLUDEPATH += $$PWD/sdk
DEPENDPATH += $$PWD/sdk
```

This file will be included in each `.pro` plugin. It aims to tell the compiler where it can find the headers of the SDK and where to look to resolve dependencies between headers and sources. This will enhance the modification detection and properly compile the sources when needed.

To see this file in the project, we have to add it to the `OTHER_FILES` macro in `ch08-image-animation.pro`:

```
OTHER_FILES += \
            sdk/Filter.h \
            plugins-common.pri
```

The most straightforward plugin to build is `filter-plugin-original` as it does not perform any specific processing on the image. Let's create this plugin with the following steps:

1. Create a new **Subproject** in `ch08-image-animation`
2. Select **Library** | **C++ Library** | **Choose...**
3. Choose a **Shared Library**, name it `filter-plugin-original`, and then click on **Next**

4. Select **QtCore** and **QtWidgets**, and click on **Next**
5. Name the created class `FilterOriginal` and click on **Next**
6. Add it as a **subproject** to `ch08-image-animation` then click on **Finish**

Qt Creator creates a lot of boilerplate code for us, but in this case, we do not need it. Update `filter-plugin-original.pro` like so:

```
QT       += core widgets

TARGET = $$qtLibraryTarget(filter-plugin-original)
TEMPLATE = lib
CONFIG += plugin

SOURCES += \
    FilterOriginal.cpp

HEADERS += \
    FilterOriginal.h

include(../plugins-common.pri)
```

We start by specifying that `TARGET` should be properly named according to the OS convention with `$$qtLibraryTarget()`. The `TEMPLATE` property adds the `lib` directive, which tells the generated `Makefile` to include the necessary instructions to compile dll/so/dylib (pick your OS).

We removed the unnecessary `DEFINES` and `FilterOriginal_global.h`. Nothing specific to the plugin should be exposed to the caller, and therefore, there is no need to handle the symbol export.

We can now proceed to `FilterOriginal.h`:

```
#include <QObject>

#include <Filter.h>

class FilterOriginal : public QObject, Filter
{
    Q_OBJECT
    Q_PLUGIN_METADATA(IID "org.masteringqt.imageanimation.filters.Filter")
    Q_INTERFACES(Filter)

public:
    FilterOriginal(QObject* parent = 0);
    ~FilterOriginal();
```

```
    QString name() const override;
    QImage process(const QImage& image) override;
};
```

The `FilterOriginal` class must first inherit `QObject`. When the plugin is loaded, it will be at first available through a `QObject*` pointer, then we will be able cast it to the `Filter*` type.

The `Q_PLUGIN_METADATA` macro is stated to export the proper implemented interface identifier to Qt. It annotates the class to let the Qt metasystem know about it. We meet the unique identifier we defined in `Filter.h` again.

The `Q_INTERFACES` macro tells the Qt metaobject system which interface the class implements.

Finally, `FilterOriginal.cpp` barely deserves to be printed:

```
FilterOriginal::FilterOriginal(QObject* parent) :
    QObject(parent)
{
}

FilterOriginal::~FilterOriginal()
{
}

QString FilterOriginal::name() const
{
    return "Original";
}

QImage FilterOriginal::process(const QImage& image)
{
    return image;
}
```

As you can see, its implementation is a no-op. The only thing we added to the version from `Chapter 7`, *Third-Party Libraries Without a Headache,* is the `name()` function, which returns `Original`.

We will now implement the grayscale filter. As we did in `Chapter 7`, *Third-Party Libraries Without a Headache,* we will rely on the OpenCV library to process the picture. The same can be said for the following plugin, the blur.

Since these two projects have their own `.pro` file, you can already foresee that the OpenCV linking will be the same. This is a perfect use-case for a `.pri` file.

Inside the `ch08-image-animation` directory, create a new file called `plugins-common-opencv.pri`. Do not forget to add it to `OTHER_FILES` in `ch08-image-animation.pro`:

```
OTHER_FILES += \
            sdk/Filter.h \
            plugins-common.pri \
            plugins-common-opencv.pri
```

Here is the content of `plugins-common-opencv.pri`:

```
windows {
    INCLUDEPATH += $$(OPENCV_HOME)/../../include
    LIBS += -L$$(OPENCV_HOME)/lib \
        -lopencv_core320 \
        -lopencv_imgproc320
}

linux {
    CONFIG += link_pkgconfig
    PKGCONFIG += opencv
}

macx {
    INCLUDEPATH += /usr/local/Cellar/opencv/3.2.0/include/

    LIBS += -L/usr/local/lib \
        -lopencv_core \
        -lopencv_imgproc
}
```

The content of `plugins-common-opencv.pri` is a direct copy of what we made in `Chapter 7`, *Third-Party Libraries Without a Headache*.

All the plumbing is now ready; we can now go ahead with the `filter-plugin-grayscale` project. As with `filter-plugin-original`, we will build it in the following way:

1. Create a **C++ Library Subproject** of `ch08-image-animation` with the **Shared Library** type
2. In the **Required Modules**, select **QtCore** and **QWidgets**
3. Create a class named `FilterGrayscale`

Here is the updated version of `filter-plugin-grayscale.pro`:

```
QT       += core widgets

TARGET = $$qtLibraryTarget(filter-plugin-grayscale)
TEMPLATE = lib
CONFIG += plugin

SOURCES += \
    FilterGrayscale.cpp

HEADERS += \
    FilterGrayscale.h

include(../plugins-common.pri)
include(../plugins-common-opencv.pri)
```

The content is very much like `filter-plugin-original.pro`. We only added `plugins-common-opencv.pri` to let our plugin link with OpenCV.

As for `FilterGrayscale`, the header is exactly like `FilterOriginal.h`. Here are the relevant pieces on `FilterGrayscale.cpp`:

```
#include <opencv/cv.h>

// Constructor & Destructor here
...

QString FilterGrayscale::name() const
{
    return "Grayscale";
}

QImage FilterGrayscale::process(const QImage& image)
{
    // QImage => cv::mat
    cv::Mat tmp(image.height(),
                image.width(),
                CV_8UC4,
                (uchar*)image.bits(),
                image.bytesPerLine());

    cv::Mat resultMat;
    cv::cvtColor(tmp, resultMat, CV_BGR2GRAY);

    // cv::mat => QImage
    QImage resultImage((const uchar *) resultMat.data,
                        resultMat.cols,
```

```
                                resultMat.rows,
                                resultMat.step,
                                QImage::Format_Grayscale8);
        return resultImage.copy();
    }
```

The inclusion of `plugins-common-opencv.pri` lets us properly include the `cv.h` header.

The last filter we will implement is the blur plugin. Once again, create a **C++ Library Subproject** and create the `FilterBlur` class. The project structure and the content of the `.pro` file are almost the same. You only need to adapt the `TARGET` and source code file names.

Here is `FilterBlur.cpp`:

```
    QString FilterBlur::name() const
    {
        return "Blur";
    }

    QImage FilterBlur::process(const QImage& image)
    {
        // QImage => cv::mat
        cv::Mat tmp(image.height(),
                    image.width(),
                    CV_8UC4,
                    (uchar*)image.bits(),
                    image.bytesPerLine());

        int blur = 17;
        cv::Mat resultMat;
        cv::GaussianBlur(tmp,
                         resultMat,
                         cv::Size(blur, blur),
                         0.0,
                         0.0);

        // cv::mat => QImage
        QImage resultImage((const uchar *) resultMat.data,
                           resultMat.cols,
                           resultMat.rows,
                           resultMat.step,
                           QImage::Format_RGB32);
        return resultImage.copy();
    }
```

The amount of blur is hardcoded at `17`. In a production application, it could have been compelling to make this amount settable from the application.

If you want to push the project further, try to include an API in the SDK that contains a way to configure the plugin properties.

Loading your plugins dynamically

We will now deal with the application that loads these plugins:

1. Create a new **Subproject** inside `ch08-image-animation`
2. Select the **Qt Widgets Application** type
3. Name it `image-animation` and accept the default **Class Information settings**

We have a few last things to do in the `.pro` files. First, `image-animation` will try to load the plugins from somewhere in its output directory. Because each filter-plugin project is independent, its output directory is separated from `image-animation`. Thus, each time you modify a plugin, you will have to copy the compiled shared library inside the proper `image-animation` directory. This works to make it available to the `image-animation` application, but we are lazy developers, right?

We can automate this by updating `plugins-common-pri`, like so:

```
INCLUDEPATH += $$PWD/sdk
DEPENDPATH += $$PWD/sdk

windows {
    CONFIG(debug, debug|release) {
        target_install_path = $$OUT_PWD/../image-animation/debug/plugins/
    } else {
        target_install_path = $$OUT_PWD/../image-animation/release/plugins/
    }

} else {
    target_install_path = $$OUT_PWD/../image-animation/plugins/
}

# Check Qt file 'spec_post.prf' for more information about
'$$QMAKE_MKDIR_CMD'
createPluginsDir.path = $$target_install_path
createPluginsDir.commands = $$QMAKE_MKDIR_CMD $$createPluginsDir.path
```

```
INSTALLS += createPluginsDir

target.path = $$target_install_path
INSTALLS += target
```

In a nutshell, the output library is deployed in the output `image-animation/plugins` directory. Windows has a different output project structure, which is why we have to have a platform-specific section.

Even better, the `plugins` directory is automatically created with the `createPluginsDir.commands = $$QMAKE_MKDIR_CMD $$createPluginsDir.path` instruction. Instead of using a system command (`mkdir`), we have to use the special `$$QMAKE_MKDIR_CMD` command. Qt will then replace it with the correct shell command (depending on your OS) to create the directory only if it does not already exist. Don't forget to add the `make install` build step to execute this task!

The last thing to do in the `.pro` files concerns `image-animation`. The application will manipulate `Filter` instances. As a consequence, it needs to access the SDK. Add the following to `image-animation.pro`:

```
INCLUDEPATH += $$PWD/../sdk
DEPENDPATH += $$PWD/../sdk
```

Fasten your seatbelt. We will now load our freshly baked plugins. In `image-animation`, create a new class named `FilterLoader`. Here is the `FilterLoader.h` content:

```
#include <memory>
#include <vector>

#include <Filter.h>

class FilterLoader
{

public:
    FilterLoader();
    void loadFilters();

    const std::vector<std::unique_ptr<Filter>>& filters() const;

private:
    std::vector<std::unique_ptr<Filter>> mFilters;
};
```

This class is responsible for loading the plugins. Once again, we rely on C++11 smart pointers with `unique_ptr` to explicate the ownership of the `Filter` instances. The `FilterLoader` class will be the owner with `mFilters` and provides a getter to the `vector` with `filters()`.

Note that `filter()` returns `const&` to the `vector`. This semantic brings two benefits:

- The reference makes sure that the `vector` is not copied. Without it, the compiler would have barked something such as, "`FilterLoader` is not the owner anymore of `mFilters` content!" at us. Of course, because it deals with C++ templates, the compiler error would have looked rather like an astounding insult to the English language.
- The `const` keyword makes sure that the `vector` type cannot be modified by callers.

Now we can create the `FilterLoader.cpp` file:

```
#include "FilterLoader.h"

#include <QApplication>
#include <QDir>
#include <QPluginLoader>

FilterLoader::FilterLoader() :
    mFilters()
{
}

void FilterLoader::loadFilters()
{
    QDir pluginsDir(QApplication::applicationDirPath());
#ifdef Q_OS_MAC
    pluginsDir.cdUp();
    pluginsDir.cdUp();
    pluginsDir.cdUp();
#endif
    pluginsDir.cd("plugins");

    for(QString fileName: pluginsDir.entryList(QDir::Files)) {
        QPluginLoader pluginLoader(
                    pluginsDir.absoluteFilePath(fileName));
        QObject* plugin = pluginLoader.instance();
        if (plugin) {
            mFilters.push_back(std::unique_ptr<Filter>(
                        qobject_cast<Filter*>(plugin)
            ));
```

```
            }
        }
    }

    const std::vector<std::unique_ptr<Filter>>& FilterLoader::filters() const
    {
        return mFilters;
    }
```

The meat of the class lies in `loadFilter()`. We start by moving the `plugins` directory in with `pluginsDir`, located in the output directory of `image-animation`. A special case is handled for the Mac platform: `QApplication::applicationDirPath()` returns a path inside the bundle of the generated application. One way to get out is to climb our way up three times with the `cdUp()` instruction.

For each `fileName` in this directory, we try to load a `QPluginLoader` loader. `QPluginLoader` provides access to a Qt plugin. It is the cross-platform way to load a shared library. Moreover, the `QPluginLoader` loader has the following benefits:

- It checks that the plugin is linked with the same version of Qt as the host application
- It simplifies the loading of the plugin by providing direct access to the plugin via `instance()` rather than relying on C functions

We then try to load the plugin using `pluginLoader.instance()`. This will try to load the root component of the plugin. In our case, the root component is either `FilerOriginal`, `FilterGrayscale`, or `FilterBlur`. This function always returns a `QObject*`; if the plugin could not be loaded, it returns `nullptr`. This is the reason we inherited the `QObject` class in our custom plugins.

The call to `instance()` implicitly tries to load the plugin. From here, we cast the plugin to `Filter*` using `qobject_cast()`.

The `qobject_cast()` function behaves similarly to the standard C++ `dynamic_cast()`; the difference is that it does not require **runtime type information (RTTI)**.

Last but not least, the `Filter*` casted `plugin` is wrapped inside `unique_ptr` and added to the `mFilters` vector.

Using the plugins inside the application

Now that the plugins are properly loaded, they have to be reachable from the UI of the application. To do so, we are going to take some inspiration (shameless stealing) from the `FilterWidget` class of `Chapter 7`, *Third-Party Libraries Without a Headache*.

Create a new Qt Designer **Form Class** using the **Widget** template named `FilterWidget`. The `FilterWidget.ui` file is exactly the same as the one completed in `Chapter 7`, *Third-Party Libraries Without a Headache*.

Create the `FilterWidget.h` file like this:

```
#include <QWidget>
#include <QImage>

namespace Ui {
class FilterWidget;
}

class Filter;

class FilterWidget : public QWidget
{
    Q_OBJECT

public:
    explicit FilterWidget(Filter& filter, QWidget *parent = 0);
    ~FilterWidget();

    void process();

    void setSourcePicture(const QImage& sourcePicture);
    void setSourceThumbnail(const QImage& sourceThumbnail);
    void updateThumbnail();

    QString title() const;

signals:
    void pictureProcessed(const QImage& picture);

protected:
    void mousePressEvent(QMouseEvent*) override;

private:
    Ui::FilterWidget *ui;
    Filter& mFilter;
```

```
    QImage mDefaultSourcePicture;
    QImage mSourcePicture;
    QImage mSourceThumbnail;

    QImage mFilteredPicture;
    QImage mFilteredThumbnail;
};
```

Overall, we trimmed everything concerning the Qt Designer plugin and simply passed the `mFilter` value by reference to the constructor. The `FilterWidget` class is not the owner of the `Filter` anymore; instead, it is the client that calls it. Remember that the owner of `Filter` (that is, the plugin) is `FilterLoader`.

The other modification is the new `setThumbnail()` function. It should be called in place of the old `updateThumbnail()`. The new `updateThumbnail()` now only performs the thumbnail-processing and does not touch the source thumbnail. This division is done to prepare the work for the coming animation section. The thumbnail update will be done only once the animation has been finished.

Please refer to this chapter's source code to see `FilterWidget.cpp`.

All the low layers have been completed. The next step is to fill `MainWindow`. Once again, it follows the same pattern we covered in `Chapter 7`, *Third-Party Libraries Without a Headache*. The sole difference with `MainWindow.ui` is that `filtersLayout` is empty. Obviously, the plugin is loaded dynamically, so we have nothing to put inside it at compile time.

Let's cover `MainWindow.h`:

```
#include <QMainWindow>
#include <QImage>
#include <QVector>

#include "FilterLoader.h"

namespace Ui {
class MainWindow;
}

class FilterWidget;

class MainWindow : public QMainWindow
{
    Q_OBJECT
```

```
public:
    explicit MainWindow(QWidget *parent = 0);
    ~MainWindow();

    void loadPicture();

protected:
    void resizeEvent(QResizeEvent* event) override;

private slots:
    void displayPicture(const QImage& picture);
    void saveAsPicture();

private:
    void initFilters();
    void updatePicturePixmap();

private:
    Ui::MainWindow *ui;
    QImage mSourcePicture;
    QImage mSourceThumbnail;
    QImage& mFilteredPicture;
    QPixmap mCurrentPixmap;

    FilterLoader mFilterLoader;
    FilterWidget* mCurrentFilter;
    QVector<FilterWidget*> mFilters;
};
```

The only notable thing is the addition of `mFilterLoader` as a member variable. In `MainWindow.cpp`, we will focus on the changes only:

```
void MainWindow::initFilters()
{
    mFilterLoader.loadFilters();

    auto& filters = mFilterLoader.filters();
    for(auto& filter : filters) {
        FilterWidget* filterWidget = new FilterWidget(*filter);
        ui->filtersLayout->addWidget(filterWidget);
        connect(filterWidget, &FilterWidget::pictureProcessed,
                this, &MainWindow::displayPicture);
        mFilters.append(filterWidget);
    }
```

```
        if (mFilters.length() > 0) {
            mCurrentFilter = mFilters[0];
        }
    }
```

The `initFilters()` function does not load the filters from the `ui` content. Rather, it starts by calling the `mFilterLoader.loadFilters()` function to dynamically load the plugins from the `plugins` directory.

After that, an `auto&` filter is assigned to `mFilterLoader.filters()`. Generally, it is much more readable to use the `auto` keyword. The real type is `const std::vector<std::unique_ptr<Filter>>&`, which looks more like a cryptic incantation than a simple object type.

For each of these filters, we create `FilterWidget*` and pass it the reference of `filter`. Here, `filter` is effectively `unique_ptr`. The people behind C++11 wisely modified the dereferencing operator, making it transparent to the new `FilterWidget(*filter)`. The combination of the `auto` keyword and the overload of the `->` operator, or the dereference operator, makes the use of new C++ features much more enjoyable.

Look at the *for* loop. For each `filter`, we do the following tasks:

1. Create a `FilterWidget` object
2. Add the `FilterWidget` object to the `filtersLayout` children
3. Connect the `FilterWidget::pictureProcessed` signal to the `MainWindow::displayPicture` slot
4. Add the new `FilterWidget` object to the `QVector` named `mFilters`

In the end, the first `FilterWidget` is selected.

The only other modification to `MainWindow.cpp` is the implementation of `loadPicture()`:

```
void MainWindow::loadPicture()
{
    ...
    for (int i = 0; i < mFilters.size(); ++i) {
        mFilters[i]->setSourcePicture(mSourcePicture);
        mFilters[i]->setSourceThumbnail(mSourceThumbnail);
        mFilters[i]->updateThumbnail();
    }
    mCurrentFilter->process();
}
```

The `updateThumbnail()` function has been split into two functions.

The application can now be tested. You should be able to execute it and see the dynamic plugins loaded and displaying the processed default Lenna picture.

Discovering the Animation Framework

Your application works like a charm. It's now time to look at how we can make it jump and move, or, in a word: live. The Qt Animation Framework can be used to create and start animations of Qt properties. The property value will be smoothly interpolated by an internal global timer handled by Qt. You can animate anything as long as it is a Qt property. You can even create a property for your own object using `Q_PROPERTY`. If you don't remember much about `Q_PROPERTY`, please refer to `Chapter 7`, *Third-Party Libraries Without a Headache*.

Three main classes are provided to build animations:

- `QPropertyAnimation`: Animates one Qt property animation
- `QParallelAnimationGroup`: Performs multiple animations in parallel (all the animations start together)
- `QSequentialAnimationGroup`: Performs multiple animations in sequence (the animations run one by one in a defined order)

All those classes inherit `QAbstractAnimation`. Here is a diagram from the official Qt documentation:

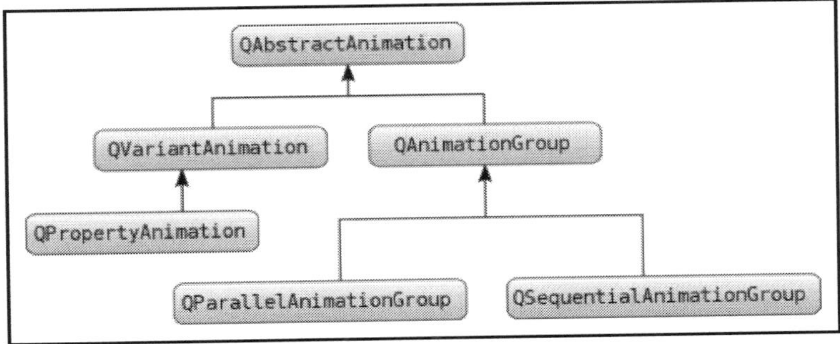

Please notice that `QAbstractAnimation`, `QVariantAnimation`, and `QAnimationGroup` are abstract classes. Here is a simple example of a Qt animation:

```
QLabel label;
QPropertyAnimation animation;

label.show();
animation.setTargetObject(&label);
animation.setPropertyName("geometry");
animation.setDuration(4000);
animation.setStartValue(QRect(0, 0, 150, 50));
animation.setEndValue(QRect(300, 200, 150, 50));
animation.start();
```

The preceding snippet moves a `QLabel` label from the (0; 0) position to (300; 200) in 4 seconds. First, let's define the target object and its property. In our case, the target object is `label` and we want to animate the property called `geometry`. Then, we set the animation duration in milliseconds: `4000` milliseconds for 4 seconds. Finally, we can decide the start and end values of the `geometry` property, which is `QRect`, defined like this:

```
QRect(x, y, width, height)
```

The `label` object starts with the (0; 0) position and ends with (300; 200). In this example, the size is fixed to 150 x 50, but you can also animate the width and the height if you want.

Finally, we call the `start()` function to begin the animation. In 4 seconds, the animation smoothly moves the label from the (0; 0) position to (300; 200). By default, the animation uses a linear interpolation to provide intermediate values, so, after two seconds, the `label` will be at the (150; 100) position. The linear interpolation of the value looks like the following schema:

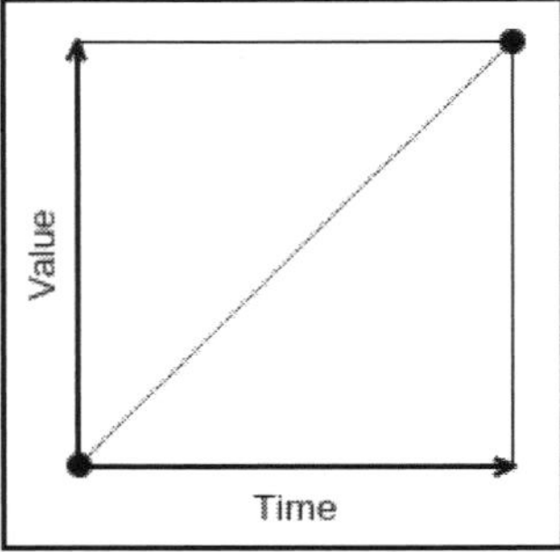

In our case, the `label` object will move with a constant speed from the start to the end position. An easing function is a mathematical function that describes the evolution of a value over time. The easing curve is the visual representation of the mathematical function. The default linear interpolation is a good start, but Qt provides plenty of easing curves to control the speed behavior of your animation. Here is the updated example:

```
QLabel label;
QPropertyAnimation animation(&label, "geometry");

label.show();
animation.setDuration(4000);
animation.setStartValue(QRect(0, 0, 150, 50));
animation.setEndValue(QRect(300, 200, 150, 50));
animation.setEasingCurve(QEasingCurve::InCirc);
animation.start();
```

You can set the target object and the property name directly using the `QPropertyAnimation` constructor. As a result, we removed the `setTargetObject()` and `setPropertyName()` functions. After that, we use `setEasingCurve()` to specify a curve for this animation. The `InCirc` looks like the following:

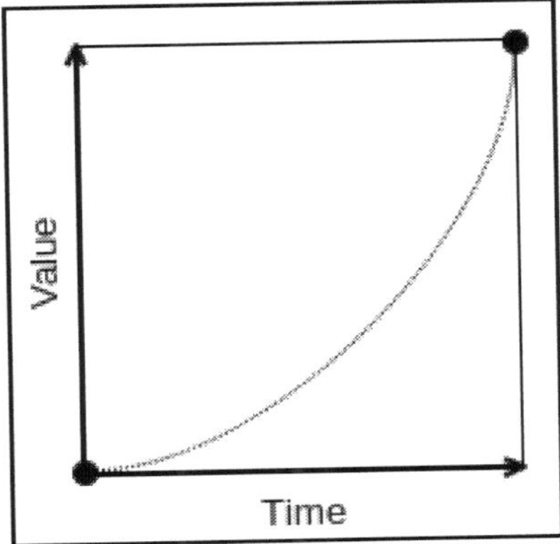

With this easing curve, the label starts to move really slowly but accelerates progressively during the animation.

Another way is to define the intermediate key steps yourself, using the `setKeyValueAt()` function. Let's update our example:

```
QLabel label;
QPropertyAnimation animation(&label, "geometry");

label.show();
```

```
animation.setDuration(4000);
animation.setKeyValueAt(0, QRect(0, 0, 150, 50));
animation.setKeyValueAt(0.25, QRect(225, 112.5, 150, 50));
animation.setKeyValueAt(1, QRect(300, 200, 150, 50));
animation.start();
```

We are now setting key frames using `setKeyValueAt()`. The first argument is the time step in the 0 to 1 range. In our case, step 1 means 4 seconds. The key frames at step 0 and step 1 provide the same positions as the start/end positions of the first example. As you can see, we also add a key frame at step 0.25 (that's one second for us) with the (225; 112.5) position. The next schema illustrates this:

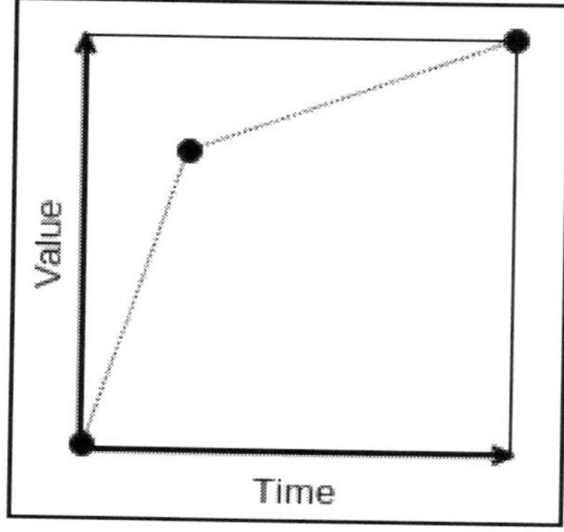

You can clearly distinguish the three key frames created with `setKeyValueAt()`. In our example, our `label` will quickly reach the (225; 112.5) position in 1 second. Then the label will slowly move to the (300; 200) position during the remaining 3 seconds.

If you have more than one `QPropertyAnimation` object, you can use groups to create more complex sequences. Let's see an example:

```
QPropertyAnimation animation1(&label1, "geometry");
QPropertyAnimation animation2(&label2, "geometry");
...
QSequentialAnimationGroup animationGroup;
animationGroup.addAnimation(&animation1);
animationGroup.addAnimation(&animation2);
animationGroup.start();
```

In this example, we are using `QSequentialAnimationGroup` to run animations one by one. First, add animations to `animationGroup`. Then, when we call `start()` on our animation group, `animation1` is `launched`. When `animation1` is finished, `animationGroup` runs `animation2`. `QSequentialAnimationGroup` is finished when the last animation of the list ends. The following schema depicts this behavior:

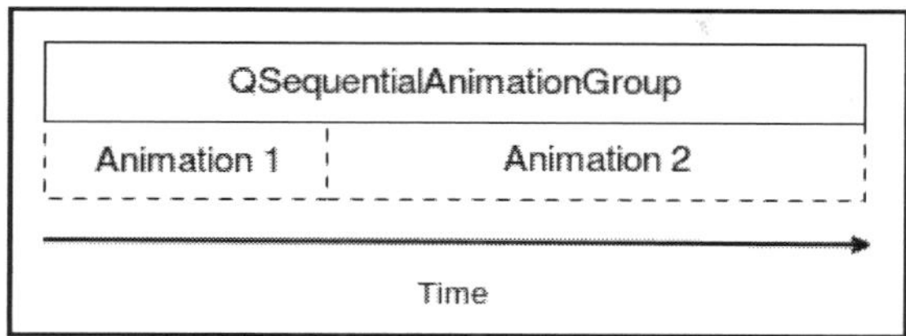

The second animation group, `QParallelAnimationGroup`, is initialized and started in the same way as `QSequentialAnimationGroup`. But the behavior is different: it starts all the animations in parallel, waiting for the longest animation to end. Here is an illustration of this:

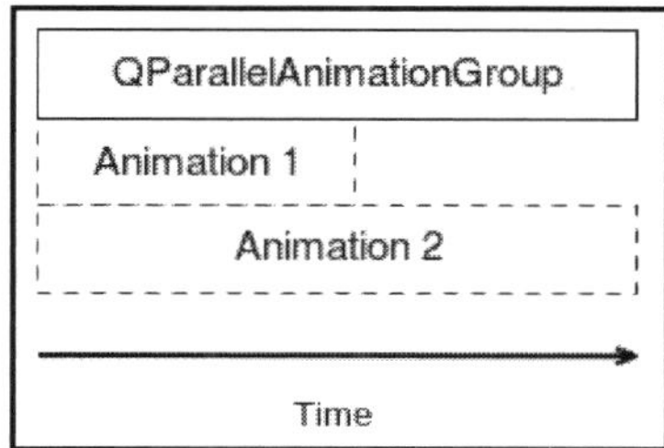

Keep in mind that an animation group is itself an animation (it inherits `QAbstractAnimation`). As a consequence, you can add animation groups to other animation groups to create a very complex animation sequence!

Making your thumbnails jump

Let's apply what we learned about the Qt Animation framework to our project. Each time the user clicks on a filter thumbnail, we want to poke it. All modifications will be done on the `FilterWidget` class. Let's start with `FilterWidget.h`:

```
#include <QPropertyAnimation>

class FilterWidget : public QWidget
```

```
{
    Q_OBJECT

public:
    explicit FilterWidget(Filter& filter, QWidget *parent = 0);
    ~FilterWidget();
    ...

private:
    void initAnimations();
    void startSelectionAnimation();
    ...
    QPropertyAnimation mSelectionAnimation;
};
```

The first function, `initAnimations()`, initializes the animations used by `FilterWidget`. The second function, `startSelectionAnimation()`, performs tasks required to start this animation correctly. As you can see, we are also using a `QPropertyAnimation` type, as covered in the previous section.

We can now update `FilterWidget.cpp`. Let's update the constructor:

```
FilterWidget::FilterWidget(Filter& filter, QWidget *parent) :
    QWidget(parent),
    ...
    mSelectionAnimation()
{
    ...
    initAnimations();
    updateThumbnail();
}
```

We initialize our `QPropertyAnimation`, called `mSelectionAnimation`. The constructor also calls `initAnimations()`. Here is its implementation:

```
void FilterWidget::initAnimations()
{
    mSelectionAnimation.setTargetObject(ui->thumbnailLabel);
    mSelectionAnimation.setPropertyName("geometry");
    mSelectionAnimation.setDuration(200);
}
```

You should be familiar with these animation initialization steps now. The target object is `thumbnailLabel`, which displays the filter-plugin preview. The property name to animate is `geometry`, because we want to update the position of this `QLabel`. Finally, we set the animation duration to 200 ms. Like jokes, keep it short and sweet.

The animation of the geometry can conflict with the automatic layout-management performed by Qt. Please be careful when you attempt to do it!

Update the existing mouse event handler like this:

```
void FilterWidget::mousePressEvent(QMouseEvent*)
{
    process();
    startSelectionAnimation();
}
```

Each time the user clicks on the thumbnail, the selection animation that moves the thumbnail will be called. We can now add this most important function, like so:

```
void FilterWidget::startSelectionAnimation()
{
    if (mSelectionAnimation.state() ==
        QAbstractAnimation::Stopped) {

        QRect currentGeometry = ui->thumbnailLabel->geometry();
        QRect targetGeometry = ui->thumbnailLabel->geometry();
        targetGeometry.setY(targetGeometry.y() - 50.0);

        mSelectionAnimation.setKeyValueAt(0, currentGeometry);
        mSelectionAnimation.setKeyValueAt(0.3, targetGeometry);
        mSelectionAnimation.setKeyValueAt(1, currentGeometry);
        mSelectionAnimation.start();
    }
}
```

First, retrieve the current geometry of `thumbnailLabel`, called `currentGeometry`. Then, we create a `targetGeometry` object with the same `x`, `width`, and `height` values. We only reduce the `y` position by 50, so the target position is always above the current position.

After that, we define our key frames:

- **At step 0**, the value is the current position.
- **At step 0.3** (60 ms, because the total duration is 200 ms), the value is the target position.
- **At step 1** (the end of the animation), we bring it to back the original position. The thumbnail will quickly reach the target position, then slowly fall down to its original position.

These key frames must be initialized before each animation starts. Because the layout is dynamic, the position (and so the geometry) could have been updated when the user resizes the main window.

Please note that we are preventing the animation from starting again if the current state is not stopped. Without this precaution, the thumbnail could move to the top again and again if the user clicks on the widget like a madman.

You can now test your application and click on a filter effect. The filter thumbnail will jump to respond to your click!

Fading in the picture

When the user opens a picture, we want to fade in the image by playing with its opacity. The `QLabel` or `QWidget` classes do not provide an opacity property. However, we can add a visual effect to any `QWidget` using `QGraphicsEffect`. For this animation, we will use `QGraphicsOpacityEffect` to provide an `opacity` property.

Here is a schema to describe the role of each one:

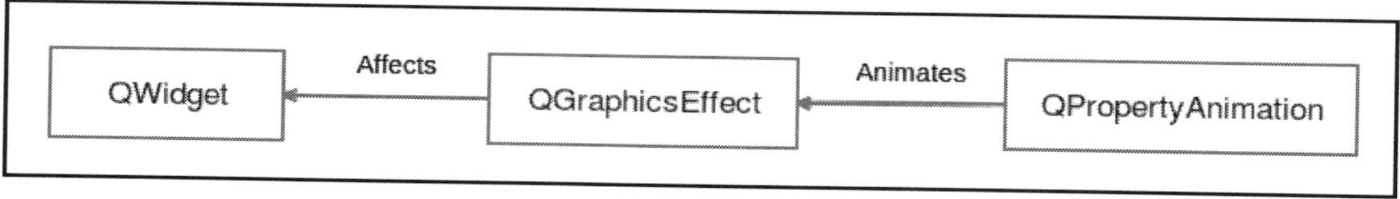

In our case, the `QWidget` class is our `QLabel` and the `QGraphicsEffect` class is `QGraphicsOpacityEffect`. Qt provides the graphics effect system to alter the rendering of a `QWidget` class. The `QGraphicsEffect` abstract class has a pure virtual method, `draw()`, that is implemented by each graphic effect.

We can now update `MainWindow.h` according to the next snippet:

```
#include <QPropertyAnimation>
#include <QGraphicsOpacityEffect>

class MainWindow : public QMainWindow
{
    ...
private:
    ...
    void initAnimations();
private:
```

```
    ...
    QPropertyAnimation mLoadPictureAnimation;
    QGraphicsOpacityEffect mPictureOpacityEffect;
};
```

The `initAnimations()` private function is in charge of all the animation initializations. The `mLoadPictureAnimation` member variable performs the fade-in animation on the loaded picture. Finally, we declare `mPictureOpacityEffect`, the mandatory `QGraphicsOpacityEffect`.

Let's switch to the implementation part with the `MainWindow.cpp` constructor:

```
MainWindow::MainWindow(QWidget *parent) :
    QMainWindow(parent),
    ...
    mLoadPictureAnimation(),
    mPictureOpacityEffect()
{
    ...
    initFilters();
    initAnimations();
}
```

No surprises here. We use the initializer list to construct our two new member variables. The `MainWindow` constructor also calls `initAnimations()`.

Let's look at how this animation is initialized:

```
void MainWindow::initAnimations()
{
    ui->pictureLabel->setGraphicsEffect(&mPictureOpacityEffect);
    mLoadPictureAnimation.setTargetObject(&mPictureOpacityEffect);
    mLoadPictureAnimation.setPropertyName("opacity");
    mLoadPictureAnimation.setDuration(500);
    mLoadPictureAnimation.setStartValue(0);
    mLoadPictureAnimation.setEndValue(1);
    mLoadPictureAnimation.setEasingCurve(QEasingCurve::InCubic);
}
```

First, let's link our `QGraphicsOpacityEffect` with our `QLabel`. This can be easily done by calling the `setGraphicsEffect()` function on `pictureLabel`.

Now we can set our animation up. In this case, `mLoadPictureAnimation` targets `mPictureOpacityEffect` and will affect its property, named `opacity`. The animation duration is `500` milliseconds. Next, we set the opacity value when the animation starts and ends:

- At the beginning, the picture is completely transparent (`opacity` value is `0`)
- At the end, the picture is fully visible (`opacity` value is `1`)

For this animation, we use the `InCubic` easing curve. This curve looks like this:

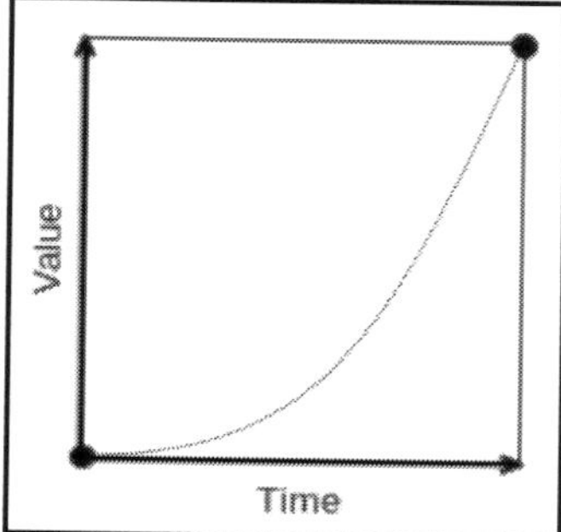

Feel free to try other curves to find the one that works the best for you.

You can get the list of all easing curves, along with a visual preview, at `http://doc.qt.io/qt-5/qeasingcurve.html`

The last step is to start the animation at the right place:

```
void MainWindow::loadPicture()
{
    ...
    mCurrentFilter->process();
    mLoadPictureAnimation.start();
}
```

You can now start your application and load a picture. You should see your picture fade in over 500 milliseconds!

Flashing the thumbnail in a sequence

For this last animation, we want to display a blue flash on each filter preview when the thumbnail is updated. We do not want to flash all previews at the same time, but in a sequence, one by one. This feature will be achieved in two parts:

- Create a color animation in `FilterWidget` to display a blue flash
- Build a sequential animation group in `MainWindow` containing all `FilterWidget` color animations

Let's start to add the color animation. Update `FilterWidget.h` as shown in the following snippet:

```
#include <QGraphicsColorizeEffect>

class FilterWidget : public QWidget
{
    Q_OBJECT

public:
    explicit FilterWidget(Filter& filter, QWidget *parent = 0);
    ~FilterWidget();
    ...
    QPropertyAnimation* colorAnimation();

private:
    ...
    QPropertyAnimation mSelectionAnimation;
    QPropertyAnimation* mColorAnimation;
    QGraphicsColorizeEffect mColorEffect;
};
```

This time, we do not want to affect the opacity, but rather colorize the thumbnail in blue. Thus, we use another Qt standard effect: `QGraphicsColorizeEffect`. We also declare a new `QPropertyAnimation`, named `mColorAnimation`, and its corresponding getter, `colorAnimation()`. We declare `mColorAnimation` as a pointer because the ownership will be taken by the animation group of `MainWindow`. This topic will be covered soon.

Let's update the constructor in `FilterWidget.cpp`:

```
FilterWidget::FilterWidget(Filter& filter, QWidget *parent) :
    QWidget(parent),
    ...
    mColorAnimation(new QPropertyAnimation()),
```

```
    mColorEffect()
{
    ...
}
```

We just have to construct our two new member variables, `mColorAnimation` and `mColorEffect`. Let's look at the amazing complexity of the getter:

```
QPropertyAnimation* FilterWidget::colorAnimation()
{
    return mColorAnimation;
}
```

It was a lie: we always try to write comprehensive code!

Now that the preliminaries are done, we can initialize the color animation by updating the `initAnimations()` function:

```
void FilterWidget::initAnimations()
{
    ...
    mColorEffect.setColor(QColor(0, 150, 150));
    mColorEffect.setStrength(0.0);
    ui->thumbnailLabel->setGraphicsEffect(&mColorEffect);

    mColorAnimation->setTargetObject(&mColorEffect);
    mColorAnimation->setPropertyName("strength");
    mColorAnimation->setDuration(200);
    mColorAnimation->setStartValue(1.0);
    mColorAnimation->setEndValue(0.0);
}
```

The first part sets the color filter up. Here, we chose a turquoise color for the flash effect. The colorize effect is handled by its `strength` property. By default, the value is `1.0`, so, we set it to `0.0` to keep it from affecting our default thumbnail of Lenna. Finally, we link `thumbnailLabel` with this `mColorEffect` by calling `setGraphicsEffect()`.

The second part is the color-animation preparation. This animation targets the color effect and its property, named `strength`. This is a short flash; `200` milliseconds is enough:

- We want to start with a full strength effect, so we put the start value at `1.0`
- During the animation, the colorize effect will decrease until it reaches `0.0`

The default linear interpolation is fine here, so we do not need to create a custom easing curve.

Here we are. The color effect/animation is initialized and we provided a `colorAnimation()` getter. We can now begin the second part of this feature, updating `MainWindow.h`:

```
#include <QSequentialAnimationGroup>

class MainWindow : public QMainWindow
{
    Q_OBJECT
    ...

private:
    ...
    QSequentialAnimationGroup mFiltersGroupAnimation;
};
```

We declare a `QSequentialAnimationGroup` class to trigger, one by one, all `FilterWidget` color animations displaying the blue flash. Let's update the constructor in `MainWindow.cpp`:

```
MainWindow::MainWindow(QWidget *parent) :
    QMainWindow(parent),
    ...
    mFiltersGroupAnimation()
{
    ...
}
```

A new member variable means a new construction in the initializer list: that is the rule!

We can now update `initAnimations()` to prepare our animation group:

```
void MainWindow::initAnimations()
{
    ...
    for (FilterWidget* filterWidget : mFilters) {
        mFiltersGroupAnimation.addAnimation(
            filterWidget->colorAnimation());
    }
}
```

Do you remember that an animation group is only an animation container? As a consequence, we iterate on every `FilterWidget` to get its color animation and fill our `mFiltersGroupAnimation` by calling `addAnimation()`. Thanks to C++11's range-based `for` loop, it is really readable. Keep in mind that when you add an animation to an animation group, the group takes ownership of this animation.

Our animation group is ready. We can now start it:

```
void MainWindow::loadPicture()
{
    ...
    mCurrentFilter->process();
    mLoadPictureAnimation.start();
    mFiltersGroupAnimation.start();
}
```

Start your application and open a picture. You can see that all filter thumbnails will flash one by one from left to right. This is what we intended, but it's still not perfect because all the thumbnails are already updated before the flashes. We have this behavior because the `loadPicture()` function actually sets and updates all thumbnails, and then finally starts the sequential animation group. Here is a schema illustrating the current behavior:

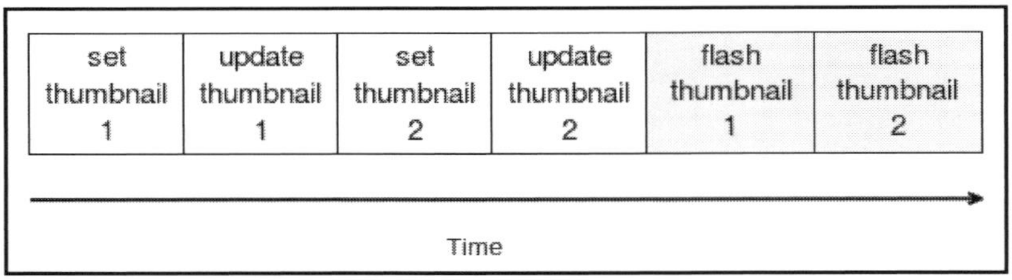

set thumbnail 1	update thumbnail 1	set thumbnail 2	update thumbnail 2	flash thumbnail 1	flash thumbnail 2

Time →

The schema only describes the behavior for two thumbnails, but the principle is the same with three thumbnails. Here is the targeted behavior:

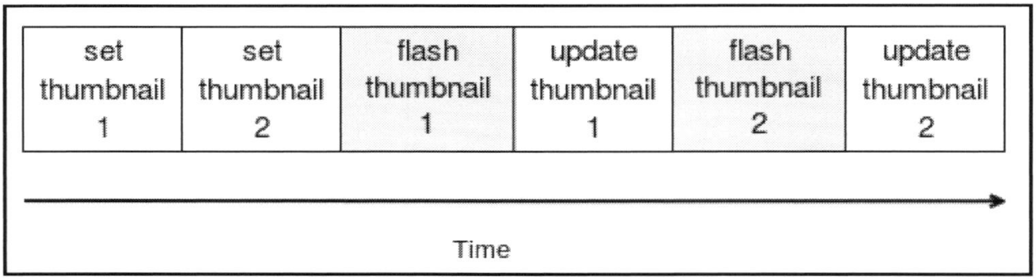

set thumbnail 1	set thumbnail 2	flash thumbnail 1	update thumbnail 1	flash thumbnail 2	update thumbnail 2

Time →

We must only update the thumbnail when the flash animation is over. Fortunately, `QPropertyAnimation` emits the `finished` signal when the animation is over, so we only have to make a few changes. Update the `loadPicture()` function from `MainWindow.cpp`:

```
void MainWindow::loadPicture()
{
    ...
    for (int i = 0; i <mFilters.size(); ++i) {
```

```
            mFilters[i]->setSourcePicture(mSourcePicture);
            mFilters[i]->setSourceThumbnail(mSourceThumbnail);
            //mFilters[i]->updateThumbnail();
        }
        ...
    }
```

As you can see, we kept the set and only removed the update thumbnail when a new picture is opened by the user. At this stage, all `FilterWidget` instances have the correct thumbnail, but they don't display it. Let's fix this by updating `FilterWidget.cpp`:

```
void FilterWidget::initAnimations()
{
    ...
    mColorAnimation->setTargetObject(&mColorEffect);
    mColorAnimation->setPropertyName("strength");
    mColorAnimation->setDuration(200);
    mColorAnimation->setStartValue(1.0);
    mColorAnimation->setEndValue(0.0);
    connect(mColorAnimation, &QPropertyAnimation::finished, [this]
    {
        updateThumbnail();
    });
}
```

We connect a `lambda` function to the finished signal of the color animation. This `lambda` simply updates the thumbnail. You can now start your application again and load a picture. You should see that we not only animate the sequential blue flash, but also the thumbnail update.

Summary

In this chapter, you learned how to define a `Filter` interface in your own SDK. Your filters are now plugins. You know how to create and load a new plugin, so your application is now modular and can be easily extended. We have also enhanced the application with the Qt Animation framework. You know how to animate the position, the color, and the opacity of any `QWidget`, using `QGraphicsEffect` if necessary. We created a sequential animation that starts three animations, one by one, with `QSequentialAnimationGroup`.

In the next chapter, we will talk about a big subject: threading. The Qt framework can help you build a robust and reliable multithreading application. To illustrate this concept, we will create a Mandelbrot fractal generator using threadpools.

9

Keeping Your Sanity with Multithreading

In previous chapters, we managed to write code without ever relying on threads. It is time to face the beast and truly understand how threading works in Qt. In this chapter, you will develop a multithreaded application that displays a Mandelbrot fractal. It is a heavy computational process that will bring tears to your CPU cores.

In the example project, the user can see the Mandelbrot fractal, zoom in on the picture, and pan around to discover the magic of fractals.

This chapter will cover the following topics:

- Discovering QThread
- Flying over Qt multithreading technologies
- Architecting the Mandelbrot project
- Defining a `Job` class with `QRunnable`
- Using `QThreadPool` in `MandelbrotCalculator`
- Displaying the fractal with `MandelbrotWidget`

Discovering QThread

Qt provides a sophisticated threading system. We assume you already know threading basics and the associated issues (deadlocks, threads synchronization, resource sharing, and so on) and we will focus on how Qt implements it.

`QThread` is the central class of the Qt threading system. A `QThread` instance manages one thread of execution within the program.

You can subclass `QThread` to override the `run()` function, which will be executed in the `QThread` framework. Here is how you can create and start `QThread*`:

```
QThread* thread = new QThread();
thread->start();
```

The `start()` function will automatically call the `run()` function of the thread and emit the `started()` signal. Only at this point will the new thread of execution be created. When `run()` is completed, the `thread` object will emit the `finished()` signal.

This brings us to a fundamental aspect of `QThread`: it works seamlessly with the signal/slot mechanism. Qt is an event-driven framework, where a main event loop (or the GUI loop) processes events (user input, graphical, and so on) to refresh the UI.

Each `QThread` comes with its own event loop that can process events outside the main loop. If not overridden, `run()` calls the `QThread::exec()` function, which starts the `thread` object's event loop. You can also override `QThread` and call yourself `exec()`, like so:

```
class Thread : public QThread
{
Q_OBJECT
protected:
    void run() override
    {
      Object* myObject = new Object();
        connect(myObject, &Object::started,
                this, &Thread::doWork);
        exec();
    }

private slots:
    void doWork();
};
```

The `started()` signal will be processed by the `Thread` event loop only upon the `exec()` call. It will block and wait until `QThread::exit()` is called.

A crucial thing to note is that a thread event loop delivers events for all `QObjects` that are living in that thread. This includes all objects created in that thread or moved to that thread. This is referred to as the thread affinity of an object. Let's see an example:

```
class Thread : public QThread
```

```
{
    Thread() :
        myObject(new QObject())
    {
    }
private :
    QObject* myObject;
};

// Somewhere in MainWindow
Thread thread;
thread.start();
```

In this snippet, `myObject` is constructed in the `Thread` class's constructor, which is created in turn in `MainWindow`. At this point, `thread` is living in the GUI thread. Hence, `myObject` is also living in the GUI thread.

An object created before a `QCoreApplication` object has no thread affinity. As a consequence, no event will be dispatched to it.

It is great to be able to handle signals and slots in our own `QThread`, but how can we control signals across multiple threads? A classic example is a long-running process that is executed in a separate thread that has to notify the UI to update some state:

```
class Thread : public QThread
{
    Q_OBJECT

public:
    Thread(QObject* parent) : QThread(parent) {}

protected:
    void run() override {
        // long running operation
        emit result("I <3 threads");
    }
signals:
    void result(QString data);
};

// Somewhere in MainWindow
Thread* thread = new Thread(this);
connect(thread, &Thread::result, this, &MainWindow::handleResult);
connect(thread, &Thread::finished, thread, &QObject::deleteLater);
thread->start();
```

Intuitively, we assume that the first `connect` sends the signal across multiple threads (to have results available in `MainWindow::handleResult`), whereas the second `connect` should work on the main thread only.

Fortunately, this is the case due to a default argument in the `connect()` function's signature: the connection type. Let's see the complete signature:

```
QObject::connect(
    const QObject *sender, const char *signal,
    const QObject *receiver, const char *method,
    Qt::ConnectionType type = Qt::AutoConnection)
```

The `type` keyword takes `Qt::AutoConnection` as a default value. Let's review the possible values of the `Qt::ConectionType` enum, as the official Qt documentation states:

- `Qt::AutoConnection`: If the receiver lives in the thread that emits the signal, `Qt::DirectConnection` is used. Otherwise, `Qt::QueuedConnection` is used. The connection type is determined when the signal is emitted.
- `Qt::DirectConnection`: This slot is invoked immediately when the signal is emitted. The slot is executed in the signaling thread.
- `Qt::QueuedConnection`: This slot is invoked when control returns to the receiver thread's event loop. The slot is executed in the receiver's thread.
- `Qt::BlockingQueuedConnection`: This is the same as `Qt::QueuedConnection`, except that the signaling thread blocks until the slot returns. This connection must not be used if the receiver lives in the signaling thread, or else the application will deadlock.
- `Qt::UniqueConnection`: This is a flag that can be combined with any one of the previous connection types, using a bitwise OR. When `Qt::UniqueConnection` is set, `QObject::connect()` will fail if the connection already exists (that is, if the same signal is already connected to the same slot for the same pair of objects).

When using `Qt::AutoConnection`, the final `ConnectionType` is resolved only when the signal is effectively emitted. If you look again at our example, it is at the first `connect()`:

```
connect(thread, &Thread::result,
        this, &MainWindow::handleResult);
```

When `result()` is emitted, Qt will look at the receiver's thread affinity, which is different from the thread that emitted the `result()` signal. The `thread` object is living in the main thread (remember that it has been created in `MainWindow`). But the `result()` signal has been emitted in the `run()` function, which is running in a different thread of execution. As a result, a `Qt::QueuedConnection` slot will be used.

We can now take a look at the second `connect()`:

```
connect(thread, &Thread::finished, thread, &QObject::deleteLater);
```

Here, `deleteLater()` belongs to an object that lives in the main thread. But the `finished()` signal is emitted from the tread. So, the connection is `Qt::QueuedConnection` in this case.

It is crucial that you understand that Qt does not care about the emitting object-thread affinity, it looks only at the signal's "context of execution."

With this knowledge, we can take another look at our first `QThread` class example to have a full understanding of this system:

```
class Thread : public QThread
{
Q_OBJECT
protected:
    void run() override
    {
        Object* myObject = new Object();
        connect(myObject, &Object::started,
                this, &Thread::doWork);
        exec();
    }

private slots:
    void doWork();
};
```

When the `Object::started()` function is emitted, a `Qt::QueuedConnection` slot will be used. This is where your brain freezes. The `Thread::doWork()` function lives in another thread than `Object::started()`, which has been created in `run()`. If thread has been instantiated in the UI thread, this is where `doWork()` would have belonged.

This system is powerful, but complex. To make things simpler, Qt favors the worker model. It splits the threading plumbing from the real processing. Here is an example:

```
class Worker : public QObject
{
    Q_OBJECT
public slots:
    void doWork()
    {
        emit resultReady("workers are the best");
    }

signals:
    void result(QString data);
};

// Somewhere in MainWindow
QThread* thread = new QThread(this);
Worker* worker = new Worker();
worker->moveToThread(thread);

connect(thread, &QThread::finished,
        worker, &QObject::deleteLater);
connect(this, &MainWindow::startWork,
        worker, &Worker::doWork);
connect(worker, &Worker::resultReady,
        this, &MainWindow::handleResult);

thread->start();

// later on, to stop the thread
thread->quit();
thread->wait();
```

We start by creating a `Worker` class that has:

- A `doWork()` slot that contains the code we want to execute in a separate thread
- A `result()` signal that will emit the resulting data

Next, in the `MainWindow` class, we create a simple `thread` object and an instance of `Worker`. `worker->moveToThread(thread)` is where the magic happens. It changes the affinity of the `worker` object. `worker` now lives in the `thread` object.

You can only push an object from your current thread to another thread. Conversely, you cannot pull an object that lives in another thread. You cannot change the thread affinity of an object if the object does not live in your thread. Once `thread->start()` is executed, we cannot call `worker->moveToThread(this)` unless we are doing it from this new thread.

After that, we do three `connect()` actions:

- We handle the `worker` life cycle by reaping it when the thread is finished. This signal will use `Qt::DirectConnection`.
- We start `Worker::doWork()` upon a possible UI event. This signal will use `Qt::QueuedConnection`.
- We process the resulting data in the UI thread with `handleResult()`. This signal will use `Qt::QueuedConnection`.

To sum up, `QThread` can be either subclassed or used in conjunction with a `worker` class. Generally, the worker approach is favored because it separates more cleanly the threading-affinity plumbing from the actual operation you want to execute in parallel.

Flying over Qt multithreading technologies

Built upon `QThread`, several threading technologies are available in Qt. First, to synchronize threads, the usual approach is to use a mutual exclusion (mutex) that will apply for a given resource. Qt provides it by means of the `QMutex` class. Its usage is straightforward:

```
QMutex mutex;
int number = 1;

mutex.lock();
number *= 2;
mutex.unlock();
```

From the `mutex.lock()` instruction, any other thread trying to lock `mutex` will wait until `mutex.unlock()` has been called.

The locking/unlocking mechanism is error-prone in complex code. You can easily forget to unlock a mutex in a specific exit condition, causing a deadlock. To simplify this situation, Qt provides `QMutexLocker`, which should be used where `QMutex` needs to be locked:

```
QMutex mutex;
QMutexLocker locker(&mutex);
```

```
int number = 1;
number *= 2;
if (overlyComplicatedCondition) {
    return;
} else if (notSoSimple) {
    return;
}
```

`mutex` is locked when the `locker` object is created and will be unlocked when the `locker` object is destroyed; for example, when it goes out of scope. This is the case for every condition we stated where the `return` statement appears. It makes the code simpler and more readable.

You may need to create and destroy threads frequently, as managing `QThread` instances by hand can become cumbersome. For this, you can use the `QThreadPool` class, which manages a pool of reusable `QThreads`.

To execute code within threads managed by a `QThreadPool` class, you will use a pattern very close to the worker we covered earlier. The main difference is that the processing class has to extend the `QRunnable` class. Here is how it looks:

```
class Job : public QRunnable
{
    void run() override
    {
        // long running operation
    }
}

Job* job = new Job();
QThreadPool::globalInstance()->start(job);
```

Just override the `run()` function and ask `QThreadPool` to execute your job in a separate thread. `QThreadPool::globalInstance()` is a static helper function that gives you access to an application's global instance. You can create your own `QThreadPool` if you need to have finer control over the `QThreadPool` life cycle.

Note that the `QThreadPool::start()` function takes the ownership of `job` and will automatically delete it when `run()` finishes. Watch out, this does not change the thread affinity like `QObject::moveToThread()` does with workers! A `QRunnable` class cannot be reused, it has to be a freshly baked instance.

If you fire up several jobs, `QThreadPool` automatically allocates the ideal number of threads based on the core count of your CPU. The maximum number of threads that the `QThreadPool` class can start can be retrieved with `QThreadPool::maxThreadCount()`.

If you need to manage threads by hand, but you want to base it on the number of cores of your CPU, you can use the handy static function, `QThread::idealThreadCount()`.

Another approach to multithreaded development is available with the Qt Concurrent framework. It is a higher-level API that avoids the use of mutexes/lock/wait conditions and promotes the distribution of processing among CPU cores.

Qt Concurrent relies on the `QFuture` class to execute a function and expects a result later on:

```
// In .pro file
QT += concurrent

// The source code
void longRunningFunction();
QFuture<void> future = QtConcurrent::run(longRunningFunction);
```

The `longRunningFunction()` function will be executed in a separated thread obtained from the default `QThreadPool` class.

To pass parameters to a `QFuture` class and retrieve the result of the operation, use the following code:

```
QImage processGrayscale(QImage& image);
QImage lenna;

QFuture<QImage> future = QtConcurrent::run(processGrayscale,
    lenna);

QImage grayscaleLenna = future.result();
```

Here we pass `lenna` as a parameter to the `processGrayscale()` function. Because we want `QImage` as a result, we declare the `QFuture` class with the `QImage` template type. After that, `future.result()` blocks the current thread and waits for the operation to be completed to return the final `QImage`.

To avoid blocking, `QFutureWatcher` comes to the rescue:

```
QFutureWatcher<QImage> watcher;
connect(&watcher, &QFutureWatcher<QImage>::finished,
        this, &QObject::handleGrayscale);

QImage processGrayscale(const QImage& image);
QImage lenna;
QFuture<QImage> future = QtConcurrent::run(processGrayscale, lenna);
watcher.setFuture(future);
```

We start by declaring a `QFutureWatcher` class with the template argument matching the one used for `QFuture`. Then simply connect the `QFutureWatcher::finished` signal to the slot you want to be called when the operation has been completed.

The last step is to tell the `watcher` object to watch the future object with `watcher.setFuture(future)`. This statement looks almost like it comes from a science-fiction movie.

Qt Concurrent also provides a `Map` (Map-Reduce) and `Filter` (Filter-Reduce) implementation. Map-Reduce is a programming model that basically does two things:

- Maps or distributes the processing of the dataset among multiple cores of the CPU
- Reduces or aggregates the results to provide it to the caller

This technique was first promoted by Google to be able to process huge datasets within a cluster of CPUs.

Here is an example of a simple map operation:

```
QList<QImage> images = ...;

void processGrayscale(const QImage& image);
QFuture<QImage> future = QtConcurrent::map(
                                    images, processGrayscale);
```

Instead of `QtConcurrent::run()`, we use the `map` function that takes a list and the function to apply to each element in multiple threads simultaneously.

The operation can be made to block by using `QtConcurrent::blockingMap()` instead of `QtConcurrent::map()`.

Finally, a Map-Reduce operation looks like this:

```
QList<QImage> images = ...;

QImage processGrayscale(const QImage& image);
void combineImage(QImage& finalImage, const QImage& inputImage);

QFuture<QImage> future = QtConcurrent::mappedReduced(
                                            images,
                                            processGrayscale,
                                            combineImage);
```

Here, we added a `combineImage()` function that will be called for each result returned by the map function, `processGrayscale()`. It will merge the intermediate data, `inputImage`, into `finalImage`. Only one thread at a time will call the reduce function. So the reduce function won't be executed concurrently and does not require a mutex.

Filter-Reduce follows exactly the same pattern; the filter function simply allows you to filter the input list instead of transforming it.

Architecting the Mandelbrot project

The example project of this chapter is the multithreaded calculation of a Mandelbrot fractal. The user will see the fractal and will be able to pan and zoom in on that window.

Before diving into the code, we need a broad understanding of a fractal and how we are going to achieve its calculation.

The Mandelbrot fractal is a numerical set that works with complex numbers (a + bi). Each pixel is associated with a value calculated through iterations. If this iterated value diverges toward infinity, then the pixel is out of the Mandelbrot set. If not, then the pixel is inside the Mandelbrot set.

A visual representation of the Mandelbrot fractal looks like this:

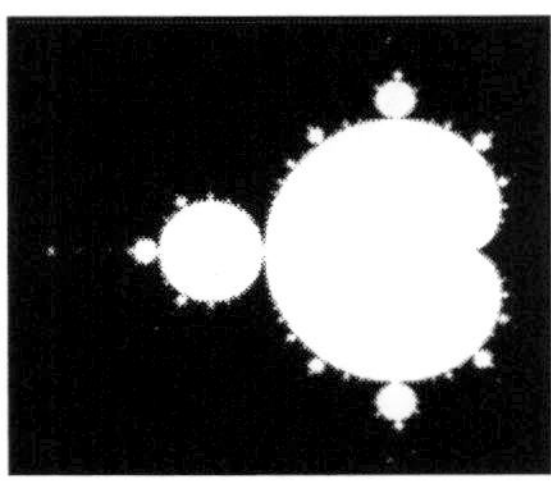

Every black pixel in this image corresponds to a complex number for which the sequence tends to diverge to an infinite value. The white pixels correspond to complex numbers bounded to a finite value. The white pixels belong to the Mandelbrot set.

What makes it interesting from a multithreaded perspective is that to determine whether the pixel belongs to the Mandelbrot set, we have to iterate on a formula to be able to hypothesize its divergence. The more iterations we perform, the safer we are in claiming, "Yes, this pixel is in the Mandelbrot set; it is a white pixel."

For even more fun, we can take any value in the graphical plot and apply the Mandelbrot formula to deduce whether the pixel should be black or white. As a consequence, you can zoom in endlessly inside the graphics of your fractal. There are only two limitations:

- The power of your CPU hinders the picture-generation speed.
- The floating-number precision of your CPU architecture limits the zoom. If you keep zooming, you will get visual artifacts because the scale factor can only handle 15 to 17 significant digits.

The architecture of the application has to be carefully designed. Because we are working with threads, it is very easy to cause deadlocks, starve threads, or even worse, freeze the UI.

We really want to maximize the use of the CPU. To do so, we will have one thread per logical CPU. Each thread will be responsible for calculating a part of the Mandelbrot set before giving back its result.

The architecture of the application is as follows:

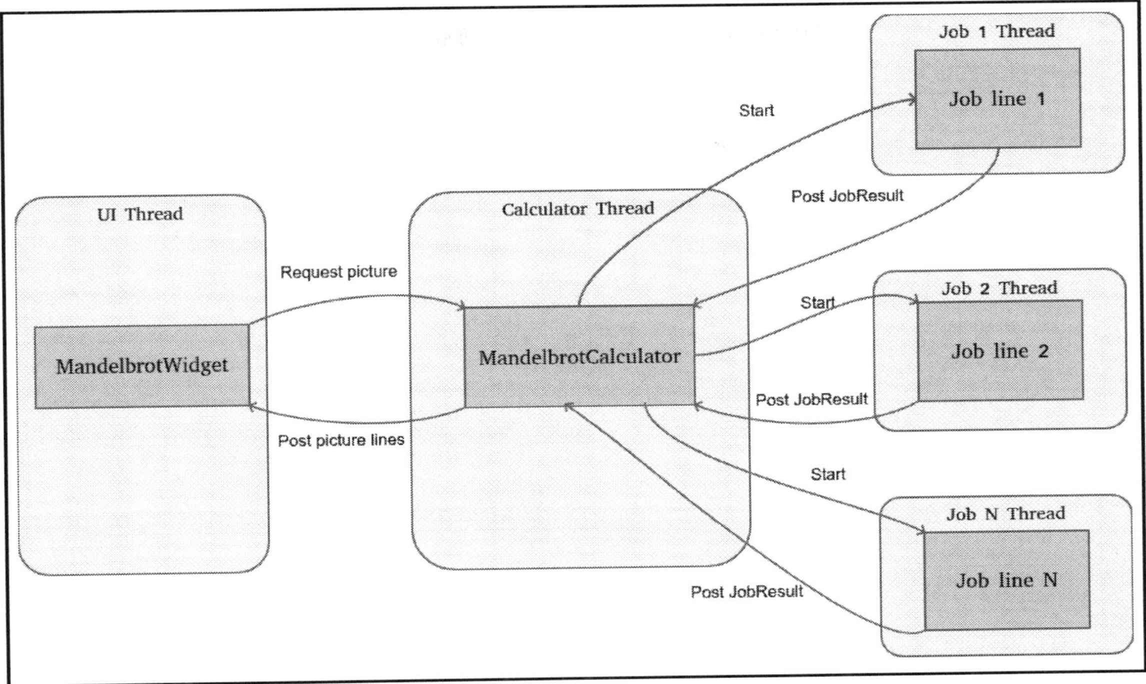

The application is divided into three parts:

- `MandelbrotWidget`: Requests a picture to display. It handles the drawing and the user interaction. This object lives in the UI thread.
- `MandelbrotCalculator`: Handles the picture requests and aggregates the resulting `JobResults` before sending it back to `MandelbrotWidget`. This object lives in its own thread.
- `Job`: Calculates a part of the final picture before transmitting the result back to `MandelbrotCalculator`. Each job lives in its own thread.

The `MandelbrotCalculator` thread will use a `QThreadPool` class to dispatch jobs in their own thread. This will scale perfectly according to your CPU cores. Each job will calculate a single line of the final picture before sending it back to `MandelbrotCalculator` through a `JobResult` object.

The `MandelbrotCalculator` thread is really the orchestrator of the calculation. Consider a user that zooms in to the picture before the calculation is complete; `MandelbrotWidget` will request a new picture to `MandelbrotCalculator`, which in turn has to cancel all the current jobs before dispatching new jobs.

We will add a last constraint to this project: it has to be mutex-free. Mutexes are very convenient tools, but they force threads to wait for each other and are error-prone. To do this, we will rely on multiple concepts and technologies provided by Qt, such as multithreaded signal/slots and implicit sharing.

By minimizing the sharing state between our threads, we will be able to let them execute as fast as they possibly can. That is why we are here, to burn some CPU cores, right?

Now that the broad picture is clearer, we can start the implementation. Create a new **Qt Widget Application** project, named `ch09-mandelbrot-threadpool`. Remember to add `CONFIG += c++14` to the `.pro` file.

Defining a Job class with QRunnable

Let's dive into the project's core. To speed up the Mandelbrot picture-generation, we will split the whole computation into multiple jobs. A `Job` is a request of a specific task. Depending the number of your CPU cores, several jobs will be executed simultaneously. A `Job` class produces a `JobResult` function that contains result values. In our project, a `Job` class generates values for one line of the complete picture. For example, an image resolution of 800 x 600 requires 600 jobs, each one generating 800 values.

Create a C++ header file called `JobResult.h`:

```
#include <QSize>
#include <QVector>
#include <QPointF>
#include <QMetaType>

struct JobResult
{
    JobResult(int valueCount = 1) :
        areaSize(0, 0),
```

```
        pixelPositionY(0),
        moveOffset(0, 0),
        scaleFactor(0.0),
        values(valueCount)
    {
    }

    QSize areaSize;
    int pixelPositionY;
    QPointF moveOffset;
    double scaleFactor;

    QVector<int> values;
};

Q_DECLARE_METATYPE(JobResult)
```

This structure contains two parts:

- Input data (`areaSize`, `pixelPositionY`, ...)
- Result `values` generated by a `Job` class

The `Q_DECLARE_METATYPE()` Qt macro is required to let the Qt meta-object system know about `JobResult`. This will allow us to use `JobResult` in signals and slots in this applications.

We can now create the `Job` class itself. Create a C++ `Job` class using the next snippet of `Job.h` for the content:

```
#include <QObject>
#include <QRunnable>

#include "JobResult.h"
class Job : public QObject, public QRunnable
{
    Q_OBJECT
public:
    Job(QObject *parent = 0);
    void run() override;
};
```

This Job class is QRunnable, so we can override run() to implement the Mandelbrot picture algorithm. As you can see, Job also inherits from QObject, allowing us to use the signal/slot feature of Qt. The algorithm requires some input data. Update your Job.h like this:

```
#include <QObject>
#include <QRunnable>
#include <QPointF>
#include <QSize>
#include <QAtomicInteger>
class Job : public QObject, public QRunnable
{
    Q_OBJECT
public:
    Job(QObject *parent = 0);
    void run() override;

    void setPixelPositionY(int value);
    void setMoveOffset(const QPointF& value);
    void setScaleFactor(double value);
    void setAreaSize(const QSize& value);
    void setIterationMax(int value);

private:
    int mPixelPositionY;
    QPointF mMoveOffset;
    double mScaleFactor;
    QSize mAreaSize;
    int mIterationMax;
};
```

Let's talk about these variables:

- The mPixelPositionY variable is the picture-height index. Because each Job generates data only for one picture line, we need this information.
- The mMoveOffset variable is the MandelbrotWidget origin offset. The user can pan the picture, so the origin will not always be (0; 0).
- The mScaleFactor variable is the MandelbrotWidget scale value. The user can also zoom into the picture.
- The mAreaSize variable is the final picture's size in pixels.

- The `mIterationMax` variable is the count of iterations allowed to determine the Mandelbrot result for one pixel.

We can now add a signal, `jobCompleted()`, and the abort feature to `Job.h`:

```
#include <QObject>
#include <QRunnable>
#include <QPointF>
#include <QSize>
#include <QAtomicInteger>

#include "JobResult.h"

class Job : public QObject, public QRunnable
{
    Q_OBJECT
public:
    ...
signals:
    void jobCompleted(JobResult jobResult);

public slots:
    void abort();

private:
    QAtomicInteger<bool> mAbort;
    ...
};
```

The `jobCompleted()` signal will be emitted when the algorithm is over. The `jobResult` parameter contains the result values. The `abort()` slot will allow us to stop the job updating the `mIsAbort` flag value. Notice that `mAbort` is not a classic `bool`, but `QAtomicInteger<bool>`. This Qt cross-platform type allows us to perform atomic operations without interruption. You could use a mutex or another synchronization mechanism to do the job, but using an atomic variable is a fast way to safely update and access a variable from different threads.

It's time to switch to the implementation part with `Job.cpp`. Here is the `Job` class's constructor:

```
#include "Job.h"

Job::Job(QObject* parent) :
    QObject(parent),
    mAbort(false),
    mPixelPositionY(0),
```

```
        mMoveOffset(0.0, 0.0),
        mScaleFactor(0.0),
        mAreaSize(0, 0),
        mIterationMax(1)
    {
    }
```

This is a classic initialization: don't forget to call the `QObject` constructor.

We can now implement the `run()` function:

```
    void Job::run()
    {
        JobResult jobResult(mAreaSize.width());
        jobResult.areaSize = mAreaSize;
        jobResult.pixelPositionY = mPixelPositionY;
        jobResult.moveOffset = mMoveOffset;
        jobResult.scaleFactor = mScaleFactor;
        ...
    }
```

In this first part, we initialize a `JobResult` variable. The width of the area size is used to construct `JobResult::values` as a `QVector` with the correct initial size. Other input data is copied from `Job` to `JobResult` to let the receiver of `JobResult` get the result with the context input data.

Then we can update the `run()` function with the Mandelbrot algorithm:

```
    void Job::run()
    {
        ...
        double imageHalfWidth = mAreaSize.width() / 2.0;
        double imageHalfHeight = mAreaSize.height() / 2.0;
        for (int imageX = 0; imageX < mAreaSize.width(); ++imageX) {
            if (mAbort.load()) {
                return;
            }
            int iteration = 0;
            double x0 = (imageX - imageHalfWidth)
                      * mScaleFactor + mMoveOffset.x();
            double y0 = (mPixelPositionY - imageHalfHeight)
                      * mScaleFactor - mMoveOffset.y();
            double x = 0.0;
            double y = 0.0;
            do {
                double nextX = (x * x) - (y * y) + x0;
                y = 2.0 * x * y + y0;
```

```
            x = nextX;
            iteration++;

        } while(iteration < mIterationMax
                && (x * x) + (y * y) < 4.0);

        jobResult.values[imageX] = iteration;
    }

    emit jobCompleted(jobResult);
}
```

This algorithm used to calculate the Mandelbrot set itself is beyond the scope of this book. But you have to understand the main purpose of this `run()` function. Let's break it down:

- The for loop iterates over all `x` positions of pixels over one line
- The pixel position is converted into complex plane coordinates
- If the trial count exceeds the maximum authorized iteration, the algorithm ends with `iteration` to the `mIterationMax` value
- If the "algorithm check" condition is true, the algorithm ends with `iteration < mIterationMax`
- In any case, for each pixel, the iteration count is stored in `values` of `JobResult`
- The `jobCompleted()` signal is emitted with the result values of this algorithm
- We perform an atomic read with `mAbort.load()`; notice that if the return value is `true`, the algorithm is aborted and nothing is emitted

The last function is the `abort()` slot:

```
void Job::abort()
{
    mAbort.store(true);
}
```

This method performs an atomic write of the value, `true`. The atomic mechanism ensures that we can call `abort()` from multiple threads without disrupting the `mAbort` read in the `run()` function.

In our case, `run()` lives in the thread affected by `QThreadPool` (we will cover it soon), while the `abort()` slot will be called in the `MandelbrotCalculator` thread context.

You might want to secure the operations on `mAbort` with `QMutex`. However, keep in mind that locking and unlocking a mutex can become a costly operation if you do it often. Using a `QAtomicInteger` class here presents only advantages: the access to `mAbort` is thread-safe and we avoid an expensive lock.

The end of the `Job` implementation only contains setter functions. Please refer to the complete source code if you have any doubts.

Using QThreadPool in MandelbrotCalculator

Now that our `Job` class is ready to be used, we need to create a class to manage the jobs. Please create a new class, `MandelbrotCalculator`. Let's see what we need in the `MandelbrotCalculator.h` file:

```
#include <QObject>
#include <QSize>
#include <QPointF>
#include <QElapsedTimer>
#include <QList>

#include "JobResult.h"

class Job;

class MandelbrotCalculator : public QObject
{
    Q_OBJECT
public:
    explicit MandelbrotCalculator(QObject *parent = 0);
    void init(QSize imageSize);

private:
    QPointF mMoveOffset;
    double mScaleFactor;
    QSize mAreaSize;
    int mIterationMax;
    int mReceivedJobResults;
    QList<JobResult> mJobResults;
    QElapsedTimer mTimer;
};
```

We have already discussed `mMoveOffset`, `mScaleFactor`, `mAreaSize`, and `mIterationMax` in the previous section. We also have some new variables:

- The `mReceivedJobResults` variable is the count of the `JobResult` received, which was sent by the jobs
- The `mJobResults` variable is a list that contains the received `JobResult`
- The `mTimer` variable calculates the elapsed time to run all jobs for a requested picture

Now that you have a better picture of all the member variables, we can add the signals, slots, and private methods. Update your `MandelbrotCalculator.h` file:

```
...
class MandelbrotCalculator : public QObject
{
    Q_OBJECT
public:
    explicit MandelbrotCalculator(QObject *parent = 0);
    void init(QSize imageSize);

signals:
    void pictureLinesGenerated(QList<JobResult> jobResults);
    void abortAllJobs();

public slots:
    void generatePicture(QSize areaSize, QPointF moveOffset,
                         double scaleFactor, int iterationMax);
    void process(JobResult jobResult);

private:
    Job* createJob(int pixelPositionY);
    void clearJobs();

private:
    ...
};
```

Let's see the roles for each of these:

- `generatePicture()`: This slot is used by the caller to request a new Mandelbrot picture. This function prepares and starts jobs.
- `process()`: This slot handles a single result generated by a job.
- `pictureLinesGenerated()`: This signal is regularly triggered to dispatch results.

- `abortAllJobs()`: This signal is used to abort all active jobs.
- `createJob()`: This is a helper function to create and configure a new job.
- `clearJobs()`: This slot removes queued jobs and aborts active jobs.

The header file is completed and we can now perform the implementation. Here is the beginning of the `MandelbrotCalculator.cpp` implementation:

```
#include <QDebug>
#include <QThreadPool>

#include "Job.h"

const int JOB_RESULT_THRESHOLD = 10;

MandelbrotCalculator::MandelbrotCalculator(QObject *parent)
    : QObject(parent),
      mMoveOffset(0.0, 0.0),
      mScaleFactor(0.005),
      mAreaSize(0, 0),
      mIterationMax(10),
      mReceivedJobResults(0),
      mJobResults(),
      mTimer()
{
}
```

As always, we are using the initializer list with default values for our member variables. The role of `JOB_RESULT_THRESHOLD` will be covered soon. Here is the `generatePicture()` slot:

```
void MandelbrotCalculator::generatePicture(QSize areaSize, QPointF
moveOffset, double scaleFactor, int iterationMax)
{
    if (areaSize.isEmpty()) {
        return;
    }

    mTimer.start();
    clearJobs();

    mAreaSize = areaSize;
    mMoveOffset = moveOffset;
    mScaleFactor = scaleFactor;
    mIterationMax = iterationMax;

    for(int pixelPositionY = 0;
        pixelPositionY < mAreaSize.height(); pixelPositionY++) {
```

```
        QThreadPool::globalInstance()->
            start(createJob(pixelPositionY));
    }
}
```

If the areaSize width or height is 0, we have nothing to do. If the request is valid, we can start mTimer to track the whole generation duration. Each new picture-generation will first cancel existing jobs by calling clearJobs(). Then we set our member variables with the ones provided. Finally, we create a new Job class for each vertical picture line. The createJob() function that returns a Job* value will be covered soon.

QThreadPool::globalInstance() is a static function that gives us the optimal global thread pool depending on the core count of our CPU. Even if we call start() for all the Job classes, only a few of them start immediately. Others are added to the pool queue waiting for an available thread.

Let's see now how a Job class is created with the createJob() function:

```
Job* MandelbrotCalculator::createJob(int pixelPositionY)
{
    Job* job = new Job();

    job->setPixelPositionY(pixelPositionY);
    job->setMoveOffset(mMoveOffset);
    job->setScaleFactor(mScaleFactor);
    job->setAreaSize(mAreaSize);
    job->setIterationMax(mIterationMax);

    connect(this, &MandelbrotCalculator::abortAllJobs,
            job, &Job::abort);

    connect(job, &Job::jobCompleted,
            this, &MandelbrotCalculator::process);

    return job;
}
```

As you can see, the jobs are allocated on the heap. This operation takes some time in the MandelbrotCalculator thread. But the results are worth it; the overhead is being compensated by the multi-threading system. Notice that when we call QThreadPool::start(), the thread pool takes ownership of the job.

As a consequence, it will be deleted by the thread pool when `Job::run()` ends. We set the input data of the `Job` class required by the Mandelbrot algorithm.

To go further, here are some ways to reduce the overhead: not allocated on the head, use `setAutoDelete(false)` on the `Job` objects, remove the `Job` inheritance to `QObject`.

Then two connections are performed:

- Emitting our `abortAllJobs()` signal will call the `abort()` slot of all jobs
- Our `process()` slot is executed each time a `Job` completes its task

Finally, the `Job` pointer is returned to the caller, in our case, the `generatePicture()` slot.

The last helper function is `clearJobs()`. Add it to your `MandelbrotCalculator.cpp`:

```
void MandelbrotCalculator::clearJobs()
{
    mReceivedJobResults = 0;
    emit abortAllJobs();
    QThreadPool::globalInstance()->clear();
}
```

The counter of received job results is reset. We emit our signal to abort all active jobs. Finally, we remove queued jobs waiting for an available thread in the thread pool.

The last function of this class is `process()`, which is maybe the most important function. Update your code with the following snippet:

```
void MandelbrotCalculator::process(JobResult jobResult)
{
    if (jobResult.areaSize != mAreaSize ||
            jobResult.moveOffset != mMoveOffset ||
            jobResult.scaleFactor != mScaleFactor) {
        return;
    }

    mReceivedJobResults++;
    mJobResults.append(jobResult);

    if (mJobResults.size() >= JOB_RESULT_THRESHOLD ||
            mReceivedJobResults == mAreaSize.height()) {
        emit pictureLinesGenerated(mJobResults);
        mJobResults.clear();
    }
```

```
        if (mReceivedJobResults == mAreaSize.height()) {
            qDebug() << "Generated in " << mTimer.elapsed() << " ms";
        }
    }
```

This slot will be called each time a job completes its task. The first thing to check is that the current `JobResult` is still valid with the current input data. When a new picture is requested, we clear the jobs queue and abort the active jobs. However, if an old `JobResult` is still sent to this `process()` slot, we must ignore it.

After that, we can increment the `mReceivedJobResults` counter and append this `JobResult` to our member queue, `mJobResults`. The calculator waits to get `JOB_RESULT_THRESHOLD` (that is, 10) results before dispatching them by emitting the `pictureLinesGenerated()` signal. You can try to tweak this value with caution:

- A lower value, for example 1, will dispatch each line of data to the widget as soon as the calculator gets it. But the widget will be slower than the calculator to handle each line. Moreover, you will flood the main thread's event loop.
- A higher value relieves the widget's event loop. But the user will wait longer before seeing something happening. A continuous partial frame update gives a better user experience.

Also notice that when the event is dispatched, the `QList` class with the job result is sent by copy. But Qt performs implicit sharing with `QList`, so we only send a shallow copy, not a costly deep copy. Then we clear the current `QList` of the calculator.

Finally, if the processed `JobResult` is the last one in the area, we display a debug message with the elapsed time since the user call, `generatePicture()`.

You can set the thread count used by the `QThreadPool` class with `setMaxThreadCount(x)`, where `x` is the thread count.

Displaying the fractal with MandelbrotWidget

Here we are, the Mandelbrot algorithm is done and the multithreading system is ready to compute complex fractals over all your CPU cores. We can now create the widget that will convert all the `JobResult` to display a pretty picture.

Create a new C++ class called `MandelbrotWidget`. For this widget, we will handle the painting ourselves. Thus, we do not need any `.ui Qt Designer Form` file. Let's begin with the `MandelbrotWidget.h` file:

```
#include <memory>

#include <QWidget>
#include <QPoint>
#include <QThread>
#include <QList>

#include "MandelbrotCalculator.h"

class QResizeEvent;

class MandelbrotWidget : public QWidget
{
    Q_OBJECT

public:
    explicit MandelbrotWidget(QWidget *parent = 0);
    ~MandelbrotWidget();

private:
    MandelbrotCalculator mMandelbrotCalculator;
    QThread mThreadCalculator;
    double mScaleFactor;
    QPoint mLastMouseMovePosition;
    QPointF mMoveOffset;
    QSize mAreaSize;
    int mIterationMax;
    std::unique_ptr<QImage> mImage;
};
```

You should recognize some of the variable names, such as `mScaleFactor`, `mMoveOffset`, `mAreaSize`, and `mIterationMax`. We have already covered them in the `JobResult` and `Job` implementation. Here are the real new ones:

- The `mMandelbrotCalculator` variable is our multithreaded `Job` manager. The widget will make requests to it and wait for the results.
- The `mThreadCalculator` variable allows the Mandelbrot calculator to run in its own thread.
- The `mLastMouseMovePosition` variable is used by the widget to handle user events for the pan feature.

- The `mImage` variable is the current picture displayed by the widget. It is a `unique_ptr` pointer, so `MandelbrotWidget` is the owner of `mImage`.

We can now add the functions. Update your code like this:

```
class MandelbrotWidget : public QWidget
{
...
public slots:
    void processJobResults(QList<JobResult> jobResults);

signals:
    void requestPicture(QSize areaSize, QPointF moveOffset, double
scaleFactor, int iterationMax);

protected:
    void paintEvent(QPaintEvent*) override;
    void resizeEvent(QResizeEvent* event) override;
    void wheelEvent(QWheelEvent* event) override;
    void mousePressEvent(QMouseEvent* event) override;
    void mouseMoveEvent(QMouseEvent* event) override;

private:
    QRgb generateColorFromIteration(int iteration);

private:
    ...
};
```

Before we dive into the implementation, let's talk about these functions:

- The `processJobResults()` function will handle the `JobResult` list dispatched by `MandelbrotCalculator`.
- The `requestPicture()` signal is emitted each time the user changes the input data (offset, scale, or area size).
- The `paintEvent()` function draws the widget with the current `mImage`.
- The `resizeEvent()` function resizes the Mandelbrot area size when the user resizes the window.
- The `wheelEvent()` function handles the user's mouse-wheel event to apply a scale factor.
- The `mousePressEvent()` and `mouseMoveEvent()` functions retrieve user's mouse events to move the Mandelbrot picture.
- `generateColorFromIteration()` is a helper function to colorize the Mandelbrot picture. The iteration value by pixel is converted into a color value.

We can now implement the `MandelbrotWidget` class. Here is the beginning of the `MandelbrotWidget.cpp` file:

```
#include "MandelbrotWidget.h"

#include <QResizeEvent>
#include <QImage>
#include <QPainter>
#include <QtMath>

const int ITERATION_MAX = 4000;
const double DEFAULT_SCALE = 0.005;
const double DEFAULT_OFFSET_X = -0.74364390249094747;
const double DEFAULT_OFFSET_Y = 0.13182589977450967;

MandelbrotWidget::MandelbrotWidget(QWidget *parent) :
    QWidget(parent),
    mMandelbrotCalculator(),
    mThreadCalculator(this),
    mScaleFactor(DEFAULT_SCALE),
    mLastMouseMovePosition(),
    mMoveOffset(DEFAULT_OFFSET_X, DEFAULT_OFFSET_Y),
    mAreaSize(),
    mIterationMax(ITERATION_MAX)
{
    mMandelbrotCalculator.moveToThread(&mThreadCalculator);

    connect(this, &MandelbrotWidget::requestPicture,
        &mMandelbrotCalculator,
        &MandelbrotCalculator::generatePicture);

    connect(&mMandelbrotCalculator,
        &MandelbrotCalculator::pictureLinesGenerated,
        this, &MandelbrotWidget::processJobResults);

    mThreadCalculator.start();
}
```

At the top of the snippet, we set some constant default values. Feel free to tweak these values if you want a different view when you start the application. The first thing the constructor does is change the thread affinity of the `mMandelbrotCalculator` class. That way, the processing performed by the calculator (creating and starting jobs, aggregating job results, and clearing jobs) does not disturb the UI thread. Then we perform connections with the signal and slot of `MandelbrotCalculator`.

Because the widget and the calculator have a different thread affinity, the connection will be automatically a `Qt::QueuedConnection` type. Finally, we can start the thread of `mThreadCalculator`. We can now add the destructor:

```
MandelbrotWidget::~MandelbrotWidget()
{
    mThreadCalculator.quit();
    mThreadCalculator.wait(1000);
    if (!mThreadCalculator.isFinished()) {
        mThreadCalculator.terminate();
    }
}
```

The `QThread::terminate()` function is dangerous and must be used sparingly. Check that it does not cause any issues in your application.

We need to request the calculator thread to quit. When the calculator thread event loop handles our request, the thread will return a code 0. We wait 1,000 ms for the thread to end. We can continue this implementation with all the cases that request a new picture. Here is the `resizeEvent()` slot:

```
void MandelbrotWidget::resizeEvent(QResizeEvent* event)
{
    mAreaSize = event->size();

    mImage = std::make_unique<QImage>(mAreaSize,
        QImage::Format_RGB32);
    mImage->fill(Qt::black);

    emit requestPicture(mAreaSize, mMoveOffset, mScaleFactor,
        mIterationMax);
}
```

We update `mAreaSize` with the new widget size. Then, a new black `QImage` is created with the correct dimensions. Finally, we request a picture computation to `MandelbrotCalculator`. Let's see how the mouse wheel is handled:

```
void MandelbrotWidget::wheelEvent(QWheelEvent* event)
{
    int delta = event->delta();
    mScaleFactor *= qPow(0.75, delta / 120.0);
    emit requestPicture(mAreaSize, mMoveOffset, mScaleFactor,
        mIterationMax);
}
```

The mouse wheel value can be retrieved from `QWheelEvent::delta()`. We use a power function to apply a coherent value on `mScaleFactor` and we request an updated picture. We can now implement the pan feature:

```
void MandelbrotWidget::mousePressEvent(QMouseEvent* event)
{
    if (event->buttons() & Qt::LeftButton) {
        mLastMouseMovePosition = event->pos();
    }
}
```

The first function stores the mouse position where the user begins the move gesture. Then the next function will use `mLastMouseMovePosition` to create an offset:

```
void MandelbrotWidget::mouseMoveEvent(QMouseEvent* event)
{
    if (event->buttons() & Qt::LeftButton) {
        QPointF offset = mLastMouseMovePosition - event->pos();
        mLastMouseMovePosition = event->pos();
        offset.setY(-offset.y());
        mMoveOffset += offset * mScaleFactor;
        emit requestPicture(mAreaSize, mMoveOffset, mScaleFactor,
            mIterationMax);
    }
}
```

The difference between the new and the old mouse position gives us the pan offset. Notice that we invert a *y* axis value because the mouse event is in a top-left referential, whereas the Mandelbrot algorithm relies on a bottom-left referential. Finally, we request a picture with updated input values. We covered all the user events that emit a `requestPicture()` signal. Let's see now how we handle `JobResult` dispatched by `MandelbrotCalculator`:

```
void MandelbrotWidget::processJobResults(QList<JobResult> jobResults)
{
    int yMin = height();
    int yMax = 0;

    for(JobResult& jobResult : jobResults) {

        if (mImage->size() != jobResult.areaSize) {
            continue;
        }

        int y = jobResult.pixelPositionY;
        QRgb* scanLine =
            reinterpret_cast<QRgb*>(mImage->scanLine(y));
```

```
            for (int x = 0; x < mAreaSize.width(); ++x) {
                scanLine[x] =
                    generateColorFromIteration(jobResult.values[x]);
            }

            if (y < yMin) {
                yMin = y;
            }

            if (y > yMax) {
                yMax = y;
            }
        }

        update(0, yMin,
               width(), yMax);
    }
```

The calculator sends us `QList` of `JobResult`. For each one, we need to check whether the concerned area size is still valid. We directly update the pixel colors of `mImage`. The `scanLine()` function returns a pointer on the pixel data. It is a fast way to update a `QImage` pixel color. The `JobResult` function contains the iteration count, and our helper function, `generateColorFromIteration()`, returns an RGB value depending on the iteration value. A complete repaint of the widget is not necessary, because we only update several lines of `QImage`. Thus, we `update` only the updated region.

Here is how we convert an iteration value in an RGB value:

```
QRgb MandelbrotWidget::generateColorFromIteration(int iteration)
{
    if (iteration == mIterationMax) {
        return qRgb(50, 50, 255);
    }

    return qRgb(0, 0, (255.0 * iteration / mIterationMax));
}
```

Coloring a Mandelbrot is an art on its own. Here, we implement a simple linear interpolation on the blue channel. A nice Mandelbrot picture depends on the maximum iteration per pixel and its color technique. Feel free to enhance it the way you want!

You can move the color-generation in `Job` to optimize the performance.

Here we are with the last, but not least, function, `paintEvent()`:

```
void MandelbrotWidget::paintEvent(QPaintEvent* event)
{
    QPainter painter(this);
    painter.save();

    QRect imageRect = event->region().boundingRect();
    painter.drawImage(imageRect, *mImage, imageRect);

    painter.setPen(Qt::white);

    painter.drawText(10, 20, QString("Size: %1 x %2")
        .arg(mImage->width())
        .arg(mImage->height()));

    painter.drawText(10, 35, QString("Offset: %1 x %2")
        .arg(mMoveOffset.x())
        .arg(mMoveOffset.y()));

    painter.drawText(10, 50, QString("Scale: %1")
        .arg(mScaleFactor));

    painter.drawText(10, 65, QString("Max iteration: %1")
        .arg(ITERATION_MAX));

    painter.restore();
}
```

We must override this function because we handle the widget-drawing ourselves. First, we need to draw the updated region of the image. The `QPaintEvent` object contains the region that needs to be updated. The `QPainter` class makes the drawing easy. Finally, we draw some information texts of the current input data in white.

Creating multiple `QStrings` objects in `paintEvent()` is not optimized. In a real application, consider using labels for texts, and the `qDebug()` function for debugging purposes.

You now have a complete overview of the progressive picture display line by line. Let's sum up the workflow of this feature:

1. Each `Job::run()` generates a `JobResult` object
2. The `MandelbrotCalculator::process()` signal aggregates the `JobResult` object and dispatches them by groups (by default, 10)

3. The `MandelbrotWidget::processJobResults()` signal updates only concerned lines of the picture and requests a partial `update` of the widget
4. The `MandelbrotWidget::paintEvent()` signal only redraws the picture with the new values

This feature causes a little overhead, but the user experience is smoother. Indeed, the application reacts quickly to the user events: the first lines are updated almost immediately. The user does not have to wait for the full picture-generation to see something happening.

The widget is ready, don't forget to add it to `MainWindow`. Promoting a custom widget should be an easy task for you now. If you have any doubt, check `Chapter 4`, *Conquering the Desktop UI*, or the complete source code for this chapter.

The last step is to edit the `main.cpp` file:

```
#include "MainWindow.h"

#include <QApplication>
#include <QList>

#include "JobResult.h"

int main(int argc, char *argv[])
{
    QApplication a(argc, argv);
    qRegisterMetaType<JobResult>();
    qRegisterMetaType<QList<JobResult>>();

    MainWindow w;
    w.show();

    return a.exec();
}
```

We employ the `qRegisterMetaType()` function to be able to use the Qt signals/slots mechanism with our `JobResult` custom class.

You should now be able to display and navigate into your multithreaded Mandelbrot set!

If you start the application, you should see something like this:

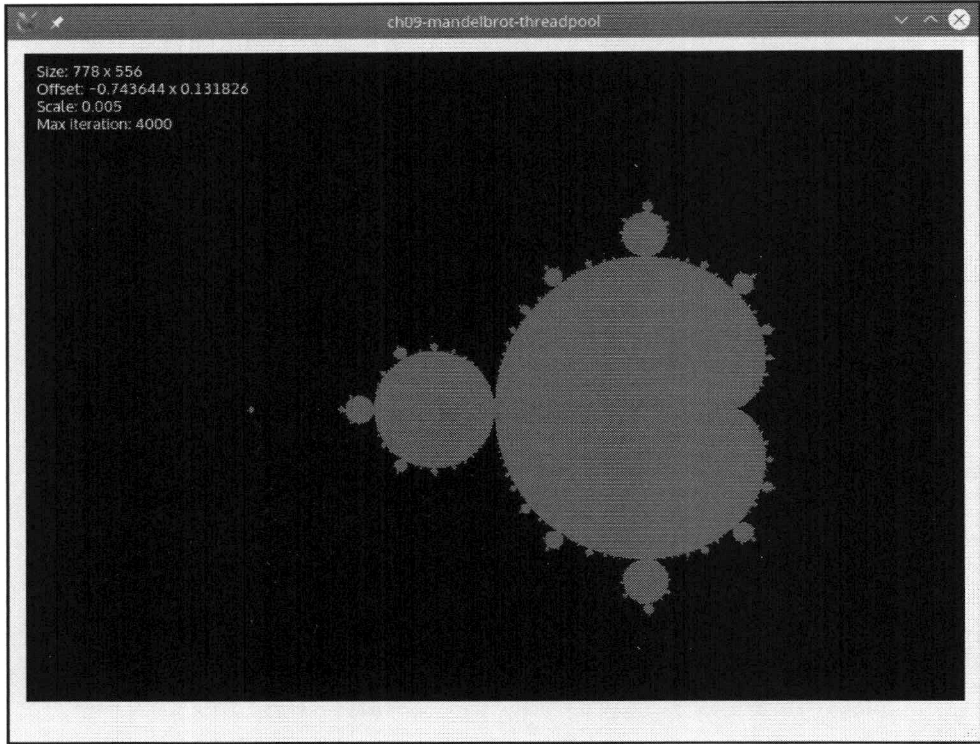

Try to zoom in now and pan into the Mandelbrot set. You should find some funny places, such as this one:

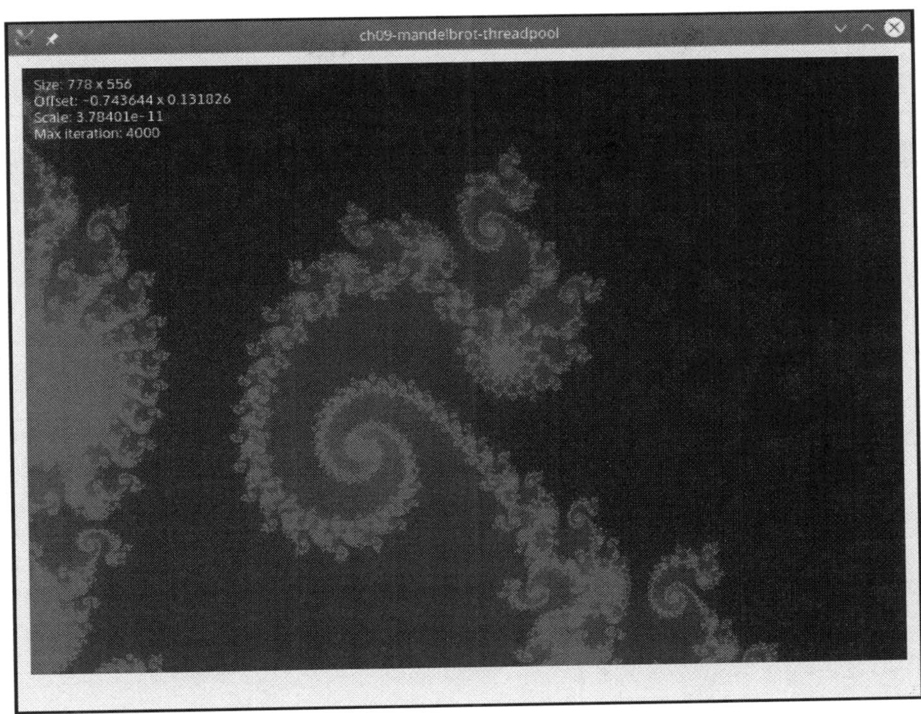

Summary

In this chapter, you discovered how a `QThread` class works and learned how to efficiently use tools provided by Qt to create a powerful multithreaded application. Your Mandelbrot application is able to use all the cores of your CPU to compute a picture quickly.

Creating a multithreaded application presents a lot of pitfalls (such as deadlock, event-loop flood, orphan threads, and overhead). The application architecture is important. If you are able to isolate the heavy code that you want to parallelize, everything should go well. Nevertheless, the user experience is of the utmost importance; you will sometimes have to accept a little overhead if your application gives the user a smoother feeling.

In the next chapter, we will see several ways to implement an Inter-Process Communication (IPC) between applications. The project example will enhance your current Mandelbrot application with a TCP/IP socket system; the Mandelbrot generator will compute pictures over several CPU cores from multiple computers!

10
Need IPC? Get Your Minions to Work

In the previous chapter, you learned how to send information across threads of the same process. In this chapter, you will look at how to share data between threads of different processes. We will even share information between applications running on different physical computers. We will enhance the Mandelbrot generator application from `Chapter 9`, *Keeping Your Sanity with Multithreading*. The Mandelbrot application will now only display results processed by the worker programs. These minions have only one mission: compute the tasks as fast as possible and return a result to your main application.

The following topics will be covered in this chapter:

- Inter-process communication techniques
- Architecturing an IPC project
- Laying down the foundations with an SDK
- Working with QDataStream and QTcpSocket
- Building your own QTcpServer

Inter-process communication techniques

An **Inter-Process Communication** (**IPC**) is a communication between two or more processes. They can be instances of the same application or different applications. The Qt framework provides multiple modules to help you implement a communication between your applications. Most of these modules are cross-platform. Let's talk about the IPC tools that can be used in a Qt application.

The first tools are the TCP/IP sockets. They provide a bidirectional data exchange over a network. Therefore, you can use them to talk with processes on different computers. Moreover, the `loopback` interface allows you to communicate with processes running on the same computer. All the required classes are inside the `QtNetwork` module. This technique relies on a client-server architecture. Here is an example of the server part:

```
QTcpServer* tcpServer = new QTcpServer(this);
tcpServer->listen(QHostAddress::Any, 5000);

connect(tcpServer, &QTcpServer::newConnection, [tcpServer] {
    QTcpSocket *tcpSocket = tcpServer->nextPendingConnection();
    QByteArray response = QString("Hello").toLatin1();
    tcpSocket->write(response);
    tcpSocket->disconnectFromHost();
    qDebug() << "Send response and close the socket";
});
```

The first step is to instantiate a `QTcpServer` class. It deals with the new incoming TCP connections. Then, we call the `listen()` function. You can provide a network interface and specify the port on which the server must listen for incoming connections. In this example, we listen on all network addresses (such as `127.0.0.1` and `192.168.1.4`) on port `5000`. When a client establishes a connection with this server, the `QTcpServer::newConnection()` signal is triggered. Let's break together this lambda slot:

1. We retrieve the `QTcpSocket` class related to this new connection with a client.
2. A `QByteArray` response is prepared with the "Hello" ASCII message. Ignore the lack of originality.
3. The message is sent to the client through the socket.
4. We close the socket. So the client, on this side, will be disconnected.

You can test a `QTcpServer` class with a telnet tool, such as Putty on Windows or the `telnet` command on Linux and macOS.

The following snippet is the client part:

```
QTcpSocket *tcpSocket = new QTcpSocket(this);
tcpSocket->connectToHost("127.0.0.1", 5000);

connect(tcpSocket, &QTcpSocket::connected, [tcpSocket] {
    qDebug() << "connected";
});
```

```
connect(tcpSocket, &QTcpSocket::readyRead, [tcpSocket] {
    qDebug() << QString::fromLatin1(tcpSocket->readAll());
});
connect(tcpSocket, &QTcpSocket::disconnected, [tcpSocket] {
    qDebug() << "disconnected";
});
```

The client also uses a `QTcpSocket` class to communicate. It turns out that the connection is initiated by the client, therefore we need to call the `connectToHost()` function with the server address and port. This class provides a lot of useful signals, such as `connected()` and `disconnected()`, that indicates the connection status. The `readyRead()` signal is emitted when new data is available for reading. The `readAll()` function returns `QByteArray` with all the available data. In our case, we know that the server sends an ASCII message to its client. Thus, we can convert this byte array into `QString` and display it.

For this example, the server writes in the TCP socket and the client reads in it. But this communication is bidirectional, so the client can also write data and the server can read it. Try to send data from the client and display it in the server. Notice that you need to keep the communication alive by removing the `disconnectFromHost()` call in the server part.

The Qt framework provides a helper class, `QDataStream`, to easily send a complex object and handle the package fragmentation. This concept will be covered later with the project example of this chapter.

Let's talk about the second IPC technique: **shared memory**. By default, different processes do not use the same memory space. The `QSharedMemory` class provides a cross-platform method to create and use a shared memory across multiple processes. Nevertheless, the processes must run on the same computer. A shared memory is identified by a key. All the processes must use the same key to share the same memory segment. The first process will create the shared memory segment and put data in it:

```
QString sharedMessage("Hello");
QByteArray sharedData = sharedMessage.toLatin1();

QSharedMemory* sharedMemory = new QSharedMemory(
    "sharedMemoryKey", this);
sharedMemory->create(sharedData.size());

sharedMemory->lock();

memcpy(sharedMemory->data(),
```

```
        sharedData.data(),
        sharedData.size());

sharedMemory->unlock();
delete sharedMemory;
```

Let's analyze all the steps:

1. We want to share the `QString` "Hello" converted into a `QByteArray` class.
2. A `QSharedMemory` class is initialized with the key, `sharedMemoryKey`. This same key should be used by the second process.
3. The first process creates the shared memory segment with a specific size in bytes. The creation also attaches the process to the shared memory segment.
4. You should now be confident with the lock/unlock system. The `QSharedMemory` class uses semaphore to protect the shared access. You must lock it before manipulating the shared memory.
5. A classic `memcpy()` function is used to copy data from the `QByteArray` class to the `QSharedMemory` class.
6. We can unlock the shared memory.

Destroying a `QShareMemory` class will call the `detach()` function, which detaches the process from the shared memory segment. If this process was the last one attached, `detach()` also destroys the shared memory segment. While an attached `QShareMemory` is alive, the shared memory segment is available for other processes. The next snippet describes how a second segment can access the shared memory:

```
QSharedMemory* sharedMemory = new QSharedMemory(
    "sharedMemoryKey", this);
sharedMemory->attach();

sharedMemory->lock();

QByteArray sharedData(sharedMemory->size(), '\0');

memcpy(sharedData.data(),
        sharedMemory->data(),
        sharedMemory->size());
sharedMemory->unlock();

QString sharedMessage = QString::fromLatin1(sharedData);
qDebug() << sharedMessage;

sharedMemory->detach();
delete sharedMemory;
```

Here are the key steps:

1. As with the first process, this second process initializes a `QSharedMemory` class with the key, `sharedMemoryKey`
2. We attach the process to the shared memory segment with the `attach()` function
3. We must lock the `QSharedMemory` class before accessing it
4. We initialize `QByteArray` with the null character, `\0`, with the size of the shared memory
5. The `memcpy()` function copies the data from `QSharedMemory` to `QByteArray`
6. We can convert `QByteArray` in `QString` and display our message
7. Call the `detach()` function to detach the process from the shared memory segment

Please notice that the `create()` and `attach()` functions specify by default a `QSharedMemory::ReadWrite` access. You can also use the `QSharedMemory::ReadOnly` access.

You can use the `QBuffer` and `QDataStream` classes to serialize a complex object in or from a bytes array.

Another IPC way is to use the `QProcess` class. The main process starts an external application as a child process. The communication is done using the standard input and output streams. Let's create a `hello` console application that relies on the standard input and output channels:

```
QTextStream out(stdout);
QTextStream in(stdin);

out << QString("Please enter your name:\n");
out.flush();

QString name = in.readLine();

out << "Hello " << name << "\n";
return 0;
```

We use the `QTextStream` class to easily work with the standards streams, `stdout` and `stdin`. The application prints the `Please enter your name:` message. Then we wait while the user types their name by calling the `readLine()` function. Finally, the program displays the `Hello` message and the user's `name`. If you start this console application, you must type your name on the keyboard to see the final hello message with your name.

The following snippet runs and communicates with the `hello` application. Further, we can programmatically control the child `hello` application:

```
QProcess* childProcess = new QProcess(this);

connect(childProcess,
    &QProcess::readyReadStandardOutput, [childProcess] {
        qDebug().noquote() << "[*]" << childProcess->readAll();
});

connect(childProcess, &QProcess::started, [childProcess] {
    childProcess->write("Sophie\n");
});

childProcess->start("/path/to/hello");
```

Here are all the steps performed by this main application:

1. We initialize a `QProcess` object that can start an external application.
2. The child process displays messages on the console and so writes in the standard output. Then, the `readyReadStandardOutput()` signal is sent. In this case, we print the message as debug text with the `[*]` prefix to identify that it comes from the child process.
3. As soon as the child process is started, the `started()` signal is sent. In our case, we write the name `Sophie` (Lenna will be jealous!) in the child standard input.
4. All is ready, we can start the `QProcess` class with the path to the `hello` console application.

If you start the main application, you should get this result in its console:

```
[*] Please enter your name:
[*] Hello Sophie
```

Mission complete! The main application is a wrapper for the `hello` application. We receive all messages from the child process and we can send it some information, such as a specific name.

The `QProcess::start()` function also accepts a second variable: the command line arguments for the child process.

The last IPC mechanism that we will cover together is the **D-Bus protocol**. Currently, the Qt D-Bus module is officially supported only on Linux. If you need to use it on Windows, you will have to compile it from Qt sources. It can be seen as a unified protocol for IPC and **remote procedure calling (RPC)**. Many forms of communication are possible, such as the following:

- One-to-one
- One-to-many
- Many-to-many

The best thing about Qt D-Bus is that you can even use the signal/slot mechanism across the bus. A signal emitted from one application can be connected to a slot from another application. Linux desktop environments, such as KDE and GNOME, use the D-Bus. That implies that you can (also) control your desktop with the D-Bus.

Here are the main concepts of the D-Bus:

- `Bus`: This is used in many-to-many communication. D-Bus defines two buses: the **system bus** and the **session bus**.
- `Service name`: This is the identifier of a service on a bus.
- `Message`: This is a message sent by one application. If a bus is used, the message contains the destination.

A Qt D-Bus Viewer tool can be found in your Qt installation folder (for example, `/Qt/5.11/gcc_64/bin/qdbusviewer`). All objects and messages from all services of the system and the session bus are displayed. Try to invoke exposed methods and retrieve a result.

Now that you have played with the Linux D-Bus services, it's time to create your own! First, we will create a simple `HelloService` object:

```
//HelloService.h
class HelloService : public QObject
{
    Q_OBJECT

public slots:
    QString sayHello(const QString &name);
```

```
};

//HelloService.cpp
QString HelloService::sayHello(const QString& name)
{
    qDebug().noquote() << name << " is here!";
    return QString("Hello %1!").arg(name);;
}
```

No big deal here, the only function is a public slot that requires a `name`, displays who is here, and returns a hello message. In the following snippet, the main application registers a new D-Bus service and the `HelloService` object:

```
HelloService helloService;
QString serviceName("org.masteringqt.QtDBus.HelloService");

QDBusConnection::sessionBus().registerService(serviceName);
QDBusConnection::sessionBus().registerObject("/",
    &helloService, QDBusConnection::ExportAllSlots);
```

The main application initializes a `HelloService` object. Then, we register a new service, named `org.masteringqt.QtDBus.HelloService`, on the session bus. Finally, we register the `HelloService` object, exposing all its slots. Notice the simple object path, `/`, used for this example. The service application part is finished. Here is the client application calling the `HelloService` object:

```
QString serviceName("org.masteringqt.QtDBus.HelloService");
QDBusInterface serviceInterface(serviceName, "/");
QDBusReply<QString> response = serviceInterface.call(
    "sayHello", "Lenna");
qDebug().noquote() << response;
```

Let's analyze the client part step by step:

1. We initialize a `QDBusInterface` object with the same service name and path as the service application.
2. We call the remote method, `sayHello()` on `HelloService`, with the `Lenna` parameter (wait, where is Sophie?!).
3. The response is stored in a `QDBusReply` object. In our case, type `QString`.
4. Finally, we display the message generated by the `HelloService` object.

If you start the service application and then the client application, you should get this console output:

```
//service application output
```

```
Lenna is here!

//client application output
Hello Lenna!
```

Use the `QDBusViewer` tool to find your D-Bus service. Select the **Session Bus** tab. Choose your service in the list. Then you can select the `sayHello` method. Right-clicking on it allows you to call the method. An input popup will ask you to fill in the method parameter, which is a name in our example. The following screenshot shows you what it looks like (it seems that Sophie is here):

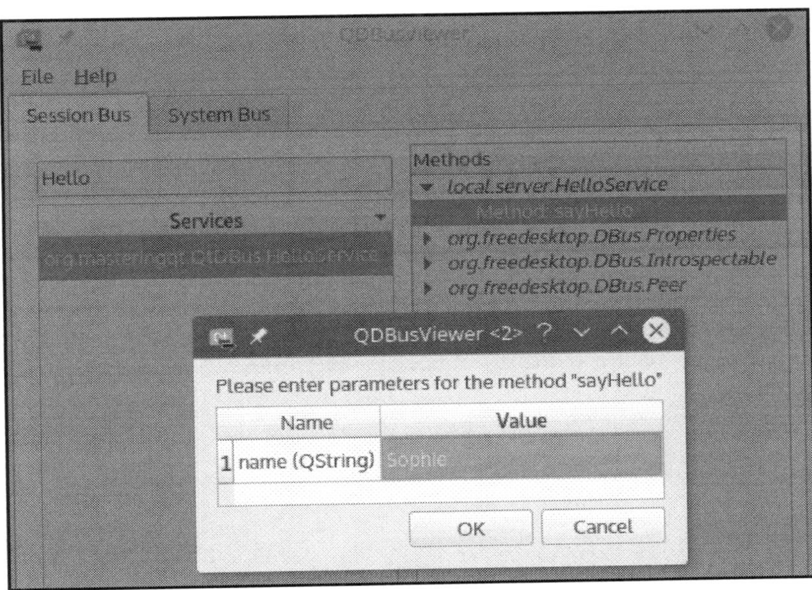

Architecturing an IPC project

The Mandelbrot picture generator from `Chapter 9`, *Keeping Your Sanity with Multithreading*, uses all the cores of your computer to speed up the computing. This time, we want to use all the cores of all of your computers! The first thing is to choose an appropriated IPC technique. For this project example, we want to establish communication between several clients acting as workers to a server running the main application. The TCP/IP sockets allow a one-to-many communication. Moreover, this IPC method is not bound to a single computer and can operate through a network on multiple computers. This project example uses sockets by implementing a multithreaded TCP server.

The following diagram describes the architecture:

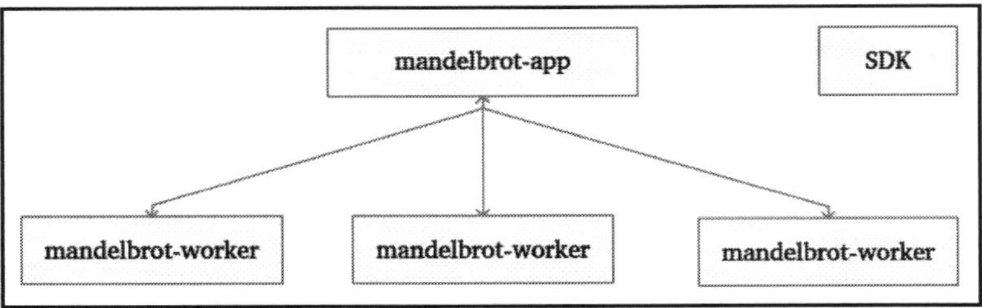

Let's talk about the global role of each actor:

- `mandelbrot-app`: This is the main application displaying the Mandelbrot picture and handling user mouse events. However, in this chapter, the application does not compute the algorithm itself but generates requests to connected workers. Then, it aggregates the results provided by the workers.
- `mandelbrot-worker`: Here is our minion! A worker is a standalone program. It is connecting to `mandelbrot-app` through a TCP socket. A worker receives a request, computes a job, and sends back a result.
- `SDK`: This regroups common code used by both applications. If the SDK changes, all the dependent applications must be updated.

As you can see, this architecture fits well with the one-to-many communication required by this project. The `mandelbrot-app` application can use one or many workers to generate the same Mandelbrot picture.

Now that you get the big picture, let's look in detail at each module. You can see all of the classes in the SDK in the following diagram:

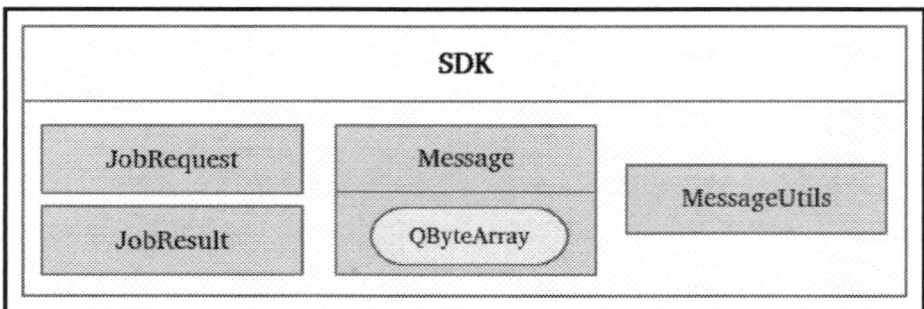

An SDK is essential when you have several modules (applications, libraries, and so on) that communicate together or need to perform the same actions. You can give the SDK to a third-party developer without compromising your main source code. In our project, `mandelbrot-app` and `mandelbrot-worker` communicate together by exchanging `Message`. The message structure must be known by both entities. A `Message` class contains a `type` and raw `data` of the type, `QByteArray`. Depending on the message `type`, the raw data can be empty or can contain an object. In this project, message `data` can be `JobRequest` or `JobResult`. `mandelbrot-app` sends `JobRequest` to `mandelbrot-worker`. Then, the worker returns `JobResult` to the main application. Finally, `MessageUtils` contains functions used by the main application and the workers to send and retrieve a `Message`.

We can now talk about `mandelbrot-worker` in more detail. The following diagram describes it:

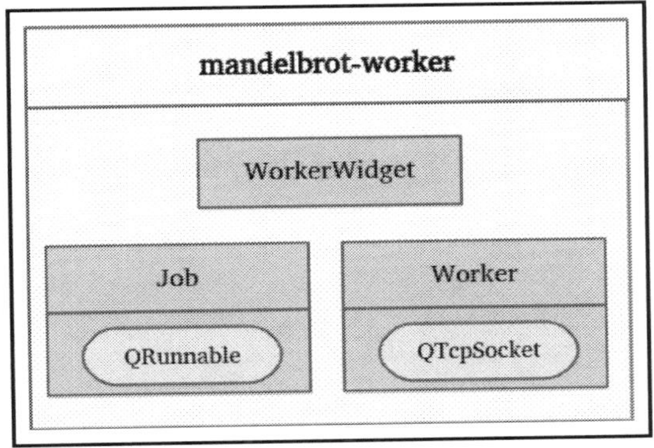

The `mandelbrot-worker` program is able to use all the CPU cores of a machine. The socket mechanism allows us to run it on multiple physical machines at the same time. The `WorkerWidget` class displays the status of the `Worker` object. The `Worker` object handles the communication with `mandelbrot-app` using `QTcpSocket`. `Job` is a `QRunnable` class that computes a task. Here is the workflow of this software:

1. Send a register `Message` to the `mandelbrot-app` application
2. Receive a `JobRequest` from `mandelbrot-app` and create several `Job` instances to complete all tasks
3. Each `Job` is running in a dedicated thread and will generate a `JobResult`
4. Send `JobResult` to `mandelbrot-app`
5. On exit, send an unregister `Message` to `mandelbrot-app`

It is now time to talk about the `mandelbrot-app` architecture. Look at the following diagram:

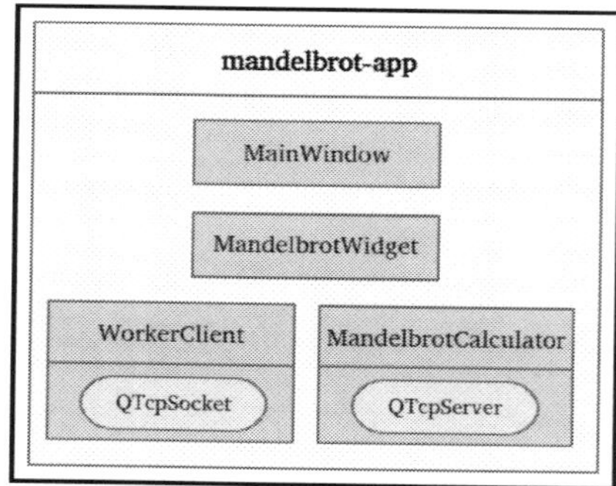

This is the main application. You can launch it on a computer with a weak CPU and the real heavy work is done by workers running the `mandelbrot-worker` software.
The `MainWindow` and `MandelbrotWidget` GUI objects are the same as those in `Chapter 9`, *Keeping Your Sanity with Multithreading*. The `MandelbrotCalculator` class is a little different in this project, because it does not run any `QRunnable` itself. It is a TCP server that handles all registered workers and dispatches tasks to those workers. Each `mandelbrot-worker` is managed by a `WorkerClient` object instance with a dedicated `QTcpSocket`.
Here is the workflow for `mandelbrot-app`:

1. Run a TCP server on a specific port
2. Receive a register `Message` and create a `WorkerClient` object for each registered worker
3. When `MandelbrotWidget` requests a generated picture, `MandelbrotCalculator` creates the `JobRequest` object required to compute the full Mandelbrot picture
4. The `JobRequest` objects are sent to the workers
5. Receive and aggregate `JobResult` from `mandelbrot-worker`
6. Transmit `JobResult` to the `MandelbrotWidget` object that displays the picture
7. If an unregister `Message` is received from a worker, the `WorkerClient` object is released and this worker will not be used for picture-generation anymore

You now have a complete overview of this project architecture. We can begin the implementation of this project. Create a **Subdirs** project called `ch10-mandelbrot-ipc`. As you might have guessed, we now create two sub-projects: `mandelbrot-app` and `mandelbrot-worker`.

The implementation in the subsequent sections follows the architecture presentation order:

1. SDK
2. `mandelbrot-worker`
3. `mandelbrot-app`

The implementation is a step up in complexity. Don't hesitate to take a break and come back to this section to keep the overall architecture clear.

Laying down the foundations with an SDK

The first step is to implement the classes that will be shared between our application and the workers. To do so, we are going to rely on a custom SDK. If you need to refresh your memory about this technique, take a look at `Chapter 8`, *Animations – It's Alive, Alive!*.

As a reminder, here is the diagram that describes the SDK:

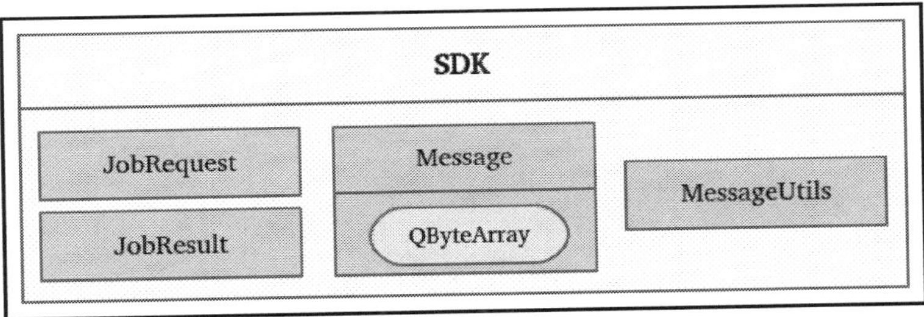

Let's look at the job of each of these components:

- The `Message` component encapsulates a piece of information that is exchanged between the application and the worker.
- The `JobRequest` component contains the necessary information to dispatch a proper job to a worker.
- The `JobResult` component contains the result of the Mandelbrot set calculation for a given line.
- The `MessageUtils` component contains helper functions to serialize/deserialize data across the TCP socket.

All these files have to be accessible from each side of our IPC mechanism (application and worker). Note that the SDK will contain only header files. We did it on purpose to simplify the SDK usage.

Let's start with `Message` implementation in the `sdk` directory. Create a `Message.h` file with the following content:

```
#include <QByteArray>

struct Message {

    enum class Type {
        WORKER_REGISTER,
        WORKER_UNREGISTER,
        ALL_JOBS_ABORT,
        JOB_REQUEST,
        JOB_RESULT,
    };

    Message(const Type type = Type::WORKER_REGISTER,
            const QByteArray& data = QByteArray()) :
        type(type),
        data(data)
    {
    }

    ~Message() {}

    Type type;
    QByteArray data;
};
```

The first thing to note is the `enum class` type, which details all the possible message types:

- `WORKER_REGISTER`: sent by the worker when it first connects to the application. The content of the message is only the number of cores of the worker's CPU. We will soon see why this is useful.
- `WORKER_UNREGISTER`: sent by the worker when it is disconnected. This lets the application know that it should remove this worker from its list and stop sending any messages to it.
- `ALL_JOBS_ABORT`: sent by the application each time a picture generation is canceled. The worker is then responsible for canceling all its current local threads.
- `JOB_REQUEST`: sent by the application to calculate a specific line of the desired picture.
- `JOB_RESULT`: sent by the worker with the calculated result from the `JOB_REQUEST` input.

A quick word about the `enum class` type, which is a C++11 addition. It is a safer version of `enum` (some might say that it is `enum` as it should have been from the beginning):

- You must use the fully qualified names with the scope qualifier. In this example, you can only reference an `enum` value with the `Message::Type::WORKER_REGISTER` syntax; no more `Message::WORKER_REGISTER` shortcuts. The good thing about this restriction is that you don't need to prefix `enum` values with `MESSAGE_TYPE_` to be sure that the name does not conflict with anything else.
- There is no implicit conversion to `int`. The `enum` class acts like a real type; to cast an `enum` class to `int`, you have to write `static_cast<int>( Message::Type::WORKER_REGISTER)`.
- There is no forward declaration. You can specify that `enum class` is a char type (with the `enum class Test : char { ... }` syntax), but the compiler will not be able to deduce the `enum` class size with a forward declaration. Therefore, it has been simply forbidden.
- `enum class` is not a `class`, it can't have members functions.

We tend to use the `enum class` whenever possible, meaning when it does not clash with the Qt `enum` usage.

As you can see, a message has only two members:

- `type`: This is the message type we just described
- `data`: This is an opaque type that contains the piece of information to be transmitted

We chose to make `data` very generic to place the responsibility of serializing/deserializing on the `Message` callers. Based on the message's `type`, they should know how to read or write the message's content.

By using this approach, we avoid a tangled class hierarchy with `MessageRegister`, `MessageUnregister`, and so on. Adding a new `Message type` is simply adding a value in `Type enum class` and doing the proper serialization/deserialization in `data` (which you have to do anyway).

To see the file in Qt Creator, don't forget to add `Message.h` in the `ch10-mandelbrot-ipc.pro` file:

```
OTHER_FILES += \
sdk/Message.h
```

The next header we will look at is `JobRequest.h`:

```
#include <QSize>
#include <QPointF>

struct JobRequest
{
    int pixelPositionY;
    QPointF moveOffset;
    double scaleFactor;
    QSize areaSize;
    int iterationMax;
};

Q_DECLARE_METATYPE(JobRequest)

// In ch10-mandelbrot-ipc
OTHER_FILES += \
    sdk/Message.h \
    sdk/JobRequest.h
```

This `struct` element contains all the necessary data for the worker to calculate a line of the target Mandelbrot picture. Because the application and the worker(s) will live in different memory spaces (or even different physical machines), the parameters to calculate the Mandelbrot set have to be transmitted somehow. This is the purpose of `JobRequest`. The meaning of each field is the same as `JobResult` from `Chapter 9`, *Keeping Your Sanity with Multithreading*.

Note the presence of the `Q_DECLARE_METATYPE(JobRequest)` macro. This macro is used to let the Qt meta-object system know about `JobRequest`. This is needed to be able to use the class in conjunction with `QVariant`. We will not use `QVariant` directly, but rather through `QDataStream`, which relies on `QVariant`.

Speaking of `JobResult`, here is the new `JobResult.h`:

```
#include <QSize>
#include <QVector>
#include <QPointF>

struct JobResult
{
    JobResult(int valueCount = 1) :
        areaSize(0, 0),
        pixelPositionY(0),
        moveOffset(0, 0),
        scaleFactor(0.0),
```

```
        values(valueCount)
    {
    }

    QSize areaSize;
    int pixelPositionY;
    QPointF moveOffset;
    double scaleFactor;

    QVector<int> values;
};

Q_DECLARE_METATYPE(JobResult)

// In ch10-mandelbrot-ipc
OTHER_FILES += \
    sdk/Message.h \
    sdk/JobRequest.h \
    sdk/JobResult.h
```

The new version is a shameless copy-paste (with the small `Q_DECLARE_METATYPE` addition) of the project example of `Chapter 9`, *Keeping Your Sanity with Multithreading*.

Working with QDataStream and QTcpSocket

The missing piece of the SDK is `MesssageUtils`. It deserves a dedicated section because it covers two major topics: serialization and `QDataStream` transactions.

We will start with the serialization. We already know that `Message` stores only an opaque `QByteArray` data member. As a consequence, the desired data has to be serialized as `QByteArray` before being passed to `Message`.

If we take the example of a `JobRequest` object, it is not directly sent. We first put it in a generic `Message` object with the appropriate `Message` type. The following diagram summarizes the sequence of actions to be done:

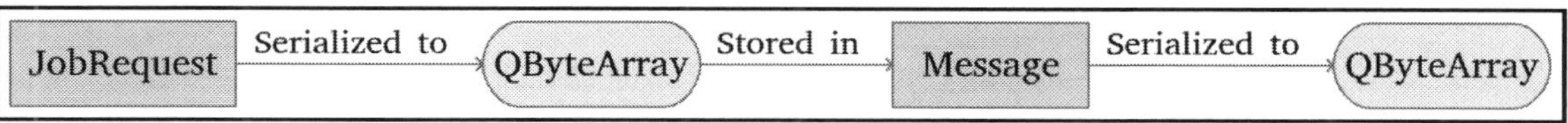

The `JobRequest` object is first serialized to a `QByteArray` class. It is then passed to a `Message` instance, which is in turn serialized to a final `QByteArray`. The deserialization process is the exact opposite of this sequence (from right to left).

Serializing data brings a lot of questions. How can we do it in a generic fashion? How do we handle the possible endianness of the CPU architecture? How do we specify the length of the data to be able to deserialize it properly?

Once again, the Qt folks did a great job and provided us with a great tool to deal with these issues: `QDataStream`.

The `QDataStream` class enables you to serialize binary data to any `QIODevice` (`QAbstractSocket`, `QProcess`, `QFileDevice`, `QSerialPort`, and so on). The great advantage of `QDataStream` is that it encodes the information in a platform-agnostic format. You don't have to worry about the byte order, the operating system, or the CPU.

The `QDataStream` class implements the serialization of C++ primitive types and several Qt types (`QBrush`, `QColor`, `QString`, and so on). Here is an example of a basic write:

```
QFile file("myfile");
file.open(QIODevice::WriteOnly);
QDataStream out(&file);
out << QString("QDataStream saved my day");
out << (qint32)42;
```

As you can see, `QDataStream` relies on the overload of the << operator to write data. To read information, open the file with the correct mode and read with the >> operator.

Back to our case: we want to serialize custom classes, such as `JobRequest`. To do so, we have to overload the << operator for `JobRequest`. The signature of the function will be like this:

```
QDataStream& operator<<(QDataStream& out,
                        const JobRequest& jobRequest)
```

We want to overload the `out << jobRequest` operator call with our custom version. By doing so, we intend to fill the `out` object with the content of `jobRequest`.
Because `QDataStream` already supports the serialization of primitive types, all we have to do is serialize them.

Here is the updated version of `JobRequest.h`:

```
#include <QSize>
#include <QPointF>
#include <QDataStream>

struct JobRequest
{
    ...
```

```
};

inline QDataStream& operator<<(QDataStream& out,
                               const JobRequest& jobRequest)
{
    out << jobRequest.pixelPositionY
        << jobRequest.moveOffset
        << jobRequest.scaleFactor
        << jobRequest.areaSize
        << jobRequest.iterationMax;
    return out;
}

inline QDataStream& operator>>(QDataStream& in,
                               JobRequest& jobRequest)
{
    in >> jobRequest.pixelPositionY;
    in >> jobRequest.moveOffset;
    in >> jobRequest.scaleFactor;
    in >> jobRequest.areaSize;
    in >> jobRequest.iterationMax;
    return in;
}
```

We include `QDataStream` and overload << very easily. The returned `out` will be updated with the platform-agnostic content of the passed `jobRequest`. The >> operator overload follows the same pattern: we fill the `jobRequest` parameter with the content of the `in` variable. Behind the scenes, `QDataStream` stores the variable size in the serialized data to be able to read it afterward.

Be careful to serialize and deserialize the members in the same order. If you do not pay attention to this, you might encounter very peculiar values in `JobRequest`.

The `JobResult` operators overload follows the same pattern, and it does not deserve to be included in the chapter. Look at the source code of the project if you have any doubts about its implementation.

On the other hand, the `Message` operator overload needs to be covered:

```
#include <QByteArray>
#include <QDataStream>

#include <QByteArray>
#include <QDataStream>

struct Message {
    ...
```

```
};

inline QDataStream &operator<<(QDataStream &out, const Message &message)
{
    out <<  static_cast<qint8>(message.type)
        << message.data;
    return out;
}

inline QDataStream &operator>>(QDataStream &in, Message &message)
{
    qint8 type;
    in >> type;
    in >> message.data;

    message.type = static_cast<Message::Type>(type);
    return in;
}
```

Because the `Message::Type enum class` signal does not have an implicit conversion to `int`, we need to explicitly convert it to be able to serialize it. We know that there will not be more than 255 message types, therefore we can safely cast it to a `qint8` type.

The same story applies to the reading part. We start by declaring a `qint8 type` variable that will be filled with `in >> type`, and then, the `type` variable is cast to `Message::Type` in `message`.

Our SDK classes are ready to be serialized and deserialized. Let's see this in action in `MessageUtils` with the serialization of a message and its writing to a `QTcpSocket` class.

While still in the `sdk` directory, create a `MessageUtils.h` header with the following content:

```
#include <QByteArray>
#include <QTcpSocket>
#include <QDataStream>

#include "Message.h"

namespace MessageUtils {

inline void sendMessage(QTcpSocket& socket,
                        Message::Type messageType,
                        QByteArray& data,
                        bool forceFlush = false)
{
    Message message(messageType, data);
```

```
        QByteArray byteArray;
        QDataStream stream(&byteArray, QIODevice::WriteOnly);
        stream << message;
        socket.write(byteArray);
        if (forceFlush) {
            socket.flush();
        }
    }
```

There is no need to instantiate a `MessageUtils` class, as it does not hold any state. Here we used a `MessageUtils` namespace to simply protect our function against any name collision.

The meat of the snippet lies in `sendMessage()`. Let's look at the parameters:

- `socket`: This is the `QTcpSocket` class in which the message will be sent. It is the responsibility of the caller to ensure that it is properly opened.
- `messageType`: This is the type of the message to be sent.
- `data`: This is the serialized data to be included in the message. It is a `QByteArray` class, meaning that the caller already serialized its custom class or data.
- `forceFlush`: This is a flag to force the socket to flush upon the message shipment. The OS keeps socket buffers that wait to be filled before being sent across the wire. Some messages need to be delivered immediately, such as an "abort all jobs" message.

In the function itself, we start by creating a message with the passed parameters. Then, a `QByteArray` class is created. This `byteArray` will be the receptacle of the serialized data.

As a matter of fact, `byteArray` is passed in the constructor of the `QDataStream` stream, which is opened in the `QIODevice::WriteOnly` mode. It means that the stream will output its data to `byteArray`.

After that, the message is elegantly serialized to stream with `stream << message` and the modified `byteArray` is written to the socket with `socket.write(byteArray)`.

Finally, if the `forceFlush` flag is set to `true`, the socket is flushed with `socket.flush()`.

Some messages will not have any associated payload. For this reason, we add a small helper function for this purpose:

```
inline void sendMessage(QTcpSocket& socket,
                        Message::Type messageType,
                        bool forceFlush = false) {
```

```
        QByteArray data;
        sendMessage(socket, messageType, data, forceFlush);
    }
```

Now that the `sendMessage()` is done, let's turn to `readMessages()`. Because we are working in IPC and more specifically with sockets, interesting issues arise when we want to read and parse messages.

When something is ready to be read in the socket, a signal will notify us. But how do we know how much we need to read? In the case of a `WORKER_DISCONNECT` message, there is no payload. On the other hand, a `JOB_RESULT` message can be very heavy. Even worse, several `JOB_RESULT` messages can line up in the socket, waiting to be read.

To make things more difficult, we have to acknowledge the fact that we are working with the network. Packets can be lost, retransmitted, incomplete, or whatever. Sure, TCP ensures that we eventually get all of the information, but it can be delayed.

If we had to do it ourselves, it would have implied a custom message header, with a payload size and a footer for each message.

A feature introduced in Qt 5.7 comes to the rescue: the `QDataStream` transaction. The idea is the following: when you start reading on a `QIODevice` class, you already know how much you have to read (based on the size of the object you want to fill). However, you might not get all the data in a single read.

If the read is not complete, `QDataStream` stores what was already read in a temporary buffer and restores it upon the next read. The next read will contain what was already loaded plus the content of the new read. You can see it as a checkpoint in the read stream that can be loaded later.

This process can be repeated until the data is read. The official documentation provides a simple enough example:

```
in.startTransaction();
qint8 messageType;
QByteArray messageData;
in >> messageType >> messageData;

if (!in.commitTransaction())
    return;
```

In the `QDataStream` class in which we want to read, `in.startTransaction()` marks the checkpoint in the stream. It will then try to read `messageType` and `messageData` atomically. If it cannot do it, `in.commitTransaction()` returns `false` and the read data is copied in an internal buffer.

Upon the next call to this code (more data to read), `in.startTransaction()` will restore the preceding buffer and try to finish the atomic read.

In our `readMessages()` situation, we can receive several messages at once. This is why the code is a bit more complex. Here is the updated version of `MessageUtils`:

```
#include <memory>
#include <vector>
#include <QByteArray>
#include <QTcpSocket>
#include <QDataStream>

#include "Message.h"

...

inline std::unique_ptr<std::vector<std::unique_ptr<Message>>>
readMessages(QDataStream& stream)
{
    auto messages =
std::make_unique<std::vector<std::unique_ptr<Message>>>();
    bool commitTransaction = true;
    while (commitTransaction
                    && stream.device()->bytesAvailable() > 0) {
        stream.startTransaction();
        auto message = std::make_unique<Message>();
        stream >> *message;
        commitTransaction = stream.commitTransaction();
        if (commitTransaction) {
            messages->push_back(std::move(message));
        }
    }
    return messages;
}
```

In the function, the parameter is only a `QDataStream`. We assume that the caller linked the stream with the socket with `stream.setDevice(socket)`.

Because we do not know the length of the content to be read, we prepare ourselves to read several messages. To explicitly indicate ownership and avoid any memory leaks, we return `vector<unique_ptr<Message>>`. This `vector` has to be a `unique_ptr` pointer to be able to allocate it on the heap and avoid any copy during the return of the function.

In the function itself, we start by declaring the `vector`. After that, a `while` loop is executed. The two conditions to stay in the loop are:

- `commitTransaction == true`: This an atomic read in the stream that has been performed; a complete `message` has been read
- `stream.device().bytesAvailable() > 0`: This states that there is still data to read in the stream

In the `while` loop, we start by marking the stream with `stream.startTransaction()`. After that, we try to perform an atomic read of a `*message` signal and see the result with `stream.commitTransaction()`. If it succeeded, the new `message` is added to the `messages` vector. This is repeated until we read all the content of the stream with the `bytesAvailable() > 0` test.

Let's study a use case to understand what will happen. Consider that we receive multiple messages in `readMessages()`:

1. The `stream` object will try to read it into `message`.
2. The `commitTransaction` variable will be set to `true` and the first message will be added to `messages`.
3. If there are still bytes to read in the `stream`, repeat step one. Otherwise, exit the loop.

To sum up, working with sockets raises its own set of questions. On the one hand, it is a very powerful IPC mechanism with a lot of flexibility. On the other hand, it brings a lot of complexity due to the nature of the network itself. Luckily, Qt (and moreover, Qt 5.7) brings great classes to help us.

Keep in mind that we tolerate the `QDataStream` serialization and transaction overhead because it fits our needs. If you are working on a constrained embedded platform, you might not have so much liberty about serializing overhead and buffer copies. However, you will still have to rebuild messages by hand for incoming bytes.

Interacting with sockets in the worker

Now that the SDK is completed, we can turn to the worker. The project is complex enough; we can refresh our memory with the `mandelbrot-worker` architecture:

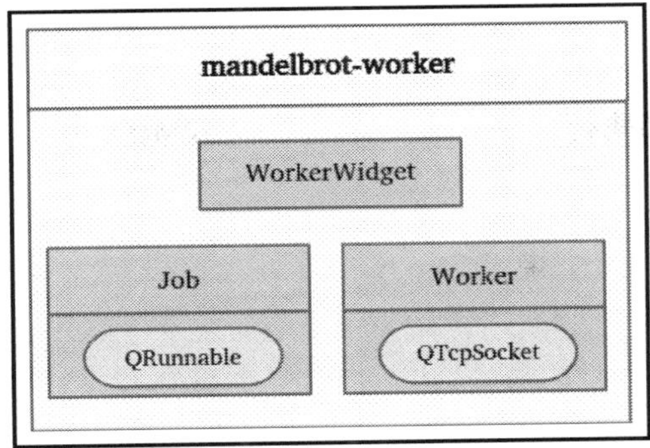

We will start by implementing the `Job` class. Inside the `mandelbrot-worker` project, create a new C++ class named `Job`. Here is the `Job.h` content:

```
#include <QObject>
#include <QRunnable>
#include <QAtomicInteger>

#include "JobRequest.h"
#include "JobResult.h"

class Job : public QObject, public QRunnable
{
    Q_OBJECT
public:
    explicit Job(const JobRequest& jobRequest,
                 QObject *parent = 0);
    void run() override;

signals:
    void jobCompleted(JobResult jobResult);

public slots:
    void abort();

private:
    QAtomicInteger<bool> mAbort;
    JobRequest mJobRequest;
};
```

If you remember the `Job` class from `Chapter 9`, *Keeping Your Sanity with Multithreading*, this header should ring a bell. The only difference is that the parameters of the job (area size, scale factor, and so on) are extracted from the `JobRequest` object rather than stored directly as member variables.

As you can see, the `JobRequest` object is provided in the constructor of `Job`. We will not cover `Job.cpp`, as it is very like the version of it in `Chapter 9`, *Keeping Your Sanity with Multithreading*.

We now proceed to the `Worker` class. This class has the following roles:

- It interacts with `mandelbrot-app` using a `QTcpSocket` class
- It dispatches `JobRequests` to a `QThreadPool` class, aggregates the results, and sends them back to the `mandelbrot-app` application through the `QTcpSocket` class

We will start by studying the interaction with the `QTcpSocket` class. Create a new class named `Worker` with the following header:

```
#include <QObject>
#include <QTcpSocket>
#include <QDataStream>

#include "Message.h"
#include "JobResult.h"

class Worker : public QObject
{
    Q_OBJECT
public:
    Worker(QObject* parent = 0);
    ~Worker();

private:
    void sendRegister();

private:
    QTcpSocket mSocket;
};
```

The `Worker` class is the owner of `mSocket`. The first thing we will implement is the connection with `mandelbrot-app`. Here is the constructor of `Worker` in `Worker.cpp`:

```
#include "Worker.h"

#include <QThread>
#include <QDebug>
#include <QHostAddress>

#include "JobRequest.h"
#include "MessageUtils.h"
```

```
Worker::Worker(QObject* parent) :
    QObject(parent),
    mSocket(this)
{
    connect(&mSocket, &QTcpSocket::connected, [this] {
        qDebug() << "Connected";
        sendRegister();
    });
    connect(&mSocket, &QTcpSocket::disconnected, [] {
        qDebug() << "Disconnected";
    });

    mSocket.connectToHost(QHostAddress::LocalHost, 5000);
}
```

The constructor initializes `mSocket` with `this` as the parent and it then proceeds to connect the relevant `mSocket` signals to lambdas:

- `QTcpSocket::connected`: When the socket is connected, it will send its register message. We will soon cover this function.
- `QTcpSocket::disconnected`: When the socket is disconnected, it simply prints a message in the console.

Finally, `mSocket` tries to connect on `localhost` on port `5000`. In the code example, we assume that you execute the worker and the application on the same machine. Feel free to change this value if you run the worker and the application on different machines.

The body of the `sendRegister()` function looks like this:

```
void Worker::sendRegister()
{
    QByteArray data;
    QDataStream out(&data, QIODevice::WriteOnly);
    out << QThread::idealThreadCount();
    MessageUtils::sendMessage(mSocket,
                              Message::Type::WORKER_REGISTER,
                              data);
}
```

A `QByteArray` class is filled with the `idealThreadCount` function of the worker's machine. After that, we call `MessageUtils::sendMessage` to serialize the message and send it through our `mSocket`.

Once the worker is registered, it will start to receive job requests, process them, and send job results back. Here is the updated `Worker.h`:

```
class Worker : public QObject
{
    ...
signals:
    void abortAllJobs();

private slots:
    void readMessages();

private:
    void handleJobRequest(Message& message);
    void handleAllJobsAbort(Message& message);
    void sendRegister();
    void sendJobResult(JobResult jobResult);
    void sendUnregister();
    Job* createJob(const JobRequest& jobRequest);

private:
    QTcpSocket mSocket;
    QDataStream mSocketReader;
    int mReceivedJobsCounter;
    int mSentJobsCounter;
};
```

Let's review the role of each one of these new members:

- `mSocketReader`: This is the `QDataStream` class through which we will read the `mSocket` content. It will be passed as a parameter to our `MessageUtils::readMessages()` function.
- `mReceivedJobsCounter`: This is incremented each time a new `JobRequest` is received from `mandelbrot-app`.
- `mSentJobsCounter`: This is incremented each time a new `JobResult` is sent to `mandelbrot-app`.

Now for the new functions:

- `abortAllJobs()`: This is a signal emitted when the `Worker` class receives the appropriate message.
- `readMessages()`: This is the slot called each time there is something to read in `mTcpSocket`. It parses the messages and, for each message type, will call the corresponding function.

- `handleJobRequest()`: This function creates and dispatches a `Job` class according to the `JobRequest` object contained in the message parameter.
- `handleAllJobsAbort()`: This function cancels all the current jobs and clears the thread queue.
- `sendJobResult()`: This function sends the `JobResult` object to `mandelbrot-app`.
- `sendUnregister()`: This function sends the unregister message to `mandelbrot-app`.
- `createJob()`: This is a helper function to create and properly connect the signals of a new `Job`.

The header is now complete. We can proceed to the updated constructor in `Worker.cpp`:

```
Worker::Worker(QObject* parent) :
    QObject(parent),
    mSocket(this),
    mSocketReader(&mSocket),
    mReceivedJobsCounter(0),
    mSentJobsCounter(0)
{
    ...
    connect(&mSocket, &QTcpSocket::readyRead,
            this, &Worker::readMessages);

    mSocket.connectToHost(QHostAddress::LocalHost, 5000);
}
```

The `QDataStream mSocketReader` variable is initialized with the address of `mSocket`. This means that it will read its content from the `QIODevice` class. After that, we add the new connect to the `QTcpSocket` signal, `readyRead()`. Each time that data is available to read on the socket, our slot, `readMessages()`, will be called.

Here is the implementation of `readMessages()`:

```
void Worker::readMessages()
{
    auto messages = MessageUtils::readMessages(mSocketReader);
    for(auto& message : *messages) {
        switch (message->type) {
            case Message::Type::JOB_REQUEST:
                handleJobRequest(*message);
                break;
            case Message::Type::ALL_JOBS_ABORT:
                handleAllJobsAbort(*message);
```

```
                break;
            default:
                break;
        }
    }
}
```

The messages are parsed with the `MessageUtils::readMessages()` function. Note the use of C++11 semantics with `auto`, which elegantly hides the smart pointers syntax and still handles the memory for us.

For each parsed `message`, it is handled in the `switch` case. Let's review `handleJobRequest()`:

```
void Worker::handleJobRequest(Message& message)
{
     QDataStream in(&message.data, QIODevice::ReadOnly);
     QList<JobRequest> requests;
     in >> requests;

     mReceivedJobsCounter += requests.size();
     for(const JobRequest& jobRequest : requests) {
         QThreadPool::globalInstance()
                    ->start(createJob(jobRequest));
     }
}
```

In this function, the `message` object is already deserialized. However, `message.data` still needs to be deserialized. To achieve this, we create `QDataStream` in a variable that will read from `message.data`.

From here, we parse the requests `QList`. Because `QList` already overrides the `>>` operator, it works in cascade and calls our `JobRequest >>` operator overload. Deserializing data has never been so easy!

After that, we increment `mReceivedJobsCounter` and start processing these `JobRequests`. For each one, we create a `Job` class and dispatch it to the global `QThreadPool` class. If you have a doubt about `QThreadPool`, go back to `Chapter 9`, *Keeping Your Sanity with Multithreading*.

The `createJob()` function is straightforward to implement:

```
Job* Worker::createJob(const JobRequest& jobRequest)
{
    Job* job = new Job(jobRequest);
    connect(this, &Worker::abortAllJobs,
```

```
            job, &Job::abort);
    connect(job, &Job::jobCompleted,
            this, &Worker::sendJobResult);
    return job;
}
```

A new Job class is created and its signals are properly connected.
When Worker::abortAllJobs is emitted, every running Job should be canceled with the Job::abort slot.

The second signal, Job::jobCompleted is emitted when the Job class has finished calculating its values. Let's see the connected slot, sendJobResult():

```
void Worker::sendJobResult(JobResult jobResult)
{
    mSentJobsCounter++;
    QByteArray data;
    QDataStream out(&data, QIODevice::WriteOnly);
    out << jobResult;
    MessageUtils::sendMessage(mSocket,
                              Message::Type::JOB_RESULT,
                              data);
}
```

We first increment mSentJobsCounter and then serialize JobResult to a QByteArray data that is passed to MessageUtils::sendMessage().

We've completed the tour of handling JobRequest and the following JobResult shipment. We still have to cover handleAllJobsAbort(), which is called from readMessages():

```
void Worker::handleAllJobsAbort(Message& /*message*/)
{
    emit abortAllJobs();
    QThreadPool::globalInstance()->clear();
    mReceivedJobsCounter = 0;
    mSentJobsCounter = 0;
}
```

The abortAllJobs() signal is emitted first to tell all the running jobs to cancel their process. After that, the QThreadPool class is cleared and the counters are reset.

The last piece of `Worker` is `sendUnregister()`, which is called in the `Worker` destructor:

```
Worker::~Worker()
{
    sendUnregister();
}

void Worker::sendUnregister()
{
    MessageUtils::sendMessage(mSocket,
                              Message::Type::WORKER_UNREGISTER,
                              true);
}
```

The `sendUnregister()` function just calls `sendMessage` without any data to serialize. Note that it passes the `forceFlush` flag to `true` to make sure that the socket is flushed and that the `mandelbrot-app` application will receive the message as fast as possible.

The `Worker` instance will be managed by a widget that will display the progress of the current calculation. Create a new class named `WorkerWidget` and update `WorkerWidget.h`, like so:

```
#include <QWidget>
#include <QThread>
#include <QProgressBar>
#include <QTimer>

#include "Worker.h"

class WorkerWidget : public QWidget
{
    Q_OBJECT
public:
    explicit WorkerWidget(QWidget *parent = 0);
    ~WorkerWidget();

private:
    QProgressBar mStatus;
    Worker mWorker;
    QThread mWorkerThread;
    QTimer mRefreshTimer;
};
```

The members of `WorkerWidget` are:

- `mStatus`: `QProgressBar` that will display the percentage of processed the `JobRequest`.
- `mWorker`: The `Worker` instance owned and started by `WorkerWidget`.
- `mWorkerThread`: The `QThread` class in which `mWorker` will be executed.
- `mRefreshTimer`: The `QTimer` class that will periodically poll `mWorker` to know the status of the process.

We can proceed to `WorkerWidget.cpp`:

```
#include "WorkerWidget.h"

#include <QVBoxLayout>

WorkerWidget::WorkerWidget(QWidget *parent) :
    QWidget(parent),
    mStatus(this),
    mWorker(),
    mWorkerThread(this),
    mRefreshTimer()
{
    QVBoxLayout* layout = new QVBoxLayout(this);
    layout->addWidget(&mStatus);

    mWorker.moveToThread(&mWorkerThread);

    connect(&mRefreshTimer, &QTimer::timeout, [this] {
        mStatus.setMaximum(mWorker.receivedJobsCounter());
        mStatus.setValue(mWorker.sentJobCounter());
    });

    mWorkerThread.start();
    mRefreshTimer.start(100);
}

WorkerWidget::~WorkerWidget()
{
    mWorkerThread.quit();
    mWorkerThread.wait(1000);
}
```

First, the `mStatus` variable is added to the `WorkerWidget` layout. Then, the `mWorker` thread affinity is moved to `mWorkerThread`, and `mRefreshTimer` is configured to poll `mWorker` and updates `mStatus` data.

Finally, `mWorkerThread` is started, triggering the `mWorker` process. The `mRefreshTimer` object is also started with an interval of 100 milliseconds between each timeout.

The last thing to cover in `mandelbrot-worker` is `main.cpp`:

```
#include <QApplication>

#include "JobResult.h"

#include "WorkerWidget.h"

int main(int argc, char *argv[])
{
    qRegisterMetaType<JobResult>();

    QApplication a(argc, argv);
    WorkerWidget workerWidget;

    workerWidget.show();
    return a.exec();
}
```

We start by registering `JobResult` with `qRegisterMetaType` because it is used in the signal/slot mechanism. After that, we instantiate a `WorkerWidget` layout and display it.

Interacting with sockets from the application

The next project to complete is `mandelbrot-app`. It will contain `QTcpServer`, which will interact with the workers and the picture drawing of the Mandelbrot set. As a reminder, the diagram of the `mandelbrot-app` architecture is shown here:

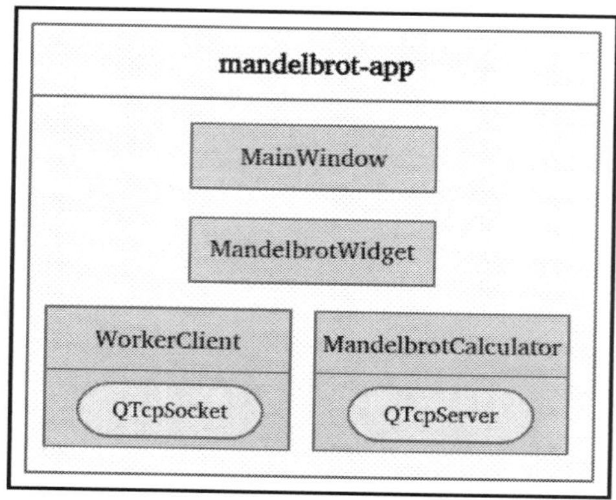

We will build this application from the ground up. Let's start with the class responsible for maintaining the connection with a specific `Worker`: `WorkerClient`. This class will live in its specific `QThread` and will interact with a `Worker` class using the same `QTcpSocket`/`QDataStream` mechanism we covered in the last section.

In `mandelbrot-app`, create a new C++ class named `WorkerClient` and update `WorkerClient.h` like so:

```
#include <QTcpSocket>
#include <QList>
#include <QDataStream>

#include "JobRequest.h"
#include "JobResult.h"
#include "Message.h"

class WorkerClient : public QObject
{
    Q_OBJECT
public:
    WorkerClient(int socketDescriptor);

private:
    int mSocketDescriptor;
    int mCpuCoreCount;
    QTcpSocket mSocket;
    QDataStream mSocketReader;
};

Q_DECLARE_METATYPE(WorkerClient*)
```

It looks very similar to `Worker`. Yet it may behave differently from a life cycle point of view. Each time a new `Worker` connects to our `QTcpServer`, a new `WorkerClient` will be spawned with an associated `QThread`. The `WorkerClient` object will take the responsibility of interacting with the `Worker` class through `mSocket`.

If `Worker` disconnects, the `WorkerClient` object will be deleted and removed from the `QTcpServer` class.

Let's review the content of this header, starting with the members:

- `mSocketDescriptor`: This is the unique integer assigned by the system to interact with the socket. `stdin`, `stdout`, and `stderr` are also descriptors that point to specific streams in your application. For a given socket, the value will be retrieved in `QTcpServer`. More on this later.

- `mCpuCoreCount`: This is the CPU core count for the connected `Worker`. This field will be initialized when the `Worker` sends the `WORKER_REGISTER` message.
- `mSocket`: This is the `QTcpSocket` used to interact with the `Worker` class.
- `mSocketReader`: This has the same role it had in `Worker`—it reads the `mSocket` content.

Now we can add the functions to `WorkerClient.h`:

```
class WorkerClient : public QObject
{
    Q_OBJECT
public:
    WorkerClient(int socketDescriptor);
    int cpuCoreCount() const;

signals:
    void unregistered(WorkerClient* workerClient);
    void jobCompleted(WorkerClient* workerClient,
                      JobResult jobResult);
    void sendJobRequests(QList<JobRequest> requests);

public slots:
    void start();
    void abortJob();

private slots:
    void readMessages();
    void doSendJobRequests(QList<JobRequest> requests);

private:
    void handleWorkerRegistered(Message& message);
    void handleWorkerUnregistered(Message& message);
    void handleJobResult(Message& message);

    ...
};
```

Let's see what each function does:

- `WorkerClient()`: This function expects `socketDescriptor` as a parameter. As a consequence, a `WorkerClient` function cannot be initialized without a valid socket.
- `cpuCoreCount()`: This function is a simple getter to let the owner of `WorkerClient` know how many cores the `Worker` has.

The class has three signals:

- `unregister()`: sent by `WorkerClient` when it receives the `WORKER_UNREGISTER` message.
- `jobCompleted()`: sent by `WorkerClient` when it receives the `JOB_RESULT` message. It will pass by copying the deserialized `JobResult`.
- `sendJobRequests()`: emitted from the owner of `WorkerClient` to pass `JobRequests` in a queued connection to the proper slot: `doSendJobRequests()`.

Here are the details of the slots:

- `start()`: called when `WorkerClient` can start its process. Typically, it will be connected to the `start` signal of the `QThread` associated with `WorkerClient`.
- `abortJob()`: triggers the shipment of the `ALL_JOBS_ABORT` message to `Worker`.
- `readMessages()`: called each time there is something to read in the socket.
- `doSendJobRequests()`: the real slot that triggers the shipment of `JobRequests` to `Worker`.

And finally, here are the details of the private functions:

- `handleWorkerRegistered()`: processes the `WORKER_REGISTER` message and initializes `mCpuCoreCount`
- `handleWorkerUnregistered()`: processes the `WORKER_UNREGISTER` message and emits the `unregistered()` signal
- `handleJobResult()`: processes the `JOB_RESULT` message and dispatches the content through the `jobCompleted()` signal

The implementation in `WorkerClient.cpp` should be quite familiar. Here is the constructor:

```
#include "MessageUtils.h"

WorkerClient::WorkerClient(int socketDescriptor) :
    QObject(),
    mSocketDescriptor(socketDescriptor),
    mSocket(this),
    mSocketReader(&mSocket)
{
    connect(this, &WorkerClient::sendJobRequests,
            this, &WorkerClient::doSendJobRequests);
}
```

The fields are initialized in the initialization list and the `sendJobRequests` signal is connected to the private slot, `doSendJobRequests`. This trick is used to still have a queued connection across threads, while avoiding multiple functions declarations.

We will proceed with the `start()` function:

```
void WorkerClient::start()
{
    connect(&mSocket, &QTcpSocket::readyRead,
            this, &WorkerClient::readMessages);
    mSocket.setSocketDescriptor(mSocketDescriptor);
}
```

This is very short indeed. It first connects the `readyRead()` signal from the socket to our `readMessages()` slot. After that, `mSocket` is properly configured with `mSocketDescriptor`.

The connect has to be done in `start()` because it should be executed in the `QThread` class associated with our `WorkerClient`. By doing so, we know that the connect will be a direct connection and that `mSocket` will not have to queue signals to interact with `WorkerClient`.

Note that at the end of the function, the associated `QThread` is not terminated. On the contrary, it is executing its event loop with `QThread::exec()`. The `QThread` class will continue to run its event loop until someone calls `QThread::exit()`.

The only purpose of the `start()` function is to do the `mSocket` connect work in the right thread affinity. After that, we rely solely on the Qt signal/slot mechanism to process data. There is no need for a busy `while` loop.

The `readMessages()` class is waiting for us; let's see it:

```
void WorkerClient::readMessages()
{
    auto messages = MessageUtils::readMessages(mSocketReader);
    for(auto& message : *messages) {
        switch (message->type) {
            case Message::Type::WORKER_REGISTER:
                handleWorkerRegistered(*message);
                break;
            case Message::Type::WORKER_UNREGISTER:
                handleWorkerUnregistered(*message);
                break;
            case Message::Type::JOB_RESULT:
                handleJobResult(*message);
```

```
                break;
            default:
                break;
        }
    }
}
```

No surprise here. It's exactly like we did for `Worker`. `Messages` are deserialized using `MessageUtils::readMessages()` and, for each message type, the appropriate function is called.

Here is the content of each of these functions, starting with `handleWorkerRegistered()`:

```
void WorkerClient::handleWorkerRegistered(Message& message)
{
    QDataStream in(&message.data, QIODevice::ReadOnly);
    in >> mCpuCoreCount;
}
```

For the `WORKER_REGISTER` message, `Worker` only serialized `int` in `message.data`, so we can initialize `mCpuCoreCount` on the spot with `in >> mCpuCoreCount`.

Here is the body of `handleWorkerUnregistered()`:

```
void WorkerClient::handleWorkerUnregistered(Message& /*message*/)
{
    emit unregistered(this);
}
```

It is a relay to send the `unregistered()` signal, which will be picked up by the owner of `WorkerClient`.

The last "read" function is `handleJobResult()`:

```
void WorkerClient::handleJobResult(Message& message)
{
    QDataStream in(&message.data, QIODevice::ReadOnly);
    JobResult jobResult;
    in >> jobResult;
    emit jobCompleted(this, jobResult);
}
```

This is deceptively short. It only deserializes the `jobResult` component from `message.data` and emits the `jobCompleted()` signal.

The "write-to-socket" functions are `abortJob()` and `doSendJobRequest()`:

```
void WorkerClient::abortJob()
{
    MessageUtils::sendMessage(mSocket,
                              Message::Type::ALL_JOBS_ABORT,
                              true);
}

void WorkerClient::doSendJobRequests(QList<JobRequest> requests)
{
    QByteArray data;
    QDataStream stream(&data, QIODevice::WriteOnly);
    stream << requests;

    MessageUtils::sendMessage(mSocket,
                              Message::Type::JOB_REQUEST,
                              data);
}
```

The `abortJob()` function sends the `ALL_JOBS_ABORT` message with the `forceFlush` flag set to `true`, and `doSendJobRequests()` serializes the `requests` to stream before sending them using `MessageUtils::sendMessage()`.

Building your own QTcpServer

Everything is ready to read and write in our sockets. We still need a server to orchestrate all these instances. To do so, we will develop a modified version of the `MandelbrotCalculator` class, which was covered in `Chapter 9`, *Keeping Your Sanity with Multithreading*.

The idea is to respect the same interface, in order to keep `MandelbrotWidget` oblivious to the fact that the Mandelbrot picture-generation is deported on different processes/machines.

The main difference between the old `MandelbrotCalculator` and the new one is that we replaced the `QThreadPool` class with `QTcpServer`. The `MandelbrotCalculator` class now only has the responsibility to dispatch `JobRequests` to Workers and aggregate the results. It will no longer interact with a `QThreadPool` class.

Create a new C++ class named `MandelbrotCalculator.cpp` and update `MandelbrotCalculator.h` to match this:

```
#include <memory>
#include <vector>

#include <QTcpServer>
#include <QList>
#include <QThread>
#include <QMap>
#include <QElapsedTimer>

#include "WorkerClient.h"
#include "JobResult.h"
#include "JobRequest.h"

class MandelbrotCalculator : public QTcpServer
{
    Q_OBJECT
public:
    MandelbrotCalculator(QObject* parent = 0);
    ~MandelbrotCalculator();

signals:
    void pictureLinesGenerated(QList<JobResult> jobResults);
    void abortAllJobs();

public slots:
    void generatePicture(QSize areaSize, QPointF moveOffset,
                         double scaleFactor, int iterationMax);

private slots:
    void process(WorkerClient* workerClient, JobResult jobResult);
    void removeWorkerClient(WorkerClient* workerClient);

protected:
    void incomingConnection(qintptr socketDescriptor) override;

private:
    std::unique_ptr<JobRequest> createJobRequest(
                                        int pixelPositionY);
    void sendJobRequests(WorkerClient& client,
                         int jobRequestCount = 1);
    void clearJobs();

private:
    QPointF mMoveOffset;
    double mScaleFactor;
```

```
    QSize mAreaSize;
    int mIterationMax;
    int mReceivedJobResults;
    QList<JobResult> mJobResults;
    QMap<WorkerClient*, QThread*> mWorkerClients;
    std::vector<std::unique_ptr<JobRequest>> mJobRequests;
    QElapsedTimer mTimer;
};
```

The modified (or new) data is highlighted. First, note that the class now inherits from `QTcpServer` rather than `QObject`. The `MandelbrotCalculator` class is now a `QTcpServer` and is able to accept and manage connections. Before digging into this topic, we can review the new members:

- `mWorkerClients`: This is a `QMap` that stores the `WorkerClient` and `QThread` pair. Each time a `WorkerClient` is created, an associated `QThread` is also spawned and both of them are stored in `mWorkerClients`.
- `mJobRequests`: This is the list of the `JobRequest` for the current picture. Each time a picture-generation is requested, the full list of `JobRequest` is generated, ready to be dispatched to `WorkerClients` (that is, to the `Worker` on the other side of the socket).

And the functions are:

- `process()`: a slightly modified version of the one seen in `Chapter 9`, *Keeping Your Sanity with Multithreading*. It not only aggregates the `JobResult` before sending them with the `pictureLinesGenerated()` signal, but also dispatches `JobRequest` to the passed `WorkerClient` to keep them busy.
- `removeWorkerClient()`: removes and deletes the given `WorkerClient` from `mWorkerClients`.
- `incomingConnection()`: an overloaded function from `QTcpServer`. It is called each time a new client tries to connect to `MandelbrotCalculator`.
- `createJobRequest()`: a helper function that creates a `JobRequest` that is added to `mJobRequests`.
- `sendJobRequests()`: is responsible for sending a list of the `JobRequest` to the specified `WorkerClient`.

Let's turn to `MandelbrotCalculator.cpp` with the constructor:

```
#include <QDebug>
#include <QThread>

using namespace std;

const int JOB_RESULT_THRESHOLD = 10;

MandelbrotCalculator::MandelbrotCalculator(QObject* parent) :
    QTcpServer(parent),
     mMoveOffset(),
    mScaleFactor(),
    mAreaSize(),
    mIterationMax(),
    mReceivedJobResults(0),
    mWorkerClients(),
    mJobRequests(),
    mTimer()
{
    listen(QHostAddress::Any, 5000);
}
```

This is the common initialization list with the `listen()` instruction in the body. Because we are subclassing `QTcpServer`, we can call listen on ourselves. Note that `QHostAddress::Any` works either with IPv4 or IPv6.

Let's see the overloaded function, `incomingConnection()`:

```
void MandelbrotCalculator::incomingConnection( qintptr socketDescriptor)
{
    qDebug() << "Connected workerClient";
    QThread* thread = new QThread(this);
    WorkerClient* client = new WorkerClient(socketDescriptor);
    int workerClientsCount = mWorkerClients.keys().size();
    mWorkerClients.insert(client, thread);
    client->moveToThread(thread);

    connect(this, &MandelbrotCalculator::abortAllJobs,
            client, &WorkerClient::abortJob);

    connect(client, &WorkerClient::unregistered,
            this, &MandelbrotCalculator::removeWorkerClient);
    connect(client, &WorkerClient::jobCompleted,
            this, &MandelbrotCalculator::process);

    connect(thread, &QThread::started,
            client, &WorkerClient::start);
```

```
        thread->start();

        if(workerClientsCount == 0 &&
            mWorkerClients.size() == 1) {
            generatePicture(mAreaSize, mMoveOffset,
                            mScaleFactor, mIterationMax);
        }
    }
```

Once `listen()` has been called, each time someone connects to our IP/port pair, `incomingConnection()` will be triggered with `socketDescriptor` passed as a parameter.

You can test this on your machine connection with a simple `telnet 127.0.0.1 5000` command. You should see the `Connected workerClient` log in `mandelbrot-app`.

We start by creating a `QThread` class and a `WorkerClient`. This pair is immediately inserted in the `mWorkerClients` map and the `client` thread affinity is changed to `thread`.

Then, we do all the `connect` to manage the `client` (`abortJob`, `unregister`, and `jobCompleted`). We continue with the `QThread::started()` signal, which is connected to the `WorkerClient::start()` slot and finally, `thread` is started.

The last part of the function is used to trigger a picture-generation upon the first `client` connection. If we did not do this, the screen would have remained black until we panned or zoomed.

We have covered the `WorkerClient` creation. Let's finish its life cycle with its destruction with `removeWorkerClient()`:

```
void MandelbrotCalculator::removeWorkerClient(WorkerClient* workerClient)
{
    qDebug() << "Removing workerClient";
    QThread* thread = mWorkerClients.take(workerClient);
    thread->quit();
    thread->wait(1000);
    delete thread;
    delete workerClient;
}
```

The workerClient/thread pair is removed from mWorkerClients and cleanly deleted. Note that this function can be called from the WorkerClient::unregistered signal or in the MandelbrotCalculator destructor:

```
MandelbrotCalculator::~MandelbrotCalculator()
{
    while (!mWorkerClients.empty()) {
        removeWorkerClient(mWorkerClients.firstKey());
    }
}
```

When MandelbrotCalculator is deleted, mWorkerClients has to be properly emptied. The iterator-style while loop does a good job of calling removeWorkerClient().

In this new version of MandelbrotCalculator, the generatePicture() function does not have exactly the same behavior:

```
void MandelbrotCalculator::generatePicture(
                              QSize areaSize, QPointF moveOffset,
                              double scaleFactor, int iterationMax)
{
    // sanity check & members initization
    ...

    for(int pixelPositionY = mAreaSize.height() - 1;
        pixelPositionY >= 0; pixelPositionY--) {
        mJobRequests.push_back(move(
                              createJobRequest(pixelPositionY)));
    }

    for(WorkerClient* client : mWorkerClients.keys()) {
        sendJobRequests(*client, client->cpuCoreCount() * 2);
    }
}
```

The beginning is the same. However, the end is quite different. Rather than creating Jobs and giving them to QThreadPool, MandelbrotCalculator now:

- Creates JobRequests to generate the whole picture. Note that they are created in reverse order. We will soon see why.
- Dispatches a number of JobRequests to each WorkerClient it owns.

The second point deserves a strong emphasis. If we want to maximize the speed of our system, we have to use multiple workers, each one having multiple cores to process multiple jobs at the same time.

Even though a `Worker` class can process multiple jobs at the same time, it can only send us `JobResults` one by one (through `WorkerClient::jobCompleted`). Each time we process a `JobResult` object from a `WorkerClient`, we will dispatch a single `JobRequest` to it.

Assume that the `Worker` class has eight cores. If we send `JobRequests` one by one, the `Worker` will always have seven cores idle. We are here to heat up your CPUs, not to let them drink mojitos on the beach!

To mitigate this, the first batch of `JobResults` we send to a worker has to be higher than its `coreCount()`. By doing so, we ensure that is always has a queue of `JobRequests` to process until we generate the whole picture. This is why we send `client->cpuCoreCount() * two` initial `JobRequests`. If you play with this value, you will see that:

- If `jobCount < cpuCoreCount()`, some cores of your `Worker` will be idle and you will not leverage the full power of its CPU
- If `jobCount > cpuCoreCount()` by too much, you might overload the queue of one of the `Workers`

Remember that this system is flexible enough to have multiple workers. If you have a RaspberryPI and an x86 with 16 cores, the RaspberryPI will lag behind the x86 CPU. By giving too many initial `JobRequests`, the RaspberryPI will hinder the whole picture-generation while the x86 CPU has already finished all its jobs.

Let's cover the remaining functions of `MandelbrotCalculator`, starting with `createJobRequest()`:

```
std::unique_ptr<JobRequest> MandelbrotCalculator::createJobRequest(int
pixelPositionY)
{
    auto jobRequest = make_unique<JobRequest>();
    jobRequest->pixelPositionY = pixelPositionY;
    jobRequest->moveOffset = mMoveOffset;
    jobRequest->scaleFactor = mScaleFactor;
    jobRequest->areaSize = mAreaSize;
    jobRequest->iterationMax = mIterationMax;
    return jobRequest;
}
```

This is a simple creation of `jobRequest` with the member fields of `MandelbrotCalculator`. Again, we use `unique_ptr` to explicitly indicate the ownership of `jobRequest` and avoid any memory leaks.

Next, here is the implementation of the `sendJobRequests()` function:

```
void MandelbrotCalculator::sendJobRequests(WorkerClient& client, int
jobRequestCount)
{
    QList<JobRequest> listJobRequest;
    for (int i = 0; i < jobRequestCount; ++i) {
        if (mJobRequests.empty()) {
            break;
        }

        auto jobRequest = move(mJobRequests.back());
        mJobRequests.pop_back();
        listJobRequest.append(*jobRequest);
    }

    if (!listJobRequest.empty()) {
        emit client.sendJobRequests(listJobRequest);
    }
}
```

Because we can send multiple `JobRequests` at the same time, we loop on `jobRequestCount` by taking the last `jobRequest` of `mJobRequests` and adding it to `listJobRequest`. This is the reason for which we had to fill `mJobRequests` in the reverse order.

Finally, the `client.sendJobRequests()` signal is emitted, which in turns triggers the `WorkerClient::doSendJobRequests()` slot.

We are now going to see the modified version of `process()`:

```
void MandelbrotCalculator::process(WorkerClient* workerClient,
                                   JobResult jobResult)

{
    // Sanity check and JobResult aggregation

    if (mReceivedJobResults < mAreaSize.height()) {
        sendJobRequests(*workerClient);
    } else {
        qDebug() << "Generated in" << mTimer.elapsed() << "ms";
    }
}
```

In this version, we pass `workerClient` as a parameter. This is used at the end of the function, to be able to dispatch a new `JobRequest` to the given `workerClient`.

Finally, here is the updated version of `abortAllJobs()`:

```
void MandelbrotCalculator::clearJobs()
{
    mReceivedJobResults = 0;
    mJobRequests.clear();
    emit abortAllJobs();
}
```

This simply cleared `mJobRequests` instead of emptying `QThreadPool`.

The `MandelbrotCalculator` class is completed! You can copy and paste `MandelBrotWidget` and `MainWindow` (`.ui` file included) from `Chapter 9`, *Keeping Your Sanity with Multithreading*. We designed it to be plug-and-play, without knowing who generates the picture: a local `QThreadPool` with `QRunnable` or minions through an IPC mechanism.

There is only a tiny difference in `main.cpp`:

```
#include <QApplication>
#include <QList>

#include "JobRequest.h"
#include "JobResult.h"
#include "WorkerClient.h"

int main(int argc, char *argv[])
{
    qRegisterMetaType<QList<JobRequest>>();
    qRegisterMetaType<QList<JobResult>>();
    qRegisterMetaType<WorkerClient*>();

    QApplication a(argc, argv);
    MainWindow w;
    w.show();

    return a.exec();
}
```

You can now launch `mandelbrot-app` and after that, the one or many `mandelbrot-worker` programs that will connect to the application. It should automatically trigger a picture-generation. The Mandelbrot picture-generation is now working across multiple processes! Because we chose to use sockets, you can start the application and the workers on different physical machines.

Using IPv6, you may very easily test the app/worker connection in different locations. If you don't have a high-speed internet connection, you will see how the network hinders the picture-generation.

You may want to take some time to deploy the application on multiple machines and see how this cluster behaves. During our tests, we ramped our cluster up to 18 cores with very heterogeneous machines (PC, laptop, Macbook, and so on).

Summary

IPC is a fundamental mechanism in computer science. In this chapter, you learned the various techniques offered by Qt to do IPC and how to create an application that uses sockets to interact, send, and receive commands. You took the original `mandelbrot-threadpool` application to the next level by enabling it to generate pictures on a cluster of machines.

Adding IPC on top of a multithreaded application brings some issues. You have many more possible bottlenecks, chances of leaking memory, and having an inefficient calculation. Qt provides multiple mechanisms to do IPC. Since Qt 5.7, the addition of transactions that makes the serialization/deserialization part much easier.

In the next chapter, you will discover the Qt Multimedia framework and how to save and load a C++ object from a file. The project example will be a virtual drum machine. You will be able to save and load your tracks.

11
Having Fun with Multimedia and Serialization

The previous chapter was a firework of threads, sockets, and workers. We hope that your minions have been working hard. In this chapter, we will turn our attention to serialization with Qt. You will learn how to serialize data in multiple formats with a flexible system. The example project will be a virtual drum machine, in which you can compose you own drum beat, record it, play it, save it, and load it. Your drum beat will probably be so awesome that you will want to share it, and you will now be able to do this in various formats.

This chapter will cover the following topics:

- Architecting the drum machine project
- Creating a drum track
- Making your objects serializable with `QVariant`
- Playing low-latency sounds with `QSoundEffect`
- Triggering a `QButton` with your keyboard
- Accepting mouse drag-and-drop events

Architecting the drum machine project

As usual, before diving into the code, let's study the structure of the project. The aim of the project is to be able to do the following:

- Play and record a sound track from a drum machine
- Save this track to a file and load it to play it back

To play a sound, we will lay out four big buttons that will play a specific drum sound upon being clicked (or upon a keyboard event): a kick, a snare, a hi-hat, and a cymbal crash. These sounds will be `.wav` files that are loaded by the application. The user will be able to record their sequence of sounds and replay it.

For the serialization, we do not just want to save the track to a single file format—we would rather save it to the following three file formats:

- **JavaScript Object Notation** (**JSON**)
- **eXtensible Markup Language** (**XML**)
- **Binary**

Not only is it more fun to cover three formats, but it also gives us the opportunity to understand the advantages and limitations of each one and how it fits within the Qt framework. The architecture we are going to implement will be flexible enough to handle future evolutions. You never know how a project can evolve!

The classes' organization looks like the arrangement shown in the following diagram:

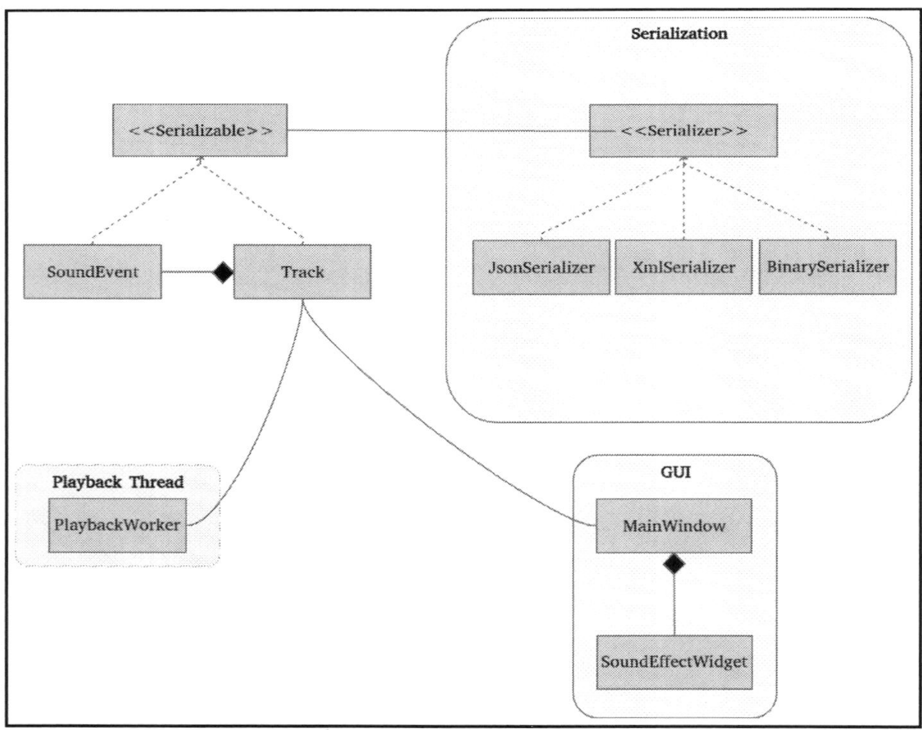

Let's review the roles of these classes:

- The `SoundEvent` class is the basic building block of a track. It is a simple class containing `timestamp` (when the sound has been played) and `soundId` (what sound has been played) variables.
- The `Track` class contains a list of `SoundEvents`, a duration, and a state (playing, recording, stopped). Each time the user plays a sound, a `SoundEvent` class is created and added to the `Track` class.
- The `PlaybackWorker` class is a worker class that runs in a different thread. It is responsible for looping through the `Track` class' `soundEvents` and triggering the proper sound when its `timestamp` has been reached.
- The `Serializable` class is an interface that must be implemented by each class that wants to be serialized (in our case, `SoundEvent` and `Track`).
- The `Serializer` class is an interface that must be implemented by each format-specific implementation class.
- The `JsonSerializer`, `XmlSerializer`, and `BinarySerializer` code phrases are the subclasses of the `Serializer` class that perform the format-specific job of serializing/deserializing a `Serializable` instance.
- The `SoundEffectWidget` class is the widget that holds the information needed to play a single sound. It displays the button for one of our four sounds. It also owns a `QSoundEffect` class that sends the sound to the audio card.
- The `MainWindow` class holds everything together. It owns the `Track` class, spawns the `PlaybackWorker` thread, and triggers the serialization/deserialization.

The output format should be easily swapped. To achieve this, we will rely on a modified version of the bridge design pattern that will allow the `Serializable` and `Serializer` classes to evolve independently.

The whole project revolves around this notion of independence between modules. This notion extends to the point that a sound can be replaced on the spot during a playback. Let's say that you listen to your incredible beat, and you want to try another snare sound. You will be able to replace it with a simple drag and drop of a `.wav` file on the `SoundEffectWidget` class holding the snare sound.

Creating a drum track

Let's buckle up and do this project! Create a new **Qt Widgets Application** project named `ch11-drum-machine`. As usual, add the `CONFIG += c++14` in `ch11-drum-machine.pro`.

Now, create a new C++ class named `SoundEvent`. Here is `SoundEvent.h` stripped of its functions:

```
#include <QtGlobal>

class SoundEvent
{

public:
    SoundEvent(qint64 timestamp = 0, int soundId = 0);
    ~SoundEvent();

    qint64 timestamp;
    int soundId;
};
```

This class contains only two public members:

- `timestamp`: A `qint64` (of the `long long` type) that contains the current time of the `SoundEvent` in milliseconds since the beginning of the track
- `soundId`: The ID of the sound that has been played

In recording mode, each time the user plays a sound, a `SoundEvent` is created with the appropriate data. The content of the `SoundEvent.cpp` file is so boring that we will not inflict it on you.

The next class to build is `Track`. Again, create the new C++ class. Let's look at `Track.h` with its members only:

```
#include <QObject>
#include <QVector>
#include <QElapsedTimer>

#include "SoundEvent.h"

class Track : public QObject
{
    Q_OBJECT
public:
    enum class State {
```

```
        STOPPED,
        PLAYING,
        RECORDING,
    };

    explicit Track(QObject *parent = 0);
    ~Track();

private:
    qint64 mDuration;
    std::vector<std::unique_ptr<SoundEvent>> mSoundEvents;
    QElapsedTimer mTimer;
    State mState;
    State mPreviousState;
};
```

We can now go into detail about them:

- `mDuration`: This variable holds the duration of the `Track` class. This member is reset to `0` when a recording is started and updated when the recording is stopped.
- `mSoundEvents`: This variable is the list of `SoundEvents` for the given `Track`. As the `unique_ptr` semantic states it, `Track` is the owner of the sound events.
- `mTimer`: This variable is started each time `Track` is played or recorded.
- `mState`: This variable is the current `State` of the `Track` class, which can have three possible values: `STOPPED`, `PLAYING`, and `RECORDING`.
- `mPreviousState`: This variable is the previous `State` of `Track`. This is useful when you want to know which action to perform on a new `STOPPEDState`. We will have to stop the playback if `mPreviousState` is in the `PLAYING` state.

The `Track` class is the pivot of the business logic of the project. It holds `mState`, which is the state of the whole application. Its content will be read during a playback of your awesome musical performance, and will also be serialized to a file.

Let's enrich `Track.h` with functions:

```
class Track : public QObject
{
    Q_OBJECT
public:
    ...
    qint64 duration() const;
    State state() const;
    State previousState() const;
    quint64 elapsedTime() const;
```

```
    const std::vector<std::unique_ptr<SoundEvent>>& soundEvents() const;

signals:
    void stateChanged(State state);

public slots:
    void play();
    void record();
    void stop();
    void addSoundEvent(int soundEventId);

private:
    void clear();
    void setState(State state);

private:
    ...
};
```

We will skip the simple getters and concentrate on the important functions:

- `elapsedTime()`: This returns the value of the `mTimer.elapsed()`.
- `soundEvents()`: This is a getter that's a little more complicated. The `Track` class is the owner of the `mSoundEvents` content, and we really want to enforce it. For this, the getter returns a `const &` to `mSoundEvents`.
- `stateChanged()`: This is emitted when the `mState` value is updated. The new `State` is passed as a parameter.
- `play()`: This is a slot that starts to play the `Track`. This play function is purely logical—the real playback will be triggered by `PlaybackWorker`.
- `record()`: This is a slot that starts the recording state of `Track`.
- `stop()`: This is a slot that stops the current start or record state.
- `addSoundEvent()`: This creates a new `SoundEvent` with the given `soundId` and adds it to `mSoundEvents`.
- `clear()`: This resets the content of `Track`: It clears `mSoundEvents` and sets `mDuration` to `0`.
- `setState()`: This is a private helper function that updates `mState` and `mPreviousState`, and emits the `stateChanged()` signal.

Now that the header has been covered, we can study the interesting parts of `Track.cpp`:

```
void Track::play()
{
    setState(State::PLAYING);
    mTimer.start();
}
```

Calling `Track.play()` simply updates the state to `PLAYING` and starts `mTimer`. The `Track` class does not hold anything related to the Qt Multimedia API; it is limited to an evolved data holder (as it also manages a state).

Now for `record()`, which brings a lot of surprises:

```
void Track::record()
{
    clearSoundEvents();
    setState(State::RECORDING);
    mTimer.start();
}
```

It starts by clearing the data, sets the state to `RECORDING`, and also starts `mTimer`. Now consider `stop()`, which is a slight variation of the `record()` function:

```
void Track::stop()
{
    if (mState == State::RECORDING) {
        mDuration = mTimer.elapsed();
    }
    setState(State::STOPPED);
}
```

If we stop while in the `RECORDING` state, `mDuration` is updated. Nothing very fancy here. We saw three times the `setState()` call without seeing its body:

```
void Track::setState(Track::State state)
{
    mPreviousState = mState;
    mState = state;
    emit stateChanged(mState);
}
```

The current value of `mState` is stored in `mPreviousState` before being updated. Finally, `stateChanged()` is emitted with the new value.

The state system of `Track` is completely covered. The last missing part is the `SoundEvents` interactions. We can start with the `addSoundEvent()` snippet:

```
void Track::addSoundEvent(int soundEventId)
{
    if (mState != State::RECORDING) {
        return;
    }
    mSoundEvents.push_back(make_unique<SoundEvent>(
                                mTimer.elapsed(),
                                soundEventId));
}
```

A `soundEvent` is created only if we are in the `RECORDING` state. After that, a `SoundEvent` is added to `mSoundEvents` with the current elapsed time of `mTimer` and the passed `soundEventId`.

Now for the `clear()` function:

```
void Track::clear()
{
    mSoundEvents.clear();
    mDuration = 0;
}
```

Because we use `unique_ptr<SoundEvent>` in `mSoundEvents`, the `mSoundEvents.clear()` function is enough to empty the vector and also delete each `SoundEvent`. This is one less thing you have to worry about with smart pointers.

The `SoundEvent` and `Track` classes are the base classes that hold the information about your future beat. We are going to see the class responsible for reading this data in order to play it: `PlaybackWorker`.

Create a new C++ class and update `PlaybackWorker.h`, like so:

```
#include <QObject>
#include <QAtomicInteger>

class Track;

class PlaybackWorker : public QObject
{
    Q_OBJECT
public:
    explicit PlaybackWorker(const Track& track, QObject *parent = 0);
```

```
signals:
    void playSound(int soundId);
    void trackFinished();

public slots:
    void play();
    void stop();

private:
    const Track& mTrack;
    QAtomicInteger<bool> mIsPlaying;
};
```

The `PlaybackWorker` class will be running in a different thread. If your memory needs to be refreshed, go back to `Chapter 9`, *Keeping Your Sanity with Multithreading*. Its role is to iterate through the `Track` class's content to trigger the sounds. Let's break down this header:

- `mTrack`: This is the reference to the `Track` class on which `PlaybackWorker` is working. It is passed in the constructor as a `const` reference. With this information, you already know that `PlaybackWorker` cannot modify `mTrack` in any way.
- `mIsPlaying`: This is a flag that is used so that you can stop the worker from another thread. It is a `QAtomicInteger` to guarantee an atomic access to the variable.
- `playSound()`: This is emitted by `PlaybackWorker` each time a sound needs to be played.
- `trackFinished()`: This is emitted when the playback has been played until the end. If it has been stopped along the way, this signal will not be emitted.
- `play()`: This is the main function of `PlaybackWorker`. In it, `mTrack` content will be queried to trigger sounds.
- `stop()`: This is the function that updates the `mIsPlaying` flag and causes `play()` to exit its loop.

The meat of the class lies in the `play()` function, as shown in the following code:

```
void PlaybackWorker::play()
{
    mIsPlaying.store(true);
    QElapsedTimer timer;
    size_t soundEventIndex = 0;
    const auto& soundEvents = mTrack.soundEvents();
```

```
        timer.start();
        while(timer.elapsed() <= mTrack.duration()
               && mIsPlaying.load()) {
            if (soundEventIndex < soundEvents.size()) {
                const auto& soundEvent =
                                      soundEvents.at(soundEventIndex);

                if (timer.elapsed() >= soundEvent->timestamp) {
                    emit playSound(soundEvent->soundId);
                    soundEventIndex++;
                }
            }
            QThread::msleep(1);
        }

        if (soundEventIndex >= soundEvents.size()) {
            emit trackFinished();
        }
    }
```

The first thing that the `play()` function does is to prepare its reading: `mIsPlaying` is set to `true`, a `QElapsedTimer` class is declared, and a `soundEventIndex` is initialized. Each time `timer.elapsed()` is called, we will know whether a sound should be played.

To know which sound should be played, `soundEventIndex` will be used to know where we are in the `soundEvents` vector.

Right after that, the `timer` object is started and we enter in the `while` loop. This loop has two conditions that are needed to continue:

- `timer.elapsed() <= mTrack.duration()`: This condition states that we did not finish playing the track
- `mIsPlaying.load()`: This condition returns `true` while nobody asks `PlaybackWorker` to stop

Intuitively, you might have added the `soundEventIndex < soundEvents.size()` condition in the `while` condition. By doing so, you would have exited `PlaybackWorker` as soon as the last sound was played. Technically it works, but that would not have respected what the user recorded.

Let's say that a user created a complex beat (do not underestimate what you can do with four sounds!) and decided on a long pause of five seconds at the end of the song. When he clicks on the **Stop** button, the time display indicates 00:55 (for 55 seconds). However, when he plays back his performance, the last sound finishes at 00:50. The playback stops at 00:50 and the program does not respect what he recorded.

For this reason, the `soundEventIndex < size()` test is moved inside the `while` loop and is used only as a fuse for the `soundEvents` readthrough.

Inside this condition, we retrieve the reference to the current `soundEvent`. We then compare the elapsed time to the `timestamp` of the `soundEvent`. If `timer.elapsed()` is greater or equal to `soundEvent->timestamp`, then the `playSound()` signal is emitted with the `soundId`.

This is only a request to play a sound. The `PlaybackWorker` class limits itself to read through `soundEvents` and trigger a `playSound()` at the proper moment. The real sound will be handled later on, with the `SoundEffectWidget` class.

At each iteration in the `while` loop, a `QThread::msleep(1)` is performed to avoid a busy loop. We minimize the sleep because we want the playback to be as faithful as possible to the original score. The longer the sleep, the more discrepancies we may encounter in the playback timing.

Finally, if the whole `soundEvents` has been processed, the `trackFinished` signal is emitted.

Making your objects serializable with QVariant

Now that we have implemented the logic in our business classes, we have to think about what we are going to serialize and how we are going to do it. The user interacts with a `Track` class that contains all the data to be recorded and played back.

Starting from here, we can assume that the object to be serialized is `Track`, which in turn should somehow bring along its `mSoundEvents` containing a list of `SoundEvent` instances. To achieve this, we will rely heavily on the `QVariant` class.

You might have worked with `QVariant` before. It is a generic placeholder for any primitive type (`char`, `int`, `double`, and so on), but also for complex types (`QString`, `QDate`, `QPoint`, and many more).

The complete list of QVariant-supported types is available at `http://doc.qt.io/qt-5/qmetatype.html#Type-enum`.

A simple example of QVariant is as follows:

```
QVariant variant(21);

int answer = variant.toInt() * 2;

qDebug() << "what is the meaning of the universe,
             life and everything?"
         << answer;
```

We store 21 in variant. From here, we can ask for variant to have a copy of the value cast to our desired type. Here, we want an int value, so we call variant.toInt(). There are a lot of conversions already available with the variant.toX() syntax.

We can take a very quick peek at what happens behind the curtain in QVariant. How does it store all we feed it? The answer lies in the C++ union type. The QVariant class is a kind of super union.

A union is a special class type that can hold only one of its nonstatic data members at a time, as illustrated in the following short code snippet:

```
union Sound
{
    int duration;
    char code;
};

Sound s = 10;
qDebug() << "Sound duration:" << s.duration;
// output= Sound duration: 10

s.code = 'K';
qDebug() << "Sound code:" << s.code;
// output= Sound code: K
```

First, a union class is declared like a struct. By default, all the members are public. The specificity of the union is that it takes only the largest member size in memory.
Here, Sound will take only as much as the int duration space in memory.

Because union takes only this specific space, every member variable shares the same memory space. Therefore, only one member is available at a time, unless you want to have undefined behaviors.

When using the `Sound` snippet, we start by initializing with the value `10` (by default, the first member is initialized). From here, `s.duration` is accessible, but `s.code` is considered undefined.

Once we assign a value to `s.code`, `s.duration` becomes undefined and `s.code` is now accessible.

The `union` class makes the memory usage very efficient. In `QVariant`, when you store a value, it is stored in a private `union`, as shown in the following code:

```
union Data
{
    char c;
    uchar uc;
    short s;
    signed char sc;
    ushort us;
    ...
    qulonglong ull;
    QObject *o;
    void *ptr;
    PrivateShared *shared;
} data;
```

Note the list of primitive types, and the complex types at the end: `QObject*` and `void*`.

Besides `Data`, a `QMetaType` object is initialized to know the type of the stored object. The combination of `union` and `QMetaType` lets `QVariant` know which `Data` member it should use to cast the value and give it back to the caller.

Now that you know what a `union` is and how `QVariant` uses it, you might ask "Why make a `QVariant` class at all?". Would a simple `union` not have been enough?

The answer is no. It is not enough because a `union` class cannot have members that do not have a default constructor. It drastically reduces the number of classes you can put in a `union`. The Qt folks wanted to include many classes that did not have a default constructor in `union`. To mitigate this, `QVariant` was born.

What makes `QVariant` very interesting is that it is possible to store custom types. If we wanted to convert the `SoundEvent` class to a `QVariant` class, we would have added the following in `SoundEvent.h`:

```
class SoundEvent
{
    ...
};
Q_DECLARE_METATYPE(SoundEvent);
```

We already used the `Q_DECLARE_METATYPE` macro in `Chapter 10`, *Need IPC? Get Your Minions to Work*. This macro effectively registers `SoundEvent` to the `QMetaType` register, making it available for `QVariant`. Because `QDataStream` relies on `QVariant`, we had to use this macro in the previous chapter.

Now, to convert back and forth with a `QVariant`, we use the following:

```
SoundEvent soundEvent(4365, 0);
QVariant stored;
stored.setValue(soundEvent);

SoundEvent newEvent = stored.value<SoundEvent>();
qDebug() << newEvent.timestamp;
```

As you can guess, the output of this snippet is `4365`, the original `timestamp` stored in `soundEvent`.

This approach would have been perfect if we wanted to do only binary serialization. Data can be easily written and read from. However, we want to output our `Track` and `SoundEvents` to standard formats: JSON and XML.

There is a major issue with the `Q_DECLARE_METATYPE`/`QVariant` combo: It does not store any key for the fields of the serialized class. We can already foresee that the JSON object of a `SoundEvent` class will look like the following:

```
{
    "timestamp": 4365,
    "soundId": 0
}
```

There is no way the `QVariant` class could know that we want a `timestamp` key. It will only store the raw binary data. The same principle applies for its XML counterpart.

For this reason, we are going to use a variation of a `QVariant` with a `QVariantMap`. The `QVariantMap` class is only a `typedef` on `QMap<QString, QVariant>`. This map will be used to store the key names of the fields and the value in the `QVariant` class. In turn, these keys will be used by the JSON and XML serialization system to output a pretty file.

Because we aim to have a flexible serialization system, we have to be able to serialize and deserialize this `QVariantMap` in multiple formats. To achieve this, we will define an interface that provides the ability for a class to serialize/deserialize its content in a `QVariantMap`.

This `QVariantMap` will be used as an intermediate format, agnostic of the final JSON, XML, or binary file.

Create a C++ header named `Serializer.h` with the following content:

```
#include <QVariant>

class Serializable {
public:
    virtual ~Serializable() {}
    virtual QVariant toVariant() const = 0;
    virtual void fromVariant(const QVariant& variant) = 0;
};
```

By implementing this abstract base class, the class will be `Serializable`. There are only two pure virtual functions:

- The `toVariant()` function, in which the class must return a `QVariant` (or more precisely, a `QVariantMap`, which can be cast to a `QVariant` thanks to the `QMetaType` system)
- The `fromVariant()` function, in which the class must initialize its members from the variant passed as a parameter

By doing so, we give the responsibility to the final class to load and save its content. After all, who knows `SoundEvent` better than `SoundEvent` itself?

Let's see `Serializable` in action with `SoundEvent`. Update `SoundEvent.h`, as shown in the following code:

```
#include "Serializable.h"

class SoundEvent : public Serializable
{
    SoundEvent(qint64 timestamp = 0, int soundId = 0);
    ~SoundEvent();

    QVariant toVariant() const override;
    void fromVariant(const QVariant& variant) override;

    ...
};
```

The `SoundEvent` class is now `Serializable`. Let's do the real work in `SoundEvent.cpp`, as shown in the following code:

```
QVariant SoundEvent::toVariant() const
{
    QVariantMap map;
    map.insert("timestamp", timestamp);
    map.insert("soundId", soundId);
    return map;
}

void SoundEvent::fromVariant(const QVariant& variant)
{
    QVariantMap map = variant.toMap();
    timestamp = map.value("timestamp").toLongLong();
    soundId = map.value("soundId").toInt();
}
```

In `toVariant()`, we simply declare a `QVariantMap` object that gets filled with `timestamp` and `soundId`.

On the other side, in `fromVariant()`, we convert `variant` to a `QVariantMap` and retrieve its content with the same keys that we used in `toVariant()`. It is as simple as that!

The next class that has to be `Serializable` is `Track`. After making `Track` inherit from `Serializable`, update `Track.cpp`, as shown in the following code:

```
QVariant Track::toVariant() const
{
    QVariantMap map;
    map.insert("duration", mDuration);
```

```
    QVariantList list;
    for (const auto& soundEvent : mSoundEvents) {
        list.append(soundEvent->toVariant());
    }
    map.insert("soundEvents", list);

    return map;
}
```

The principle is the same, although a bit more complex. The `mDuration` variable is stored in the `map` object, as we saw for `SoundEvent`. For `mSoundEvents`, we have to generate a list of `QVariant` (a `QVariantList`) where each item is the converted `QVariant` version of a `soundEvent` key.

To do so, we simply loop over `mSoundEvents` and fill `list` with the `soundEvent->toVariant()` result we covered earlier in this section.

Now for `fromVariant()`:

```
void Track::fromVariant(const QVariant& variant)
{
    QVariantMap map = variant.toMap();
    mDuration = map.value("duration").toLongLong();

    QVariantList list = map.value("soundEvents").toList();
    for(const QVariant& data : list) {
        auto soundEvent = make_unique<SoundEvent>();
        soundEvent->fromVariant(data);
        mSoundEvents.push_back(move(soundEvent));
    }
}
```

Here, for each element of the `soundEvents` key, we create a new `SoundEvent`, load it with the content of `data`, and finally add it to the `mSoundEvents` vector.

Serializing objects in JSON format

The `Track` and `SoundEvent` classes can now be converted to a common Qt format, `QVariant`. We now need to write a `Track` (and its `SoundEvent` objects) class in a file with a text or a binary format. This example project allows you to handle all the formats. It will allow you to switch the saved file format in one line.

So where should we put the specific format code? That is the million-dollar question! One primary approach is shown in the following diagram:

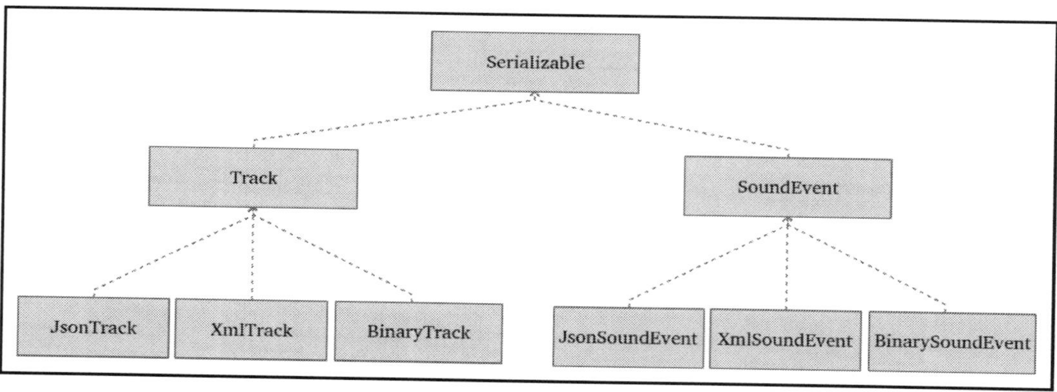

In this proposition, the specific file format serialization code is inside a dedicated child class. Well, it works, but what would the hierarchy look like if we added two new file formats? Moreover, each time we add a new object to serialize, we have to create all these child classes to handle the different serialization file formats. This massive inheritance tree can quickly become a sticky mess. The code will be unmaintainable. You do not want to do that. So, here is where the bridge pattern can be a good solution, as shown in the following diagram:

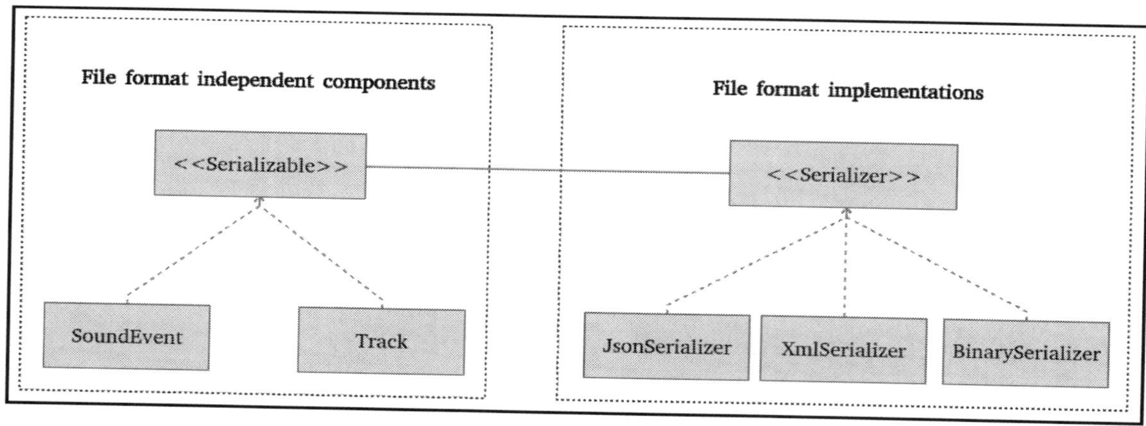

In a bridge pattern, we decouple the classes in two inheritance hierarchies:

- The components that are independent from the file format. The `SoundEvent` and `Track` objects do not care about JSON, XML, or binary formats.

- The file format implementations. The `JsonSerializer`, `XmlSerializer`, and `BinarySerializer` handle a generic format, `Serializable`, not specific components, such as `SoundEvent` or `Track`.

Note that, in a classic bridge pattern, an abstraction (`Serializable`) should contain an implementor (`Serializer`) variable. The caller only deals with the abstraction. However, in this example project, `MainWindow` has the ownership of `Serializable` and also of `Serializer`. This is a personal choice to use the power of the design pattern while keeping uncoupled functional classes.

The architecture of `Serializable` and `Serializer` is clear. The `Serializable` class is already implemented, so you can now create a new C++ header file called `Serializer.h`:

```
#include <QString>

#include "Serializable.h"

class Serializer
{
public:
    virtual ~Serializer() {}

    virtual void save(const Serializable& serializable,
        const QString& filepath,
        const QString& rootName = "") = 0;
    virtual void load(Serializable& serializable,
        const QString& filepath) = 0;
};
```

The `Serializer` class is an interface, an abstract class with only pure virtual functions and no data. Let's talk about the `save()` function:

- This function saves `Serializable` to a file on the hard disk drive.
- The `Serializable` class is `const` and cannot be modified by this function.
- The `filepath` function indicates the destination file to create.
- Some `Serializer` implementations can use the `rootName` variable. For example, if we request to save a `Track` object, the `rootName` variable could be the `track` string. This is the label used to write the root element. The XML implementation requires this information.

The `load()` function is also easy to understand:

- This function loads data from a file to fill a `Serializable` class
- The `Serializable` class will be updated by this function
- The `filepath` function indicates which file to read

The `Serializer` interface is ready and waiting for some implementations! Let's start with JSON. Create a C++ class called `JsonSerializer`. The following code shows the header for `JsonSerializer.h`:

```
#include "Serializer.h"

class JsonSerializer : public Serializer
{
public:
    JsonSerializer();

    void save(const Serializable& serializable,
        const QString& filepath,
        const QString& rootName) override;
    void load(Serializable& serializable,
        const QString& filepath) override;
};
```

No difficulties here: We have to provide an implementation of `save()` and `load()`. The following code shows the `save()` implementation:

```
void JsonSerializer::save(const Serializable& serializable,
    const QString& filepath, const QString& /*rootName*/)
{
    QJsonDocument doc =
        QJsonDocument::fromVariant(serializable.toVariant());
    QFile file(filepath);
    file.open(QFile::WriteOnly);
    file.write(doc.toJson());
    file.close();
}
```

The Qt framework provides a nice way to read and write a JSON file with the `QJsonDocument` class. We can create a `QJsonDocument` class from a `QVariant` class. Note that the `QVariant` accepted by `QJsonDocument` must be a `QVariantMap`, `QVariantList`, or `QStringList`. No worries—the `toVariant()` function of the `Track` class and `SoundEvent` generates a `QVariantMap`. Then, we can create a `QFile` file with the destination `filepath`. The `QJsonDocument::toJson()` function converts it to a UTF-8-encoded text representation. We write this result to the `QFile` file and close the file.

The `QJsonDocument::toJson()` function can produce an `Indented` or a `Compact` JSON format. By default, the format is `QJsonDocument::Indented`.

The `load()` implementation is also short, as shown in the following code:

```
void JsonSerializer::load(Serializable& serializable,
    const QString& filepath)
{
    QFile file(filepath);
    file.open(QFile::ReadOnly);
    QJsonDocument doc = QJsonDocument::fromJson(file.readAll());
    file.close();
    serializable.fromVariant(doc.toVariant());
}
```

We open a `QFile` with the source `filepath`. We read all the data with `QFile::readAll()`. Then we can create a `QJsonDocument` class with the `QJsonDocument::fromJson()` function. Finally, we can fill our `Serializable` destination with the `QJsonDocument`, converted to a `QVariant` class. Note that the `QJsonDocument::toVariant()` function can return `QVariantList` or a `QVariantMap`, depending on the nature of the JSON document. In a real application, you will have to handle the possible errors (for example, file not found).

The following is an example of a `Track` class saved with this `JsonSerializer`:

```
{
    "duration": 6205,
    "soundEvents": [
        {
            "soundId": 0,
            "timestamp": 2689
        },
        {
            "soundId": 2,
            "timestamp": 2690
        },
        {
            "soundId": 2,
            "timestamp": 3067
        }
    ]
}
```

The root element is a JSON object, represented by a map with two keys:

- `Duration`: A simple integer value
- `soundEvents`: An array of objects

Each `soundEvents` object is a map with the following keys:

- `soundId`: An integer
- `timestamp`: An integer

Serializing objects in XML format

The JSON serialization was a direct representation of the C++ objects, and Qt already provides all we need. However, the serialization of a C++ object can be done with various representations in an XML format. So we have to write the XML from/to `QVariant` conversion ourselves. We have decided to use the following XML representation:

```
<[name]> type="[type]">[data]</[name]>
```

For example, the `soundId` type gives the following XML representation:

```
<soundId type="int">2</soundId>
```

Create a C++ `XmlSerializer` class that also inherits from `Serializer`. Let's begin with the `save()` function. The following is `XmlSerializer.h`:

```
#include <QXmlStreamWriter>
#include <QXmlStreamReader>

#include "Serializer.h"

class XmlSerializer : public Serializer
{
public:
    XmlSerializer();

    void save(const Serializable& serializable,
        const QString& filepath,
        const QString& rootName) override;
};
```

Now we can see the `save()` implementation in `XmlSerializer.cpp`:

```
void XmlSerializer::save(const Serializable& serializable, const QString&
filepath, const QString& rootName)
{
    QFile file(filepath);
    file.open(QFile::WriteOnly);
    QXmlStreamWriter stream(&file);
    stream.setAutoFormatting(true);
    stream.writeStartDocument();
    writeVariantToStream(rootName, serializable.toVariant(),
        stream);
    stream.writeEndDocument();
    file.close();
}
```

We create a `QFile` file with the `filepath` destination. We construct a `QXmlStreamWriter` object that writes in the `QFile`. By default, the writer will produce a compact XML; you can generate a pretty XML with the `QXmlStreamWriter::setAutoFormatting()` function. The `QXmlStreamWriter::writeStartDocument()` function writes the XML version and the encoding. We write our `QVariant` in the XML stream with our `writeVariantToStream()` function. Finally, we end the document and close the `QFile`. As already explained, writing a `QVariant` to an XML stream depends on how you want to represent the data, so we have to write the conversion function. Update your class with `writeVariantToStream()`, as shown in the following code:

```
//XmlSerializer.h
private:
    void writeVariantToStream(const QString& nodeName,
        const QVariant& variant, QXmlStreamWriter& stream);

//XmlSerializer.cpp
void XmlSerializer::writeVariantToStream(const QString& nodeName,
    const QVariant& variant, QXmlStreamWriter& stream)
{
    stream.writeStartElement(nodeName);
    stream.writeAttribute("type", variant.typeName());

    switch (variant.type()) {
        case QMetaType::QVariantList:
            writeVariantListToStream(variant, stream);
            break;
        case QMetaType::QVariantMap:
            writeVariantMapToStream(variant, stream);
            break;
        default:
```

```
            writeVariantValueToStream(variant, stream);
            break;
    }

    stream.writeEndElement();
}
```

This `writeVariantToStream()` function is a generic entry point. It will be called each time we want to put a `QVariant` in the XML stream. The `QVariant` class could be a list, a map, or data, so we apply a specific treatment if the `QVariant` is a container (`QVariantList` or `QVariantMap`). All the other cases are considered to be data values.

The following are the steps of this function:

1. Start a new XML element with the `writeStartElement()` function. The `nodeName` will be used to create the XML tag—for example, `<soundId`.
2. Write an XML attribute called `type` in the current element. We use the name of the type stored in the `QVariant`—for example, `<soundId type="int"`.
3. Depending on the `QVariant` data type, we call one of our XML serialization functions—for example, `<soundId type="int">2`.
4. Finally, we end the current XML element with `writeEndElement()`: the final result is `<soundId type="int">2</soundId>`.

In this function, we call three helper functions, which we are going to create now. The easiest one is `writeVariantValueToStream()`. Update your `XmlSerializer` class with the following:

```
//XmlSerializer.h
void writeVariantValueToStream(const QVariant& variant,
    QXmlStreamWriter& stream);

//XmlSerializer.cpp
void XmlSerializer::writeVariantValueToStream(
    const QVariant& variant, QXmlStreamWriter& stream)
{
    stream.writeCharacters(variant.toString());
}
```

If the `QVariant` is a simple type, we retrieve its `QString` representation. Then we use `QXmlStreamWriter::writeCharacters()` to write this `QString` in the XML stream.

The second helper function is `writeVariantListToStream()`. The following code shows its implementation:

```
//XmlSerializer.h
private:
    void writeVariantListToStream(const QVariant& variant,
        QXmlStreamWriter& stream);

//XmlSerializer.cpp
void XmlSerializer::writeVariantListToStream(
    const QVariant& variant, QXmlStreamWriter& stream)
{
    QVariantList list = variant.toList();

    for(const QVariant& element : list) {
        writeVariantToStream("item", element, stream);
    }
}
```

At this step, we already know that the `QVariant` is a `QVariantList`. We call `QVariant::toList()` to retrieve the list. Then we iterate over all elements of the list and call our generic entry point, `writeVariantToStream()`.

Note that we retrieve the elements from a list, so we do not have an element name. But the tag name does not matter for a list item serialization, so insert the arbitrary label `item`.

The last write helper function is `writeVariantMapToStream()`:

```
//XmlSerializer.h
private:
    void writeVariantMapToStream(const QVariant& variant,
        QXmlStreamWriter& stream);

//XmlSerializer.cpp
void XmlSerializer::writeVariantMapToStream(
    const QVariant& variant, QXmlStreamWriter& stream)
{
    QVariantMap map = variant.toMap();
    QMapIterator<QString, QVariant> i(map);

    while (i.hasNext()) {
        i.next();
        writeVariantToStream(i.key(), i.value(), stream);
    }
}
```

The `QVariant` phrase is also a container, but a `QVariantMap` this time. We call `writeVariantToStream()` for each element found. The tag name is important because this is a map. We use the map key from `QMapIterator::key()` as the node name.

The saving part is over. We can now implement the loading part. Its architecture follows the same spirit as the saving functions. Let's begin with the `load()` function:

```
//XmlSerializer.h
public:
    void load(Serializable& serializable,
        const QString& filepath) override;

//XmlSerializer.cpp
void XmlSerializer::load(Serializable& serializable,
    const QString& filepath)
{
    QFile file(filepath);
    file.open(QFile::ReadOnly);
    QXmlStreamReader stream(&file);
    stream.readNextStartElement();
    serializable.fromVariant(readVariantFromStream(stream));
}
```

The first thing to do is to create a `QFile` with the source `filepath`. We construct a `QXmlStreamReader` with the `QFile`. The `QXmlStreamReader::readNextStartElement()` function reads until the next start element in the XML stream. Then we can use our read helper function, `readVariantFromStream()`, to create a `QVariant` class from an XML stream. Finally, we can use our `Serializable::fromVariant()` to fill the `serializable` destination. Let's implement the helper function, `readVariantFromStream()`, using the following code:

```
//XmlSerializer.h
private:
    QVariant readVariantFromStream(QXmlStreamReader& stream);

//XmlSerializer.cpp
QVariant XmlSerializer::readVariantFromStream(QXmlStreamReader& stream)
{
    QXmlStreamAttributes attributes = stream.attributes();
    QString typeString = attributes.value("type").toString();

    QVariant variant;
    switch (QVariant::nameToType(
            typeString.toStdString().c_str())) {
        case QMetaType::QVariantList:
            variant = readVariantListFromStream(stream);
```

```
            break;
        case QMetaType::QVariantMap:
            variant = readVariantMapFromStream(stream);
            break;
        default:
            variant = readVariantValueFromStream(stream);
            break;
    }

    return variant;
}
```

The role of this function is to create a `QVariant`. Firstly, we retrieve the `type` from the XML attributes. In our case, we have only one attribute to handle. Then, depending on the type, we will call one of our three read helper functions. Let's implement the `readVariantValueFromStream()` function using the following code:

```
//XmlSerializer.h
private:
    QVariant readVariantValueFromStream(QXmlStreamReader& stream);

//XmlSerializer.cpp
QVariant XmlSerializer::readVariantValueFromStream(
    QXmlStreamReader& stream)
{
    QXmlStreamAttributes attributes = stream.attributes();
    QString typeString = attributes.value("type").toString();
    QString dataString = stream.readElementText();

    QVariant variant(dataString);
    variant.convert(QVariant::nameToType(
        typeString.toStdString().c_str()));
    return variant;
}
```

This function creates a `QVariant` with its data depending on the type. As with the previous function, we retrieve the type from the XML attribute. We also read the data as a text with the `QXmlStreamReader::readElementText()` function. A `QVariant` class is created with this `QString` data. At this stage, the `QVariant` type is a `QString`, so we use the `QVariant::convert()` function to convert the `QVariant` to the real type (`int`, `qlonglong`, and so on).

The second read helper function is `readVariantListFromStream()`, as shown in the following code:

```
//XmlSerializer.h
private:
    QVariant readVariantListFromStream(QXmlStreamReader& stream);

//XmlSerializer.cpp
QVariant XmlSerializer::readVariantListFromStream(QXmlStreamReader& stream)
{
    QVariantList list;
    while(stream.readNextStartElement()) {
        list.append(readVariantFromStream(stream));
    }
    return list;
}
```

We know that the stream element contains an array, so this function creates and returns a `QVariantList`. The `QXmlStreamReader::readNextStartElement()` function reads until the next start element and returns `true` if a start element is found within the current element. We call the `readVariantFromStream()` entry-point function for each element. Finally, we return the `QVariantList`.

The last helper function to cover is `readVariantMapFromStream()`. Update your file with the following code snippet:

```
//XmlSerializer.h
private:
    QVariant readVariantMapFromStream(QXmlStreamReader& stream);

//XmlSerializer.cpp
QVariant XmlSerializer::readVariantMapFromStream(
    QXmlStreamReader& stream)
{
    QVariantMap map;
    while(stream.readNextStartElement()) {
        map.insert(stream.name().toString(),
                   readVariantFromStream(stream));
    }
    return map;
}
```

This function sounds like the `readVariantListFromStream()`. This time, we have to create a `QVariantMap`. The key used for inserting a new item is the element name. We retrieve the name with the `QXmlStreamReader::name()` function.

A `Track` class serialized with the `XmlSerializer` looks like the following:

```
<?xml version="1.0" encoding="UTF-8"?>
<track type="QVariantMap">
    <duration type="qlonglong">6205</duration>
    <soundEvents type="QVariantList">
        <item type="QVariantMap">
            <soundId type="int">0</soundId>
            <timestamp type="qlonglong">2689</timestamp>
        </item>
        <item type="QVariantMap">
            <soundId type="int">2</soundId>
            <timestamp type="qlonglong">2690</timestamp>
        </item>
        <item type="QVariantMap">
            <soundId type="int">2</soundId>
            <timestamp type="qlonglong">3067</timestamp>
        </item>
    </soundEvents>
</track>
```

Serializing objects in binary format

The XML serialization is fully functional! We can now switch to the last type of serialization covered in this chapter.

Binary serialization is easier because Qt provides a direct way to do it. Create a `BinarySerializer` class that inherits from `Serializer`. The header is common; we only have the override functions `save()` and `load()`. Here is the implementation of the `save()` function:

```
void BinarySerializer::save(const Serializable& serializable,
    const QString& filepath, const QString& /*rootName*/)
{
    QFile file(filepath);
    file.open(QFile::WriteOnly);
    QDataStream dataStream(&file);
    dataStream << serializable.toVariant();
    file.close();
}
```

We hope you recognized the `QDataStream` class used in `Chapter 10`, *Need IPC? Get Your Minions to Work*. This time, we use this class to serialize binary data in a destination `QFile`. A `QDataStream` class accepts a `QVariant` class with the << operator. Note that the `rootName` variable is not used in the binary serializer.

The following is the `load()` function:

```
void BinarySerializer::load(Serializable& serializable, const QString&
filepath)
{
    QFile file(filepath);
    file.open(QFile::ReadOnly);
    QDataStream dataStream(&file);
    QVariant variant;
    dataStream >> variant;
    serializable.fromVariant(variant);
    file.close();
}
```

Thanks to the `QVariant` and the `QDataStream` mechanism, the task is easy. We open the `QFile` with the source `filepath`. We construct a `QDatastream` class with this `QFile`. Then, we use the >> operator to read the root `QVariant`. Finally, we fill the source `Serializable` with our `Serializable::fromVariant()` function.

Do not worry—we will not include an example of a `Track` class serialized with the `BinarySerializer` class.

The serialization is completed. The GUI part of this example project has been covered many times during the previous chapters of this book. The following sections will only cover specific features used in our `MainWindow` and `SoundEffectWidget` classes. Check the source code if you need the complete C++ classes.

Playing low-latency sounds with QSoundEffect

The project application `ch11-drum-machine` displays four `SoundEffectWidget` widgets: `kickWidget, snareWidget, hihatWidget,` and `crashWidget.`

Each `SoundEffectWidget` widget displays a `QLabel` and a `QPushButton`. The label displays the sound name. If the button is clicked, a sound is played.

The Qt Multimedia module provides two main ways to play an audio file:

- `QMediaPlayer`: This file can play songs, movies, and internet radio with various input formats
- `QSoundEffect`: This file can play low-latency `.wav` files

This project example is a virtual drum machine, so we are using a `QSoundEffect` object. The first step to using a `QSoundEffect` is to update your `.pro` file as shown in the following code:

```
QT       += core gui multimedia
```

Then you can initialize the sound. Here is an example of how to do this:

```
QUrl urlKick("qrc:/sounds/kick.wav");
QUrl urlBetterKick = QUrl::fromLocalFile("/home/better-kick.wav");

QSoundEffect soundEffect;
QSoundEffect.setSource(urlBetterKick);
```

The first step is to create a valid `QUrl` for your sound file. The `urlKick` is initialized from a `.qrc` resource's file path, while `urlBetterKick` is created from a local file path. Then we can create `QSoundEffect` and set the URL sound to play with the `QSoundEffect::setSource()` function.

Now that we have a `QSoundEffect` object initialized, we can play the sound with the following code snippet:

```
soundEffect.setVolume(1.0f);
soundEffect.play();
```

Triggering a QButton with your keyboard

Let's explore the public slot, `triggerPlayButton()`, in the `SoundEffectWidget` class:

```
//SoundEffectWidget.h
class SoundEffectWidget : public QWidget
{
...
public slots:
    void triggerPlayButton();
```

```
    ...

private:
    QPushButton* mPlayButton;
    ...
};

//SoundEffectWidget.cpp
void SoundEffectWidget::triggerPlayButton()
{
   mPlayButton->animateClick();
}
```

This widget has a `QPushButton` called `mPlayButton`. The `triggerPlayButton()` slot calls the `QPushButton::animateClick()` function, which simulates a click on the button over 100 ms by default. All signals will be sent in the same way that a real click is sent. The button really appears to be down. If you do not want the animation, you can call `QPushButton::click()`.

Let's now see how to trigger this slot with a key. Each `SoundEffectWidget` has a `Qt:Key`:

```
//SoundEffectWidget.h
class SoundEffectWidget : public QWidget
{
...
public:
    Qt::Key triggerKey() const;
    void setTriggerKey(const Qt::Key& triggerKey);
};

//SoundEffectWidget.cpp
Qt::Key SoundEffectWidget::triggerKey() const
{
    return mTriggerKey;
}

void SoundEffectWidget::setTriggerKey(const Qt::Key& triggerKey)
{
    mTriggerKey = triggerKey;
}
```

The `SoundEffectWidget` class provides a getter and a setter for the member variable, `mTriggerKey`.

The MainWindow class initializes the keys of its four SoundEffectWidget widgets, as follows:

```
ui->kickWidget->setTriggerKey(Qt::Key_H);
ui->snareWidget->setTriggerKey(Qt::Key_J);
ui->hihatWidget->setTriggerKey(Qt::Key_K);
ui->crashWidget->setTriggerKey(Qt::Key_L);
```

By default, the QObject::eventFilter() function is not called. To enable it and intercept these events, we need to install an event filter on the MainWindow:

```
installEventFilter(this);
```

So each time the MainWindow receives an event, the MainWindow::eventFilter() function is called.

The following is the MainWindow.h header:

```
class MainWindow : public QMainWindow
{
    Q_OBJECT
public:
    ...
    bool eventFilter(QObject* watched, QEvent* event) override;

private:
    QVector<SoundEffectWidget*> mSoundEffectWidgets;
    ...
};
```

The MainWindow class has a QVector with the four SoundEffectWidget widgets (kickWidget, snareWidget, hihatWidget, and crashWidget). Let's see the implementation in MainWindow.cpp:

```
bool MainWindow::eventFilter(QObject* watched, QEvent* event)
{
    if (event->type() == QEvent::KeyPress) {
        QKeyEvent* keyEvent = static_cast<QKeyEvent*>(event);
        for(SoundEffectWidget* widget : mSoundEffectWidgets) {
            if (keyEvent->key() == widget->triggerKey()) {
                widget->triggerPlayButton();
                return true;
            }
        }
    }
    return QObject::eventFilter(watched, event);
}
```

The first thing to do is to check that the `QEvent` class is a `KeyPress` type. We do not care about other event types. If the event type is correct, we proceed to go through the following steps:

1. Cast the `QEvent` class to `QKeyEvent`.
2. Check whether the pressed key belongs to the `SoundEffectWidget` class.
3. If a `SoundEffectWidget` class corresponds to the key, we call our `SoundEffectWidget::triggerPlayButton()` function, and we return `true` to indicate that we consumed the event and that it must not be propagated to other classes. Otherwise, we call the `QObject` class implementation of `eventFilter()`.

Another way to support the keyboard inputs is to use the `QShortcut` class. Some widgets also automatically create an Alt shortcut (automnemonic) in which you put a `&` in front of a character. For more information, go to `http://doc.qt.io/qt-5/qshortcut.html#details`.

Bringing PlaybackWorker to life

The user can play a sound live with a mouse click or the press of a keyboard's button. But when they record an awesome beat, the application must be able to play it again with the `PlaybackWorker` class. Let's see how `MainWindow` uses this worker. The following is the `MainWindow.h` related to the `PlaybackWorker` class:

```
class MainWindow : public QMainWindow
{
...
private slots:
    void playSoundEffect(int soundId);
    void clearPlayback();
    void stopPlayback();
    ...

private:
    void startPlayback();
    ...

private:
    PlaybackWorker* mPlaybackWorker;
    QThread* mPlaybackThread;
    ...
};
```

As you can see, `MainWindow` has the `PlaybackWorker` and `QThread` member variables. Let's look at the implementation of `startPlayback()`:

```
void MainWindow::startPlayback()
{
    clearPlayback();

    mPlaybackThread = new QThread();

    mPlaybackWorker = new PlaybackWorker(mTrack);
    mPlaybackWorker->moveToThread(mPlaybackThread);

    connect(mPlaybackThread, &QThread::started,
            mPlaybackWorker, &PlaybackWorker::play);
    connect(mPlaybackThread, &QThread::finished,
            mPlaybackWorker, &QObject::deleteLater);

    connect(mPlaybackWorker, &PlaybackWorker::playSound,
            this, &MainWindow::playSoundEffect);

    connect(mPlaybackWorker, &PlaybackWorker::trackFinished,
            &mTrack, &Track::stop);

    mPlaybackThread->start(QThread::HighPriority);
}
```

Let's go through the steps:

1. We clear the current playback with the `clearPlayback()` function, which we will look at soon.
2. The new `QThread` and `PlaybackWorker` are constructed. The current track is given to the worker at this moment. As usual, the worker is then moved to its dedicated thread.
3. We want to play the track as soon as possible, so when the `QThread` emits the `started()` signal, the `PlaybackWorker::play()` slot is called.
4. We do not want to worry about the `PlaybackWorker` memory, so when the `QThread` is over and it has sent the `finished()` signal, we call the `QObject::deleteLater()` slot, which schedules the worker for deletion.
5. When the `PlaybackWorker` class needs to play a sound, the `playSound()` signal is emitted and our `MainWindow:playSoundEffect()` slot is called.
6. The last `connect` covers when the `PlaybackWorker` class finishes playing the whole track. A `trackFinished()` signal is emitted and we call the `Track::Stop()` slot.

7. Finally, the thread is started with a high priority. Note that some operating systems (for example, Linux) do not support thread priorities.

We can now see the `stopPlayback()` body:

```
void MainWindow::stopPlayback()
{
    mPlaybackWorker->stop();
    clearPlayback();
}
```

We call the `stop()` function of the `PlaybackWorker` from our thread. Because we use a `QAtomicInteger` in `stop()`, the function is thread-safe and can be directly called. Finally, we call our helper function, `clearPlayback()`. This is the second time that we use `clearPlayback()`, so let's implement it, as shown in the following code:

```
void MainWindow::clearPlayback()
{
    if (mPlaybackThread) {
        mPlaybackThread->quit();
        mPlaybackThread->wait(1000);
        mPlaybackThread = nullptr;
        mPlaybackWorker = nullptr;
    }
}
```

No surprises here. If the thread is valid, we ask the thread to exit and wait one second. Then, we set the thread and the worker to `nullptr`.

The `PlaybackWorker::PlaySound` signal is connected to `MainWindow::playSoundEffect()`. The following is the implementation:

```
void MainWindow::playSoundEffect(int soundId)
{
   mSoundEffectWidgets[soundId]->triggerPlayButton();
}
```

This slot retrieves the `SoundEffectWidget` class corresponding to the `soundId`. Then, we call the `triggerPlayButton()`, the same method that is called when you press the trigger key on your keyboard.

So, when you click on the button, press a key, or when the `PlaybackWorker` class requests to play a sound, the `QPushButton` of `SoundEffectWidget` emits the `clicked()` signal. This signal is connected to our `SoundEffectWidget::play()` slot. The next code snippet shows this slot:

```
void SoundEffectWidget::play()
{
    mSoundEffect.play();
    emit soundPlayed(mId);
}
```

Nothing fancy here. We call the `play()` function on the `QSoundEffect` that we already looked at. Finally, we emit the `soundPlayed()` signal that is used by `Track` to add a new `SoundEvent` if we are in the `RECORDING` state.

Accepting mouse drag-and-drop events

In this project example, if you drag and drop a `.wav` file on a `SoundEffectWidget`, you can change the sound being played. The constructor of `SoundEffectWidget` performs a specific task to allow you to drag and drop:

```
setAcceptDrops(true);
```

We can now override the drag-and-drop callbacks. Let's start with the `dragEnterEvent()` function:

```
//SoundEffectWidget.h
class SoundEffectWidget : public QWidget
{
...
protected:
    void dragEnterEvent(QDragEnterEvent* event) override;
...
};

//SoundEffectWidget.cpp
void SoundEffectWidget::dragEnterEvent(QDragEnterEvent* event)
{
    if (event->mimeData()->hasFormat("text/uri-list")) {
        event->acceptProposedAction();
    }
}
```

The `dragEnterEvent()` function is called each time the user drags an object on the widget. In our case, we only want to allow dragging and dropping on files that are of the *MIME* type: `"text/uri-list"` (a list of URIs, which can be `file://`, `http://`, and so on). In this case, though, we can call the `QDragEnterEvent::acceptProposedAction()` function to show that we enable this object to be dragged and dropped.

We can now add a second function, `dropEvent()`, as shown in the following code:

```
//SoundEffectWidget.h
class SoundEffectWidget : public QWidget
{
...
protected:
    void dropEvent(QDropEvent* event) override;
...
};

//SoundEffectWidget.cpp
void SoundEffectWidget::dropEvent(QDropEvent* event)
{
    const QMimeData* mimeData = event->mimeData();
    if (!mimeData->hasUrls()) {
        return;
    }
    const QUrl url = mimeData->urls().first();
    QMimeType mime = QMimeDatabase().mimeTypeForUrl(url);
    if (mime.inherits("audio/wav")) {
        loadSound(url);
    }
}
```

The first step is a sanity check. If the event does not have a URL, we do nothing. The `QMimeData::hasUrls()` function returns `true` only with the MIME type: `"text/uri-text"`. Note that a user can drag and drop multiple files at once. In our case, we only handle the first URL. You can check that the file is a `.wav` file with its MIME type. If the MIME type is `"audio/wav"`, we call the `loadSound()` function, which updates the sound assigned to this `SoundEffectWidget`.

The following screenshot shows the complete application for `ch11-drum-machine`:

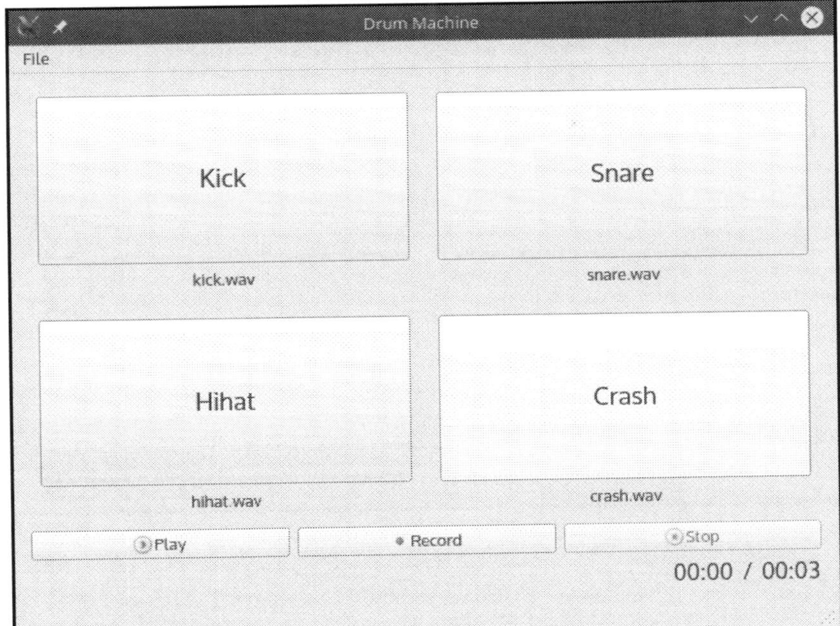

Summary

Serialization is a good way to make your data persistent when you close your application. In this chapter, you learned how to make your C++ objects serializable with `QVariant`. You created a flexible serialization structure with the bridge pattern. You saved an object in different text formats, namely the JSON, XML, and binary formats.

You also learned how to use the Qt Multimedia module to play some sound effects. These sounds can be triggered by a mouse click or by pressing a keyboard key. You implemented a friendly user interaction, allowing you to load a new sound by dragging and dropping a file.

In the next chapter, we will discover the `QTest` framework and how you can organize your project so it has a clean application/test separation.

12
You Shall (Not) Pass with QTest

In the previous chapter, we created a drum machine software with some serialization features. In this chapter, we will write the unit tests for this application. Unit testing will help us to verify each part of the source code. We will easily be able to spot an error during software development. To achieve this goal, we will use Qt Test, a dedicated test module for Qt applications.

The example project is a test application using CLI commands to execute and generate a test report. We will cover different types of tests, including datasets, GUI, signals, and benchmarking.

In this chapter, we will cover the following topics:

- Discovering Qt Test
- Executing your tests
- Writing factorized tests with datasets
- Benchmarking your code
- Testing your GUI
- Spying on your application with `QSignalSpy`

Discovering Qt Test

The Qt framework provides Qt Test, a complete API to create your unit tests in C++. A test executes the code of your application and performs verification on it. Usually, a test compares a variable with an expected value. If the variable does not match the specific value, the test fails. If you wish to go further, you can benchmark your code and get the time/CPU tick/events required by your code. Clicking over and over on a GUI to test it can quickly become boring. Qt Test offers you the possibility to simulate keyboard entries and mouse events on your widgets to completely check your software.

In our case, we want to create a unit test program named `drum-machine-test`. This console application will check the code of our famous drum machine from the previous chapter. Create a `subdirs` project, called `ch12-drum-machine-test`, with the following topology:

- `drum-machine`:
    - `drum-machine.pro`
- `drum-machine-test`:
    - `drum-machine-test.pro`
- `ch12-drum-machine-test.pro`
- `drum-machine-src.pri`

The `drum-machine` and `drum-machine-test` projects share the same source code. So all common files are put in a project include file: `drum-machine-src.pri`. Here is the updated `drum-machine.pro`:

```
QT += core gui multimedia widgets
CONFIG += c++14

TARGET = drum-machine
TEMPLATE = app

include(../drum-machine-src.pri)

SOURCES += main.cpp
```

As you can see, we only perform a refactoring task; the project drum-machine is not affected by the drum-machine-test application. You can now create the `drum-machine-test.pro` file like this:

```
QT += core gui multimedia widgets testlib
CONFIG += c++14 console
```

```
TARGET = drum-machine-test
TEMPLATE = app

include(../drum-machine-src.pri)

DRUM_MACHINE_PATH = ../drum-machine
INCLUDEPATH += $$DRUM_MACHINE_PATH
DEPENDPATH += $$DRUM_MACHINE_PATH

SOURCES += main.cpp
```

The first thing to notice is that we need to enable the `testlib` module. Then, even if we are creating a console application, we want to perform a test on the GUI so the modules (`gui`, `multimedia`, and `widgets`) used by the primary application are also required here. Finally, we include the project include file with all application files (sources, headers, forms, and resources). The `drum-machine-test` application will also contain new source files, so we must correctly set the `INCLUDEPATH` and `DEPENDPATH` variables to the source files folder.

Qt Test is easy to use and relies on some simple assumptions:

- A test case is a `QObject` class
- A private slot is a test function
- A test case can contain several test functions

Notice that the private slots with the following names are not test functions, but special functions automatically called to initialize and clean up your test:

- `initTestCase()`: Called before the first test function
- `init()`: Called before each test function
- `cleanup()`: Called after each test function
- `cleanupTestCase()`: Called after the last test function

Alright, we are ready to write our first test case in the `drum-machine-test` application. The serialization of the `drum-machine` object is an important part. A bad modification on the save feature can easily break the load feature. It can produce no errors at compile time, but it can lead to an unusable application. That is why tests are important. The first thing is to validate the serialization/deserialization process. Create a new C++ class, `DummySerializable`. Here is the header file:

```
#include "Serializable.h"

class DummySerializable : public Serializable
{
```

```
public:
    DummySerializable();

    QVariant toVariant() const override;
    void fromVariant(const QVariant& variant) override;

    int myInt = 0;
    double myDouble = 0.0;
    QString myString = "";
    bool myBool = false;
};
```

It is a simple class that implements our `Serializable` interface created in `Chapter 11`, *Having Fun with Serialization*. This class will be helpful to validate the lower layer in our serialization process. As you can see, the class contains some variables with various types to ensure a complete functioning serialization. Let's see the file, `DummySerializable.cpp`:

```
#include "DummySerializable.h"

DummySerializable::DummySerializable() :
    Serializable()
{
}

QVariant DummySerializable::toVariant() const
{
    QVariantMap map;
    map.insert("myInt", myInt);
    map.insert("myDouble", myDouble);
    map.insert("myString", myString);
    map.insert("myBool", myBool);
    return map;
}

void DummySerializable::fromVariant(const QVariant& variant)
{
    QVariantMap map = variant.toMap();
    myInt = map.value("myInt").toInt();
    myDouble = map.value("myDouble").toDouble();
    myString = map.value("myString").toString();
    myBool = map.value("myBool").toBool();
}
```

No surprise here; we perform our operation with `QVariantMap`, as already performed in the previous chapter. Our dummy class is ready; create a new C++ class, `TestJsonSerializer`, with the following header:

```
#include <QtTest/QTest>

#include "JsonSerializer.h"

class TestJsonSerializer : public QObject
{
    Q_OBJECT

public:
    TestJsonSerializer(QObject* parent = nullptr);

private slots:
    void cleanup();
    void saveDummy();
    void loadDummy();

private:
    QString loadFileContent();

private:
    JsonSerializer mSerializer;
};
```

Here we are, our first test case! This test case performs verifications on our class, `JsonSerializer`. You can see two test functions, `saveDummy()` and `loadDummy()`. The `cleanup()` slot is the special Qt Test slot that we covered earlier, which is executed after each test function. We can now write the implementation in `TestJsonSerializer.cpp`:

```
#include "DummySerializable.h"

const QString FILENAME = "test.json";
const QString DUMMY_FILE_CONTENT = "{\n    "myBool": true,\n    "myDouble":
5.2,\n    "myInt": 1,\n    "myString": "hello"\n}\n";

TestJsonSerializer::TestJsonSerializer(QObject* parent) :
    QObject(parent),
    mSerializer()
{
}
```

Two constants are created here:

- `FILENAME`: This is the filename used to test the save and load
- `DUMMY_FILE_CONTENT`: This is the referential file content used by the test functions, `saveDummy()` and `loadDummy()`

Let's implement the `saveDummy()` test function:

```
void TestJsonSerializer::saveDummy()
{
    DummySerializable dummy;
    dummy.myInt = 1;
    dummy.myDouble = 5.2;
    dummy.myString = "hello";
    dummy.myBool = true;

    mSerializer.save(dummy, FILENAME);

    QString data = loadFileContent();
    QVERIFY(data == DUMMY_FILE_CONTENT);
}
```

The first step is to instantiate a `DummySerializable` class with some hardcoded values. So, we call the function to test, `JsonSerializer::save()`, that will serialize our dummy object in the `test.json` file. Then, we call a helper function, `loadFileContent()`, to get the text contained in the `test.json` file. Finally, we use a Qt Test macro, `QVERIFY()`, to perform the verification that the text saved by the JSON serializer is the same as the expected value in `DUMMY_FILE_CONTENT`. If `data` equals the expected value, the test function succeeds. Here is the log output:

```
PASS   : TestJsonSerializer::saveDummy()
```

If the data is different, the test fails and an error is displayed in the console log:

```
FAIL!  : TestJsonSerializer::saveDummy()
'data == DUMMY_FILE_CONTENT' returned FALSE. ()
Loc: [../../ch12-drum-machine-test/drum-machine-
test/TestJsonSerializer.cpp(31)]
```

Let's briefly see the helper function, `loadFileContent()`:

```
QString TestJsonSerializer::loadFileContent()
{
    QFile file(FILENAME);
    file.open(QFile::ReadOnly);
    QString content = file.readAll();
```

```
        file.close();
        return content;
    }
```

No big deal here. We open the file, `test.json`, read all the text content, and return the corresponding `QString`.

The `QVERIFY()` macro is great for checking a Boolean value, but Qt Test provides a better macro when you want to compare data to an expected value. Let's discover `QCOMPARE()` with the `loadDummy()` test function:

```
void TestJsonSerializer::loadDummy()
{
    QFile file(FILENAME);
    file.open(QFile::WriteOnly | QIODevice::Text);
    QTextStream out(&file);
    out << DUMMY_FILE_CONTENT;
    file.close();

    DummySerializable dummy;
    mSerializer.load(dummy, FILENAME);

    QCOMPARE(dummy.myInt, 1);
    QCOMPARE(dummy.myDouble, 5.2);
    QCOMPARE(dummy.myString, QString("hello"));
    QCOMPARE(dummy.myBool, true);
}
```

The first part creates a `test.json` file, with a referential content. Then we create an empty `DymmySerializable` and call the function to test `Serializable::load()`. Finally, we use the Qt Test macro, `QCOMPARE()`. The syntax is simple:

```
QCOMPARE(actual_value, expected_value);
```

We can now test each field of the dummy loaded from JSON. The test function, `loadDummmy()`, will only succeed if all `QCOMPARE()` calls succeed. An error with `QCOMPARE()` is much more detailed:

```
FAIL!  : TestJsonSerializer::loadDummy() Compared values are not the same
   Actual   (dummy.myInt): 0
   Expected (1)          : 1
Loc: [../../ch12-drum-machine-test/drum-machine-
test/TestJsonSerializer.cpp(45)]
```

Each time a test function is executed, the special `cleanup()` slot is called. Let's update your file, `TestJsonSerializable.cpp`, like this:

```
void TestJsonSerializer::cleanup()
{
    QFile(FILENAME).remove();
}
```

This is a simple security that will remove the `test.json` file after each test function and prevent the save and load tests from colliding.

Qt also provides `QTemporaryFile`, a convenient way to create a unique temporary file that will be automatically removed by the `QTemporaryFile` destructor.

Executing your tests

We wrote a test case, `TestJsonSerializer`, with some test functions. We need a `main()` function in our `drum-machine-test` application. We will explore three possibilities:

- The `QTEST_MAIN()` function
- Writing our own simple `main()` function
- Writing our own enhanced `main()` function that supports multiple test classes

The `QTest` module provides an interesting macro, `QTEST_MAIN()`. This macro generates a complete `main()` function for your application. This generated method runs all the test functions of your test case. To use it, add the following snippet at the end of the `TestJsonSerializer.cpp` file:

```
QTEST_MAIN(TestJsonSerializer)
```

Moreover, if you declare and implement your test class only in the `.cpp` file (without a header file), you need to include the generated moc file after the `QTEST_MAIN` macro:

```
QTEST_MAIN(TestJsonSerializer)
#include "testjsonserializer.moc"
```

If you use the `QTEST_MAIN()` macro, don't forget to remove the existing `main.cpp`. Otherwise, you will have two `main()` functions and a compilation error will occur.

You can now try to run your drum-machine-test application and look at the application output. You should see something similar to this:

```
$ ./drum-machine-test
********* Start testing of TestJsonSerializer *********
Config: Using QtTest library 5.7.0, Qt 5.7.0 (x86_64-little_endian-lp64
shared (dynamic) release build; by GCC 4.9.1 20140922 (Red Hat 4.9.1-10))
PASS   : TestJsonSerializer::initTestCase()
PASS   : TestJsonSerializer::saveDummy()
PASS   : TestJsonSerializer::loadDummy()
PASS   : TestJsonSerializer::cleanupTestCase()
Totals: 4 passed, 0 failed, 0 skipped, 0 blacklisted, 1ms
********* Finished testing of TestJsonSerializer *********
```

Our test functions, `saveDummy()` and `loadDummy()`, are executed in the declaration order. Both succeed with the `PASS` status. The generated test application handles some options. Commonly, you can display the help menu by executing this command:

```
$ ./drum-machine-test -help
```

Let's see some cool features. We can execute only one function with its name. The following command only executes the `saveDummy` test function:

```
$ ./drum-machine-test saveDummy
```

You can also execute several test functions by separating their names with a space.

The QTest application provides multiple log detail options:

- `-silent` for silent. Only displays fatal errors and summary messages.
- `-v1` for verbose. Shows that the test function entered information.
- `-v2` for extended verbose. Shows each `QCOMPARE()` and `QVERIFY()`.
- `-vs` for verbose signal. Shows the emitted signal and the connected slot.

For example, we can display details of the execution of `loadDummy` with the following command:

```
$ ./drum-machine-test -v2 loadDummy
********* Start testing of TestJsonSerializer *********
Config: Using QtTest library 5.7.0, Qt 5.7.0 (x86_64-little_endian-lp64
shared (dynamic) release build; by GCC 4.9.1 20140922 (Red Hat 4.9.1-10))
INFO   : TestJsonSerializer::initTestCase() entering
PASS   : TestJsonSerializer::initTestCase()
INFO   : TestJsonSerializer::loadDummy() entering
INFO   : TestJsonSerializer::loadDummy() QCOMPARE(dummy.myInt, 1)
   Loc: [../../ch12-drum-machine-test/drum-machine-
```

```
test/TestJsonSerializer.cpp(45)]
    INFO   : TestJsonSerializer::loadDummy() QCOMPARE(dummy.myDouble, 5.2)
       Loc: [../../ch12-drum-machine-test/drum-machine-
test/TestJsonSerializer.cpp(46)]
    INFO   : TestJsonSerializer::loadDummy() QCOMPARE(dummy.myString,
QString("hello"))
       Loc: [../../ch12-drum-machine-test/drum-machine-
test/TestJsonSerializer.cpp(47)]
    INFO   : TestJsonSerializer::loadDummy() QCOMPARE(dummy.myBool, true)
       Loc: [../../ch12-drum-machine-test/drum-machine-
test/TestJsonSerializer.cpp(48)]
    PASS   : TestJsonSerializer::loadDummy()
    INFO   : TestJsonSerializer::cleanupTestCase() entering
    PASS   : TestJsonSerializer::cleanupTestCase()
    Totals: 3 passed, 0 failed, 0 skipped, 0 blacklisted, 1ms
    ********* Finished testing of TestJsonSerializer *********
```

Another great feature is the logging output format. You can create a test report file with various formats (such as `.txt`, `.xml`, and `.csv`). The syntax requires a filename and a file format separated by a comma:

```
$ ./drum-machine-test -o <filename>,<format>
```

In the following example, we create an XML report named `test-report.xml`:

```
$ ./drum-machine-test -o test-report.xml,xml
```

Notice that some log level affects only the plain text output. Moreover, the CSV format can be used only with the `QBENCHMARK` test macro, which is covered later in this chapter.

If you want to customize the generated test application, you can write the `main()` function. Remove the `QTEST_MAIN` macro in `TestJsonSerializer.cpp`. Then create `main.cpp`, like this:

```
#include "TestJsonSerializer.h"

int main(int argc, char *argv[])
{
    TestJsonSerializer test;
    QStringList arguments = QCoreApplication::arguments();
    return QTest::qExec(&test, arguments);
}
```

In this case, we are using the static function, `QTest::qExec()`, to start a `TestJsonSerializer` test. Don't forget to provide the command-line arguments to enjoy the QTest CLI options.

If you wrote your test functions in different test classes, you would have created one application per test class. If you keep one test class per test application, you can even use the `QTEST_MAIN` macro to generate the main functions.

Sometimes, you want to create only one test application to handle all your test classes. In this case, you have multiple test classes in the same application, so you cannot use the `QTEST_MAIN` macro because you don't want to generate several *main* functions for each test class.

Let's see a simple way to call all your test classes in a unique application:

```
int main(int argc, char *argv[])
{
    int status = 0;
    TestFoo testFoo;
    TestBar testBar;
    status |= QTest::qExec(&testFoo);
    status |= QTest::qExec(&testBar);
    return status;
}
```

In this simple custom `main()` function, we are executing the `TestFoo` and `TestBar` tests. But we are losing the CLI options. Indeed, executing the `QTest::qExec()` function with command-line arguments more than once will lead to errors and bad behavior. Let's take an example. You want to execute only one specific test function from `TestBar`. The execution of `TestFoo` will not find the test function, display an error message, and stop the application.

Here is a workaround to handle several test classes in a unique application: we will create a new CLI option, `-select`, to our test application. This option allows you to select a specific test class to execute. Here is a syntax example:

```
$ ./drum-machine-test -select foo fooTestFunction
```

The `-select` option, if used, must be at the beginning of the command followed by the test class name (`foo`, in this example). Then, we can optionally add Qt Test options. To achieve this goal, we will create an enhanced `main()` function that parses the new `select` option and executes the corresponding test class.

We will create our enhanced `main()` function together:

```
QApplication app(argc, argv);
QStringList arguments = QCoreApplication::arguments();

map<QString, unique_ptr<QObject>> tests;
```

```
tests.emplace("jsonserializer",
    make_unique<TestJsonSerializer>());
tests.emplace("foo", make_unique<TestFoo>());
tests.emplace("bar", make_unique<TestBar>());
```

The `QApplication` will be required later by our other GUI test cases. We retrieve the command-line arguments for later use. The `std::map` template, named `tests`, contains the smart pointers of the test classes and a `QString` label is used as a key. Notice that we are using the `map::emplace()` function that does not copy the source to the map, but creates it in place. Using the `map::insert()` function leads to an error due to the illegal copy of a smart pointer. Another syntax that could be used with a `std::map` template and `make_unique` is:

```
tests["bar"] = make_unique<TestBar>();
```

We can now parse the command-line arguments:

```
if (arguments.size() >= 3 && arguments[1] == "-select") {
    QString testName = arguments[2];
    auto iter = tests.begin();
    while(iter != tests.end()) {
        if (iter->first != testName) {
            iter = tests.erase(iter);
        } else {
            ++iter;
        }
    }
    arguments.removeOne("-select");
    arguments.removeOne(testName);
}
```

If the `-select` option is used, this snippet performs two important tasks:

- Remove `tests` from the map, the test classes that do not match the test name.
- Remove the arguments from the `-select` option and the `testName` variable to provide cleaned arguments to the `QTest::qExec()` function.

We can now add the final step to execute the test classes:

```
int status = 0;
for(auto& test : tests) {
    status |= QTest::qExec(test.second.get(), arguments);
}

return status;
```

Without the `-select` option, all the test classes will be performed. If we use the `-select` option with a test class name, only this one will be executed.

Writing factorized tests with datasets

We will now turn our attention to testing the `Track` class. We will focus specifically on the different states a `Track` class can have: `STOPPED`, `PLAYING`, and `RECORDING`. For each of these states, we want to make sure that adding `SoundEvents` works only if we are in the proper state (`RECORDING`).

To do so, we could write the following test functions:

- `testAddSoundEvent()`: This function puts `Track` in the `STOPPED` state, calls `track.addSoundEvent(0)`, and checks `track.soundEvents().size == 0`
- `testAddSoundEvent()`: This function puts `Track` in the `PLAYING` state, calls `track.addSoundEvent(0)`, and checks `track.soundEvents().size == 0`
- `testAddSoundEvent()`: This function puts `Track` in the `RECORDING` state, calls `track.addSoundEvent(0)`, and checks `track.soundEvents().size == 1`

As you can see, the logic is the same, we simply change the input and the desired output. To factorize this, Qt Test provides another module: datasets.

A dataset can be seen as a two-dimensional table where each row is a test, and the columns are the input and expected output. For our `Track` state test, it would look like this:

index	name	input (Track::State)	result (soundEvents count)
0	STOPPED	State::STOPPED	0
1	PLAYING	State::PLAYING	0
2	RECORDING	State::RECORDING	1

With this approach, you write a single `addSoundEvent()` test function and Qt Test takes care of iterating over this table and comparing the result. Right now, it seems like magic. Let's implement it!

Create a new C++ class named `TestTrack`, following the same pattern used for the `TestJsonSerializer` class (inherits `QObject`, includes `QTest`). Update `TestTrack.h` like so:

```
class TestTrack : public QObject
{
    Q_OBJECT
public:
    explicit TestTrack(QObject *parent = 0);

private slots:
    void addSoundEvent_data();
    void addSoundEvent();
};
```

Here, we added two functions:

- `addSoundEvent_data()`: Fills the dataset for the real test
- `addSoundEvent()`: Executes the test

As you can see, the function that fills the dataset for a given `xxx()` function must be named `xxx_data()`. Let's see the implementation of `addSoundEvent_data()`:

```
void TestTrack::addSoundEvent_data()
{
    QTest::addColumn<int>("trackState");
    QTest::addColumn<int>("soundEventCount");

    QTest::newRow("STOPPED")
                << static_cast<int>(Track::State::STOPPED)
                << 0;
    QTest::newRow("PLAYING")
                << static_cast<int>(Track::State::PLAYING)
                << 0;
    QTest::newRow("RECORDING")
                << static_cast<int>(Track::State::RECORDING)
                << 1;
}
```

As you can see, a dataset is constructed like a table. We start by defining the structure of the table with the `trackState` and `soundEventCount` columns. Note that `QTest::addColumn` relies on templating to know the type of the variable (`int` in both cases).

After that, a row is appended to the table with the `QTest::newRow()` function, which has the name of the test passed as a parameter. The `QTest::newRow` syntax supports the `<<` operator, making it very easy to pack all the data for a given row.

Note that each row added to the dataset corresponds to an execution of the `addSoundEvent()` function in which the data of the row will be available.

We can now turn our attention to `addSoundEvent()`:

```
void TestTrack::addSoundEvent()
{
    QFETCH(int, trackState);
    QFETCH(int, soundEventCount);

    Track track;
    switch (static_cast<Track::State>(trackState)) {
        case Track::State::STOPPED:
            track.stop();
            break;
        case Track::State::PLAYING:
            track.play();
            break;
        case Track::State::RECORDING:
            track.record();
            break;
        default:
            break;
    }

    track.addSoundEvent(0);
    track.stop();

    QCOMPARE(track.soundEvents().size(),
             static_cast<size_t>(soundEventCount));
}
```

Because `addSoundEvent()` is executed by QTest and is fed the dataset data, we can safely access the current row of the dataset like we would do with a cursor on a database. `QFETCH(int, trackState)` is a helpful macro that does two things:

- Declares an `int` variable named `trackState`
- Fetches the current column index data of the dataset and stores its content in `trackState`

The same principle is applied to `soundEventCount`. Now that we have our desired track state and the expected sound events count, we can proceed to the real test:

1. Put the track in the proper state according to `trackState`. Remember that the `Track::setState()` function is private, because the `Track` keyword handles the `trackState` variable alone, based on the caller instruction (`stop()`, `play()`, or `record()`).
2. Try to add a `SoundEvent` to the track.
3. Stop the track.
4. Compare the number of `SoundEvents` in the track to what is expected in `soundEventCount`.

Don't forget to add the `TestTrack` class in `main.cpp`:

```
#include "TestJsonSerializer.h"
#include "TestTrack.h"

...

int main(int argc, char *argv[])
{
    ...
    map<QString, unique_ptr<QObject>> tests;
    tests.emplace("jsonserializer",
                  make_unique<TestJsonSerializer>());
    tests.emplace("track",
                  make_unique<TestTrack>());
    ...
}
```

You can now run the tests and see the result output of the three tests done with `addSoundEvent()` in the console:

```
PASS   : TestTrack::addSoundEvent(STOPPED)
PASS   : TestTrack::addSoundEvent(PLAYING)
PASS   : TestTrack::addSoundEvent(RECORDING)
```

Datasets make the writing of tests less dull, by factorizing variations of data for a single test.

You can also run a single test for a specific entry of a dataset using the command line:

```
$ ./drum-machine-test <testfunction>:<dataset entry>
```

Let's say we want to execute the `addSoundEvent()` test function from `TestTrack` with only the `RECORDING` state. Here is the command line to run:

```
$ ./drum-machine-test -select track addSoundEvent:RECORDING
```

Benchmarking your code

Qt Test also provides a very easy-to-use semantic to benchmark the execution speed of your code. To see it in action, we will benchmark the time it takes to save `Track` in the JSON format. The duration of the serialization depends of the track length (the number of `SoundEvents`).

Of course, it is more interesting to benchmark this feature with different track lengths and see whether the time saved is linear. Datasets come to the rescue! It is not only useful to run the same function with expected input and output, but also to run the same function with different parameters.

We will start by creating the dataset function in `TestJsonSerializer`:

```
class TestJsonSerializer : public QObject
{
    ...

private slots:
    void cleanup();
    void saveDummy();
    void loadDummy();

    void saveTrack_data();
    ...
};

void TestJsonSerializer::saveTrack_data()
{
    QTest::addColumn<int>("soundEventCount");

    QTest::newRow("1") << 1;
    QTest::newRow("100") << 100;
    QTest::newRow("1000") << 1000;
}
```

The `saveTrack_data()` function simply stores the number of `SoundEvent` to be added to a `Track` class before it is saved. The `"1"`, `"100"`, and `"1000"` strings are here to have a clear label in the test-execution output. These strings will be displayed in each execution of `saveTrack()`. Feel free to tweak these numbers!

Now, for the real test with the benchmark call:

```
class TestJsonSerializer : public QObject
{
    ...
    void saveTrack_data();
    void saveTrack();
    ...
};

void TestJsonSerializer::saveTrack()
{
    QFETCH(int, soundEventCount);
    Track track;
    track.record();
    for (int i = 0; i < soundEventCount; ++i) {
        track.addSoundEvent(i % 4);
    }
    track.stop();

    QBENCHMARK {
        mSerializer.save(track, FILENAME);
    }
}
```

The `saveTrack()` function starts by fetching the `soundEventCount` column from its dataset. After that, it adds the correct number of `soundEvent` (with the proper `record()` state!) and benchmarks the serialization in the JSON format.

You can see that the benchmark itself is simply a macro that looks like this:

```
QBENCHMARK {
    // instructions to benchmark
}
```

The instructions enclosed in the `QBENCHMARK` macro will be executed multiple times to perform the measure automatically. If you execute the test with the updated `TestJsonSerializer` class, you should see an output similar to this:

```
PASS   : TestJsonSerializer::saveTrack(1)
RESULT : TestJsonSerializer::saveTrack():"1":
     0.041 msecs per iteration (total: 84, iterations: 2048)
```

```
PASS   : TestJsonSerializer::saveTrack(100)
RESULT : TestJsonSerializer::saveTrack():"100":
     0.23 msecs per iteration (total: 59, iterations: 256)
PASS   : TestJsonSerializer::saveTrack(1000)
RESULT : TestJsonSerializer::saveTrack():"1000":
     2.0 msecs per iteration (total: 66, iterations: 32)
```

As you can see, the `QBENCHMARK` macro makes Qt Test output very interesting data. To save a `Track` class with a single `SoundEvent`, it took 0.041 milliseconds. Qt Test repeated this test 2,048 times and it took a total of 84 milliseconds.

The power of the `QBENCHMARK` macro starts to become visible in the following test. Here, the `saveTrack()` function tried to save a `Track` class with 100 `SoundEvent`. It took 0.23 milliseconds to do so and it repeated the instruction 256 times. This shows you that the Qt Test benchmark automatically adjusts the number of iterations based on the average time a single iteration takes.

The `QBENCHMARK` macro has this behavior because a metric tends to be more accurate if it is repeated multiple times (to avoid possible external noise).

If you want your test to be benchmarked without multiple iterations, use `QBENCHMARK_ONCE`.

If you execute the test using the command line, you can provide additional metrics to `QBENCHMARK`. Here is the table recapitulating the available options:

Name	Command-line argument	Availability
Walltime	(default)	All platforms
CPU tick counter	`-tickcounter`	Windows, OS X, Linux, many UNIX-like systems
Event Counter	`-eventcounter`	All platforms
Valgrind Callgrind	`-callgrind`	Linux (if installed)
Linux Perf	`-perf`	Linux

Each one of these options will replace the selected backend used to measure the execution time of the benchmarked code. For example, if you run `drum-machine-test` with the `-tickcounter` argument:

```
$ ./drum-machine-test -tickcounter
...
RESULT : TestJsonSerializer::saveTrack():"1":
     88,062 CPU cycles per iteration (total: 88,062, iterations: 1)
PASS   : TestJsonSerializer::saveTrack(100)
RESULT : TestJsonSerializer::saveTrack():"100":
     868,706 CPU cycles per iteration (total: 868,706, iterations: 1)
PASS   : TestJsonSerializer::saveTrack(1000)
RESULT : TestJsonSerializer::saveTrack():"1000":
     7,839,871 CPU cycles per iteration (total: 7,839,871, iterations:
1)
...
```

You can see that the wall time, measured in milliseconds, has been replaced by the number of CPU cycles completed for each iteration.

Another interesting option is `-eventcounter`, which measures the numbers that were received by the event loop before they are sent to their corresponding target. This could be an interesting way to check that your code emits the proper number of signals.

Testing your GUI

It is now time to see how you can test your GUI using the Qt Test API. The `QTest` class offers several functions to simulate keys and mouse events.

To demonstrate it, we will stay with the notion of testing a `Track` state, but on an upper level. Rather than testing the `Track` state itself, we will check that the UI state of the `drum-machine` application is properly updated when the `Track` state is changed. Namely, the control buttons (play, stop, record) should be in a specific state when a recording is started.

Start by creating a `TestGui` class in the `drum-machine-test` project. Don't forget to add the `TestGui` class in the `tests` map of `main.cpp`. As usual, make it inherit `QObject` and update `TestGui.h` like so:

```
#include <QTest>

#include "MainWindow.h"

class TestGui : public QObject
{
```

```
    Q_OBJECT
public:
    TestGui(QObject* parent = 0);

private:
    MainWindow mMainWindow;
};
```

In this header, we have a member, `mMainWindow`, which is an instance of the `MainWindow` keyword from the `drum-machine` project. Throughout the tests of `TestGui`, a single `MainWindow` will be used, in which we will inject events and check how it reacts.

Let's switch to the `TestGui` constructor:

```
#include <QtTest/QtTest>

TestGui::TestGui(QObject* parent) :
    QObject(parent),
    mMainWindow()
{
    QTestEventLoop::instance().enterLoop(1);
}
```

The constructor initializes the `mMainWindow` variable. Notice that `mMainWindow` is never shown (using `mMainWindow.show()`). We do not need to display it, we just want to test its states.

Here, we use a rather obscure function call (`QTestEventLoop` is not documented at all) to force the event loop to be started after one second.

The reason why we have to do this lies in the `QSoundEffect` class. The `QSoundEffect` class is initialized when the `QSoundEffect::setSource()` function is called (in `MainWindow`, this is done at the initialization of `SoundEffectWidgets`). If we omit the explicit `enterLoop()` call, the `drum-machine-test` execution will crash with a segmentation fault.

It seems that the event loop has to be explicitly entered to let the `QSoundEffect` class properly complete its initialization. We found this undocumented workaround by studying the Qt unit tests of the `QSoundEffect` class.

Now for the real GUI test! To test the control buttons, update `TestGui`:

```
// In TestGui.h
class TestGui : public QObject
{
    ...
private slots:
    void controlButtonState();
    ...
};

// In TestGui.cpp
#include <QtTest/QtTest>
#include <QPushButton>
...
void TestGui::controlButtonState()
{
    QPushButton* stopButton =
        mMainWindow.findChild<QPushButton*>("stopButton");
    QPushButton* playButton =
        mMainWindow.findChild<QPushButton*>("playButton");
    QPushButton* recordButton =
        mMainWindow.findChild<QPushButton*>("recordButton");

    QTest::mouseClick(recordButton, Qt::LeftButton);

    QCOMPARE(stopButton->isEnabled(), true);
    QCOMPARE(playButton->isEnabled(), false);
    QCOMPARE(recordButton->isEnabled(), false);
}
```

In the `controlButtonState()` function, we start by retrieving our buttons using the handy `mMainWindow.findChild()` function. This function is available in `QObject`, and the passed name corresponds to the `objectName` variable we used for each button in Qt Designer when we created `MainWindow.ui`.

Once we retrieve all the buttons, we inject a mouse-click event using the `QTest::mouseClick()` function. It takes a `QWidget*` parameter as a target and the button that should be clicked. You can even pass keyboard modifiers (*Ctrl*, *Shift*, and so on) and a possible click delay in milliseconds.

Once `recordButton` has been clicked, we test the states of all the control buttons to make sure they are in the desired enabled state.

This function can be easily extended to test all the states (`PLAYING`, `STOPPED`, `RECORDING`) with a dataset where the input is the desired state and the output are the expected buttons states.

The `QTest` class offers many useful functions to inject events, including:

- `keyEvent()`: Simulates a key event
- `keyPress()`: Simulates a key-press event
- `keyRelease()`: Simulates a key-release event
- `mouseClick()`: Simulates a key-click event
- `mouseDClick()`: Simulates a mouse double-click event
- `mouseMove()`: Simulates a mouse-move event

Spying on your application with QSignalSpy

The last part we will cover in the Qt Test framework is the ability to spy on signals with `QSignalSpy`. This class allows you to do the introspection of the emitted signal of any `QObject`.

Let's see it in action with `SoundEffectWidget`. We will test `QSignalSpy` when the `SoundEffectWidget::play()` function is called, the `soundPlayed` signal is emitted with the correct `soundId` parameter.

Here is the `playSound()` function of `TestGui`:

```
#include <QTest>

#include "MainWindow.h"

// In TestGui.h
class TestGui : public QObject
{
    ...
    void controlButtonState();
    void playSound();
    ...
};

// In TestGui.cpp
#include <QPushButton>
#include <QtTest/QtTest>
```

```
#include "SoundEffectWidget.h"
...
void TestGui::playSound()
{
    SoundEffectWidget widget;
    QSignalSpy spy(&widget, &SoundEffectWidget::soundPlayed);
    widget.setId(2);
    widget.play();

    QCOMPARE(spy.count(), 1);
    QList<QVariant> arguments = spy.takeFirst();
    QCOMPARE(arguments.at(0).toInt(), 2);
}
```

We start by initializing a `SoundEffectWidget` widget and a `QSignalSpy` class. The `spy` class' constructor takes the pointer to the object to spy and the pointer to the member function of the signal to be watched. Here, we want to check the `SoundEffectWidget::soundPlayed()` signal.

Right after, `widget` is configured with an arbitrary `soundId` (`2`) and `widget.play()` is called. This is where it gets interesting: `spy` stores the signal's emitted parameters in `QVariantList`. Each time `soundPlayed()` is emitted, a new `QVariantList` is created in `spy`, which contains the emitted parameters.

The first step is to check that the signal is emitted only once, by comparing `spy.count()` to `1`. After that, we store the parameters of this signal in `arguments` and check that it has the value of `2`, the initial `soundId` that `widget` was configured with.

As you can see, `QSignalSpy` is simple to use; you can create as many as you need for each signal you want to spy on.

Summary

The Qt Test module helps us to easily create a test application. In this chapter, you learned to organize your project with a standalone test application. You are able to compare and verify a specific value in your simple tests. For your complex tests, you could use the datasets. You implemented a simple benchmark, recording the time or the CPU ticks required to execute a function. You have simulated GUI events and spied on Qt signals to ensure that your application works well.

Your application is created and your unit tests indicate a PASS status. In the next chapter, you will learn how to deploy your application.

13
All Packed and Ready to Deploy

In the previous chapter, you learned how to create a robust application with unit tests. The final step for an application is packaging. The Qt framework enables you to develop cross-platform applications, but packaging is really a platform-specific task. Moreover, when your application is ready to be shipped, you need a one-step procedure to generate and pack your application.

In this chapter, we will reuse the gallery application (both on desktop and mobile platforms) to learn the steps required to package a Qt application. There are many ways to prepare the packaging of an application. In this chapter, we want to package the gallery application from `Chapter 4`, *Conquering the Desktop UI*, and `Chapter 5`, *Dominating the Mobile UI*, on the supported platforms (Windows, Linux, macOS, Android, and iOS).

The following topics will be covered in this chapter:

- Packaging for Windows
- Packaging for Linux with a distribution package
- Packaging for Linux with AppImage
- Packaging for macOS
- Packaging for Android
- Packaging for iOS

Packaging your application

For each platform, you will create a dedicated script to perform all the tasks required to build a standalone application. Depending on the OS type, the packaged application will be `gallery-desktop` or `gallery-mobile`. Because the whole gallery project has to be compiled, it also has to include `gallery-core`. Therefore, we will create a parent project with `gallery-core`, `gallery-desktop`, and `gallery-mobile`.

For each platform, we will prepare the project to be packaged and create a specific script. All the scripts follow the same workflow:

1. Set the input and output directories
2. Create makefiles with `qmake`
3. Build the project
4. Regroup only the necessary files in the output directory
5. Package the application with platform-specific tasks
6. Store the packed application in the output directory

These scripts could run on a developer computer or on a continuous-integration server running software such as Jenkins, as long as the packaging computer OS matches the script target OS (except for mobile platforms). In other words, you need to run the Windows script on a computer that runs Windows to be able to package a Qt application for Windows.

Technically, you can perform cross compilation (given the appropriate toolchain and libraries), but this is beyond the scope of this book. It is easy to cross compile for a Raspberry Pi when you are on Linux, but the same cannot be said when you want to compile for macOS and you are on Windows.

From Linux, you can cross compile Qt for Windows with tools such as MXE at `http://mxe.cc/`.

Create a new `subdirs` project named `ch13-gallery-packaging` with the following hierarchy:

- `ch13-gallery-packaging`:
    - `gallery-core`

- `gallery-desktop`
- `gallery-mobile`

Even if you are now an expert on Qt `subdirs` projects, here is the `ch13-gallery-packaging.pro` file:

```
TEMPLATE = subdirs

SUBDIRS += \
    gallery-core \
    gallery-desktop \
    gallery-mobile

gallery-desktop.depends = gallery-core
gallery-mobile.depends = gallery-core
```

You are now ready to work through any of the following sections, depending on the platform you are targeting.

Packaging for Windows

To package a standalone application on Windows, you need to provide all the dependencies of your executable. The `gallery-core.dll` file, the Qt libraries (for example, `Qt5Core.dll`), and the compiler-specific libraries (for example, `libstdc++-6.dll`) are some examples of the dependencies required by our executable. If you forget to provide a library, an error will be displayed when you run the `gallery-desktop.exe` program.

On Windows, you can use the Dependency Walker utility (`depends`). It will give you a list of all the libraries required by your application. You can download it at `www.dependencywalker.com`.

For this section, we will create a script to build the project via the command-line interface. Then we will use the Qt tool `windeployqt` to gather all dependencies required by our application. This example is for a MinGW compiler, but you can easily adapt it for a MSVC compiler.

In the case of the MSVC compiler, the `windeployqt` tool will not deploy certain libraries (for example, `msvcrt`). Always double-check that your final application can run on a non-developer computer.

The following is a list of the required files and folders gathered by `winqtdeploy` to properly run `gallery-desktop` on Windows:

- `iconengines`:
    - `qsvgicon.dll`
- `imageformats`:
    - `qjpeg.dll`
    - `qwbmp.dll`
    - `...`
- `platforms`:
    - `qwindows.dll`
- `translations`:
    - `qt_en.qm`
    - `qt_fr.qm`
    - `...`
- `D3Dcompiler_47.dll`
- `gallery-core.dll`
- `gallery-desktop.exe`
- `libEGL.dll`
- `libgcc_s_dw2-1.dll`
- `libGLESV2.dll`
- `libstdc++-6.dll`
- `libwinpthread-1.dll`
- `opengl32sw.dll`
- `Qt5Core.dll`
- `Qt5Gui.dll`
- `Qt5Svg.dll`
- `Qt5Widgets.dll`

Check that your environment variables are correctly set, as shown in the following table:

Name	Example
`QTDIR`	`C:\Qt\5.11\mingw49_32`
`MINGWROOT`	`C:\Qt\Tools\mingw492_32`

Create a file called `package-windows.bat` in the `scripts` directory:

```
@ECHO off

set DIST_DIR=dist\desktop-windows
set BUILD_DIR=build
set OUT_DIR=gallery

mkdir %DIST_DIR% && pushd %DIST_DIR%
mkdir %BUILD_DIR% %OUT_DIR%

pushd %BUILD_DIR%
%QTDIR%\bin\qmake.exe ^
  -spec win32-g++ ^
  "CONFIG += release" ^
  ..\..\..\ch13-gallery-packaging.pro

%MINGWROOT%\bin\mingw32-make.exe qmake_all

pushd gallery-core
%MINGWROOT%\bin\mingw32-make.exe && popd

pushd gallery-desktop
%MINGWROOT%\bin\mingw32-make.exe && popd

popd
copy %BUILD_DIR%\gallery-core\release\gallery-core.dll %OUT_DIR%
copy %BUILD_DIR%\gallery-desktop\release\gallery-desktop.exe %OUT_DIR%
%QTDIR%\bin\windeployqt %OUT_DIR%\gallery-desktop.exe %OUT_DIR%\gallery-
core.dll

popd
```

Let's go through the steps that are involved:

1. Set the main path variables. The output directory is `DIST_DIR`. All files are generated in the `dist/desktop-windows/build` directory.
2. Create all directories and launch `dist/desktop-windows/build`.
3. Execute `qmake` in release mode for the Win32 platform to generate the parent project, `Makefile`. The spec `win32-g++` is for the MinGW compiler. You should use the spec `win32-msvc` if you want to use the MSVC compiler.
4. Run the `mingw32-make qmake_all` command to generate the subproject makefiles. You must replace `mingw32-make` with `nmake` or `jom` using an MSVC compiler.
5. Run the `mingw32-make` commands to build each required subproject.

6. Copy the generated files, `gallery-desktop.exe` and `gallery-core.dll`, into the `gallery` directory.
7. Call the Qt tool, `windeployqt`, on both files and copy all required dependencies (for example, `Qt5Core.dll`, `Qt5Sql.dll`, `libstdc++-6.dll`, `qwindows.dll`, and so on).

Packaging for Linux with a distribution package

Packaging an application for a Linux distribution is a bumpy road. Because each distribution can have its own packaging format (`.deb`, `.rpm`, and so on), the first question to answer is which distribution do you wish to target? Covering every major packaging format would take several chapters. Even detailing a single distribution could be unfair (you wanted to package for RHEL? Too bad—we only covered Arch Linux!). After all, from a Qt application developer's perspective, what you want is to ship your product to your users; you are not (yet) aiming to become an official Debian repository maintainer.

With all this in mind, we decided to focus on a tool that packages the application for you for each distribution. That is right: You do not need to learn the internals of Debian or Red Hat! We will still explain the common principles in the packaging systems without going into excessive detail.

For our purposes, we will demonstrate how packaging can be done using the `.deb` format on an Ubuntu machine, but as you will see, it can be easily updated to generate a `.rpm` package.

The tool we are going to use is named `fpm` (**eFfing Package Management**).

The `fpm` tool is available at `https://github.com/jordansissel/fpm`.

The `fpm` tool is a Ruby application that aims to do exactly what we need: take care of the distribution-specific details and generate the final package. First, take the time to install `fpm` on your machine and make sure that it is working.

In a nutshell, a Linux package is a file format that contains all the files you want to deploy with a lot of metadata. It can contain a description of the content, a changelog, a license file, the list of dependencies, checksums, pre- and post-installation triggers, and much, much more.

If you want to learn how to package a Debian binary by hand, go to `http://tldp.org/HOWTO/html_single/Debian-Binary-Package-Building-HOWTO/`.

In our case, we still have to do some project preparation to allow `fpm` to do its job. The files we want to deploy have to match the target filesystem. Here is how the deployment should look:

- `gallery-desktop`: This binary should be deployed in `/usr/bin`
- `libgallery-core.so`: This library should be deployed in `/usr/lib`

To achieve this, we are going to organize our outputs in `dist/desktop-linux` like so:

- The `build` directory will contain the compiled project (it is our release shadow build)
- The `root` directory will contain the to-be-packaged files, meaning the binary and library files in the proper hierarchy (`usr/bin` and `usr/lib`)

To generate the root directories, we will rely on Qt and the power of the `.pro` files. When compiling a Qt project, the target files are already tracked. All we have to do is to add an additional install target for `gallery-core` and `gallery-desktop`.

Add the following scope in `gallery-core/gallery-core.pro`:

```
linux {
    target.path = $$_PRO_FILE_PWD_/../dist/desktop-linux/root/usr/lib/
    INSTALLS += target
}
```

Here, we define a new `target.path` that is going to deploy the `DISTFILES` (the `.so` files) to our desired root tree. Note the use of `$$_PRO_FILE_PWD_`, which points to the directory where the current `.pro` file is stored.

Almost the same procedure is carried out in `gallery-desktop/gallery-desktop.pro`:

```
linux {
    target.path = $$_PRO_FILE_PWD_/../dist/desktop-linux/root/usr/bin/
    INSTALLS += target
}
```

With these lines, when we do the `make install` shell command, the files are going to be deployed in `dist/desktop-linux/root/....`

Now that the project configuration is completed, we can switch to the packaging script. We will cover the script in two parts:

- Project compilation and `root` preparation
- The `.deb` package generation with `fpm`

First, check that your environment variables are correctly set, as shown in the following table:

Name	Example
QTDIR	$HOME/qt/5.11/gcc_64

Create `scripts/package-linux-deb.sh` with the following content:

```
#!/bin/bash

DIST_DIR=dist/desktop-linux
BUILD_DIR=build
ROOT_DIR=root

BIN_DIR=$ROOT_DIR/usr/bin
LIB_DIR=$ROOT_DIR/usr/lib

mkdir -p $DIST_DIR && cd $DIST_DIR
mkdir -p $BIN_DIR $LIB_DIR $BUILD_DIR

pushd $BUILD_DIR
$QTDIR/bin/qmake \
    -spec linux-g++ \
    "CONFIG += release" \
    ../../../ch13-gallery-packaging.pro

make qmake_all
pushd gallery-core && make && make install ; popd
pushd gallery-desktop && make && make install ; popd
popd
```

Let's break this down:

1. Set the main path variables. The output directory is `DIST_DIR`. All files are generated in the `dist/desktop-linux/build` folder.
2. Create all the directories and launch `dist/desktop-linux/build`.
3. Execute `qmake` in release mode for the Linux platform to generate the parent project, `Makefile`.
4. Run the `make qmake_all` command to generate the subprojects `Makefile` files.
5. Perform the `make` commands to build each required subproject.
6. Use the `make install` command to deploy the binary and the libraries to the `dist/desktop-linux/root` directory.

If you execute `scripts/package-linux-deb.sh`, the final file tree in `dist/desktop-linux` should look like the following:

- `build/`
    - `gallery-core/*.o`
    - `gallery-desktop/*.p`
    - `Makefile`
- `root/`
    - `usr/bin/gallery-desktop`
    - `usr/lib/libgallery-core.so`

Everything is now ready for `fpm` to work. The final part of `scripts/package-linux-deb.sh` contains the following:

```
fpm --input-type dir \
    --output-type deb \
    --force \
    --name gallery-desktop \
    --version 1.0.0 \
    --vendor "Mastering Qt 5" \
    --description "A Qt gallery application to organize and manage your
pictures in albums" \
    --depends qt5-default \
    --depends libsqlite3-dev \
    --chdir $ROOT_DIR \
    --package gallery-desktop_VERSION_ARCH.deb
```

Most of the arguments are explicit enough. We will focus on the most important ones, as shown in the following list:

- `--input-type`: what `fpm` will work with. It can take `deb`, `rpm`, `gem`, `dir`, and so on, and repackage them to another format. Here, we use the `dir` option to tell `fpm` to use a directory tree as the input source.
- `--output-type`: the desired output type. Take a look at the official documentation to see how many platforms are supported.
- `--name`: the name given to the package (if you want to uninstall it, you write `apt-get remove gallery-desktop`).
- `--depends`: a library package dependency of the project. You can add as many dependencies as you want. In our case, we only depend on `qt5 -default` and `sqlite3-dev`. This option is very important, so ensure that the application will be able to run on the target platform. You can specify the version of the dependency with `--depends library >= 1.2.3`.
- `--chdir`: the base directory from which `fpm` will run. We set it to `dist/desktop-linux/root`, where our file tree is ready to be loaded!
- `--package`: the name of the final package. The `VERSION` and `ARCH` phrases are placeholders that are automatically filled based on your system.

The rest of the options are purely informative; you can specify a changelog, a license file, and much more. Just by changing the `--output-typedeb` to `rpm`, the package format is properly updated. The `fpm` tool also provides specific package format options, letting you have fine control over what is generated.

If you now execute `scripts/package-linux-deb.sh`, you should get a new `dist/desktop-linux/gallery-desktop_1.0.0_amd64.deb` file. Try to install it with the following commands:

```
sudo dpkg -i  dist/desktop-linux/gallery-desktop_1.0.0_amd64.deb
sudo apt-get install -f
```

The first command deploys the package in your system. You should now have the files named `/usr/bin/gallery-desktop` and `/usr/lib/libgallery-core.so`.

However, because we installed the package using the `dpkg` command, the dependencies are not automatically installed. This would be done if the package was provided by a Debian repository (installing the package with `apt-get install gallery-desktop`). The missing dependencies are still "marked", and the command `apt-get install -f` performs their installation.

You can now start gallery-desktop from anywhere in your system with the gallery-desktop command. At the time of writing, if you execute it on a "fresh" Ubuntu, you might run into the following issue:

```
$ gallery-desktop
gallery-desktop: /usr/lib/x86_64-linux-gnu/libQt5Core.so.5: version
`Qt_5.11' not found (required by gallery-desktop)
gallery-desktop: /usr/lib/x86_64-linux-gnu/libQt5Core.so.5: version
`Qt_5' not found (required by gallery-desktop)
...
gallery-desktop: /usr/lib/x86_64-linux-gnu/libQt5Core.so.5: version
`Qt_5' not found (required by /usr/lib/libgallery-core.so.1)
```

What happened? We installed the dependencies with apt-get install -f! Here, we encounter a major pain point in Linux package management. The dependencies we specify in our .deb could refer to a specific version of Qt, but the reality is that we depend on the package version maintained by the upstream. In other words, each time a new version of Qt is released, the distribution maintainers (Ubuntu, Fedora, and so on) have to repackage it to make it available in the official repository. This can be a long process, and the maintainers have a huge number of packages to port!

To be confident about what we are stating, let's view the library dependencies of gallery-desktop with an ldd command:

```
$ ldd /usr/bin/gallery-desktop
     libgallery-core.so.1 => /usr/lib/libgallery-core.so.1
(0x00007f8110775000)
     libQt5Widgets.so.5 => /usr/lib/x86_64-linux-gnu/libQt5Widgets.so.5
(0x00007f81100e8000)
     libQt5Gui.so.5 => /usr/lib/x86_64-linux-gnu/libQt5Gui.so.5
(0x00007f810fb9f000)
     libQt5Core.so.5 => /usr/lib/x86_64-linux-gnu/libQt5Core.so.5
(0x00007f810f6c9000)
     ...
     libXext.so.6 => /usr/lib/x86_64-linux-gnu/libXext.so.6
(0x00007f810966e000)
```

As you can see, libgallery-core.so is correctly resolved in /usr/lib, as are the Qt dependencies in /usr/lib/x86_64-linux-gnu. But which version of Qt is used? The answer lies in the details of the libraries:

```
$ ll /usr/lib/x86_64-linux-gnu/libQt5Core.*
-rw-r--r-- 1 root root    1014 may   2 15:37 libQt5Core.prl
lrwxrwxrwx 1 root root      19 may   2 15:39 libQt5Core.so ->
libQt5Core.so.5.5.1
lrwxrwxrwx 1 root root      19 may   2 15:39 libQt5Core.so.5 ->
```

```
libQt5Core.so.5.5.1
    lrwxrwxrwx 1 root root      19 may   2 15:39 libQt5Core.so.5.5 ->
libQt5Core.so.5.5.1
    -rw-r--r-- 1 root root 5052920 may   2 15:41 libQt5Core.so.5.5.1
```

The `libQt5Core.so` file is a soft link to `libQt5Core.so.5.5.1`, meaning that the system version of Qt is 5.5.1, whereas `gallery-desktop` relies on Qt 5.7. You can configure your system to have the system Qt pointing to your Qt installation (which is performed using the Qt installer). However, it is highly improbable that your customer will install Qt by hand just to have `gallery-desktop` running.

Even worse, for an older version of your distribution, the packages are usually not updated at all after some time; just try to install a Qt 5.7 Debian package on Ubuntu 14.04 to understand how complicated things can become. We didn't even mention incompatible dependencies. If we rely on a specific version of `libsqlite3-dev`, and another application needs another one, things will get ugly, and only one can survive.

A Linux package has many advantages if you want it to be available on an official repository, or if you have specific needs. Using official repositories is a common way of installing an application on Linux, and your users will not be disoriented. If you can restrict your Qt version to the one deployed on the Linux distribution, that may be a fine solution.

Unfortunately, it also brings major headaches: You need to support multiple distributions, handle the dependencies without breaking the system, make sure that your application has up-to-date dependencies, and so on.

Do not worry—everything is not lost; smart people are already resolving this issue on Linux with self-contained packages. As a matter of fact, we are going to cover a self-contained package.

Packaging for Linux with AppImage

On Windows or Mac, an application is self-sufficient; it contains all the dependencies it needs to be executed. On the one hand, this creates more file duplication, and on the other hand, it simplifies packaging for the developer.

Based on this premise, efforts have been made to have the same pattern on Linux (as opposed to a repository/distribution-specific package). Today, several solutions offer a self-contained package on Linux. We suggest you study one of these solutions: AppImage. This particular tool is gaining traction in the Linux community. There is a growing number of developers relying on AppImage to package and deploy their application.

AppImage is a file format that contains an application with all its libraries included. You download a single AppImage file, execute it, and you are done: The application is running. Behind the scenes, an AppImage is an ISO file on steroids, mounted on-the-fly when you execute it. The AppImage file itself is read-only, and can also run in a sandbox, such as Firejail (a SUID sandbox program that reduces the risk of security breaches by restricting the running environment of applications).

More information on AppImage is available at `http://appimage.org/`.

There are two major steps to package `gallery-desktop` into an AppImage:

1. Gather all the dependencies of `gallery-desktop`
2. Package `gallery-desktop` and its dependencies in the AppImage format

Fortunately, this whole process can be done by using a nifty tool: `linuxdeployqt`. It started as a hobby project and became the official way to package a Qt application in the AppImage documentation.

Get `linuxdeployqt` from `https://github.com/probonopd/linuxdeployqt/`.

The script we are going to write now assumes that the `linuxdeployqt` binary is available in your `$PATH` variable. Check that your environment variables are correctly set:

Name	Example
`QTDIR`	`$HOME/qt/5.11/gcc_64`

Create `scripts/package-linux-appimage.sh` and update it as shown in the following code:

```
#!/bin/bash

DIST_DIR=dist/desktop-linux
BUILD_DIR=build

mkdir -p $DIST_DIR && cd $DIST_DIR
mkdir -p $BUILD_DIR

pushd $BUILD_DIR
```

```
$QTDIR/bin/qmake \
    -spec linux-g++ \
    "CONFIG += release" \
    ../../../ch13-gallery-packaging.pro
make qmake_all
pushd gallery-core && make ; popd
pushd gallery-desktop && make ; popd
popd

export QT_PLUGIN_PATH=$QTDIR/plugins/
export LD_LIBRARY_PATH=$QTDIR/lib:$(pwd)/build/gallery-core

linuxdeployqt \
    build/gallery-desktop/gallery-desktop \
    -appimage

mv build/gallery-desktop.AppImage .
```

The first part is the compilation of the project, and goes through the following steps:

1. Set the main path variables. The output directory is `DIST_DIR`. All files are generated in the `dist/desktop-linux/build` folder.
2. Create all the directories and go into `dist/desktop-linux/build`.
3. Execute `qmake` in release mode for the Linux platform to generate the parent project `Makefile`.
4. Run the `make qmake_all` command to generate the subproject `Makefile` files.
5. Perform the `make` commands to build each required subproject.

The second part of the script concerns `linuxdeployqt`. We first have to export some paths to let `linuxdeployqt` properly find all the dependencies of `gallery-desktop` (the Qt libraries and the `gallery-core` library).

After that, we execute `linuxdeployqt` by specifying the source binary to work with and the target file type (AppImage). The resulting file is a single `gallery-desktop.AppImage` ready to be launched on the user's computer without any Qt package installed!

Packaging for OS X

On OS X, applications are built and run from a bundle: a single directory that contains the application binary and all its dependencies. In the finder, these bundles are viewed as `.app` special directories.

When running `gallery-desktop` from Qt Creator, the application is already bundled in a `.app` file. Because we are using a custom library, called `gallery-core`, this `gallery-desktop.app` does not contain all the dependencies, and Qt Creator handles it for us.

What we aim to create is a script that completely packages `gallery-desktop` (`gallery-core` included) in a `.dmg` file, an OS X disk image file that is mounted upon executionn and lets the user install the application with ease.

To achieve this, Qt provides the `macdeployqt` tool, which gathers the dependencies and creates the `.dmg` file.

First, check that your environment variables are correctly set, as shown in the following table:

Name	Example
`QTDIR`	`$HOME/Qt/5.11/clang_64`

Create the `scripts/package-macosx.sh` file with the following content:

```
#!/bin/bash

DIST_DIR=dist/desktop-macosx
BUILD_DIR=build

mkdir -p $DIST_DIR && cd $DIST_DIR
mkdir -p $BUILD_DIR

pushd $BUILD_DIR
$QTDIR/bin/qmake \
  -spec macx-clang \
  "CONFIG += release x86_64" \
  ../../../ch13-gallery-packaging.pro
make qmake_all
pushd gallery-core && make ; popd
pushd gallery-desktop && make ; popd

cp gallery-core/*.dylib \
    gallery-desktop/gallery-desktop.app/Contents/Frameworks/

install_name_tool -change \
  libgallery-core.1.dylib \
  @rpath/libgallery-core.1.dylib \
  gallery-desktop/gallery-desktop.app/Contents/MacOS/gallery-desktop
popd
```

```
$QTDIR/bin/macdeployqt \
    build/gallery-desktop/gallery-desktop.app \
    -dmg

mv build/gallery-desktop/gallery-desktop.dmg .
```

We can split the script in two. The first part prepares the application for `macdeployqt` and goes through the following steps:

1. Set the main path variables. The output directory is `DIST_DIR`. All files are generated in the `dist/desktop-macosx/build` folder.
2. Create all the directories and go into `dist/desktop-macosx/build`.
3. Execute `qmake` in release mode for the OS X platform to generate the parent project `Makefile`.
4. Run the `make qmake_all` command to generate the subproject `Makefile` files.
5. Perform the `make` commands to build each required subproject.

The second part includes the `gallery-core` library in the generated `gallery-desktop.app`. If we do not execute the `cp` command stated in the script and everything that comes after it, we might be quite surprised by the `gallery-desktop` binary content. Let's take a look at it by executing the following command:

```
    $ otool -L dist/desktop-macosx/build/gallery-desktop/gallery-desktop.app/Contents/MacOS/gallery-desktop
    dist/desktop-macosx/build/gallery-desktop/gallery-desktop.app/Contents/MacOS/gallery-desktop:
        libgallery-core.1.dylib (compatibility version 1.0.0, current version 1.0.0)
        @rpath/QtWidgets.framework/Versions/5/QtWidgets (compatibility version 5.7.0, current version 5.7.0)
    ...
        /usr/lib/libSystem.B.dylib (compatibility version 1.0.0, current version 1226.10.1)
```

As you can see, `libgallery-core.1.dylib` is resolved in the local path, but not in the special dependencies path, as it is for `QtWidget` with `@rpath` (namely `Contents/Frameworks/`). To mitigate this, `package-macosx.sh` copies the `.dylib` file in `gallery-desktop.app/Contents/Frameworks/` and regenerates the dependencies index of the binary with `install_name_tool`.

Finally, in `package-macosx.sh`, `macdeployqt` is called with the updated `gallery-deskop.app` and the target `dmg` format. The resulting `gallery-desktop.dmg` can be deployed on your user computer.

Packaging for Android

The aim of this section is to generate a standalone APK file for the `gallery-mobile` application. Packaging and deploying an application for Android requires multiple steps:

1. Configure the Android build details
2. Generate a `keystore` and a certificate
3. Customize the Android manifest from a template
4. Create a script to automate the packaging

You can do most of these tasks directly from Qt Creator. Under the hood, the `androiddeployqt` Qt tool is called to generate the APK file. Go to **Projects** | **Android for armeabi-v7a** | **Build Steps**. You should see a special build step: **Build Android APK**. The details look like the following screenshot:

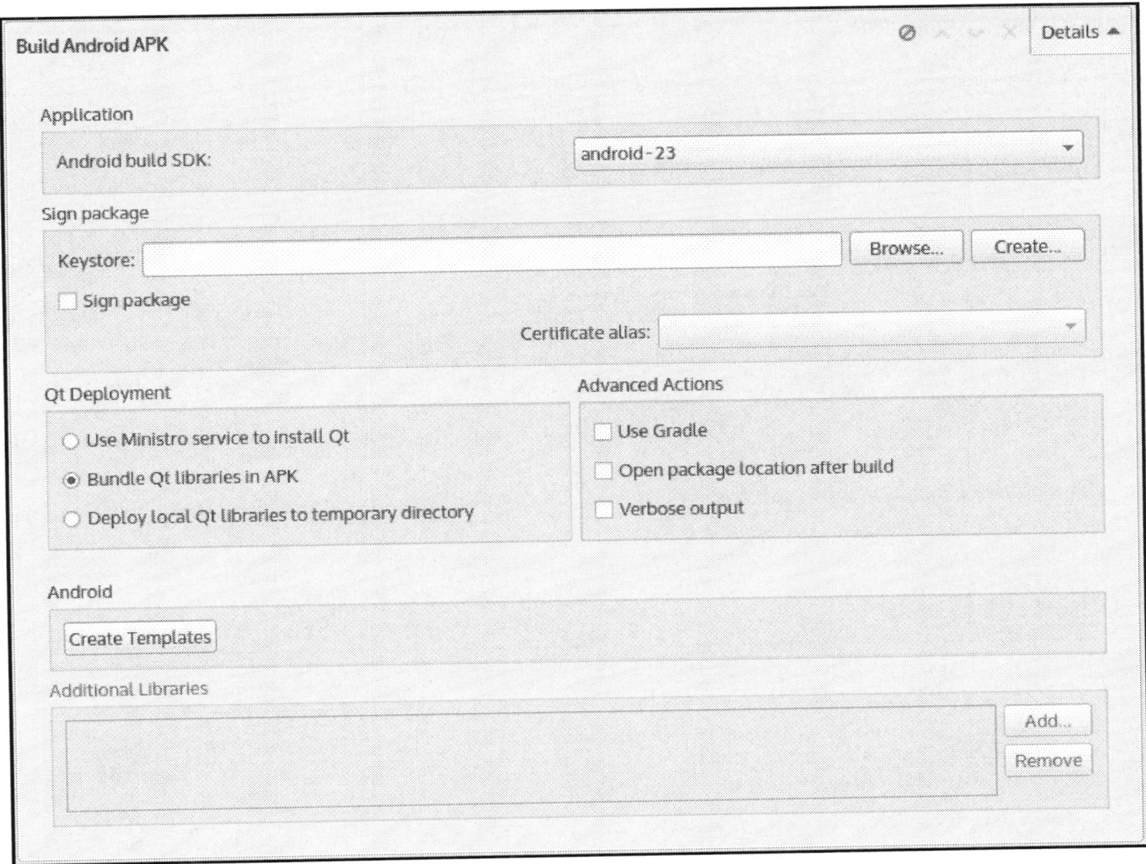

The first thing to do is to select which Android API level you want to use to generate the application. In our case, we selected **android-23** for the Android API Level 23. Always try to build your application with the latest SDK version available.

To publish your application on the Play Store, you must sign the package. To be able to update an application, the signature of the current version and the new version must be the same. This procedure is a measure to ensure that any future versions of the application were really created by you. The first time, you should create a keystore. The next time, you can reuse it with the **Browse...** button. For now, click on the **Create...** button on the **Sign package** | **Keystore** line. You will get the following popup:

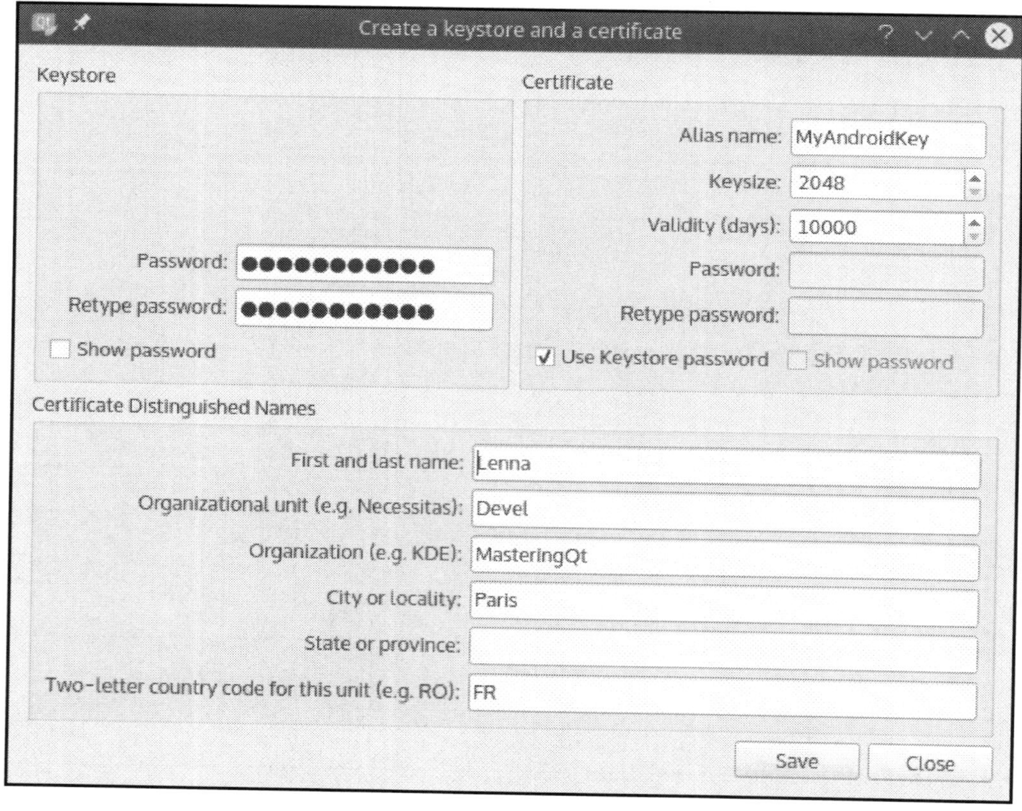

Follow these steps to generate a new `keystore`:

1. The `keystore` must be protected by a password. Do not forget it or you will not be able to use this `keystore` for a future release.
2. Specify an **Alias name** for the certificate. The default values for **Keysize** and **Validity (days)** are fine. You can specify a different password for the certificate or use the same.
3. In the **Certificate Distinguished Names** group, enter information about you and your company.
4. Save the `keystore` file in a safe place.
5. Enter the `keystore` password to validate its selection for the deployment.

The next part concerns Qt deployment. Indeed, your application needs some Qt libraries. Qt supports three kinds of deployment:

- Create a minimal APK relying on Ministro for the Qt dependencies. Ministro is an Android application that can be downloaded from the Play Store. It acts as a Qt shared libraries installer/provider for all Qt applications on Android.
- Create a standalone bundle APK that embeds the Qt libraries.
- Create an APK that relies on the fact that the Qt libraries are in a specific directory. The libraries are copied into a temporary directory during the first deployment.

During the developing and debugging phase, you should select the temporary directory method to reduce the packaging time. For a deployment, you can use the Ministro or the bundle option. In our case, we chose the standalone bundle to generate a complete APK.

The **Advanced actions** pane offers three options:

- **Use Gradle**: This option generates Gradle wrappers and a script, which is useful if you plan to customize the Java part in an IDE, such as Android Studio
- **Open package location after build**: This option opens the directory with the packages generated by `androiddeployqt`
- **Verbose Output**: This option displays additional information about the `androiddeployqt` processing

The Android build details and signing options are finished. We can now customize the Android manifest. Click on **Create Templates**, select the `gallery-mobile.pro` file, and click on **Finish**. The wizard will create an `android` subdirectory for you, with several files, such as `AndroidManifest.xml` (for example). The `gallery-mobile.pro` file has to be updated automatically with these files. However, do not forget to add the `android` scope, as shown in the following snippet:

```
TEMPLATE = app
...
android {
    contains(ANDROID_TARGET_ARCH,x86) {
        ANDROID_EXTRA_LIBS = \
            $$[QT_INSTALL_LIBS]/libQt5Sql.so
    }

    DISTFILES += \
        android/AndroidManifest.xml \
        android/gradle/wrapper/gradle-wrapper.jar \
        android/gradlew \
        android/res/values/libs.xml \
        android/build.gradle \
        android/gradle/wrapper/gradle-wrapper.properties \
        android/gradlew.bat

    ANDROID_PACKAGE_SOURCE_DIR = $$PWD/android
}
```

You can now edit the `AndroidManifest.xml` file. Qt Creator provides a dedicated editor. You can also edit it with a plain text editor, but do so carefully. You can open it from the hierarchical project view by going to **gallery-mobile** | **Other files** | **android**.

The following screenshot shows our Android manifest in Qt Creator:

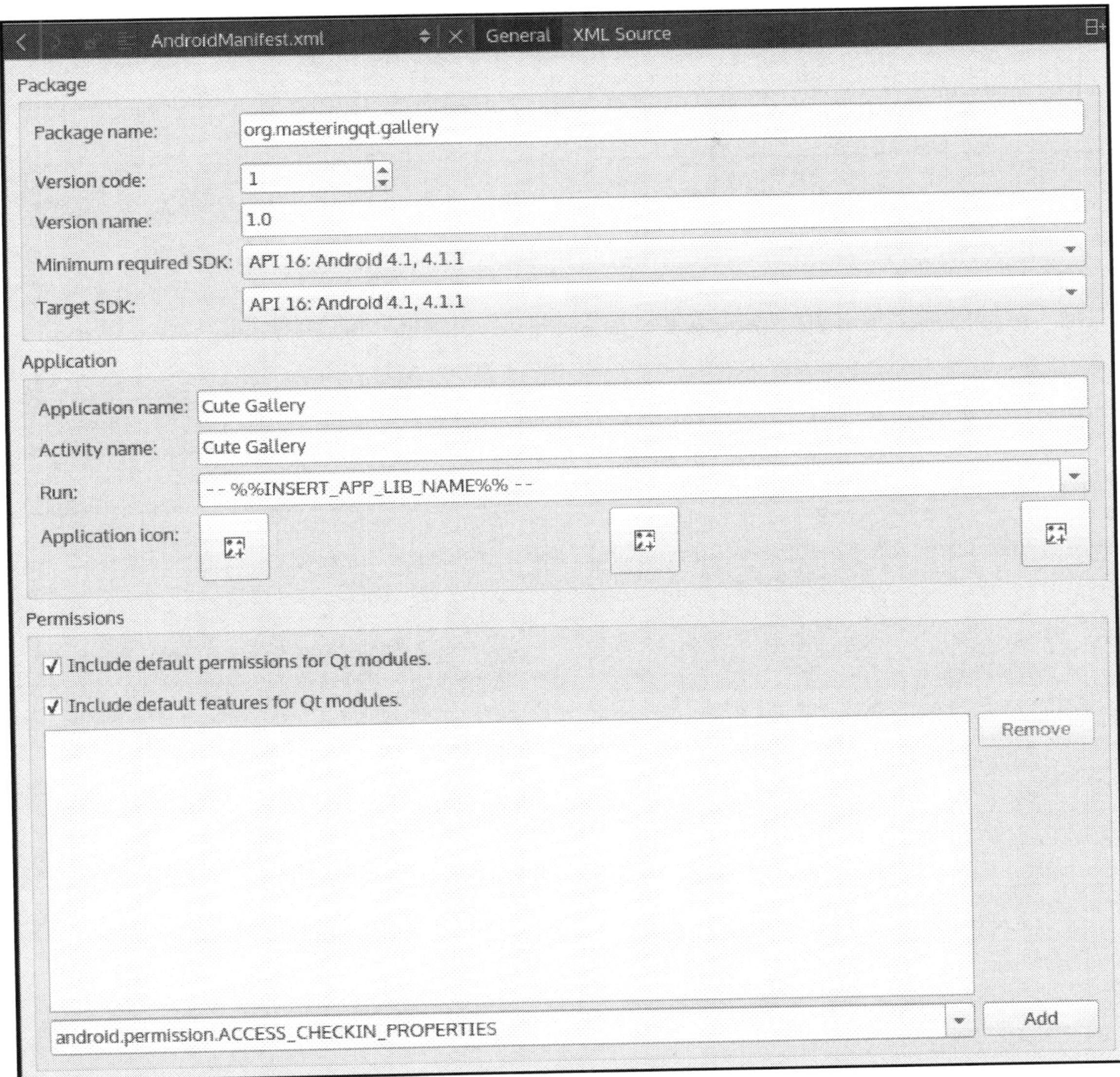

The following are the most important steps of this process:

1. Replace the default **Package name** with yours.
2. The **Version code** is an integer that must be increased for each official release. Ensure that it matches the official release.
3. The **Version name** is the displayed version for users. Ensure that it meets your requirements.
4. Select the **Minimum required SDK**. Users with an older version will not be able to install your application.
5. Select the SDK that will be used to compile your application with the **Target SDK.**
6. Change the application and activity name.
7. Select an **Application icon** depending on the screen DPI (dots per inch) icons that you require: low, medium, or high DPI icons (moving from left to right).
8. Finally, if required by your application, you can add some Android permissions.

You can already build and deploy your signed application from Qt Creator. You should see the new application name and icon on your Android phone or emulator. However, we will now create a script to easily generate and package the signed APK from the command line.

Several environment variables are required by the Android and Qt tools, but they are also required by the script itself. The following table shows a summary of this using an example:

Name	Example
`QTROOT`	`$HOME/qt/5.11`
`QTDIR_ANDROID`	`$QTROOT/android_armv7`
`JAVA_HOME`	`/usr/lib/jvm/java-8-openjdk-amd64`
`ANT_ROOT`	`/opt/apache-ant`
`ANDROID_SDK_ROOT`	`$HOME/android-sdk`
`ANDROID_NDK_ROOT`	`$HOME/android-ndk`

This example is a *bash* script, but feel free to adapt it to a `.bat` file if you are on Windows. Create a `package-android.sh` file in the `scripts` directory, as shown in the following code:

```
#!/bin/bash

DIST_DIR=dist/mobile-android
BUILD_DIR=build
APK_DIR=apk
KEYSTORE_PATH="$(pwd)/scripts/android-data"
```

```
ANDROID_BUILD_PATH="$(pwd)/$DIST_DIR/$BUILD_DIR/android-build"

mkdir -p $DIST_DIR && cd $DIST_DIR
mkdir -p $APK_DIR $BUILD_DIR

pushd $BUILD_DIR
$QTDIR_ANDROID/bin/qmake \
    -spec android-g++ \
    "CONFIG += release" \
    ../../../ch13-gallery-packaging.pro
make qmake_all
pushd gallery-core && make ; popd
pushd gallery-mobile && make ; popd
pushd gallery-mobile && make INSTALL_ROOT=$ANDROID_BUILD_PATH install ;
popd

$QTDIR_ANDROID/bin/androiddeployqt
    --input ./gallery-mobile/android-libgallery-mobile.so-deployment-
settings.json \
    --output $ANDROID_BUILD_PATH \
    --deployment bundled \
    --android-platform android-23 \
    --jdk $JAVA_HOME \
    --ant $ANT_ROOT/ant \
    --sign $KEYSTORE_PATH/android.keystore myandroidkey \
    --storepass 'masteringqt'
cp $ANDROID_BUILD_PATH/bin/QtApp-release-signed.apk ../apk/cute-gallery.apk
popd
```

Let's analyze this script together:

1. Set the main path variables. The output directory is `DIST_DIR`. All files are generated in the `dist/mobile-android/build` directory. The final signed APK is copied in the `dist/mobile-android/apk` directory.
2. Create all the directories and go into `dist/mobile-android/build`.
3. Execute `qmake` in release mode for the Android platform to generate the parent project `Makefile`.
4. Run the `make qmake_all` command to generate the subproject `Makefile` files.
5. Perform the `make` commands to build each required subproject.
6. Run the `make install` command on the `gallery-mobile` directory, specifying the `INSTALL_ROOT` to copy all binaries and files required by the APK generation.

The final part of the script calls the `androiddeployqt` binary, a Qt tool to generate the APK. Take a look at the following options:

- The `--deployment` option used here is `bundled`, like the mode we used in Qt Creator.
- The `--sign` option requires two parameters: the URL to the keystore file and the alias to the key for the certificate.
- The `--storepass` option is used to specify the keystore password. In our case the password is `masteringqt`.

Finally, the generated signed APK called `cute-gallery.apk` is copied to the `dist/mobile-android/apk` directory.

Packaging for iOS

Packaging a Qt application for iOS relies on XCode. When you build and run `gallery-mobile` from Qt Creator, XCode will be called under the hood. In the end, an `.xcodeproj` file is generated and passed to XCode.

Knowing this, the packaging part will be fairly limited. The only thing that can be automated is the generation of the `.xcodeproj` file.

First, check that your environment variables are correctly set, as shown in the following table:

Name	Example
QTDIR_IOS	$HOME/Qt/5.11/ios

Create `scripts/package-ios.sh` and add the following code snippet to it:

```
#!/bin/bash

DIST_DIR=dist/mobile-ios
BUILD_DIR=build

mkdir -p $DIST_DIR && cd $DIST_DIR
mkdir -p $BIN_DIR $LIB_DIR $BUILD_DIR

pushd $BUILD_DIR
$QTDIR_IOS/bin/qmake \
  -spec macx-ios-clang \
  "CONFIG += release iphoneos device" \
```

```
    ../../../ch13-gallery-packaging.pro
make qmake_all
pushd gallery-core && make ; popd
pushd gallery-mobile && make ; popd

popd
```

This script performs the following steps:

1. Set the main path variables. The output directory is `DIST_DIR`. All files are generated in the `dist/mobile-ios/build` folder.
2. Create all the directories and go into `dist/mobile-ios/build`.
3. Execute `qmake` in release mode for the iPhone device (as opposed to the iPhone simulator) platform to generate the parent project `Makefile`.
4. Run the `make qmake_all` command to generate the subproject `Makefile` files.
5. Perform the `make` command to build each required subproject.

Once this script has been executed, `dist/mobile-ios/build/gallery-mobile/gallery-mobile.xcodeproj` is ready to be opened in XCode. The remaining steps are entirely done in XCode:

1. Open `gallery-mobile.xcodeproj` in XCode
2. Compile the application for an iOS device
3. Follow the Apple procedure to distribute your application (through the App Store or as a standalone file)

After that, `gallery-mobile` will be ready for your users!

Summary

Even if your application runs well on your computer, your development environment can affect its behavior. Its packaging must be correct to run your application on the user's hardware. In this chapter, you learned the steps required to package an application before deploying it. Some platforms require specific tasks that must be followed carefully. You can now make a standalone package if your application is running a unique script.

The next chapter describes some tricks that can be useful for developing applications with Qt. In the next chapter, you will learn some tips concerning Qt Creator.

14
Qt Hat Tips and Tricks

In the previous chapter, we taught you how to package a Qt application on all of the major desktop and mobile platforms. That was the final step before shipping your application to your users. This chapter will gather some tips and tricks that will help you to develop your Qt applications with ease.

This chapter will cover the following topics:

- Managing your workspace with sessions
- Searching with the Locator
- Examining memory with Qt Creator
- Generating random numbers
- Generating a command-line interface
- Playing with Qt Gamepad
- Styling QML with Qt Quick Controls 2

Managing your workspace with sessions

It is common for a commercial product to be composed of several Qt projects. In this book, we regularly encountered such a practice. An example would be an application composed of a core project and a GUI project. The Qt `subdirs` project can be used to handle interdependent projects within the same application.

However, when your product grows up, you will want to open some unrelated projects in Qt Creator. In that case, you should use a **session**. A session is a complete snapshot of your workspace in Qt Creator. You can easily create a new session from **File** | **Session Manager** | **New** (do not forget to switch to the new session). For example, you could create a session, Mastering Qt5, and load all project examples into a common workspace.

Sessions are useful when you need to quickly switch between two different workspaces. The following items in Qt Creator will automatically be saved in the session:

- Opened projects of the hierarchical view
- Editor's windows (including the splits)
- Debug breakpoints and expressions views
- Bookmarks

You can switch to a different session via **File** | **Session Manager**, or by using the **Welcome** tab. A session can be destroyed without any impact on your projects.

Searching with the Locator

Another way to improve your productivity with Qt Creator is to use keyboard shortcuts. Qt Creator provides many great keyboard shortcuts. A selection is as follows:

Action	Shortcut
Comment / uncomment	Ctrl + /
Autocomplete	Ctrl + Space
View help of symbol under cursor	F1
Follow symbol under cursor	F2
Switch between header / source file	F4
Switch between function declaration and definition	Shift + F2
Switch between form / source file	Shift + F4
Rename symbol under cursor	Ctrl + Shift + R
Find usages of symbol under cursor	Ctrl + Shift + U
Select the kit	Ctrl + T
Build current project	Ctrl + B
Start / continue debugging	F5
Debugging : step over	F10
Debugging : step into	F11
Debugging : step out	Shift + F11
Run	Ctrl + R
Open next file from Open Documents	Ctrl + Tab
Open previous file from Open Documents	Ctrl + Shift + Tab
Toggle the left sidebar	Atl + 0
Toggle Issues pane	Alt + 1
Activate Locator	Ctrl + K
Auto indent the selection	Ctrl + I
Go to the line	Ctrl + L
Toggle fullscreen	Ctrl + Shift + F11
Remove current split editor	Ctrl + E, 0
Split editor horizontally	Ctrl + E, 2
Split editor vertically	Ctrl + E, 3

Some Qt Creator shortcuts depend on your OS. You can find (and edit) the complete list via **Tools** | **Options...** | **Environment** | **Keyboard**.

One of our favorite shortcuts is the Locator. Press *Ctrl* + *K* to activate it. Then, you can enjoy several features, as follows:

- Enter a filename (you can even use a partial entry) and press *Enter* to open the file. If the Locator suggests multiple files, you can use the up and down arrows to navigate.
- Prefix your search with a dot followed by a space (.) to search C++ symbols in the current document. For example, in the `Task.cpp` file of the first chapter, try to use the Locator with `. set`, and press *Enter* to go to the `Task::setName()` function.
- Enter `l` (*L* followed by a space) to go to a specific line. For example, `l 37` will bring us to line 37 of the current file.

The Locator provides plenty of features. The next time you press *Ctrl* + *K*, take a look!

Increasing the compilation speed

You can speed up the compilation on a multi-core computer. By default, when you build your project with Qt Creator, you use only one job (therefore, only one core). But `make` supports compilation with multiple jobs. You can use the `make -j N` option to allow *N* jobs at once. Do not forget to update your packaging scripts!

If you build your project from Qt Creator, you can set this option from **Projects** | **Build Steps** | **Make**. Click on **Details**, and in the **Make arguments** field, put the value `-j 8` to allow for eight jobs during the compilation, as shown in the following screenshot:

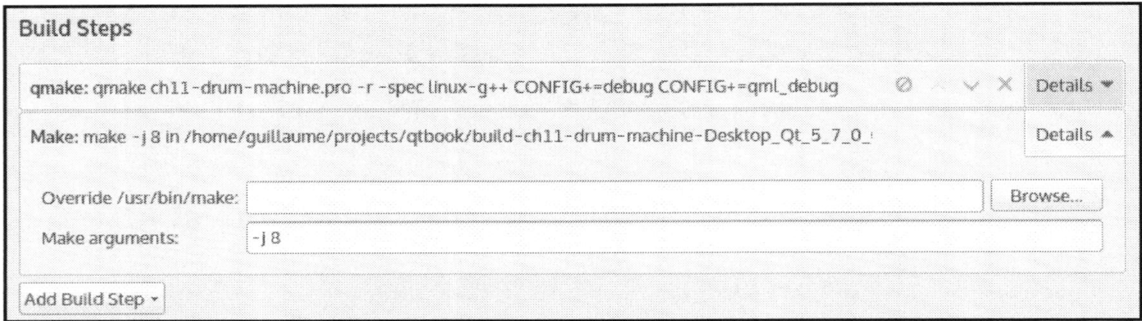

Examining memory with Qt Creator

For this section, we will use the following code snippet:

```
bool boolean = true;
int integer = 5;
char character = 'A';
int* integerPointer = &integer;

qDebug() << "boolean is:" << boolean;
qDebug() << "integer is:" << integer;
qDebug() << "character is:" << character;
qDebug() << "integerPointer is:" << integerPointer;
qDebug() << "*integerPointer is:" << *integerPointer;
qDebug() << "done!";
```

In the preceding code, we declared three primitive types: `boolean`, `integer`, and `character`. We also added an `integerPointer` pointer that refers to the `integer` variable. Put a breakpoint at the last line, and start the debugging. On the **Debug** pane, you should have the **Locals and Expressions** view. You can easily add/remove it from **Window | Views | Locals and Expressions**, as shown in the following screenshot:

Locals and Expressions

Name	Value			Type
boolean	true			bool
character	'A'	65	0x41	char
integer	5			int
integerPointer	5			int

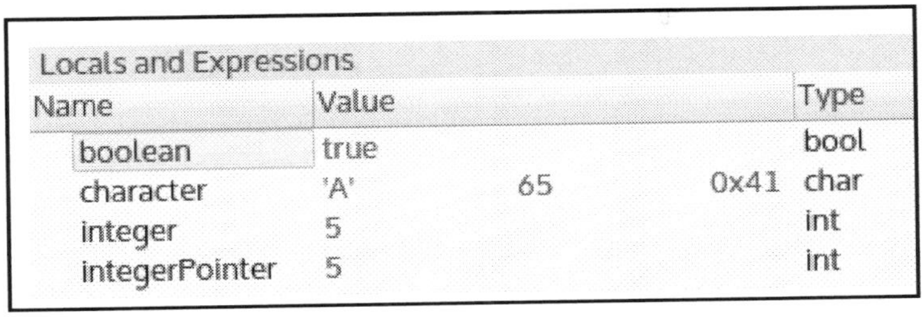

You can see that all of our local variables are displayed, along with their values. The `character` line even displays three formats (ASCII, integer, and hexadecimal) of the letter **A**. You may also notice that the `integerPointer` line displays the automatically de-referenced value, not the pointer address. You can disable it by right-clicking on the background of the **Locals and Expressions** window, and then selecting **Dereference Pointers automatically**. You can see the pointer address and the de-referenced value appear, as shown in the following screenshot:

Locals and Expressions

Name	Value			Type
boolean	true			bool
character	'A'	65	0x41	char
integer	5			int
▾ integerPointer	0x7ffe601153ac			int *
*integerPointer	5			int

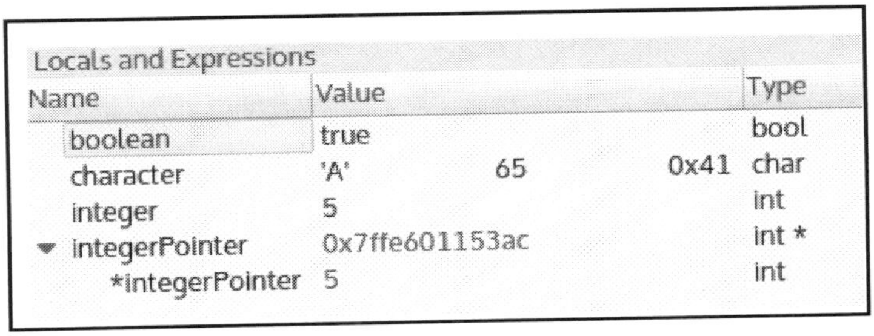

The console output displays the following information:

```
boolean is: true
integer is: 5
character is: A
integerPointer is: 0x7ffe601153ac
*integerPointer is: 5
```

You can see that we retrieve the same information in the console output. The **Locals and Expressions** view helps you to save time. You can display a lot of information without logging it with a `qDebug()` function.

Qt Creator provides a useful memory editor. You can open it with a right-click on a variable name in the **Locals and Expressions** window, by selecting **Open Memory Editor | Open Memory Editor at Object's Address**.

Within the memory editor, look at the value of the `boolean` variable:

```
0000:7ffe:6011:5390|30 55 11 60 fe 7f 00 00 58 4d 40 00 00 00 00 00 |0U·`····XM@·····
0000:7ffe:6011:53a0|20 54 11 60 fe 7f 00 00 20 54 01 41 05 00 00 00 | T·`···· T·A····
0000:7ffe:6011:53b0|30 3a 18 02 00 00 00 00 ac 53 11 60 fe 7f 00 00 |0:······S·`····
```

A hexadecimal editor appears, with three parts, as follows (from left to right):

- The memory address of the data
- The hexadecimal representation of the data
- The ASCII representation of the data

The selection in the hexadecimal representation corresponds to the variable. We can confirm that the `boolean` variable is represented in memory by one byte. Because the value is `true`, the memory representation is **0x01**.

Let's examine the `character` memory with the **Memory Editor** tool:

```
0000:7ffe:6011:5390|30 55 11 60 fe 7f 00 00 58 4d 40 00 00 00 00 00 |0U·`····XM@·····
0000:7ffe:6011:53a0|20 54 11 60 fe 7f 00 00 20 54 01 41 05 00 00 00 | T·`···· T·A····
0000:7ffe:6011:53b0|30 3a 18 02 00 00 00 00 ac 53 11 60 fe 7f 00 00 |0:······S·`····
```

The character is also stored in memory with one byte. The hexadecimal representation is **0x41**. The character is encoded with the well-known ASCII format. Note that, on the right-hand side, the ASCII representation displays the **A**.

The following is the **Memory Editor** location of the `integer` variable:

```
0000:7ffe:6011:5390|30 55 11 60 fe 7f 00 00 58 4d 40 00 00 00 00 00 |0U·`····XM@·····
0000:7ffe:6011:53a0|20 54 11 60 fe 7f 00 00 20 54 01 41 05 00 00 00 | T·`···· T·A····
0000:7ffe:6011:53b0|30 3a 18 02 00 00 00 00 ac 53 11 60 fe 7f 00 00 |0:······S·`····
```

There are two interesting facts to note here. The integer is stored on four bytes. The value **05** is stored in hexadecimal as **05 00 00 00**. The byte order depends on the endianness of your processor. We are using an Intel CPU that is Little-Endian. Another CPU architecture with a Big-Endian memory storage will display the variable as **00 00 00 05**.

Before we continue diving into the memory of our application, let's look at the last three screenshots closely. You might notice that, in this case, the three variables are contiguous in the stack memory. This behavior is not guaranteed, depending on the implementation of your compiler.

Try to open the memory editor on the `integerPointer` variable. The contextual menu offers you two different methods, as follows:

- The **Open Memory Editor at Object's Address** option de-references the pointer and brings you directly to the pointed value. You will get the same result as the integer memory view.
- The **Open Memory Editor at Pointer's Address** option displays the raw pointer data, which is a memory address to where it is pointing.

The following is the **Memory Editor** tool, showing the pointer's address of `integerPointer`:

```
0000:7ffe:6011:53a0|20 54 11 60 fe 7f 00 00 20 54 01 41 05 00 00 00| T·`····T·A····
0000:7ffe:6011:53b0|30 3a 18 02 00 00 00 00 ac 53 11 60 fe 7f 00 00|0:······S·····
0000:7ffe:6011:53c0|02 00 00 00 66 00 00 00 10 9e 40 00 00 00 00 00|····f·····@·····
```

We are on a 64-bit OS, so our pointer is stored on eight bytes. The data of this pointer is the hexadecimal value **ac 53 11 60 fe 7f 00 00** . This is the Little-Endian representation of the memory address `0x7ffe601153ac`, displayed by the **Locals and Expressions** and by our console output.

We display the memory, but we can also change it. Follow these steps:

1. Remove the current breakpoint and add a new one on the first `qDebug()` line.
2. Restart the debugging and look at the **Locals and Expressions**. If you double-click a variable's value, you can edit it. Note that the **Memory Editor** window immediately updates its representation.
3. In our case, we set the `boolean` value to false, the `character` to 68 (that is, `D`), and the `integer` to 9. When you are confident about your changes, continue the debugging.

The following is the final console output, reflecting our modifications:

```
boolean is: false
integer is: 9
character is: D
integerPointer is: 0x7fff849203dc
*integerPointer is: 9
done!
```

The **Memory Editor** is a powerful tool. You can display and change your variables' values at runtime, without changing your source code and recompiling your application.

Generating random numbers

Generating real random numbers is quite a difficult task for a computer. Commonly, we only use a **pseudo-random number generation (PRNG)**. The Qt framework provides the function `qrand()`, a thread-safe version of `std::rand()`. This function returns an integer between `0` and `RAND_MAX` (defined in `<cstdlib>`). The following code shows two pseudo-random numbers:

```
qDebug() << "first number is" << qrand() % 10;
qDebug() << "second number is" << qrand() % 10;
```

We are using a modulo operator to get a value between 0 and 9. Try to run your application several times. The numbers are always the same; in our case, the numbers are 3 and 7. That is because each time we call `qrand()`, we retrieve the next number of the pseudo-random sequence—but the sequence is always the same! Fortunately, we can use `qsrand()` to initialize the PRNG with a seed. A seed is an unsigned integer that is used to generate a sequence. Try the following snippet:

```
qsrand(3);
qDebug() << "first number is" << qrand() % 10;
qDebug() << "second number is" << qrand() % 10;
```

In this example, we are using the seed 3, and we get a different value from `qrand()`—on this computer, it is 5 and 4. Great; however, if you run this application several times, you will always have this sequence. One way of generating a different sequence each time you run your application is to use a different seed on each run. Run the following code snippet:

```
qsrand(QDateTime::currentMSecsSinceEpoch());
qDebug() << "first number is" << qrand() % 10;
qDebug() << "second number is" << qrand() % 10;
```

As you can see, we are now initializing the PRNG with the epoch time from `QDateTime`. You can try to run your application multiple times, to check that you will get different numbers each time! However, this solution is not recommended for cryptography. In that case, you should use a stronger random number engine.

Silencing unused variable warnings

If your compiler is configured to output its warnings, you will probably see the following type of log sometimes:

```
warning: unused parameter 'myVariable' [-Wunused-parameter]
```

This is a safety warning to tell the developer to keep their code clean and to avoid dead variables. It is a good practice to try to minimize this kind of warning. However, sometimes, you have no choice; you override an existing function, and you do not use all of the parameters. You now face a conundrum. On the one hand, you can silence the warning for your whole application, and on the other hand, you can let these safety warnings pile up in your compile output. There must be a better option.

Indeed, you can silence the warning for your function only. There are two ways of doing this, as follows:

- Using the C/C++ syntax
- Using a Qt macro

Let's suppose that you override `myFunction(QString name, QString myVariable)`, and you do not use `myVariable`. Using the C/C++ syntax, you just have to implement `myFunction()`, like so:

```
void myFunction(QString name, QString /*myVariable*/)
```

By commenting the variable's name, `myVariable`, in the function signature, you ensure that you will not (that is, cannot) use the variable in the function body. The compiler will also interpret it like this, and will not output any warning.

Qt also provides a way to mark unused variables with the `Q_UNUSED` macro. Let's see it in action, as follows:

```
void myFunction(QString name, QString myVariable)
{
    Q_UNUSED(myVariable)
    ...
}
```

Simply pass `myVariable` to `Q_UNUSED`, and it will remove the warning from the compiler output. Behind the curtain, `Q_UNUSED` does not do anything magical with the variable:

```
#define Q_UNUSED(x) (void)x;
```

It is a simple trick to fool the compiler; it sees `myVariable` as used, but nothing is done with it.

Logging custom objects to QDebug

When you are debugging complex objects, it is nice to output their current members' value to `qDebug()`. In other languages (such as Java), you may have encountered the `toString()` method or its equivalent, which is very convenient.

Sure, you could add a function void `toString()` to each object that you want to log, in order to write code with the following syntax:

```
qDebug() << "Object content:" << myObject.toString()
```

There must be a more natural way of doing this in C++. Moreover, Qt already provides this kind of feature:

```
QDate today = QDate::currentDate();
qDebug() << today;
// Output: QDate("2016-10-03")
```

To achieve this, we will rely on a C++ operator overload. This will look very similar to what we did with `QDataStream` operators in `Chapter 10`, *Need IPC? Get Your Minions to Work.*

Consider a `struct Person`, as follows:

```
struct Person {
    QString name;
    int age;
};
```

To add the ability to properly output to `QDebug`, you just have to override the << operator between `QDebug` and `Person`, like so:

```
#include <QDebug>

struct Person {
    ...
};

QDebug operator<<(QDebug debug, const Person& person)
{
    QDebugStateSaver saver(debug);
    debug.nospace() << "Person ("
                    << "name: " << person.name << ", "
```

```
                    << "age: " << person.age
                    << ")";
    return debug;
}
```

The QDebugStateSaver is a convenience class to save the settings of QDebug and restore them automatically upon destruction. It is good practice to always use it, to be sure that you do not break QDebug in an << operator overload.

The rest of the function is the usual way of using QDebug, and finally, returning the modified debug variable. You can now use Person, as follows:

```
Person person = { "Lenna", 66 };
qDebug() << "Person info" << person;
```

There is no need for a toString() function; simply use the person object. For those of you that wondered: yes, Lenna is really 66 at the time of writing this book (2018).

Improving log messages

Qt offers multiple methods for improving log messages. A good compromise between the result and its complexity is to combine the Qt log type with a custom message pattern.

Qt defines five log types, listed as follows, from the least to the most critical level:

- qDebug(): Custom debug messages
- qInfo(): Informational messages
- qWarning(): Warnings and recoverable errors in your applications
- qCrtical(): Critical error messages and system errors
- qFatal(): Write a last message before automatically exiting

Try to always use the most appropriate option!

By default, the message pattern is configured to only display your message without any extra data, but you can customize the pattern to display more information. This pattern can be changed at runtime by setting the QT_MESSAGE_PATTERN environment variable. You can also call the qSetMessagePattern function from your software to change the pattern. The pattern is just a string, with some placeholders.

The following are the most common placeholders that you can use:

- `%{appname}`: Your application name
- `%{file}`: The path to the source file
- `%{function}`: The function name
- `%{line}`: A line in the source file
- `%{message}`: An original message
- `%{type}`: The Qt log type (debug, info, warning, critical, or fatal)
- `%{time [format]}`: The system time when the message occurred

An easy way to use it is to edit your `main.cpp` file, as follows:

```
#include <QApplication>
#include <QDebug>
...
int main(int argc, char *argv[])
{
    qSetMessagePattern("[%{time yyyy-MM-dd hh:mm:ss}] [%{type}]
        %{function} %{message}");
    qInfo() << "Application starting...";

    QApplication a(argc, argv);
    ...
    return a.exec();
}
```

You should get something like the following in your application output:

```
[2018-10-03 10:22:40] [info] qMain Application starting...
```

Try to play around with the Qt log types and the custom message pattern, until you find a useful pattern for you.

For more complex applications, you can use the `QLoggingCategory` class to define the categories of logging. Visit `http://doc.qt.io/qt-5/qloggingcategory.html` for more information on this.

Saving your logs to a file

Developers commonly need to have logs. In some situations, you will not have access to the console output, or you will have to study the application state afterwards. In both cases, the log has to be output to a file.

Qt provides a practical way of redirecting your logs (`qDebug`, `qInfo`, `qWarning`, and so on) to any device that is convenient for you: `QtMessageHandler`. To use it, you have to register a function that will save the logs to the desired output.

For example, in your `main.cpp`, add the following function:

```
#include <QFile>
#include <QTextStream>

void messageHander(QtMsgType type,
                   const QMessageLogContext& context,
                   const QString& message) {
    QString levelText;
    switch (type) {
        case QtDebugMsg:
            levelText = "Debug";
            break;
        case QtInfoMsg:
            levelText = "Info";
            break;
        case QtWarningMsg:
            levelText = "Warning";
            break;
        case QtCriticalMsg:
            levelText = "Critical";
            break;
        case QtFatalMsg:
            levelText = "Fatal";
            break;
    }
    QString text = QString("[%1] %2")
                        .arg(levelText)
                        .arg(message);
    QFile file("app.log");
    file.open(QIODevice::WriteOnly | QIODevice::Append);
    QTextStream textStream(&file);
    textStream << text << endl;
}
```

The signature of the function must be respected to be called by Qt without any issues. Let's review the parameters:

- `QtMsgType type`: This is an `enum` that describes the function that generated the message (`qDebug()`, `qInfo()`, `qWarning()`, and so on)
- `QMessageLogContext& context`: This contains additional information about the log message (the source file where the log was produced, the name of the function, the line number, and so on)
- `const QString& message`: This is the actual message that was logged

The body of the function formats the log message before appending it to a file named `app.log`. You can easily add features in this function by adding a rotating log file, sending the logs through the network, and so on.

The last missing part is the registration of `messageHandler()`, which is done in the `main()` function, as follows:

```
int main(int argc, char *argv[])
{
    QCoreApplication a(argc, argv);
    qInstallMessageHandler(messageHander);
    ...
}
```

The call to the `qInstallMessageHander()` function is enough to reroute all of the log messages to `app.log`. Once this is done, the logs will no longer be displayed in the console output, and will be appended to `app.log` only.

If you need to de-register your custom message handler function, call `qInstallMessageHandler(nullptr)`.

Generating a command-line interface

The command-line interface can be a wonderful way to start your application with specific options. The Qt framework provides an easy way to define your options, with the `QCommandLineParser` class. You can provide a short (for example, `-t`) or a long (for example, `--test`) option name. The application version and help menu are automatically generated. You can easily check in your C++ code whether an option is set or not. An option can take a value and you can define a default value.

For example, we can create a CLI to configure the log files. We want to define three options, as follows:

- The `-debug` command, if set, enables the log file writing
- The `-f` or `--file` command defines where to write the logs
- The `-l` or `--level <level>` command specifies the minimum log level

Look at the following snippet:

```
QCoreApplication app(argc, argv);

QCoreApplication::setApplicationName("ch14-hat-tips");
QCoreApplication::setApplicationVersion("1.0.0");

QCommandLineParser parser;
parser.setApplicationDescription("CLI helper");
parser.addHelpOption();
parser.addVersionOption();

parser.addOptions({
    {"debug",
        "Enable the debug mode."},

    {{"f", "file"},
        "Write the logs into <file>.",
        "logfile"},

    {{"l", "level"},
        "Restrict the logs to level <level>. Default is 'fatal'.",
        "level",
        "fatal"},
});

parser.process(app);

qDebug() << "debug mode:" << parser.isSet("debug");
qDebug() << "file:" << parser.value("file");
qDebug() << "level:" << parser.value("level");
```

Let's discuss each step, as follows:

1. The first part uses the functions from `QCoreApplication` to set the application name and version. This information will be used by the `--version` option.
2. We instantiate a `QCommandLineParser` class. Then, we instruct it to automatically add the help (`-h` or `--help`) and version (`-v` or `--version`) options.

3. We add our options with the `QCommandLineParser::addOptions()` function.
4. We request the `QCommandLineParser` class to process the command-line arguments.
5. We retrieve and use the options.

The following are the parameters to create an option:

- `optionName`: By using this parameter, you can use single or multiple names
- `description`: In this parameter, the description of the option is displayed in the help menu
- `valueName` (optional): This shows the value name, if your option expects one
- `defaultValue` (optional): This shows the default value of the option

You can retrieve and use the option by using `QCommandLineParser::isSet()`, which returns `true` if the option was set by the user. If your option requires a value, you can retrieve it with `QCommandLineParser::value()`.

The following is a display of the generated help menu:

```
$ ./ch14-hat-tips --help
Usage: ./ch14-hat-tips [options]
Helper of the command-line interface

Options:
  -h, --help             Displays this help.
  -v, --version          Displays version information.
  --debug                Enable the debug mode.
  -f, --file <logfile>   Write the logs into <file>.
  -l, --level <level>    Restrict the logs to level <level>. Default is
'fatal'.
```

Finally, the following snippet displays the CLI in use:

```
$ ./ch14-hat-tips --debug -f log.txt --level info
debug mode:  true
file:  "log.txt"
level:  "info"
```

Sending and receiving HTTP data

Requesting information from an HTTP server is a common task. Again, the Qt folks have prepared some useful classes to make it easy for us. To achieve this, we will rely on three classes, as follows:

- `QNetworkAccessManager`: This class allows your application to send requests and receive replies
- `QNetworkRequest`: This class holds the request to be sent with all the information (headers, URLs, data, and so on)
- `QNetworkReply`: This class contains the result of a `QNetworkRequest` class, with the headers and the data

The `QNetworkAccessManager` class is the pivot point of the whole Qt HTTP API. It is built around a single `QNetworkAccessManager` object that holds the configuration of the client, proxy settings, cache information, and much more. This class is designed to be asynchronous, so you do not need to worry about blocking your current thread.

Let's see it in action in a custom `HttpRequest` class. First, the header is as follows:

```
#include <QObject>
#include <QNetworkAccessManager>
#include <QNetworkReply>

class HttpRequest : public QObject
{
    Q_OBJECT
public:
    HttpRequest(QObject* parent = 0);

    void executeGet();

private slots:
    void replyFinished(QNetworkReply* reply);

private:
    QNetworkAccessManager mAccessManager;
};
```

The `QNetworkAccessManager` class works with the signal/slot mechanism, so `HttpRequest` inherits from `QObject` and uses the `Q_OBJECT` macro. We declare the following functions and member:

- `executeGet()`: This is used to trigger an `HTTP GET` request
- `replyFinished()`: This is the slot called when the `GET` request has completed
- `mAccessManager`: This is the object that will be used for all of our asynchronous requests

Let's turn our attention to the constructor of the `HttpRequest` class in `HttpRequest.cpp`:

```
HttpRequest::HttpRequest(QObject* parent) :
    QObject(parent),
    mAccessManager()
{
    connect(&mAccessManager, &QNetworkAccessManager::finished,
            this, &HttpRequest::replyFinished);
}
```

In the body of the constructor, we connect the `finished()` signal from `mAccessManager` to our `replyFinished()` slot. This implies that every request sent through `mAccessManager` will trigger this slot.

Enough with the preparation; let's see the request and reply in action, as follows:

```
// Request
void HttpRequest::executeGet()
{
    QNetworkRequest request(QUrl("http://httpbin.org/ip"));
    mAccessManager.get(QNetworkRequest(request));
}

// Response
void HttpRequest::replyFinished(QNetworkReply* reply)
{
    int statusCode =
reply->attribute(QNetworkRequest::HttpStatusCodeAttribute).toInt();
    qDebug() << "Reponse network error" << reply->error();
    qDebug() << "Reponse HTTP status code" << statusCode;
    qDebug() << "Reply content:" << reply->readAll();
    reply->deleteLater();
}
```

The `HTTP GET` request is processed using `mAccessManager.get()`. The `QNetworkAccessManager` class provides the function for other HTTP verbs (`head()`, `post()`, `put()`, `delete()`, and so on). It expects `QNetworkRequest` access, which takes a URL in its constructor. This is the simplest form of an HTTP request.

Note that we did our request using the URL `http://httpbin.org/ip`, which will respond to the emitter's IP address in the JSON format:

```
{
  "origin": "1.2.3.4"
}
```

This website is a practical developer resource, where you can send your test requests and have useful information sent back to you. This avoids having to launch a custom web server to test only a few requests. The website is an open source project freely hosted by Runscope. Of course, you can replace the request URL with anything you wish.

Take a look at `http://httpbin.org/` to see all of the supported request types.

After the `executeGet()` function has completed, the `mAccessManager` object executes the request in a separate thread and calls our slot, `replyFinished()`, with the resulting `QNetworkReply*` object. In the preceding code snippet, you can see how to retrieve the HTTP status code and check whether any network error happened; you can also get the body of the response with `reply->readAll()`.

The `QNetworkReply` class inherits from `QIODevice`, so that you can read it all at once (with `readAll()`) or in chunks (with a loop on `read()`). This lets you adapt the reading to your needs by using a familiar `QIODevice` API.

Note that you are the owner of the `QNetworkReply*` object. You should not delete it by hand (your application might crash if you do so). Instead, it's better to use the `reply->deleteLater()` function, which will let the Qt event loop pick the appropriate moment to delete the object.

Now, let's look at a more complex example of `QNetworkReply`, with an `HTTP POST` method. There will be times when you will need to keep track of the `QNetworkReply` class and have a more fine-grained control over its life cycle.

The following is an implementation of the `HTTP POST` method that also relies on `HttpRequest::mAccessManager`:

```
void HttpRequest::executePost()
{
    QNetworkRequest request(QUrl("http://httpbin.org/post"));
    request.setHeader(QNetworkRequest::ContentTypeHeader,
                      "application/x-www-form-urlencoded");
    QUrlQuery urlQuery;
    urlQuery.addQueryItem("book", "Mastering Qt 5");

    QUrl params;
    params.setQuery(urlQuery);

    QNetworkReply* reply = mAccessManager.post(
```

```
                              request, params.toEncoded());
        connect(reply, &QNetworkReply::readyRead,
            [reply] () {
            qDebug() << "Ready to read from reply";
        });
        connect(reply, &QNetworkReply::sslErrors,
                [this] (QList<QSslError> errors) {
            qWarning() << "SSL errors" << errors;
        });
    }
```

We start by creating a `QNetworkRequest` class with a custom header; `Content-Type` is now `application/x-www-form-urlencoded`, to respect the HTTP RFC. After that, a URL form is built, ready to be sent with the request. You can add as many items as you wish to the `urlQuery` object.

The next part is interesting. When executing `mAccessManager.post()` with the request and the URL encoded form, the `QNetworkReply*` object is immediately returned to us. From here, we use some lambda slots connected directly to reply, rather than using `mAccessManage` slots. This lets you have precise control over what happens with each reply.

Note that the `QNetworkReploy::readyRead` signal comes from the `QIODevice` API, and that it does not pass the `QNetworkReply*` object in the parameter. It is your job to store the reply in a member field somewhere, or to retrieve the emitter of the signal.

Finally, this code snippet does not undo our preceding slot, `replyFinished()`, which is connected to `mAccessManager`. If you execute this code, you will get the following output sequence:

```
Ready to read from reply
Reponse network error QNetworkReply::NetworkError(NoError)
Reponse HTTP status code 200
```

The lambda connected to the `QNetworkReply::readyRead` signal is called first; then, the `HttpRequest::replyFinished` signal is called.

The last feature that we will cover on the Qt HTTP stack is synchronous requests. If you happen to need to manage the request threading yourself, the default asynchronous work mode of `QNetworkAccessManager` can get in your way. To circumvent this, you can use a custom `QEventLoop`, as follows:

```
void HttpRequest::executeBlockingGet()
{
    QNetworkAccessManager localManager;
```

```
    QEventLoop eventLoop;
    QObject::connect(
        &localManager, &QNetworkAccessManager::finished,
        &eventLoop, &QEventLoop::quit);

    QNetworkRequest request(
                QUrl("http://httpbin.org/user-agent"));
    request.setHeader(QNetworkRequest::UserAgentHeader,
                      "MasteringQt5Browser 1.0");

    QNetworkReply* reply = localManager.get(request);
    eventLoop.exec();

    qDebug() << "Blocking GET result:" << reply->readAll();
    reply->deleteLater();
}
```

In this function, we declare another `QNetworkAccessManager`, which will not interfere with the one declared in `HttpRequest`. Right after, a `QEventLoop` object is declared and connected to `localManager`. When `QNetworkAccessManager` emits the `finished()` signal, `eventLoop` will quit, and the calling function will resume.

The `request` is built as usual, the `reply` object is retrieved, and the function becomes blocked with the call to `eventLoop.exec()`. The function is blocked until `localManager` has emitted its finished signal. In other words, the request is still done asynchronously; the sole difference is that the function is blocked until the request is completed.

Finally, the `reply` object can be safely read and deleted at the end of the function. This `QEventLoop` trick can be used any time a synchronous wait for a Qt signal is needed. Use it wisely, to avoid blocking the UI thread!

Playing with Qt Gamepad

Are you tired of your common keyboard and mouse? Qt Gamepad is the solution! This module brings gamepad hardware support to your Qt game or application. Introduced as a **Technology Preview (TP)** in Qt 5.7, you can now enjoy a stable version (since Qt 5.9). Several platforms are supported, as follows:

- Windows (XInput)
- Linux (evdev / SDL2)
- Android (InputDevice)
- macOS, iOS, and tvOS (GCController)

Concerning the gamepad compatibility, the XBox controller works perfectly. Other gamepads (such as PlayStation controllers) should work, but you will have to configure the button and axis mapping. The Qt Gamepad library offers both C++ and Qt Quick API, so you can use your gamepad everywhere!

The first thing to do is to add the `gamepad` module to your `.pro` file:

```
QT += gamepad
```

Let's begin to use our gamepad in a Qt Quick application. Later, you will see how to use the C++ API. You will need to add the proper import on top of your QML file, as follows:

```
import QtGamepad 1.0
```

We can now define a `Gamepad` element:

```
Gamepad {
    id: gamepad
    deviceId: GamepadManager.connectedGamepads.length > 0 ?
        GamepadManager.connectedGamepads[0] : -1
}
```

As you can see, the `deviceId` is assigned to the first connected gamepad by using the `GamepadManager`. Thanks to the QML, you are now able to receive the input values of the axis and buttons, using the `gamepad` element. For example, you can display the `Button A` status in a `Text` element:

```
Text {
    text: "Button A: " + gamepad.buttonA
}
```

The following table shows the main `Gamepad` properties that you can use. Notice that the trigger buttons, `buttonL2` and `buttonR2`, are analog buttons, so the type is `double`, like an analog axis:

Property name	Type	Value
axisLeftX	double	[-1.0, 1.0]
axisLeftY	double	[-1.0, 1.0]
axisRightX	double	[-1.0, 1.0]
axisRightY	double	[-1.0, 1.0]
buttonUp	bool	false or true
buttonDown	bool	false or true
buttonLeft	bool	false or true
buttonRight	bool	false or true

buttonA	bool	false or true
buttonB	bool	false or true
buttonX	bool	false or true
buttonY	bool	false or true
buttonL1	bool	false or true
buttonR1	bool	false or true
buttonL2	double	[-1.0, 1.0]
buttonR2	double	[-1.0, 1.0]
buttonSelect	bool	false or true
buttonStart	bool	false or true
buttonL3	bool	false or true
buttonR3	bool	false or true
buttonGuide	bool	false or true

As you can see, the Qt Quick Gamepad API is really simple to use.

Let's look at how to do the same thing with the C++ API. Add the include on top of your .cpp file:

```
#include <QGamepad>
```

Now, let's find the connected gamepads with the QGamepadManager:

```
QList<int> deviceIds = QGamepadManager::instance()->connectedGamepads();
if (deviceIds.isEmpty()) {
    qDebug().noquote() << QString("No gamepad found!");
    return;
}
```

The function connectedGamepads() returns a list of deviceId. We can now define a new QGamepad object with the deviceId of the first connected gamepad:

```
QGamepad gamepad(deviceIds.first());
```

The preparation task is now finished. We can now connect to any signals emitted by the gamepad object. For example, you can display a log message each time the Button A status changes with the following lambda function:

```
connect(&mGamepad, &QGamepad::buttonAChanged, this, [](bool pressed) {
        qDebug() << "Button A:" << pressed;
});
```

You can refer to the preceding table of Gamepad properties to use another signal. The signal's name syntax is <propertyName>Changed.

Styling QML with Qt Quick Controls 2

The module Qt Quick Controls 2 is a growing Qt Quick add-on. Since 2016, this Technology Preview module, introduced in Qt 5.6, has been reaching, release by release, a more mature state. From Qt 5.11 (in 2018), you can use the stable version 2.4 of **Qt Quick Controls 2 (QQC2)**.

This library offers a huge list of ready-to-use QML controls. The following is a non-exhaustive list of the controls in Qt Quick Controls 2 version 2.4:

- **Buttons**: Button, CheckBox, RadioButton, Switch, and so on
- **Containers**: ApplicationWindow, GroupBox, Page, ScrollView, ToolBar, and so on
- **Indicators**: BusyIndicator, ProgressBar, PageIndicator, ScrollBar, and so on
- **Input**: ComboBox, RangeSlider, TextArea, TextField, Tumbler, and so on
- **Menus**: Action, Menu, and MenuBar
- **Navigations**: StackView, SwipeView, Drawer, and so on
- **Popups**: Dialog, Drawer, Menu, Popup, ToolTip, and so on

Remember that in `Chapter 5`, *Dominating the Mobile UI*, we used some controls from Qt Quick Controls 2: `ApplicationWindow`, `Page`, `ToolBar`, and `StackView`.

Version 2 is designed to target the desktop, embedded, and mobile platforms. So, you can even use it on a Raspberry Pi! However, some controls from version 1 are still missing in version 2.4 of Qt 5.11. For example, `Calendar`, `TableView`, `SplitView`, and the `Pickers` (date, time, and color). Some are in progress, and should be released in the next Qt versions.

An impressive feature of Qt Quick Controls 2 is styling. A style is a kind of theme that will be applied to all of the QQC2 controls in your application. The Qt framework currently provides five styles, as follows:

- The **Default** style: This is a basic style, focusing on drawing performance. You should be able to run it everywhere—even on a cheap embedded platform:

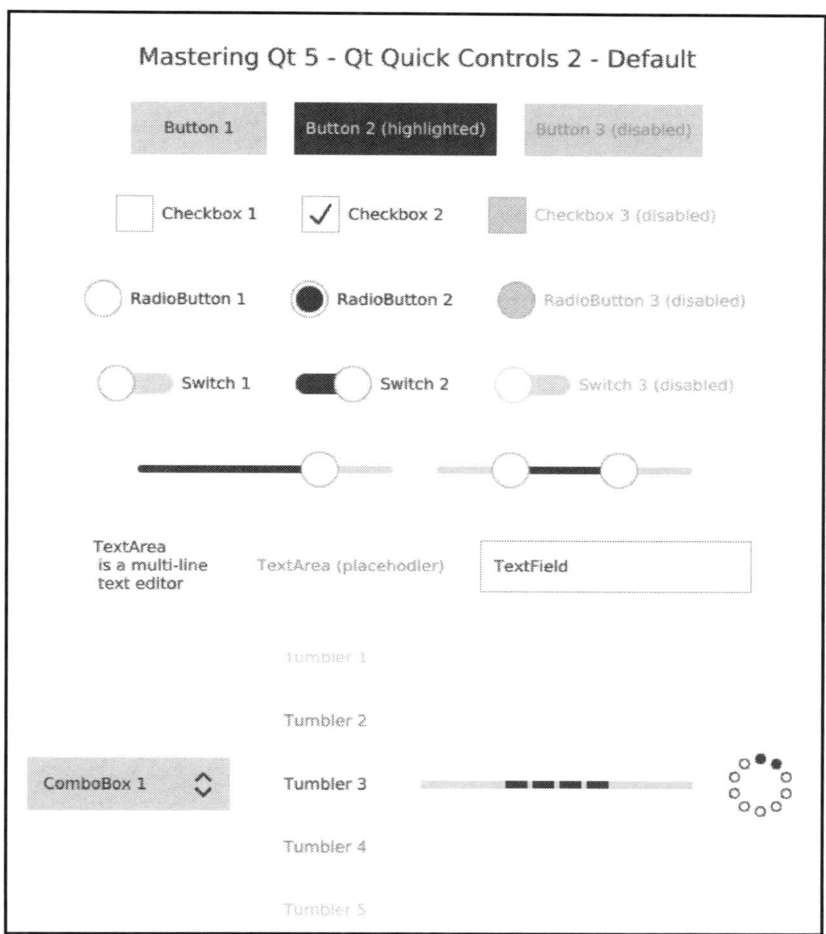

- The **Fusion** style: This style is a platform-agnostic desktop style. So, your application looks the same on all of the targets (Windows, Linux, macOS, and so on). You can use the `palettes` to customize it:

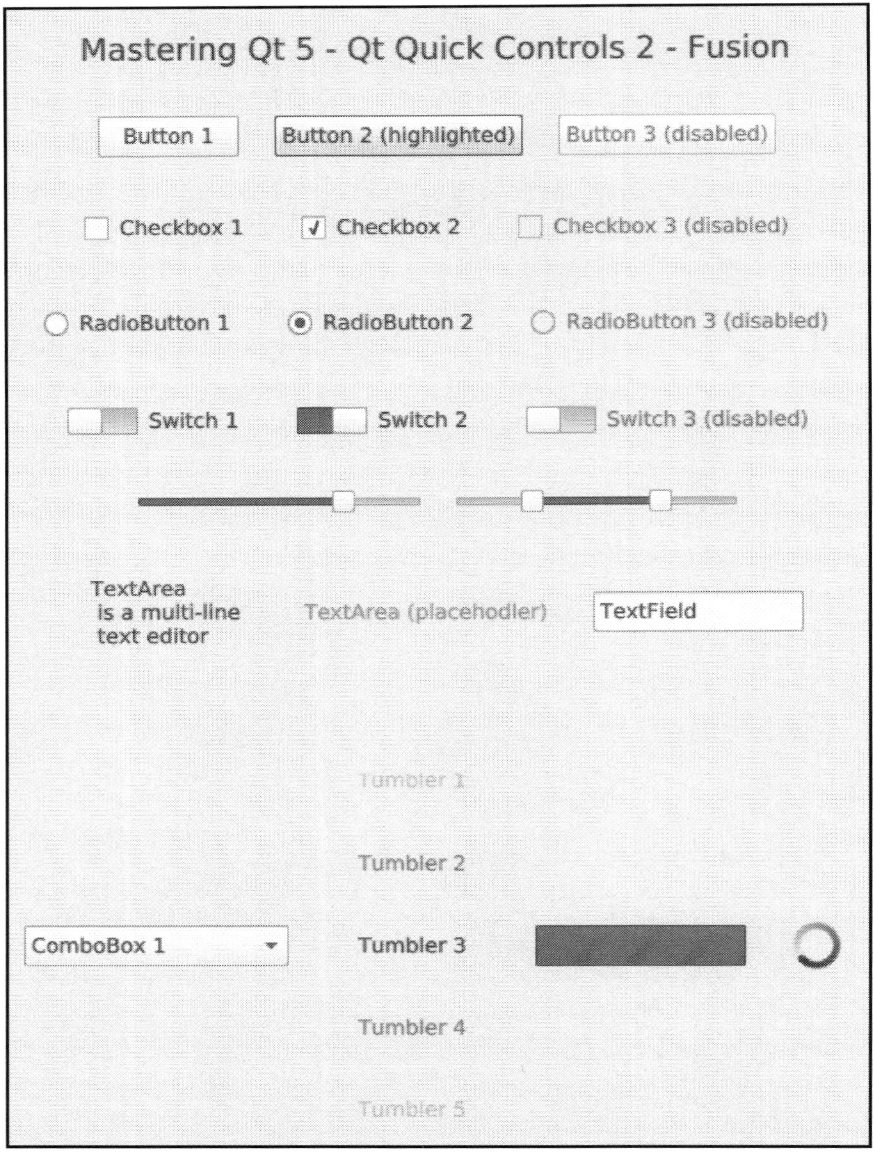

- The **Imagine** style: This has been constructed on image assets, so you can easily ask a designer working on Photoshop, Krita, or Sketch to customize this style:

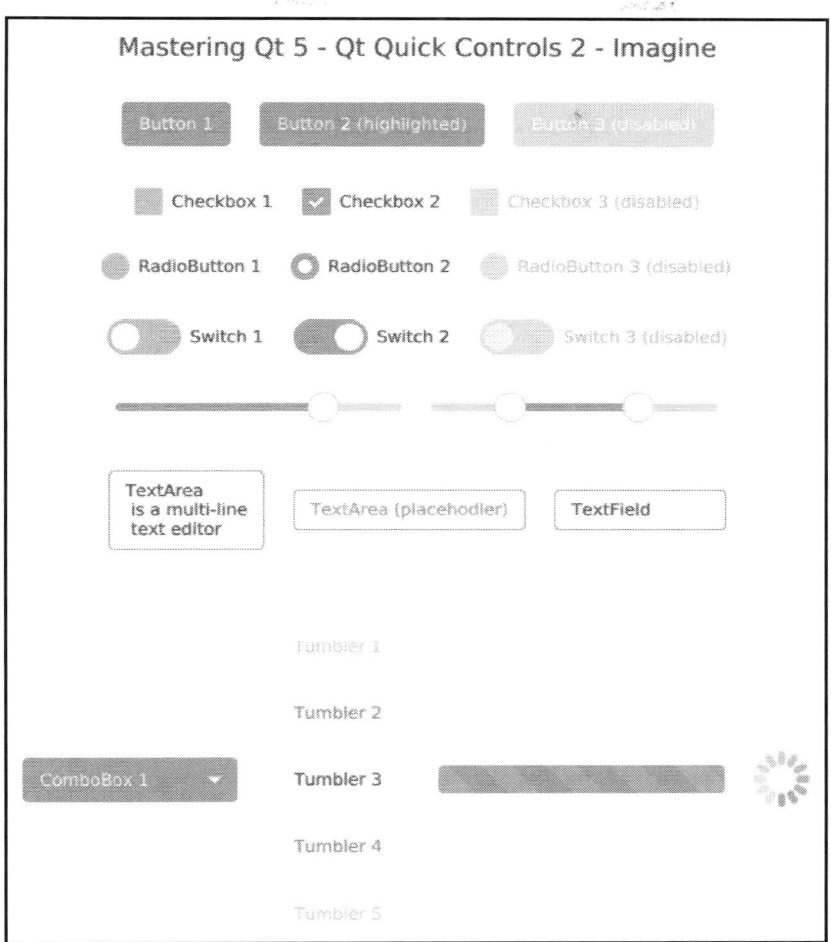

- The **Material** style: This design is based on the Google Material Design Guidelines used on Android. You can customize the main theme (light or dark) and provide an `accent` color:

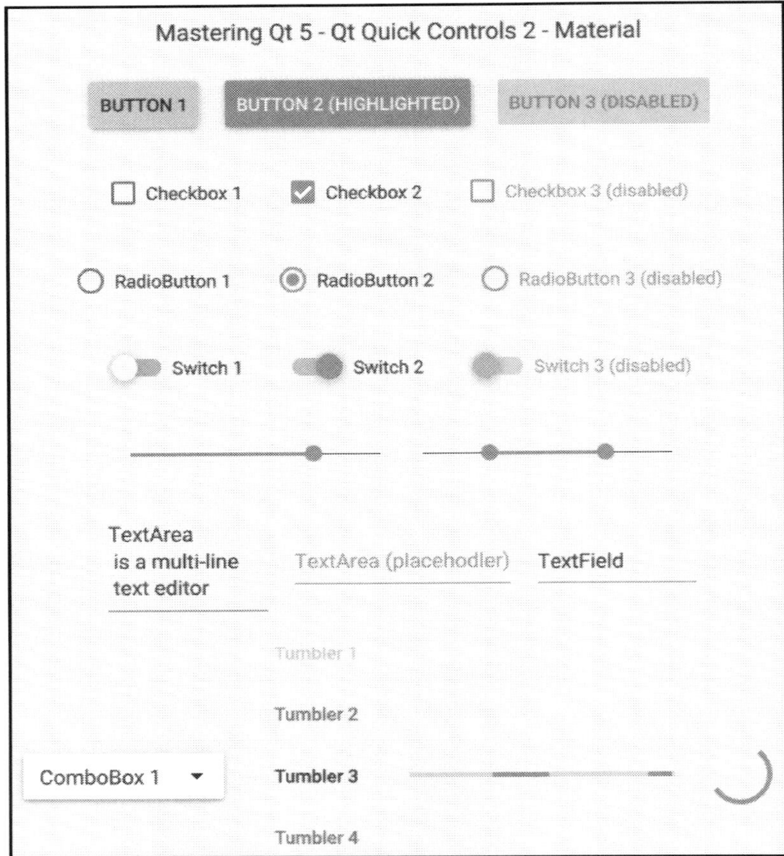

- The **Universal** style: This style is based on the Microsoft Universal Design Guidelines used on Windows. You can also customize the main theme (light or dark) and provide an accent color:

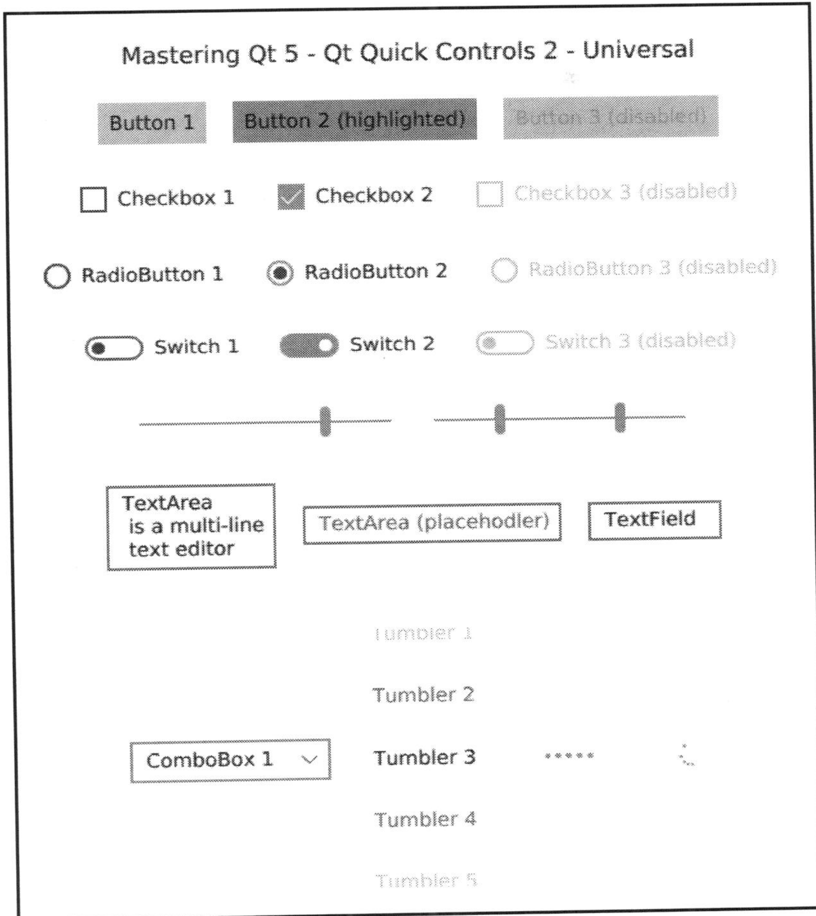

Did you pick your favorite style? Let's look at how to apply it to your Qt Quick application. First, check that you added the module in your `qmake.pro` file:

```
QT += quickcontrols2
```

Then, in the file `main.cpp`, you will need to use `QQuickStyle`:

```
#include <QGuiApplication>
#include <QQmlApplicationEngine>
#include <QQuickStyle>

int main(int argc, char *argv[])
{
    QCoreApplication::setAttribute(Qt::AA_EnableHighDpiScaling);
    QGuiApplication app(argc, argv);

    // Default, Fusion, Imagine, Material, Universal
    QQuickStyle::setStyle("Material");

    QQmlApplicationEngine engine;
    engine.load(QUrl(QStringLiteral("qrc:/main.qml")));

    if (engine.rootObjects().isEmpty())
        return -1;
    return app.exec();
}
```

Depending on the selected `Style`, you can customize some parameters. Here is an example of the `Material` style:

```
import QtQuick 2.11
import QtQuick.Window 2.11
import QtQuick.Layouts 1.3
import QtQuick.Controls 2.4
import QtQuick.Controls.Material 2.2

ApplicationWindow {
    id: window
    visible: true
    width: 6480
    height: 480

    Material.theme: Material.Dark
    Material.accent: Material.Green
    ...
}
```

And, voilà! You have a nice `Material` dark green `Style` applied to your Qt Quick application.

You can customize Qt Quick Controls 2 in so many ways, from modifying a part of a button to creating your own style from scratch! For more information, see `https://doc.qt.io/qt-5/qtquickcontrols2-customize.html`.

Another way to specify the `Style` is to create a `qtquickcontrols2.conf` file in the application's Qt resource file (`.qrc`). Then, you can fill it in as follows:

```
[Controls]
Style=Material

[Material]
Theme=Dark
Accent=Green
```

Summary

In this chapter, you learned some tips that will complement your Qt knowledge. You should now have the ability to use Qt Creator with ease and efficiency. The `QDebug` format should not hold any secrets, and you can now save your logs to a file without even blinking. You can now create a good-looking CLI interface, debug the memory of any program without shaking, and execute an HTTP request with confidence.

This journey will now come to an end. You are prepared for daily challenges. Throughout this book, you saw that the Qt framework is more than just another C++ GUI framework. We designed library/application projects. We crafted cross-platform applications. We added Qt modules, like Qt Charts, Qt 3D, and Qt Gamepad. We integrated a third-party library, with the essential OpenCV. You learned a lot of Qt Creator tips to master this underrated IDE. We sincerely hope that you had as much fun reading this book as we did writing it. In our opinion, Qt is a great framework, and it covers many areas that deserve to be explored with a book (or several books)! We hope that you keep coding C++ Qt code with pleasure, building efficient and beautifully crafted applications.

Other Books You May Enjoy

If you enjoyed this book, you may be interested in these other books by Packt:

Qt 5 Projects
Marco Piccolino

ISBN: 9781788293884

- Learn the basics of modern Qt application development
- Develop solid and maintainable applications with BDD, TDD, and Qt Test
- Master the latest UI technologies and know when to use them: Qt Quick, Controls 2, Qt 3D and Charts
- Build a desktop UI with Widgets and the Designer
- Translate your user interfaces with QTranslator and Linguist
- Get familiar with multimedia components to handle visual input and output
- Explore data manipulation and transfer: the model/view framework, JSON, Bluetooth, and network I/O
- Take advantage of existing web technologies and UI components with WebEngine

Learn QT 5
Nicholas Sherriff

ISBN: 9781788478854

- Install and configure the Qt Framework and Qt Creator IDE
- Create a new multi-project solution from scratch and control every aspect of it with QMake
- Implement a rich user interface with QML
- Learn the fundamentals of QtTest and how to integrate unit testing
- Build self-aware data entities that can serialize themselves to and from JSON
- Manage data persistence with SQLite and CRUD operations
- Reach out to the internet and consume an RSS feed
- Produce application packages for distribution to other users

Leave a review - let other readers know what you think

Please share your thoughts on this book with others by leaving a review on the site that you bought it from. If you purchased the book from Amazon, please leave us an honest review on this book's Amazon page. This is vital so that other potential readers can see and use your unbiased opinion to make purchasing decisions, we can understand what our customers think about our products, and our authors can see your feedback on the title that they have worked with Packt to create. It will only take a few minutes of your time, but is valuable to other potential customers, our authors, and Packt. Thank you!

Index

.

.pro file
  about 69
  exploring 69, 70, 71, 73

A

AlbumListWidget
  used, for listing albums 122, 124
albums
  displaying, with ListView 166, 167
  listing, with AlbumListWidget 122, 125
AlbumWidget
  used, for displaying selected album 131, 134, 135, 139
Android
  application, packaging 471, 472, 476
Animation Framework
  discovering 289, 290, 291, 292, 293
AppImage
  reference 467
  used, for application packaging with Linux 467
application
  interacting, with sockets 374, 375, 380
  packaging, for Android 471, 473, 476
  packaging, for iOS 478
  packaging, for Linux with AppImage 466
  packaging, for Linux with distribution package 460, 461, 463, 465
  packaging, for Mac OS X 469
  plugins, using 285, 288
  spying, on with QSignalSpy 453
auto type
  used, for simplifying 32, 33, 35, 36

B

binary format
  about 392
  object, serializing 419
board game
  preparing 216, 217
brew
  reference 245
built-in functions
  reference 73

C

code responsibility
  distributing 27
code
  execution speed, benchmarking 447, 448
  protecting, with smart pointer 97, 98, 100, 102, 103
command-line interface (CLI)
  about 73
  generating 494, 495
compilation speed
  increasing 484
completed task feature
  implementing 32
CpuWidget
  implementing, with Qt Charts 59, 61, 62
Create/Read/Update/Delete (CRUD) 91
cross-platform project
  designing 37, 38, 40
  Linux implementation, adding 46, 49
  Mac OS implementation, adding 51, 54
  Windows implementation, adding 40, 41, 42, 43, 45, 46
custom InputDialog
  new album, creating 174, 176, 178

custom objects
logging, to QDebug 490
custom QWidget 18, 19, 20
custom signal
emitting, with lambdas 28, 29, 31

D

D-Bus
about 347
session bus 347
system bus 347
data classes
defining 86
data
storing, in database 89, 90
database
data, storing 89, 90, 91, 94
loading, on mobile devices 172, 174
datasets
used, for writing factorized tests 443, 444, 445
Dependency Walker
reference 457
design patterns, for cross-platform project
singleton pattern 38
strategy pattern 38
distribution package
used, for packaging application for Linux 460, 461, 463, 464, 466
drum machine project
architecting 391, 393
drum track
creating 394, 397, 400

E

entities
crafting, from factory 218, 220
entity component system (ECS) 192
entry point
creating, for Qt3D code 203

F

factorized tests
writing, with datasets 443, 444, 446
factory
entities, crafting from 218
file
logs, saving 493, 494
FilterWidget
used, for designing UI 250, 251, 252, 253
foundations
laying down, with SDK 353, 354, 356
fpm (eFfing Package Management)
reference 460
fractal
displaying, with MandelbrotWidget 329, 334, 337, 338
fragment 214
full resolution images
navigating through 187, 189

G

Gallery app
composing 146, 147, 149
GridView
thumbnails, displaying 184, 187
GUI, linked to core shared library
creating 117, 118, 119, 120, 121
GUI
testing 450, 452

H

heads up display (HUD)
about 206
varying, with QML states 229, 232
HTTP data
receiving 497, 498, 500
sending 497, 498, 500

I

image-filter application
building 261, 262, 264, 266, 268
ImageProvider
used, for loading images 179, 180, 181, 183
images
loading, with ImageProvider 179, 180, 181, 184
Inter-Process Communication (IPC)
about 341
techniques 341, 343, 345, 346, 348
iOS
application, packaging 478

IPC project
architecturing 349, 350, 351, 352

J

JavaScript
snake engine, building 221
Job class
defining, with QRunnable 318, 319, 320, 322
JSON (JavaScript Object Notation) format
about 392
objects, serializing 407, 410

K

kit
compiler 198
debugger 198
device 198
Qt version 198

L

lambdas
used, for emitting custom signal 28, 29, 31
Linux Kernel
reference 50
Linux
application, packaging with AppImage 466
application, packaging with distribution package 460, 461, 463, 464
project, configuring 244
linuxdeployqt
reference 467
ListView
used, for displaying albums 166
Locator
used, for searching 482
log messages
improving 491, 492
logs
saving, to file 493, 494
low latency sounds
playing, with QSoundEffect 421

M

Mac OS X
application, packaging 468
Mac
project, configuring 245
maintainable project
designing 82, 83, 84, 85
sub-projects 82
MainWindow
structure 11, 13
Mandelbrot project
architecting 315, 316, 318
Job 317
MandelbrotCalculator 317
MandelbrotWidget 317
MandelbrotCalculator
QThreadPool, using 324, 325, 328, 329
MandelbrotWidget
used, for displaying fractal 330, 334, 337, 338
memory consumption
displaying, with QCharts 63, 65, 69
memory
examining, with Qt Creator 484, 486, 487
mobile devices
database, loading 172, 173
Model View Controller (MVC) 104
model
implementing 104, 105, 108, 109, 111, 113, 115
List Model 108
Table Model 108
Tree Model 108
mouse drag events
accepting 427, 428
mouse drop events
accepting 427, 428
MXE
reference 456

O

Object Oriented Paradigm (OOP) 87
object
serializing, in binary format 419
serializing, in JSON format 407, 410
serializing, in XML format 412, 415, 417, 419
serializing, with QVariant 401, 404, 407
ObjectVariant

used, for object serialization 403, 405, 406, 407
Open Source Computer Vision (OpenCV)
about 240
filters, implementing 246, 247, 250

P

picture
displaying, with PictureWidget 144, 146
fading in 296, 297
PictureDelegate
used, for enhancing thumbnails 140, 141, 143
PictureWidget
used, for displaying picture 144, 146
PlaybackWorker
using 424, 426
plugins
automatic loading 284
creating 275, 278, 279, 281
dynamic loading 281, 283
exposing, to Qt Designer 255, 256, 258
using, inside application 285, 288
project
configuring, for Linux 244
configuring, for Mac 245
creating 8
pseudo-random number generation (PRNG) 488

Q

Q_OBJECT 76
QButton
triggering, with keyboard 422
QCharts
used, for displaying memory consumption 63, 65, 69
used, for implementing CpuWidget 59, 60, 62
QDataStream
working with 357, 359, 363, 364
QDebug
custom objects, logging to 490, 491
QDialog
using 25
QEasingCurve class
reference 298
QLoggingCategory class
reference 492
qmake 73, 74, 76, 78
QML application
profiling 233, 234, 237
theming, with QML singleton 168, 170, 171
QML singleton
reference 170
used, for theming QML application 168, 170, 171
QML states
used, for varying HUD 229
QML
starting with 152
styling, with Qt Quick Controls 2 (QQC2) 504, 506, 508, 509
working with 153, 155, 158
QPainter
reference 142
QRunnable
used, for defining Job class 318, 319, 320, 321, 324
QShortcut class
reference 424
QSignalSpy
used, for spying on application 453
QSoundEffect
used, for playing low latency sounds 421
QString documentation
reference 36
Qt application
development environment, checking 159
Qt Charts
about 56
exploring 56, 58
reference 56
Qt Creator
about 8
used, for examining memory 484, 485, 486, 487
Qt Designer plugin
creating 240, 241, 242
using 258, 259, 261
Qt Designer
about 14
interface 14, 15
plugin, exposing 255
Qt framework

connect function 16
signals 16
slot 16
Qt Gamepad
playing with 501, 503
Qt multi-threading technologies
exploring 311, 314, 315
Qt Plugin system
used, for creating SDK 271, 273, 274
Qt project
basic structure 8, 9
Qt Quick Controls 2 (QQC2)
controls 504
reference 510
used, for styling QML 504, 505, 507, 509, 511
Qt Quick Controls application 161
Qt Quick gallery
entry point, preparing 162, 164
Qt Quick project
creating 160, 161
starting with 152, 153
working with 155, 157
Qt resource file 123
Qt Test
discovering 432, 434, 435, 437
Qt3D code
entry point, creating 203, 205
Qt3D entities
assembling 210, 213, 216
Qt3d lights
reference 205
Qt3D
discovering 191, 195
Qt
configuring, for Raspberry Pi 196, 200, 202
QTcpServer
building 380, 382, 384, 386, 387, 388, 389
QTcpSocket
working with 357
QThread
discovering 305, 306, 308, 309, 311
QThreadPool
using, in MandelbrotCalculator 324, 325, 328, 329
QVariant
supported types, references 401
used, for making objects serializable 401
used, for object serialization 401

R

random numbers
generating 488
range-based for loop
used, for simplifying 32, 33, 35, 36
Raspberry Pi
for QT, reference 196
Qt, configuring 196, 197, 200
remote procedure calling (RPC) 347
Run-time type information(RTTI) 77

S

scene
setting up 206, 208, 209, 210
SDK
preparing 271
used, for laying down foundation 353, 354, 356
selected album
displaying, with AlbumWidget 131, 134, 136, 139
sessions
used, for managing workspace 482
shared memory 343
signals 16, 17, 18, 76
singleton
SysInfo, transforming 54
slots 16, 17, 18, 76
smart pointer
used, for protecting code 97, 98, 100, 102, 103
snake engine
building, in JavaScript 221, 223, 225, 227
sockets
interacting, from application 374, 376, 380
interacting, in worker 364, 367, 369, 372, 373, 374
software development kit (SDK)
about 271
creating, with Qt Plugin system 271, 273, 274
standalone application
packaging 456
packaging, for Windows 457, 458

standard C++ documentation
  reference 24
sub-projects
  gallery-core 82
  gallery-desktop 82
  gallery-mobile 82
SysInfo
  transforming, in singleton 54

T

task
  adding 22, 23, 24, 25
Technology Preview (TP) 501
tests
  executing 438, 441, 442
ThumbnailProxyMode
  creating 131
ThumbnailProxyModel
  creating 127, 128, 129
thumbnails
  animating 293, 294, 296
  displaying, in GridView 184, 187
  enhancing, with PictureDelegate 140, 141, 142, 143
  flashing, in sequence 299, 301, 303
type information(RTTI) 284

U

UI
  designing, with FilterWidget 250, 251, 252, 253
unique_ptr pointer
  reference 103
unused variable warnings
  silencing 489
User Interface Compiler 257

V

vertex shader 214

W

What You See Is What You Get (WYSIWYG) 9
Windows API
  reference 45
Windows
  project, configuring 242, 243
  standalone application, packaging 457, 458
worker
  interacting, with sockets 364, 366, 368, 371, 373
workspace
  managing, with sessions 482

X

XML (eXtensible Markup Language) format
  about 392
  object, serializing 412, 414, 415

Printed in Great Britain
by Amazon